Teaching Cues for Sport Skills for Secondary School Students

FOURTH EDITION

Hilda Ann Fronske

UTAH STATE UNIVERSITY

PEARSON
Benjamin Cummings

San Francisco Boston New York
Cape Town Hong Kong London Madrid Mexico City
Montreal Munich Paris Singapore Sydney Tokyo Toronto

Acquisitions Editors: Deirdre McGill-Espinoza, Sandra Lindelof
Development Manager: Claire Alexander
Project Editor: Betsy Roll
Editorial Assistant: Amy Yu
Managing Editor: Deborah Cogan
Production Supervisor: Beth Masse
Production Management and Composition: GGS Book Services
Interior Designer: The Left Coast Group
Cover Designer: tani hasegawa
Director, Image Resource Center: Melinda Patelli
Image Rights and Permissions Manager: Zina Arabia
Manufacturing Buyer: Stacy Wong
Marketing Manager: Neena Chandra
Text Printer: Malloy, Inc.
Cover Printer: Phoenix Color
Cover Photo Credits: Jaime D. Travis/DK Stock/Getty Images, Mike Powell/Allsport Concepts/Getty Images, Photodisc/Getty Images

Library of Congress Cataloging-in-Publication Data

Fronske, Hilda Ann.
Teaching cues for sport skills for secondary school students / Hilda Ann Fronske.—4th ed.
p. cm.
Includes bibliographical references and index.
ISBN 0-8053-2719-3 (alk. paper)
1. Sports—Study and teaching (Secondary) 2. School sports—Coaching. I. Title.
GV361.F66 2008
796.07'7—dc22 2006031059

PEARSON
Benjamin Cummings

ISBN-13: 978-08053-2719-9
ISBN-10: 0-8053-2719-3
1 2 3 4 5 6 7 8 9 10—MAL—11 10 09 08 07
www.aw-bc.com

This book is dedicated to my beloved late grandfather and grandmother: Dr. Martin George Fronske and Hilda Ann Fronske.

Contents

Preface

Have you ever dreamed of a book that would cover teaching cues, drill progressions, and mini-games for a variety of sport skills and activities for secondary and high school students? The wait is over! Featured in this unique and exciting book are teaching cues and activities for 30 sports and physical activities. This book also features live-action pictures of athletes executing the cues.

This book will save you hours of planning time by providing you with a user-friendly format. The cues will also establish credibility with your students because you can tell them why a particular cue works and you can analyze a skill better to speed up student learning.

ACKNOWLEDGMENTS

My thanks to the awesome crew at Benjamin Cummings, especially Acquisitions Editors Deirdre Espinoza and Sandy Lindelof, Editorial Assistant Amy Yu, Production Supervisor Beth Masse, and Production Editor Emily Autumn (GGS Book Services). They provided incredible energy, inspiration, wit, enthusiasm, and editing ideas for the fourth edition. Thanks also to Edward Heath for the time, editing skills, and insights and talents that he brought to the book.

I appreciate the time, effort, and suggestions of the reviewers for this edition: Vinnie Bradford, Palo Alto College; Donna Dove, Pennsylvania State University; Paula Politte, Concordia University, Portland; Tom Stitcher, Salisbury University; Shaunna McGhie, Utah Valley State College; Lydia Garcia Crain, University of Arizona; Lindy Valdez, California State University, Sacramento.

Additionally, I am grateful to all the coaches and athletes at Utah State University and other colleges and universities in the United States who posed for the photographs used in this book.

Sport Consultants

Thank you to Debbie Tidwell, Carolyn Brook, Beth Allen, Michelle Wilson, Peter Mathesius, and John Kras for their support and assistance with the book. Thank you to Ralph and Marlene Meikle for their support and friendship. Thanks to all of the sport consultants who generously shared with me their time, knowledge, and expertise in their specific sports.

Aerobic Kickboxing: Chris Erickson, certified aerobic kickboxing instructor, second-degree black belt, elementary physical education teacher, Adams Elementary School, Logan, Utah.

Archery: Joyce Harrison, associate dean, Brigham Young University, Provo, Utah. Derek Lindley, archery manager at pro shop, Al's Sporting Goods, Logan, Utah. Val Spillet, vice president of Al's Sporting Inc., Logan, Utah.

Badminton: Peggy Savosik, Jim Leete, and Jim Stabler, USA Badminton, Colorado Springs, Colorado. Gord Smith, Badminton Canada, Gloucester, Ontario, Canada. Richard Jones, Brigham Young University, Provo, Utah. Edward Heath, professor in Physical Education, Utah State University, Logan, Utah.

Baseball: Justin Jensen, associate scout for Milwaukee Brewers, Rocky Mountain School of Baseball, Logan, Utah. Jonathan Howell, Health, Physical Education, and Recreation Department, Utah State University, Logan, Utah. Rick Thorne, Skyview High School head baseball coach, Smithfield, Utah.

Basketball: Coach Al Brown, assistant basketball coach for Lady Volunteers, University of Tennessee, Knoxville. Shanna Stevens, Utah State University club basketball coach, Logan, Utah.

Bowling: Richard Jones, professor in pedagogy and sports, Brigham Young University, Provo, Utah. Russell Boyer, undergraduate student, Utah State University, Logan, Utah.

Cycling—Mountain Biking: Quinn Bingham, bicycle technician, Al's Sporting Goods, Logan, Utah. Jeff Keller, Sunrise Cycle, Logan, Utah. Steven Gudmundson, graduate student, Utah State University, Logan, Utah. Emily Watkins, graduate student, Utah State University, Logan, Utah.

Cycling—Road Biking: Jeff Keller, Sunrise Cycle, Logan, Utah. Steven Gudmunson, graduate student, Utah State University, Logan, Utah. State Stowers, bicycle technician, Al's Sporting Goods, Logan, Utah. Emily Watking, undergraduate student, Utah State University, Logan, Utah.

Field Hockey: Laura Darling, United States Field Hockey Association, Colorado Springs, Colorado. Katie Harris and Deanie Stetson, Falmouth High School, Falmouth, Maine.

Fitness Equipment Work Out: Edward Heath, professor in Physical Education, Utah State University, Logan, Utah. Rod Hammer, MS, Icon Health and Fitness, Logan, Utah.

Floor Hockey: Ross Keys, physical education undergraduate student, and Michael Burggraf, physical education undergraduate student, Utah State

University, Logan, Utah. Gianni Maddalozzo, instructor in physical education, Department of Exercise and Sport Science, Oregon State University, Corvallis, Oregon.

Football: Bill Bauer, facility coordinator, Utah State University, Logan, Utah. Jeff Berg, football player, Utah State University, Logan, Utah. Art Erickson, player and coach, Utah State University, Logan, Utah. Ryan Allred, undergraduate physical education, Utah State University, Logan, Utah.

Golf: Robert Fronske, amateur golf player, Tempe, Arizona. Dan Roskelley, golf professional, Logan Golf and Country Club, Logan, Utah. Brett Wayment, assistant professional, Logan Golf and Country Club, Logan, Utah.

In-Line Skating: Lisa Klarich Davis, teacher, Ecker Hill Middle School, Park City, Utah. Margot Willett, program director, Skate in School, Edina, Minnesota.

Lacrosse: Roger Allen, lacrosse coach, Logan, Utah. Mason Goodhand, Utah Lacrosse Association, Salt Lake City, Utah. Heriberto "Eddie" Vega, head lacrosse coach, Utah State University, Logan, Utah. Erin Smith, US Lacrosse, Baltimore, Maryland. Photography: Erin Smith.

Pickleball: Sarah Lowe, Angela Kimball, Amy Thatcher and Jackie Ellis, tennis team at Utah State University, Logan, Utah. Tedi Searle, physical education undergraduate student, Utah State University, Logan, Utah. Doug Smith, general manager, Pickle-Ball Inc., Seattle, Washington.

Racquetball: Chris Atkins, head racquetball club coach, Utah State University, Logan, Utah. Jim Hiser, American Amateur Racquetball Association, Colorado Springs, Colorado. Susan Hill, graduate student, Health Department, Southern Illinois University, Carbondale, Illinois.

Recreational Walking, Running, and Hiking: Patrick Shane, head women's cross-country/distance coach, Brigham Young University, Provo, Utah. Kevin Prusak, assistant professor, elementary physical education, Brigham Young University, Provo, Utah. Sue Vincent, assistant professor, elementary physical education, Brigham Young University, Provo, Utah. Jesse Nelson, undergraduate student, Utah State University, Logan, Utah. Loretta Cide, undergraduate student of physical education, Utah State University, Logan, Utah.

Soccer: Chris Agnello, men's soccer coach, Department of Exercise and Sport Science, University of Utah, Salt Lake City, Utah. Brent Anderson, assistant soccer coach, Heather Carins, head women's soccer coach, Utah State University, Logan, Utah. Charles Dudschus, Health, Physical Education, and Recreation Department, Utah State University, Logan, Utah. Kelli Brooke Parsons, undergraduate physical education student, Utah State University, Logan, Utah. Jin Wang, men's soccer coach, Rockford College, Rockford, Illinois.

Softball: Lloydene Searle, women's fast-pitch head softball coach, Utah State University, Logan, Utah. Ann Schulz, softball coach, Sandridge Junior High School, Layton, Utah. Emily Watkins, graduate student, Stephanie Vasarhely, graduate teaching assistant, Nicole Downs, physical education undergraduate student, Kelly Warner, physical education undergraduate student, Utah State University, Logan, Utah.

Strength Training with Free Weights: Art Erickson and Don Gowans, Health, Physical Education and Recreation Department, Utah State University, Logan, Utah. Nicole Anastasia McKenzie, North Dakota State University, Fargo, North Dakota. Jamie Bennion, heptathlete, graduate student,

Utah State University, Logan, Utah. Peter Mathesius, fitness specialist, Utah State University, Logan, Utah. Mark Uyeyama, M.S., head strength and conditioning coach, Utah State University, Logan, Utah.

Swimming: Katrina Bingham, swimming and water aerobics instructor, Utah State University, Logan, Utah. Lisa Klarich and Steven Dunn, Health, Physical Education and Recreation Department, Utah State University, Logan, Utah.

Team Handball: Mary Phyl Dwight, cochair, Coaching and Methods Committee, United States Team Handball Federation, Kansas City, Missouri. Reita Clanton, assistant coach for women's team handball, Atlanta, Georgia. Peter Mathesius, physical education instructor, Utah State University, Logan, Utah.

Tennis: Janet Carey, tennis professional, Neversink, New York. Dan Clifton, tennis instructor for campus recreation instructional program, Utah State University, Logan, Utah. Steven Dunn, former assistant professor in physical education, Rolayne Wilson, associate professor of physical education, Joy Hartung, tennis athlete and undergraduate student, Tedi Searle, physical education undergraduate student, and Clay Stevens, former graduate student, Utah State University, Logan, Utah. Sarah Lowe, Angela Kimball, Amy Thatcher, and Jackie Ellis, tennis team at Utah State University, Logan, Utah. Christian Wright, Head Tennis Coach, Utah State University, Logan, Utah. Edward Heath, Professor, Physical Education, Utah State University, Logan, Utah.

Touch Rugby: Peter Mathesius, physical education instructor, Utah State University, Logan, Utah. Michelle Olphi, undergraduate rugby player, Utah State University, Logan, Utah.

Track and Field: Curtis Collier, track technician, Utah State University, Logan, Utah. Dayna Barrett, track and field heptathlete, and Jamie Bennion, heptathlete and graduate student, Utah State University, Logan, Utah.

Ultimate Frisbee: Ann Asbell, activity specialist, Department of Exercise and Sport Science, Oregon State University, Corvallis, Oregon. Janenne Graff, player/coach, Ultimate Frisbee Club, Utah State University, Logan, Utah.

Volleyball: Carl McGown, Department of Physical Education, Brigham Young University, Provo, Utah. Lana Moser, head volleyball coach, Preston High School, Preston, Idaho. David Cuthbert, Head Coach for Wessex Volleyball Club Junior Women, Poole, UK.

Yoga: Rachel Hebert, yoga practitioner and model, San Francisco, California. Denise "Deni" Preston, certified group exercise fitness instructor for American Council on Exercise, Brigham Young University, Provo, Utah. Jennifer Fallon, M.S., Yoga Instructor, Utah State University, Logan, Utah. Photography: Christina Pierson.

Pilates: Karen Lynn Smith, Professor and Chairman, Department of Physical Education, Washington College, Chestertown, Maryland. Photography: Karen Lynn Smith.

1

Teaching Physical Education Is Fun with the Right Tools

Have you ever found yourself asking these questions: How can I do a good job teaching physical education and have fun at the same time? What is the quickest and most efficient way to teach sport skills in the time I have been allotted? What tools do I have available to provide a positive learning environment in the sports arena and to build lasting relationships with my students?

This book answers these questions and provides a wealth of teaching cues for physical education activities in your curriculum. The benefits of this book are distinct from the skills text.

- The text answers *why* a cue is appropriate for a skill.
- The text includes photographs of students and athletes, with each cue labeled.
- The text provides cues for successfully teaching fundamental sport skills that are developmentally appropriate.
- The text reinforces the National Standards for Physical Education (NASPE, 2004).
- The text provides a resource for enrichment of the state core curricula.
- Using teaching cues addresses the three learning domains: psychomotor, cognitive, and affective.
- The cues are broken down by components and are easily modified for students with disabilities.
- The cues provide a framework for authentic assessment by teachers and students.
- The cues provide an opportunity to integrate other curricular areas.

TOOL 1: WHAT AM I SUPPOSED TO TEACH?

The National Association for Sport and Physical Education (NASPE) established six content standards and numerous benchmarks that provide curricular objectives for a physically educated person. The National Standards for Physical Education are:

1. Demonstrates competency in motor skills and movement patterns needed to perform a variety of physical activities.
2. Demonstrates understanding of movement concepts, principles, strategies, and tactics as they apply to the learning and performance of physical activities.
3. Participates regularly in physical activity.
4. Achieves and maintains a health-enhancing level of physical fitness.
5. Exhibits responsible personal and social behavior that respects self and others in physical activity settings.
6. Values physical activity for health, enjoyment, challenge, self-expression, and/or social interaction (National Association for Sport and Physical Education [NASPE] and Association of the American Alliance for Health, Physical Education, Recreation and Dance, 2004).

The NASPE (2004) content standards and your state core curriculum provide a curricular foundation for teaching physical education.

TOOL 2: WHAT ARE TEACHING CUES?

A *cue* is defined as a guiding suggestion or a stimulus that excites the imagination to action. Cues are short, catchy phrases that call the student's attention to key components of a skill. A cue projects a clear description of a skill component into the student's mind.

Cues may be verbal, serving as a short reminder of more complete information presented about a skill. A cue developed around rich visual imagery, or related to the student's previous experience, remains in cognition much longer than a lengthy discourse on the fine points of technique. A mind cluttered with many technical concepts cannot direct the muscles to achieve flawless coordination. At best, a mind concentrating on one visual or kinesthetic prompt may direct that one body part to obey the command. For example, a verbal cue for shooting a basketball is "palm up." Phrases may be more visual, with the intent of creating a picture in the learner's mind that results in correct skill performance. The "palm up" cue could be followed by "like holding a waiter's tray." These are prompts that provide a rich visual imagery for students to identify the skill component. By visualizing these familiar patterns, students are able to develop skill patterns, and if they begin to show poor form, a cue serves as a quick reminder of proper form.

Too often when teaching sport skills, the teacher overloads the student with too much information and technical jargon, which may make little sense to the student. Motor learning specialists have long noted that the simpler the instructions, the easier it is for the student to concentrate on the skill at hand. The KISS principle, "keep it short and simple," is applied.

TOOL 3: WHY DO STUDENTS NEED TO GET A CUE?

Cues are used to motivate students. Research has determined that students who receive cues appear to be more motivated to improve their performance than students who do not receive them. The self-confidence of the cued students seems to

FIGURE 1.1 Cues Poster

increase steadily with improved skill ability, as they work to improve each day. Students who do not receive cues appear to be frustrated and bored and have a difficult time staying on task (Fronske, Abendroth-Smith, & Blakemore, 1997).

Cues can help students set higher goals in skill performance. Cues arouse students to direct their efforts toward improving their performance and provide a foundation for setting goals. When students feel the success of learning one cue at a time, you can introduce other cues without intimidation until they become proficient at the complete skill component. Mastering one cue at a time gives students very specific goals to work for. By providing a cue, or a few alternative cues, students are able to choose one and work at their own pace. Create cues posters and display them in your facility for your students to refer to as they practice the skills (Figure 1.1). Cues help all students experience success with sport skills.

Physical education teachers have students for a short period of time during the week. It is imperative that this time be utilized to the fullest. The use of material, such as found in this book, on short, accurate, qualitative teaching cues can save teachers hours of preparation. Research indicates that the combination of accurate, qualitative cues; appropriate numbers of cues; and use of visual demonstrations along with verbal explanations seems to produce greater skill development gains (Rink, 1993). The cues in this book have been developed by experts in their respective areas to help teachers give accurate, qualitative cues regarding a specific sport skill. These cues *work*!

Cues also address the psychomotor, cognitive, and affective learning domains. They

- Enhance the learner's memory. (cognitive)
- Compress information and reduce words. (cognitive)
- Encourage focus on one specific component of a skill. (psychomotor)
- Help teachers and students analyze a skill performance by helping them focus on a particular component of the skill. (psychomotor)
- Strengthen correct performance. (psychomotor)
- Help teachers give positive, corrective feedback. (affective and cognitive)
- Help peers give positive, corrective feedback. (affective and cognitive)
- Motivate students to develop and refine skills. (affective and cognitive)

TOOL 4: HOW DO STUDENTS GET A CUE?

Students are visual learners and need three to five demonstrations. The use of demonstrations is the best way to teach with cues. Cues used with demonstrations help students develop a strong visual image of the skill. When demonstrating a skill, the teacher focuses the students' attention on one specific component of the skill through the use of a good verbal or visual cue. To avoid confusing students, it is important to keep verbalization to a minimum. For example, having students make an upside-down L when performing skipping A's gives them a picture upon which to base their skill. By picturing the correct pattern, they are able to develop the correct skipping patterns. If they begin to show improper form, a cue, a demonstration, or both can serve as a quick reminder of proper form.

Do not overload students with too many cues. Here are some helpful tips when teaching with cues:

- Research in motor learning indicates that students can best learn with a limited amount of new material.
- Giving students too much information or progressing to new information before students have grasped a concept may hinder the learning process.
- Too much information is worse than no information at all.
- For each component of a skill, practice the whole skill, but focus on each part in turn.
- Give students no more than one to three cues at a time.
- Following the acquisition of the motor pattern targeted to the first cue (e.g., in the football punt, "kick the fish in the belly"), teachers then move to the next phase of the motor skill.
- Additional cues should build on the previously learned skills, with no more than three cues for each teaching episode.
- Students need short bits of information that they can quickly apply to their skill.
- Practice, practice, practice; repetition, repetition, repetition.

Provide students with lots of opportunities to respond (OTRs), such as touching the ball. You want maximum activity with minimum wait time. Each student or pair is provided with a piece of equipment. This increases a student's OTRs. This book provides great drill progressions and mini-games to assist you when teaching sport skills and games that offer lots of OTRs.

Providing feedback to your students is a critical tool to help them learn sport skills. To earn your credibility as an educator, you must work hard during each class session. Giving appropriate feedback is the "heartbeat" of the class. Is it tough to give feedback in each class session? Yes. Why? Because it takes focus, intensity, time, and effort to pay attention to the performance of the students. When teachers are in tune and give appropriate corrective feedback, it helps to maintain the supportive climate. Why? Because, as Thomas Dewey states, "The deepest urge in human nature is the desire to be important" (Carnegie, 1981, p. 18). William James states, "The deepest principle in human nature is the craving to be appreciated" (Carnegie, 1981, p. 18). When teachers pay attention to students, students feel important, and when teachers give feedback, students feel appreciated.

Teachers need to notice details about their students. "What kind of details?" you might ask. Start with the effort the individual is giving when performing a skill or participating in a game. Study each student's face and body language. This takes hard work on your part, but if the students know you are paying attention to them and that you notice the small details, they will develop trust in you because they sense you care about them as individuals.

But this tool is not enough for you to earn credibility with your students. You must know the correct movement patterns to analyze the skills of your students and give technical feedback. Using cues in this book will give you a jump start in earning credibility with your students. Teaching sport skills is easier and more effective when you focus on one to three cues and then give feedback on those cues.

Just as important as technical feedback is positive communication between you and a student. Eighty percent of what a teacher communicates to students is through nonverbal behaviors, such as body language: for example, thumbs up or down, clapping, the "yes" arm pump, the raise-the-roof motion, the OK sign, facial expressions, "The Look," raising the eyebrow, a wink, the with-it-ness body stance, hands in pockets, or folded arms.

The smile is a very powerful nonverbal tool in teaching. Why? Dale Carnegie states, "Actions speak louder than words and a smile says, 'I like you, you make me happy, I am glad to see you'" (Carnegie, 1981, p. 66). People who smile, he said, "tend to manage, teach and sell more effectively and to raise happier children. There is far more information in a smile than a frown. That's why encouragement is a much more effective teaching device than punishment of other people. People rarely succeed unless you are having fun doing it" (p. 67). "The smile enriches those who receive it without impoverishing those who give it, happens in a flash and the memory of it sometimes lasts forever" (p. 70).

Another communication technique is appropriate touch, such as high fives, low fives, side fives, backward fives, and a jump with two-handed fives. Appropriate places to touch students may be the arms, shoulders, and back. Be sensitive to other cultural customs regarding appropriate touch.

There is one more tool that works when giving feedback: The Challenge. This tool is rarely discussed in the literature. The best coaches in the United States—John Wooden, Pat Summit, Phil Jackson, and many others—challenge their athletes. A Challenge is stimulating, thought provoking, something that incites or quickens actions, feelings, and thoughts; and it arouses to action or effort by encouragement. The Challenge is usually disguised. It comes with risk, but it can become a major tool for taking your students beyond what they think is their potential.

The Challenge happens only after you have built positive relationships with your students. To issue a challenge, you must know the student's backgrounds, dreams, and goals. Then and only then will The Challenge be effective.

To review, the following are five examples of feedback:

- *Effort:* "Abby, great effort on trying to throw the ball left-handed. Try making a better L for me." Or "Great effort running the bases."
- *Technical:* Give positive, specific feedback on a cue, and then correct an error. "Amanda, great L throwing on the ball. Now try to take a longer step on the target." (Figure 1.2, page 6).
- *Nonverbal:* Clear across the gym, you notice that Abby is practicing making an L with her left arm. Give her a thumbs-up and a big smile. (Figure 1.3, page 6).
- *Appropriate touch:* "Amanda, I like your long step to the target." You give Amanda a high five (Figure 1.4, page 6).
- *Challenge:* John already knows how to throw. You say to John, "Is that the hardest or farthest you can throw the ball?" Another example might be found in a game situation. You notice John jogging around the bases. You might say, "John, is that the fastest you can go around the bases? I noticed you are quite a sprinter and you outrun everyone in class. Show me how fast you can run."

FIGURE 1.2 Technical Feedback

FIGURE 1.3 Nonverbal Feedback

Carnegie (1981) sums up the importance of providing feedback: "You want the approval of those with whom you come in contact. You want recognition of your true worth. You want a feeling that you are important in your little world. You don't want to listen to cheap, insincere flattery but you do crave sincere appreciation. How? When? Where? The answer is: All the time, everywhere" (p. 101).

If you use these specific feedback tools, will it help you become a better teacher? Absolutely! Start today.

Mini-Games Increase Feedback Opportunities

Mini-games with three to six students on each team are recommended so that students have an opportunity to respond. Feedback is easier to give when your class is divided into smaller groups. More is better! More students with their

FIGURE 1.4 Appropriate Touch

FIGURE 1.5 Mini-Game

own equipment. More opportunities to practice. More feedback gives the students more skill development and more confidence to succeed (Figure 1.5).

Feedback on the cues should be given during these games. Teachers usually do not give technical feedback in the game situation but get caught up watching the game, or if they do give feedback, it is in the form of nags (negative feedback). Mini-games provide a great opportunity to gain credibility with your students. Remember: it takes effort, hard work, observation, focus, and timing to give precisely the right feedback. Try to use a variety of feedback techniques, and always give the students something to work on. Your class will be full of exciting options to help your students learn skills, have fun playing games, and develop lifetime sport skills. You will also be so absorbed in the class that time will pass very quickly, and your passion for your work will increase. The students will feel your fervor, enthusiasm, and passion when you teach. Watch the best teachers and see what *they* do.

Custom Teaching Cues for Your Students

After reading this book, you may want to design your own cues. Connie Blakemore (personal communication, January 1997) offers suggestions on how to begin the process:

- Go to various sources—skill books, skill videos, workshops, experts, and so on—to make sure the cue is accurate.
- Condense the skill analysis to a few effective words. Find the catchy words, metaphors, short phrases, and key words in the resources. Avoid long sentences.
- Determine, for example, what is critical to the task with three to five cues. Decide which is the most important cue for the skill, then the second most important, then the third, and so on.
- Design the cues for the appropriate age and learning stage.
- Cut out pictures from a sports section in the newspaper or a sports magazine, or use sports photographs of your students. Type one to three cues, place them directly onto the pictures of photos, and make photocopies. Display these pictures in the gym, the locker room, or a recreation center, or at athletic events.
- Listen to your students. They sometimes come up with creative cues. However, make sure their cues are accurate.
- If you're not already there, shift to the right side of your brain and develop your own creative cues.

TOOL 5: HOW DO I ORGANIZE A SUCCESSFUL CLASS?

Develop a Supportive Climate on the First Day

On the first day of class, the teacher needs to get to know each student—and the students need to get to know each other—before anything else is done (Figure 1.6). How do you set the stage for the first hour of class? The first protocol, or rule, is that no one talks when a student or teacher is "onstage." Ask each student to stand and talk about something they carry with them each day, or perhaps to imagine some piece of sports equipment they would like to be. Why is this activity critical on the first day? It breaks the ice between the students and the teacher. The students begin to feel comfortable with each other. They begin relating to each other's experiences. First impressions and judgments—good or bad—are replaced by feelings of warmth for the individual. The students feel more comfortable talking with each other, and they learn specific facts about their classmates. They can use this information to open a conversation. Walls come down. Relationships start to form. The teacher also benefits and has information with which to spark a later conversation.

Another reason this activity is so effective is that all students must be quiet when not onstage. This teaches respect for each other, and the teacher can begin to work on management skills, setting the tone for the rest of the year.

On the second day, have students network with a partner for about five minutes. Each student stands with a partner, and they share with the group what they have learned about each other. Once again, emphasize the rule that no one else is to talk when partners are sharing their experiences about their new friend. Respect is reinforced. You will be amazed at how well the students listen during this time. Perform this type of activity throughout the year whenever you feel a need to bond with your class. Remember, the first few days are critical in terms of what you will do the rest of your year. The benefits of a supportive climate (Patton & Griffin, 1981) include the following:

- Group members more easily accept others' influence.
- Members of the group are less suspicious of the motives of others.
- A greater degree of tolerance of deviant behavior occurs.
- When conflicts arise, the group is able to focus on the group goals rather than on defending egos.
- The group develops trust, which allows more freedom for group risk taking.
- Members of the group feel better about themselves.

FIGURE 1.6 Supportive Climate on the First Day

Establish a Supportive Climate When Teaching Sport Skills

Teachers need to establish a framework of support in order to implement teaching cues successfully. Students need to feel safe in order to reach out and try new behaviors. Creating a supportive climate promotes a safe learning environment for students. The supportive climate happens verbally, with positive, clear cues and reinforcing phrases. It also happens in a safe, nonverbal physical environment.

Nonverbal behaviors, which accompany verbal cues, also communicate to students. A teacher who says, "Nice dive," accompanied by a harsh tone of voice and disapproving facial expression, communicates, "Bad dive." The way teachers present cues—the tone of their voice, their body language, their manner of touch, or the way they dress (such as a teacher not wearing a swimsuit in a swim class)—can enhance or detract from a positive comment.

Great teachers and coaches are skillful at giving the most appropriate cue at the appropriate time, using verbal and/or nonverbal signals. Combining verbal cues and positive nonverbal cues becomes a powerful tool for providing feedback from the teacher. By creating a supportive climate, you can help students feel comfortable and become motivated to explore and learn a variety of sports.

Build Relationships and Still Get the Work Done

Hunter (1998) states this about building relationships: "If we focus only on tasks and not on the relationship, we may experience turnover, rebellion, poor quality, low commitment, low trust and other undesirable symptoms" (p. 40). Being an excellent leader maximizes the teacher's effectiveness. The first thing one must do is value those leading and strive to develop healthy and mutually respectful relationships. Hunter continues, "The key then to leadership is accomplishing the tasks at hand while building relationships" (p. 41).

How does a teacher continue to build relationships (Figure 1.7) and still get the work done? Theodore Roosevelt (as all leaders know) said that "the royal road to a person's heart is to talk about things he or she treasures most" (Carnegie, 1981, p. 94). Teachers have many opportunities to learn each day about students' lives and what they treasure. Here are some options to think about: Take time before school, at lunch, and after school to visit with your students. Interview them about their interests, dreams, and goals. Attend school functions to let them know you care about them. Let them talk about what they did over the weekend, on spring break, or during their summer vacations.

Expending the effort to build relationships with your students develops their respect and trust. They will be more willing to work for you, so work on

FIGURE 1.7 Building Relationships

building relationships daily. The best teachers do, and the work gets done in a supportive climate.

Establish Protocols and Use Management Skills

Protocols are necessary to provide a safe learning environment and to provide structure for your students. Just like any other sport skill, the protocols need to be practiced repeatedly. For further information, refer to Graham, Holt/Hale, and Parker (2000) and Pangrazi (2007a, 2007b). The following protocols are just a few to get you started.

1. Establish start and stop signals. The signals need to be different from each other. They can be auditory or visual, or a combination of both—for example, one whistle blow to start and two whistle blows to stop.
2. Establish protocols; for example (Figure 1.8):
   - Proper dress: tee shirt, shorts, tennis shoes, and socks
   - No talking while others are talking
   - A gathering place for giving instruction and talking to the entire class
   - Distributing and collecting of equipment
   - Grouping students: partners, teams, and so forth
   - Off-task behavior; for example, three strikes, you're out—one strike is a warning; second strike, the student sits out for five minutes and observes the class; third strike, the student sits out for the entire class
3. Provide a piece of developmentally appropriate equipment for each student; this is key so students have many opportunities to practice sport skills. Teachers (Figure 1.9) need to be creative in finding ways to work

FIGURE 1.8 Establishing Protocols

FIGURE 1.9 Everyone Has a Piece of Equipment

FIGURE 1.10 Establish a Home for the Equipment

their budget to buy safe, age-appropriate equipment. For example, good, inexpensive leather volleyballs can be purchased from college volleyball teams. Old tennis balls can be purchased from tennis teams or tennis clubs. Send home a letter with students at the beginning of the school year indicating your equipment needs. Enlist the help of the high school shop or an applied technology school to make equipment. Use your creativity to find solutions.

4. Establish a "home" for the equipment when giving directions: for example, students can place a basketball or softball between their feet (Figure 1.10).
5. Move around the perimeter of the area, with your back to the wall, during activities. You can observe the entire class, give instruction, and offer feedback to students.
6. Maximize activity time and minimize wait time. Mini-games are very effective in increasing OTRs and minimizing wait time.
7. Avoid having lines of students wait for their turn.
8. See Woods and Langley's concerns (1997, pp. 8–9) about circle formations:
   - Lack of practice time
   - Requirement for complex use of the skill
   - Organizational pattern that does not match game requirements
   - Potential to embarrass and discourage
   - No clear goals for success
   - Potential to increase management problems

   The authors then list six suggestions for effective student learning:

   - Adequate practice time
   - Requirement for less-complex use of skill
   - Organizational patterns that match game requirements
   - Development of student self-confidence
   - Clear goals for success
   - Effective management of student practice

Use a Successful Teaching Model

How does a teacher correctly teach a motor skill? What is a correct and successful teaching model? How do teaching cues fit into this model? The following are components of a good teaching model, with suggestions for implementing cues.

FIGURE 1.11 Demonstrate So All Can See and Hear

- Get the students' attention! Use anticipatory sets (attention getters) to motivate the students to perform the skill. Make sure they pay attention to the instructions. Be enthusiastic!
- Organize the group so that everyone can see and hear. State the lesson objective by describing what is to be learned and why it is important. Your objective should be brief, simple, and direct. This should lead to a demonstration (Figure 1.11).
- Preassess your students by asking how many of them know how to perform the skill, or ask the students to perform the skill if it is relatively safe.
- Demonstrate the entire skill three to five times. Show the skill from front, side, and back angles. Demonstrations should be performed as they would appear in a game situation. Move the class around so they can see the demonstration from different angles. The students should see a correct demonstration of the skill. Remember, a picture is worth a thousand words when learning a sport skill.
- After the demonstration, have the students practice the skill. This will give you time to assess their proficiency.
- Have the students practice the skill. You provide feedback on the cue words used in the demonstration. Use a systematic approach to giving feedback to all of your students during the class.
- Use one teaching cue at a time. This directs the students' attention to the specific area of focus.
- Provide additional demonstrations and new cues when students have mastered the previous ones.
- Review and/or demonstrate the cues during class closure. Provide the students with an opportunity to ask questions.
- Have students repeat aloud the cues for the skill. The cues will be fresh in their memories.

Develop Cues for Students with Disabilities

You might have the opportunity to teach students with disabilities. Be creative in developing cues and activities for these students. For example, you could put a bell around a ball for a blind student, integrate brightly colored equipment for the hearing impaired, and use balloons for the student in a wheelchair. Include all of the other students. Let them participate on their own levels, see their excitement in being able to participate, and feel the emotional bonding with your students.

TOOL 6: AUTHENTIC ASSESSMENT: HOW DO I KNOW THE CUES ARE WORKING?

Cues Help Instructors Analyze a Skill

Some physical education teachers tend to analyze skills excessively and tell all they know (Lockhart, 1996). Cues are short and to the point, and they focus the assessment process on giving specific feedback.

Teaching cues provide students with valuable information to accompany demonstrations. Cues aid you in focusing on correct skill performance so that appropriate feedback can be given. Incorporating cues in the teaching process makes it possible for you to identify major errors quickly. For example, when the students are performing the forehand stroke in tennis, and the cue is "swing racket low to high," it is easy to observe whether the racket head is high at the end of the stroke. It is also important to explain why it is necessary to perform a particular cue accurately.

Cues Strengthen Correct Performance

A critical component of skill acquisition is identifying the parts of the skill that are being performed correctly. You can have the students work in pairs or in small groups; in this way, they can analyze their performance and give feedback to each other on one specific cue. For example, the following three cues for throwing a ball are used: (1) Take the ball straight down and graze your shorts, (2) stretch your arm way back, and (3) make an L. Student responses might include the following:

- "Hey, I like the way you brought your arm down and grazed your shorts. That action will give you more distance."
- "Way to make an L shape with your arm! You're keeping the ball away from your head."
- "Wow! Way to stretch your arm way back! That was a great stretch. It looks like Barry Bonds's or Dale Murphy's."

This type of specific feedback increases the likelihood that the student will repeat the correct response in the near future.

Cues Help Correct Errors in Technique

"Coach, how can I get over the hurdles faster?" "How do I improve my sprint time?" "What is the best way to exchange the baton?" These are questions students might ask about track skills. Are you ready to answer these questions without criticizing or giving the student too much information?

Your challenge is to identify the cause of the problem and look for solutions. The effective use of cues avoids judgment and criticism. Cues are used to correct errors constructively. Cues help you identify the problem and provide accurate feedback to the student: for example, "Stacie, I really liked how you made a 'banana shape' when performing the long jump. This time, work on the 'jackknife position' when you land."

Cues Help Peers Correct Errors in Technique

When students are provided with correct teaching cues, they can help give feedback to other peers. Pair students and have them observe their partner's performance. For example, if the cue given on throwing is, "Stand sideways and take a long step toward the target," a student can watch her partner and assess whether she is standing sideways and taking the long step. If her partner steps too high or takes a short step, but is standing sideways, she can provide her partner with the following feedback: "Hey, Stacie, you stood sideways. Now remember to take a long step with your foot toward the target." This feedback emphasizes a student's correct performance, notifies her of the error, and suggests a specific way to correct it, providing a more positive interaction.

Cues Help Teachers to Assess Students' Performance

Cues are a valuable tool for assessing your students. You can assess them specifically on the cues you have taught. Your students know specific components of the skill they need to practice and how they will be assessed. This gives them an opportunity to practice the important cues. For example, a rubric can be designed with a four-point checklist. A rubric on the overhand throw might include the following:

- Stands sideways to the target
- Makes an L with the throwing arm
- Takes a long step with the leg closest to the target
- Throws hard

Decide how you want to mark the checklist. You might choose a yes-or-no format or a scale ranging from proficient to almost there to needs more practice.

CONCLUSION

The tools outlined in this chapter help make teaching fun and exciting. Students will appreciate your expertise and retain knowledge in a fun and caring environment. This book is intended to widen your vision about teaching. The cues in this book can be effective, motivating, and life altering when students are successful. To establish credibility quickly, incorporate the teaching cues in subsequent chapters to obtain the edge that is necessary to connect with your students. Have fun!

FYI

PUBLICATIONS

Carnegie, D. (1981). *How to win friends and influence people.* New York: Pocket Books.

Fronske, H., Abendroth-Smith, J., & Blakemore, C. (1997). The effect of critical cues on throwing efficiency of elementary school children. *The Physical Educator, 54*(2), 88–95.

Graham, G., Holt/Hale S., & Parker, M. (2000). *Children moving: A reflective approach to teaching physical education* (5th ed.). Mountain View, CA: Mayfield.

Hunter, J. C. (1998). *The servant: A simple story about the true essence of leadership.* Roseville, CA: Prima.

Lockhart, A. (1966, May). Communicating with the learner. *Quest, VI,* 57–67.

NASPE. (2004). *Moving into the future: National standards for physical education* (2nd ed.). St. Louis: Mosby.

Pangrazi, R. (2007a). *Dynamic physical education for elementary school children* (15th ed.). San Francisco: Benjamin Cummings.

Pangrazi, R. (2007b). *Dynamic physical education curriculum guide: Lesson plans for implementation* (15th ed.). San Francisco: Benjamin Cummings.

Patton, B. R., & Griffin, K. (1981). *Interpersonal communication in action: Basic text and readings* (3rd ed.). New York: Harper & Row.

Rink, J. (1993). *Teaching physical education for learning*. St. Louis: Times Mirror/Mosby.

Woods, A., & Langley, D. (1997). Circle drills: Do they accomplish your goals? *Journal of Physical Education, Recreation, and Dance, 68*(3), 8–9.

2

Aerobic Kickboxing

INTRODUCTION

Taebo, CardioKarate, Karabo, Cardio Kickboxing, or even kickboxercise all refer to the same thing: the rhythmic repetitions of traditional fighting techniques combined with elements from aerobic dance. This blending of martial-arts-based techniques, such as punches, kicks, and knee and elbow strikes, with aerobic dance music and choreography produces aerobic kickboxing.

Currently, aerobic kickboxing is one of the fastest-growing additions to the health and fitness craze in the United States. As its name implies, aerobic kickboxing is really a type of cross-training workout. An aerobic kickboxing workout incorporates all the muscles of the body and can include anaerobic components through the use of burnout drills: muscular endurance with prolonged repetition of techniques. Although aerobic kickboxing works well as a solo activity, it is a good supplement for other sports or physical activities.

Why Should Physical Educators Teach Aerobic Kickboxing?

In an effort to motivate more kids to participate in physical education classes (particularly in school districts where PE is an elective), some schools are currently experimenting with activities that high school students already choose to do in their free time. The current success of aerobic kickboxing in the health and fitness clubs and the massive media hype on aerobic kickboxing due to the success of Billy Blank's Taebo video series has made it an obvious choice for such an activity. Aerobic kickboxing is already now being offered either as a unit or as a regular class in some public schools. In both cases it is generally the regular physical education staff that ends up teaching it. It is for you, the physical education teachers of the third millennium, who will likely find yourselves teaching aerobic kickboxing at some point in your career, that this chapter has been written.

What Do I Need to Get Started?

Contrary to what many current fitness clubs and martial-arts studios advertise, you don't need experience with either aerobics or martial arts, just a basic knowledge of the techniques you plan to incorporate, an ability to keep a steady beat, and tons of energy and enthusiasm. Nevertheless, expertise with either of these activities would enhance the quality of your program.

SKILLS LISTED WITH CUES

Aerobic kickboxing involves a plethora of skills that can be used and therefore taught, which makes it impossible to cover all of them in just a few short pages. But wait! Don't panic just yet. There are a few basic skills that, once learned and performed correctly, can make any instructor look good in front of a class regardless of a lack of experience with aerobic kickboxing. What's more exciting is that not only will your class get an incredible workout, but they will more than likely have fun doing it, . . . and you will too! The techniques covered in this chapter along with their cues are the boxer's stance, center position, Roc Hop step, step-and-touch step, bob and weave, jab punch, cross punch, uppercut punch, aerobic uppercut punch, hook punch, speed bag punch, back fist strike, front kick, side kick, roundhouse kick, and back kick. Once learned, these techniques can be used as a strong backbone of any aerobic kickboxing program for all experience levels.

TIPS

1. The best way to learn to teach any aerobic class, including aerobic kickboxing, is to attend classes taught by a variety of instructors to get a feel for their teaching styles until you develop your own class.
2. If you find particular instructors or teaching formats you like, imitate them (don't directly copy them) for awhile until you feel comfortable teaching with your own style.
3. Videos can be an invaluable resource for new ideas. But remember that many of your students may also have the same video, so you'll still need your own creativity to keep the combinations from the videos fresh.
4. A good rule of thumb to use when preparing an aerobic kickboxing class is to mirror your routine on both sides of the body (i.e., what you do on one side, you have to do on the other side). This will keep your classes feeling balanced.
5. A good idea, especially for beginning aerobic kickboxing instructors, is to write out the entire workout from warm-ups to cooldowns. List the specific techniques you want to teach, in the order you want, with the approximate amount of time needed for each activity. Remember, if you do jab punches with the left hand, you'll have to do them on the right side as well.
6. It is *never* a good idea when teaching aerobic kickboxing (or any other type of aerobics class) just to roll in the video cart, plug in an aerobics video, and expect the class to follow along. Watching a video for class is boring and looks unprofessional. Either make up a routine using techniques you know, or find someone else with more experience to teach that unit.

EQUIPMENT TIPS

1. Equipment needed to teach aerobic kickboxing includes a quality stereo system, kickboxing targets or punching bags, bag gloves or hand wraps to protect the knuckles and wrists from injury, jump ropes, regular hand weights, and music. Good, clean, high-energy music and a decent sound system are critical to the overall quality of the class. If the music flops, so will your class.
2. Aerobic kickboxing requires no special clothes or equipment—just a pair of secure shorts (remember you will be bouncing on the balls of your feet a lot, so things can fall off) and a cool tee shirt.
3. Hand wraps, if used, should secure the wrist enough so that the range of motion is limited but should not restrict blood flow in the hand or forearm. Many boxing and martial arts supplies now include wrap instructions.
4. Equipment such as bags, jump ropes, and hand weights should be in place before class begins so that students can get to it in a matter of seconds, but it should also be out of the way so that it doesn't become a safety hazard.
5. If you decide to incorporate bags into your class, it is suggested that a portable heavy bag, such as the Century Wavemaster bag, be used rather than smaller bags such as handheld focus mitts or kicking shields. This way students can work alone if need be, and time will not be wasted in showing new students how to hold the smaller bags.
6. When focus mitts are used, be sure everyone knows how to hold the bag correctly for the partner. If students don't know how to hold a bag, safety problems can arise.
7. Be sure to match students of equal size and power when using focus mitts and kicking shields in order to reduce the chance that a student holding the pad will be injured by a technique too powerful for him.
8. Smaller pads can be a lot of fun. Use some creativity on how you have the class hold the smaller bags, so that both students are getting a great workout. For example, to keep students' heart rates up, have one student punch the focus mitts as many times as she can until tired; then have the pad holder do squat thrusts until tired while the puncher bounces in place. This can be done several times, in two-minute periods, with students exchanging pads.

TEACHING IDEAS

1. Teaching aerobic kickboxing is slightly different from aerobic dance classes. Aerobic kickboxing classes do not have to be taught using the standard 32-count system used in aerobic dance. (The 32-count system has students performing combinations in exactly 32 counts of music.) Aerobic kickboxing techniques are different from the dance techniques used in dance aerobics, and therefore timing is less important. If you know how to stay on count, this ability will help your classes. However, simply staying on beat (listen to the bass for help) with correct technique, lots of energy, and enthusiasm is sufficient for aerobic kickboxing.
2. Do not shortcut techniques to stay on beat with the music. If the music seems too fast, either simplify the combinations or pick slower music.
3. If you're familiar with professionally produced aerobics music, step music works really well for aerobic kickboxing. It's about a 128-count system.

4. Write your entire routine on a 3 × 5 index card so that it can be taped to a mirror, a nearby desk, or some other convenient place. If you should forget a combination, you can glance at your note card.
5. Aerobic kickboxing is aerobic in nature, meaning it is continuous. Keep the class in their target heart rate range of about 70–80 percent of their maximum heart rate. *All feedback and corrections should be done while the class stays moving.*
6. The old adage "Fake it until you make it" definitely applies to aerobic kickboxing. If you forget what comes next in your routine, fake it until you remember. Doing so will keep the class on task and their heart rates up.

A Warning

One of the scariest things about the current media push for aerobic kickboxing is the notion that aerobic kickboxing teaches self-defense. Aerobic kickboxing does not teach self-defense. While the techniques may be the same, and even technically correct, aerobic kickboxing is intended more to improve overall fitness than to teach self-defense. Techniques such as hook punches or roundhouse kicks may be the same as in self-defense class, but aerobic kickboxing does not teach students how or when to use these techniques. It would be just as fair to say that by shooting free throws, a person can learn how to play basketball. Aerobic kickboxing instructors should explain this principle to students right from the beginning.

FYI

For further information about aerobic kickboxing, consult the following organizations and resources.

ORGANIZATIONS

Promise Enterprises
P.O. Box 7654
Jackson, MS 39284
Phone: (601) 372-8313

EQUIPMENT SUPPLIES

Century Martial Supply
1705 National Boulevard
Midwest City, OK 73110-7942
Phone: (800) 626-2787
Website: www.centuryma.com

Asian World of Martial Arts
917 Arch Street
Philadelphia, PA 19154-2117
Phone: (215) 969-3500
Website: www.awma.com

PROFESSIONAL MIXED AEROBIC WORKOUT MUSIC

Aerobic and Fitness Association of America
15250 Ventura Blvd., #200
Sherman Oaks, CA 91403

Power Music
P.O. Box 27927
Salt Lake City, UT 84127-0927

Dynamix: (800) 843-6499
In-Lytes Productions: (800) 243-7867
Muscle Mixes Music: (800) 52-Mixes
Musicflex: (718) 738-6839
Sports Music, Inc.: (800) 391-7692
The Work Out Source: (800) 552-4552

PUBLICATION

Thiboutot, F., & Croteau, K. (2001, January 1). *Cardio kickboxing elite.* Roslindale, MA: YMAA Publications.

WEBSITES

www.aerobickick.com
www.artofcombat.com/aerobic2.htm

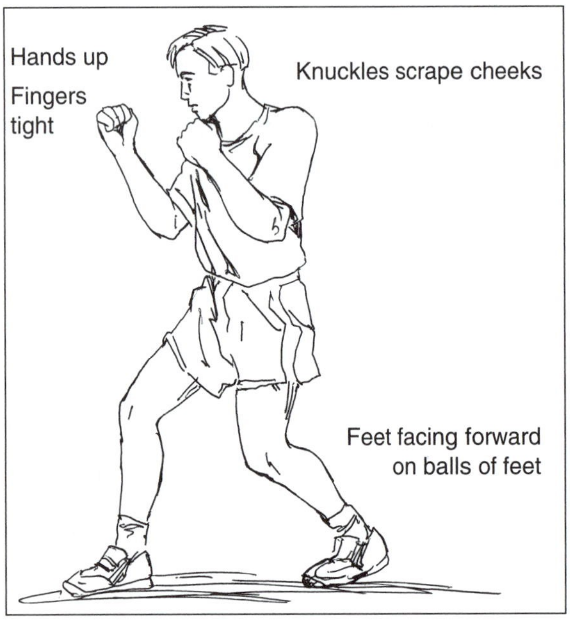

FIGURE 2.1 Boxer's Shuffle or Fighting Stance

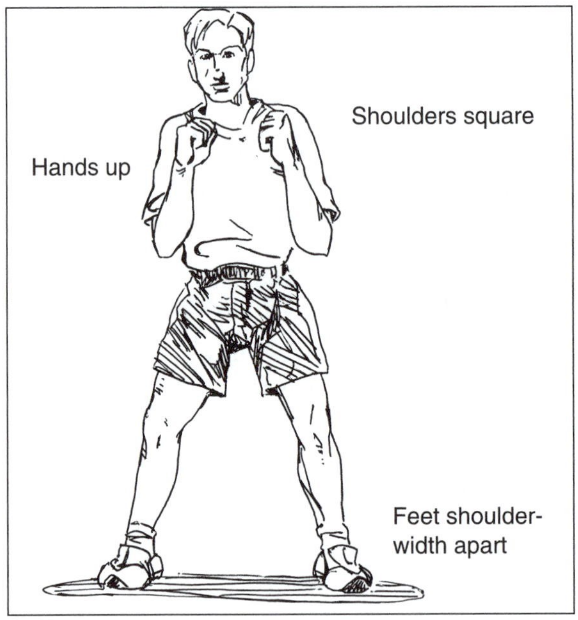

FIGURE 2.2 Center Position

STANCES AND STEPS

SKILL	CUE	WHY	COMMON ERROR
Boxer's Stance	Shoulders and hips face straight ahead	Allows boxer to hit target with maximum power and reach	Shoulders turn inward
Boxer's Shuffle (Figure 2.1)	Dominant leg steps back		Hands drop below chin
			Feet flat on floor
	Fists by cheeks; knuckles scrape cheeks	Develops good technique that protects face and ribs	Shoulders turn inward
	On balls of feet	Keeps body moving and light on feet	
		Allows boxer to move quickly	
	Shoulders and hips face straight ahead		
Center Boxing Stance Position (Figure 2.2)	Feet shoulder width apart with slight bend in knees	Allows for maximum lateral movement	Feet too close or wide
	Fists by cheeks; knuckles scrape cheeks, shoulders square	Protects face	Hands drop below chin
Roc Hop Step	Bring lead leg knee up (or kick)		
	Feet return to side by side		
	Rear leg steps back		
	Feet return to side-by-side	Step is more of a dance step that is used in conjunction with punches and kicks	Not returning feet to side-by-side
Step and Touch	Move point foot of trailing leg laterally		
	Step and touch		

continued

STANCES AND STEPS, continued			
SKILL	CUE	WHY	COMMON ERROR
Bob and Weave	Drop body, bending at knees	Allows the boxer to drop under a punch, come up chambered to center a punch	Bending over at the waist
		Can be used with or without a partner	
	Move upper body side to side		Whole body rising up all at once
	Lead with shoulder coming up		
	Keep hands and eyes up		Looking down during bob

Note: Cues for all punches except one are to be executed while in the boxer's stance. The one exception is the aerobic uppercut punch, which is always done from the center position. This punch is not intended to create any power. It is used as a burnout exercise for the arms and shoulders and should not be practiced on pads.

Here are a couple of cues to remember that apply to any punch: hands always start and end by the cheeks; the wrists should always be locked straight out; and the nonpunching hand should be kept up by the cheek at all times. A common error that many people make while learning to punch is to use only their arms and shoulders to punch. A correct punch actually uses the entire body beginning with a slight turn of the pivot foot, continued by a slight turn of the hips and shoulder, and ending when the force is finally released through the arm and fist to the target.

PUNCHES			
SKILL	**CUE**	**WHY**	**COMMON ERROR**
Jab	Extend lead arm straight out		Arm not fully extended
	Fist tight with wrist straight		Fingers loose Wrist bent
Cross Reverse	Extend rear arm straight out		Arm not fully extended
	Rear leg pivots onto ball of foot	Pivot creates power and distance for punch	Foot stays flat on ground
	Shoulders turn inward, leading with punching shoulder		Shoulders stay square
Uppercut Punch	Knees dip	Power for punch comes from hip as knees push on return back	Punch uses only shoulders
	Punching hand chambers back, held in tight 45° angle		Arm kept too vertical
	Explode off feet, pushing fist and navel through target		Punch stops at target Shoulders stay squared
Aerobic Uppercut Flutter Punch	Feet and shoulders square up		One leg stays back
	Both arms held in tight 45° angle		
	Rapid punch using just the shoulders and arms	Rapid punches are designed to burn out arms and shoulders	Arm kept too vertical
	Elbows are brushing sides		Elbows point outward
Lead Arm Hook	Lead arm drops to make a tight L between shoulder, elbow, arms, and wrist	Arm drops to be able to strike to sides of bag or partners	Wrist slightly bent
	Lead hand generally at rib or head level		
	Lead foot lifts up onto ball of foot		Foot stays flat
	Lead foot, hips, and lead shoulder pivot inward through target	Creates power punch	Only leg turns Punch stops at target

continued

PUNCHES, continued			
SKILL	**CUE**	**WHY**	**COMMON ERROR**
Back Fist Strike	1. Lead arm drops to make a tight L between shoulder, elbow, and wrist with palms facing you		Wrist slightly bent
	2. "Open the gate"	Arm extended for open gate in order to align back of hand with target	
	3. Extend arm and shoulder through target	Push through target with fist to create power	
Speed Bag Punch	One or both arms turn inward 45° so elbows point out		Arm(s) drop to make L
	Move arms in circling motion		
	First 2 knuckles should lead punch		Pinkie finger leads punch
	"Hit the back of the hand"		

Note: All kicks can be broken down into four basic parts. These parts are the *chamber* when the knee lifts up, the *extension* or kick, the *recoil* where the knee returns to the chambered position, and the *recovery* when the kicking leg returns to the ground. Be sure to watch for all four parts in your students' kicks.

As beginning kickers get excited, they tend to kick faster by shortcutting one or more of these four parts. By shortcutting a kick, students develop poor technique and will not be able to generate much power. They may also injure themselves in classes that incorporate the use of kicking bags. So watch for it!

KICKS

SKILL	CUE	WHY	COMMON ERROR
Front Kick	Bring up knee of kicking leg	Tight chamber and recoil creates power	Kicking with foot dorsiflexed
	Flex the ankle	Flex ankle to allow kick to make contact with ball of foot	
	Extend kick out		
Side Kick	Bring knee to chest, heel pointed out	Tight chamber creates power	Kick not locked out
	Extend kick straight out		Kicking with entire bottom of foot
	Push heel through target	Power for kick is maintained when sent through target rather than bouncing off target	
	Stomp your target		
Roundhouse (Figure 2.3, page 26)	Bring kicking knee up at 45° angle		
	Planted foot pivots 180°	Power from kick is created when hips are in line with target; pivoting the hips will turn them to align with target	Foot doesn't pivot
	Extend kick with toes pointed		Kicking with foot dorsiflexed

continued

KICKS, continued			
SKILL	CUE	WHY	COMMON ERROR
Back Kick	Pick up kicking knee		Kicking with entire bottom of foot
			Knee points out
	Kick straight back, hit with heel		
	Brush knees together "like a cricket"		

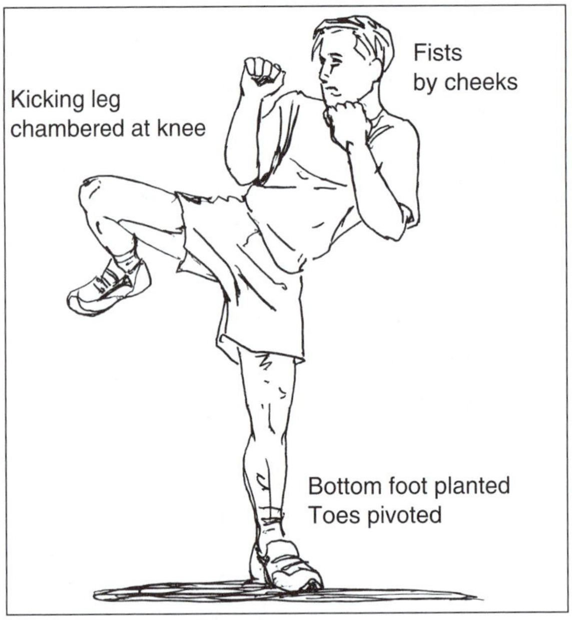

FIGURE 2.3 Chamber for Roundhouse Kick

3

Archery

INTRODUCTION

Are you looking for a new way to have fun or a new sport to add to your curricula? Archery is one of the oldest sports participated in today. Why is archery still being enjoyed by many? Young and old alike enjoy the challenge of hitting a target. Archery can be enjoyed year-round—indoors during inclement weather and outdoors in the fresh air. Archery provides opportunities for physical activity and competition. Those who join archery clubs or leagues can participate with archers of their own age and abilities. In many high schools and universities, students can join archery teams and perhaps even receive scholarships.

If students are taught the fundamental archery skills, display an interest, and experience success, teachers could then suggest they pursue related sports, which include field archery, bow hunting, bow fishing, and target archery.

By providing these archery cues, teachers might incorporate archery into their curricula. Consequently, students of all ages can learn a new sport and "be on target for fun."

SKILLS LISTED WITH CUES

In this chapter we have designed equipment cues for selecting a bow, arrows, arm guard, and finger tab. Cues are given for safety techniques and retrieving arrows from a target. The other cues cover beginning skills for the stance address, bow arm, nock, draw, anchor (target shooting), aim, release, follow-through, and adjusting the sight pin.

TIPS

1. Purchasing a peep sight (a tiny aperture the archer looks through to align the arrow with the target) and stabilizer makes the archery experience more enjoyable and successful.

2. A frequent archery error is dropping the bow arm to see where the arrow is going. This is called *peeking*. An archer gets in a hurry and peeks to see where the arrow is going, and consequently the arrow drops. Keep the arrow on the string by not peeking. Have patience and wait until the arrow is off the string.
3. If an archer has a problem with inconsistency in accuracy, go to an archery pro shop for suggestions or check for consistent anchor point and consistent draw length. If everything is done the same way each time, accuracy will result.

EQUIPMENT TIPS

1. There are a variety of bows: long bows, recurve bows, and compound bows. They can be manual or automatic.
2. Carbon graphite arrows, although more expensive than aluminum arrows, are lighter, faster, stronger, and straighter.
3. The peep site is a tiny aperture the archer looks through to align the arrow with the target. The peep sight will force the archer to anchor in the same place for each shot. Anchoring in the same place time after time increases accuracy.
4. The stabilizer assists the archer by quieting the bow and placing the pin on target. The stabilizer also prevents the archer from shaking.
5. An archery pro shop is the best place to purchase a bow because the personnel can set up the bow for proper shooting and give specific instruction.
6. The mechanical release is a pull trigger that releases the strings on a bow. The trigger provides a quicker, smoother, and more accurate release.
7. Field archers shoot in rough terrain, with three-dimensional targets, from a variety of distances.
8. Bow hunting requires arrows with different points—broad heads for larger game and blunt heads for smaller game. To hunt game birds such as quail, use flu flu arrows that have larger and more feathers to reduce the distance the arrow travels.
9. Bow fishing is another unique option, requiring solid fiberglass arrows that have fish points. A bow-fishing reel is another good idea.

RANGE SAFETY

1. Use archery equipment only in places especially designed for shooting arrows. Allow plenty of room behind the targets and to the sides.
2. Students should always point the bow and arrow downrange and never at another person.
3. Students should never shoot an arrow to where they cannot see the landing area, and they should never shoot an arrow straight up.
4. Students should not draw a bow without an arrow on it, and they should never dry-fire (release without an arrow) a bow.
5. Students should not overdraw bows.
6. Students should never shoot an arrow when someone is downrange.
7. Students should wait for the teacher's verbal command (or whistle) to shoot, and they should wait for a different command to walk beyond the shooting line and collect arrows.

8. Students should prop their bows on the target while looking for arrows behind the target.
9. All equipment should be regularly inspected by the teacher and students for damage.

TEACHING IDEAS

1. Practice without shooting and to check the proper skill cues.
2. Have partners check cues.
3. Start students with large targets that are easy to hit.
4. Use balloons for some fun targets and noise when they are popped.
5. Use cooperative groups and keep score in a group at first for a nonthreatening and fun learning environment.
6. Shoot at paper targets with a bull's-eye. Keep score. Use this idea when fundamentals are mastered.
7. Shoot to a variety of paper targets. Target shooting during the winter months maintains correct form and technique, thus increasing the archer's ability to hit the game during hunting season.
8. Getting involved in an archery club provides an opportunity to learn from the experience of other archers and to improve techniques.
9. To hunt game, an archer needs correct equipment, an in-depth knowledge of the ethical principles and laws of hunting game, and correct techniques to harvest the game as well as camouflage, scent-masking, and tracking skills.

FYI

For further information and special help, consult the following organizations and resources.

ORGANIZATIONS

Provides archery videos.

National Archery Association
One Olympic Plaza
Colorado Springs, CO 80909
Phone: (719) 866-4576
Fax: (719) 632-4733

The Athletic Institute
200 Castlewood Drive, North
Palm Beach, FL 33408

Go to the local pro archery shop for lessons and proper equipment setup.

WEBSITES

www.encarta.msn.com
www.usarchery.org
www.BearGoldenEagle.com

EQUIPMENT AND SAFETY			
SKILL	**CUE**	**WHY**	**COMMON ERROR**
Selecting Bow	Choose a bow that you can draw comfortably and hold for 10 seconds	Reduces straining	Bow too heavy
Selecting Arrow	Place nock against chest; reach with fingers; arrow should be 1 inch past fingertips (or draw a marked arrow)	Less chance of injury and better projectory	Arrow too short or too long
	Partner stands to the side and reads marking even with bow		
	Hunters add 1 inch		
Arm Guard	String should divide the arm guard in half; this varies with modern compound bows	Protection	
Finger Tab or Glove or Release	Protect fingers with tab or glove	Shoot for a longer duration and more comfortably	String hurts fingers
Safety	Do not draw or shoot a bow unless you are shooting on a line	Safety and common sense	Injuring students
	Do not release a bow without an arrow in it	Avoids breaking equipment	Bow splits along laminations
Retrieving Arrows	Stand to side of arrow; check position of other archers		Bending arrow Injuring students
	With one hand: fingers straddle arrow; press against target	Safety; for example, by pulling an arrow straight out, a student poked himself in the eye	
	With the other hand: grasp arrow close to target; rotate and pull straight back		
What Is the Dominant Eye?	Hold arms straight out, make a triangle with both hands; center a small object in the triangle, keeping the object certain; close one eye, and if the object does not move, you have found your dominant eye	Enhances shooting skills	

SHOOTING AN ARROW

SKILL	CUE	WHY	COMMON ERROR
Stance Address	Straddle the shooting line (one foot on each side)	Consistency	Standing behind the line
	Weight even		Leaning forward or backward
	Good posture		
	Feet shoulder width apart		
Bow Arm	Grip bow as if holding a soda can	More accuracy	Gripping bow too tightly
	Thumb and index finger touch	Smoother release	
	Push bow toward target		Gripping bow too lightly
	Elbow points outward at shoulder level		
Nock	Nock arrow at 90° angle	Consistency	Arrow too high or low on string
	Snap nock on bowstring under nock locator		
	Index finger points away from bow		
Draw (Figure 3.1)	Make a scout sign (3 fingers up)	Consistency	More or less than 3 fingers on string
	String in first groove of index finger		String on fingertips or hand wraps around fingers
	Keep back of hand flat		
	Elbow level with hand		Elbow too low
	Squeeze shoulder blades together		Drawing with arm only

continued

SHOOTING AN ARROW, continued			
SKILL	**CUE**	**WHY**	**COMMON ERROR**
Anchor (Target Shooting) (Figure 3.2)	Touch string to center of chin and center of nose; index finger pushes against jawbone	Consistency; doing everything the same ensures accuracy	Failing to anchor
Anchor (in bows without sights)	Touch corner of mouth with index finger of draw hand	Consistency; also allows archers to aim down the path of the arrow	Failing to adjust anchor for use of bows without sights
Aim	Look through pin to center of gold sight pen		Looking at target instead of pin
	Aim for 3–5 seconds before releasing		Releasing while drawing
	Close dominant left eye when shooting right-handed		Leaving dominant left eye open when shooting right-handed
Release	Relax fingers; string "slips" off fingers	Arrow performance; prevents left-to-right wobble	Jerking string hand back or allowing the string to "creep" forward before releasing it
Follow-Through (Hold) (Figure 3.3)	Fingers move back along side of face		Moving string hand
	Hold position until arrow hits target	Increases accuracy; prevents peeking	Moving bow arm

continued

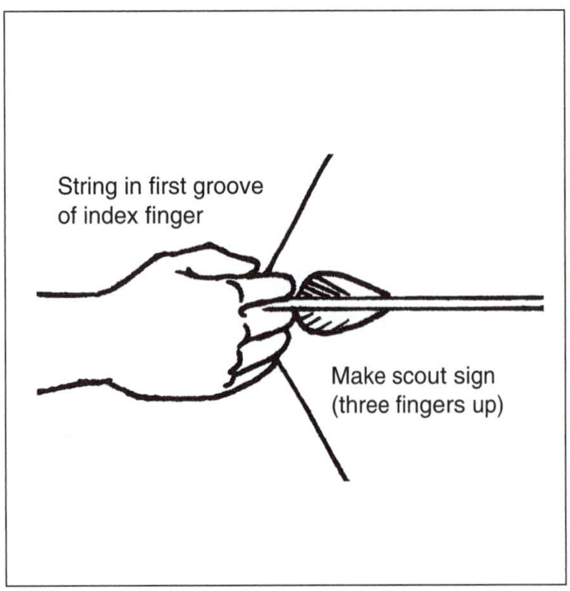

FIGURE 3.1 Draw the Arrow

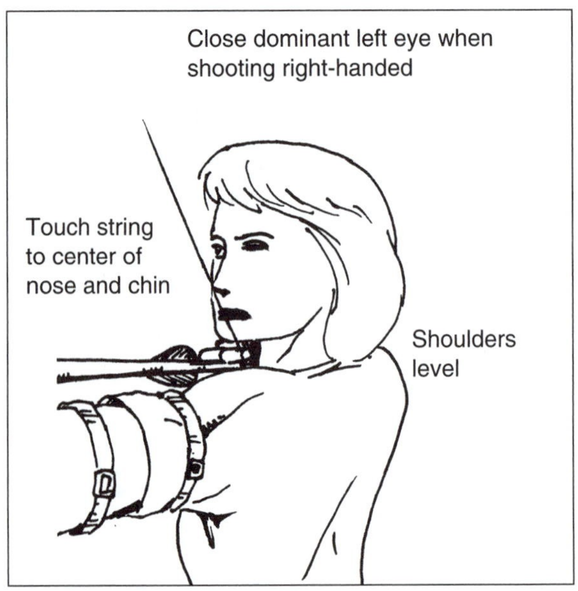

FIGURE 3.2 Anchor (Target Shooting)

SHOOTING AN ARROW, continued			
SKILL	**CUE**	**WHY**	**COMMON ERROR**
Adjust Sight Pin	Choose arrow with sight pin		Moving sight after each arrow or failing to adjust sight
	If arrows go high, move pin up		
	If arrows go low, move pin down		
	If arrows go left, move pin left		
	If arrows go right, move pin right		

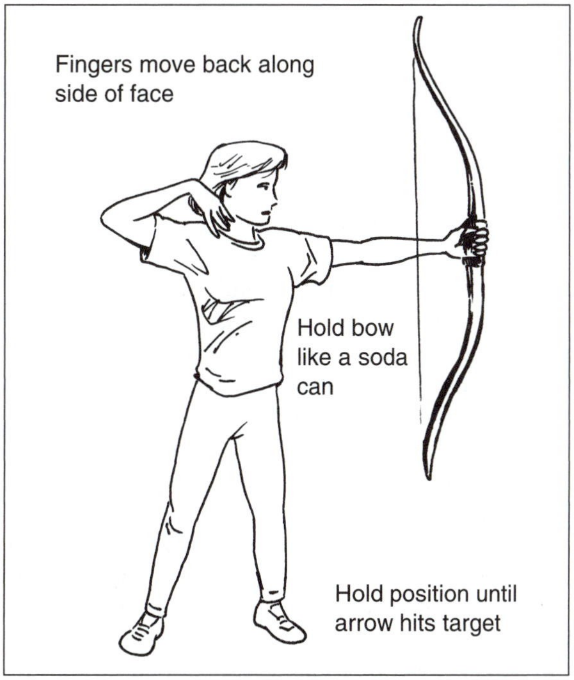

FIGURE 3.3 Follow-Through (Hold)

4

Badminton

INTRODUCTION

Badminton is a physically demanding sport that provides players with a good measure of aerobic and anaerobic power, flexibility, strength, and speed. The skill of badminton can be relatively easy to learn, especially with the correct teaching cues. When designing these cues we consulted the USA Badminton Association in Colorado Springs, Colorado, and Canadian Badminton Association for their expertise and suggestions. For example, the cue for the wrist action when teaching the badminton overhead clear is "pronate the wrist," which describes clockwise forearm rotation. Snapping the wrist would be the common error. This cue and others will provide the teacher with correct teaching techniques.

Jim Stabler, a member of Pikes Peak Badminton Club, Colorado Springs, CO, likes to think of the grip in terms of "shaking hands with the racquet." Hold the racquet with the racquet head perpendicular to the floor. Now shake hands with it. Hold it loosely with the index finger open along the handle. Do not grip it like you would a baseball bat. If your index finger is open, it is possible to use your wrist and internally pronate your arm when hitting the shuttles. If you grip it like a bat, you can't bend your wrist. The tendon to your index finger is all tied up in the grip, so you won't have the flexibility to bend your wrist and utilize the power you can generate that way. How does a baseball pitcher throw a baseball at 90 miles an hour? He uses his legs, back, arm, and wrist as he hurls the ball to the catcher. If he used only his arm, he'd have very little velocity. It is the same whip of the wrist and internal rotation of the arm that allow an advanced badminton player to hit a shuttle at 150 miles per hour or more. The shuttle weighs one-sixteenth of an ounce, so you are not hitting an object that weighs very much. You can utilize the action of your wrist and arm to hit the shuttle very hard.

Badminton is unique in that the object you're playing with can fly at 150-plus miles an hour by hard hits, or you can use a drop shot and just dink it ever so slowly over the net. No other sport employs this wide range of speeds in its game.

Jim Leete of USA Badminton has provided this chapter with some wonderful warm-up and drill progressions for the beginner to the advanced badminton player. These drills, called the "nifty fifty," come from years of experience teaching and coaching young and old alike.

SKILLS LISTED WITH CUES

A recommended teaching progression of skills before the strokes are taught is as follows: grips, flick-up, feeding, ready position, and court position. Teachers should take extra time to teach flick-up and feeding skills. The cues for the badminton skills in this chapter include this teaching progression as well as forehand/backhand underhand clear, forehand/backhand overhead clear, forehand/backhand smash, forehand/backhand drive, net shots (finesse shot), long singles serve, short doubles serve, and singles/doubles boundaries, scoring, and strategies. After each skill we have added some drills to work students' skills.

TIPS

1. Remember . . . correct grip, ready position.
2. Get into the habit of hit-move, hit-move, hit-move.
3. Move to hit the shuttle; don't wait for it.
4. Court sense for singles: after each shot, the singles player should attempt to return to base position, which is midcourt. Remember to get in ready position regardless of court position.
5. Court sense for doubles is different. Partners adopt an "up-back" arrangement and, when attacking, a "sides" arrangement. Communicating with and supporting each other is the key to playing a good doubles game.

EQUIPMENT TIPS

1. Shuttles may be made from feathers or nylon. The flight of a shuttle is what makes the game unique, since it does not soar in an arc as a ball does. Very often, cheap nylon shuttles do not "catch" the air very well and are too fast. To test the speed of a shuttle, strike it underhand as hard as possible, hitting it the length of the court fairly close to parallel to the floor. If the shuttle is moving at the correct speed, it should land on or near the doubles service line at the other end.
2. Use gym tape to mark a court. (It is not advisable to use a rope or a line for a net. It would be difficult to determine whether a shuttle went over or under the rope. Nets are not expensive and last for years if properly cared for.)
3. Court shoes are recommended.
4. You will need 100 to 200 shuttles for a class.

TEACHING IDEAS

1. Badminton is a demanding game involving lots of running, stopping, starting, and lunging. Warm up before stretching. Suggested warm-up activities: light jogging, running in place, jumping jacks, running in various directions, tag games, circuits. After the warm-up, stretch out legs, ankles, arms, and so on.

2. Partner-feed drill: One partner feeds shuttle by hand to the receiver. Receiver hits and then attempts to assume ready position and base position after each return. Cue words are "feed-hit-ready position." Instructor specifies type of hand feed. This drill can be done with or without a net.
3. Racquet-feed drill: same as the drill above, but the feeder racquet-feeds to receiver. Feeder gradually sends shuttle to more challenging positions: "further right," "further left," "in front," and "behind" specify the type of feed and type of return.
4. Triples games are designed for large badminton classes. Six can play on a court rather than four. The game is played with three players on each side. Two players from each side are in the front half of the court. Each front player must remain on his respective side of the centerline. The third player plays back and may move anywhere in the back half of court. Serve is always from right front position. Team rotates clockwise each time serve is regained.

"THE NIFTY FIFTY"

The Beginner 10: Getting Acquainted with the Racquet, Shuttle, and Court

1. Throw the shuttle over the net from short service line to short service line.
2. Catch the shuttle thrown over the net to you from the short service line.
3. Walk or run with the shuttle on the racquet cork up, palm up.
4. Do the same with the palm down (backhand).
5. Do the same with the shuttle on its side, palm up.
6. Do the same with the shuttle palm down.
7. Grip the racquet properly, using the handshake position, and in a ready position make figure eights with it.
8. Raise the racquet up, cock the wrist out, swing forward, uncock wrist.
9. Raise the racquet up, cock wrist out, swing forward, uncock wrist.
10. Hold racquet arm up just below wrist, swing forward with wrist only.

Basic Novice 10

1. Bounce shuttle, a little above your head, using forehand, palm up.
2. Repeat, alternating forehand to backhand and back.
3. Repeat, alternating backhand to forehand and back.
4. Hit shuttle overhead and straight to and from short service line.
5. Drop shuttles gently over the net from midcourt area.
6. Hit shuttles straight to and from midcourt area; like clears, but shorter.
7. Serve backhand fairly short and low.
8. Repeat, and then follow with high and clear.
9. Attitude and cooperation.
10. Sportsmanship . . . fair play and court manners, etc.

Warm-Up Exercise and Strokes

1. Hands on shoulders, full slow circles, elbows touching in front.
2. Arm up, grasp wrist, pull over with full side bend, rotate wrist.
3. Arm up, bend elbow, scratch back, cup elbow, push down, scratch again.
4. Full hip, then body, then knee circles.
5. Feet apart, slow squat elbows on knees and hands locked, rock slowly.
6. Position foot across, outside next to other foot, bend down slowly.
7. Raise, grasp, and pull leg toward chest, rotate ankle fully.
8. In place, jump, run, knees up side straddle jump rope.
9. On the court, hit clears, drops, smashes, and drives.
10. On the court, hit short and long serves and touch serves.

Moving on Court 10 Steps

1. Move up center for a short hit near T to midcourt, then run left and back.
2. Start with a long hit, then do short hit, run left and back.
3. Alternate hitting and moving for long and short shots till missing.
4. Hit in sequence from deep center, mid-right, short, mid-left.
5. Mix up by feeding longs or shorts at random.
6. Mix up by feeding longs or shorts to the four corners at random.
7. Hit from four corners in sequence as fed.
8. Hit from any corner as fed randomly, returning to midcourt each shot.
9. Move in response to a racquet pointed to any corner or spot.
10. Hit shuttle fed to any spot, any corner, or in between.

Advanced Novice or Above 10

1. Rapid midcourt drives, back and forth, low and flat.
2. Round-the-head forehand shots in preference to backhand.
3. Hit full-court, accurate high clears to middle and back alley either side.
4. Place various shots to designated corners and midcourt spots accurately.
5. Serve very low and close to T or high and deep consistently.
6. Stretch or lunge for short net shots close to net level if possible.
7. Develop a strong low and down smash, then on toes or a jump smash.
8. Develop various backhand strokes for clears, drops, drives, and smashes.
9. Perform the clear, drop, drop running stroke accurately and consistently.
10. Perform the clear, smash, drop, or block sequence as in #9 above.

A Few Important Considerations

1. Practice leads to progress, and that leads toward perfection and playing better.
2. Improving stroking skills and consistency takes concentration and practice.

FYI

For further information and special help, consult the following organizations and resources.

ORGANIZATIONS

Provides information on instructor manuals, videotapes, drills, skill progressions, program materials, awards, pictures.

USA Badminton
One Olympic Plaza
Colorado Springs, CO 80909
Phone: (719) 866-4808
Fax: (719) 866-4507
Email: usab@usabadminton.org
Website: www.usabadminton.org

VIDEO AND MANUAL

Badminton 2000 Plus Guide to Teaching Badminton. Can be purchased through USA Badminton. $39.99 plus shipping.

PUBLICATIONS

Golds, M. (2002). *Badminton (skills of the game).* Ramsbury, Wiltshire, England: Crowood Press.

Grice, T. (1996). *Badminton: Steps to success.* Champaign, IL: Human Kinetics.

USA Badminton. *Badminton official rule book.* (2001). Colorado Springs, CO: USA Badminton.

WEBSITES

www.usabadminton.org
www.worldbadminton.net

BASIC GRIPS AND STANCE

SKILL	CUE	WHY	COMMON ERROR
Forehand Grip	Heel of hand at butt of racquet		Choking up on racket
	V on top bevel		Grip too tight
	Index finger positioned to pull trigger		Incorrect placement of index finger
	Squeeze trigger finger on impact		
Backhand Grip	Turn racquet clockwise		Failure to rotate grip from forehand to backhand
	Make V on left bevel		
	Knuckle on top		
Ready Position (Figure 4.1)	Hold racquet up	If racquet is down at your ankle, it takes a good part of a second to get it back up. That part of a second is all it may take for you to be late in making a good shot.	
	Knees bent		Standing upright
	Weight on balls of feet		Weight on heels
Correct Order of Play	1. Be ready to hit the shuttle 2. SEE the shuttle 3. Hit the shuttle	Make sure you do this in order. If step 2 comes before step 1, you might be late in hitting the shuttle.	Fall backward/ fall away

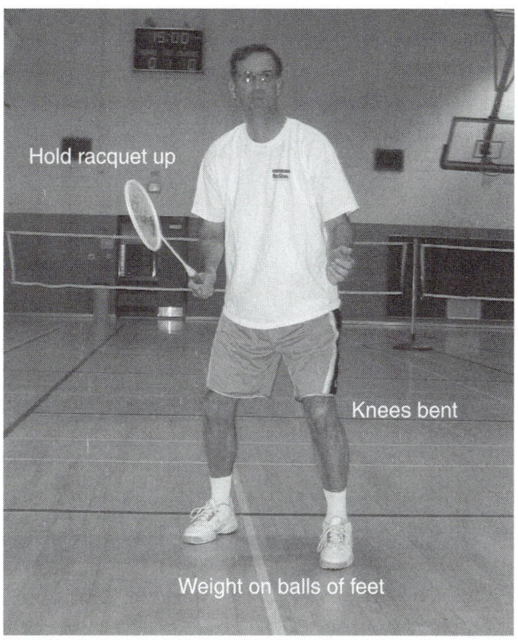

FIGURE 4.1 Ready Position

FLICK-UP AND FEEDING

SKILL	CUE	WHY	COMMON ERROR
Flick-Up			
Definition	Flick move using the racquet to scoop the shuttle from the floor (speeds game up); players must employ proper grip to do this move		
Action	Side scooping action, feel snap of wrist as racquet head turns		Forward and up action
	Raise shuttle to land on strings		Improper grip
Feeding			
Definition (See Figure 4.5 on page 45)	Serving the shuttle by racquet so that receiver has a good chance to return it		

CLEARS

SKILL	CUE	WHY	COMMON ERROR
Forehand Underhand Clear	Whip wrist and brush shorts	More power	Snapping wrist
	Contact shuttle below waist	Rule	Contacting too soon, lack of height
	Swing up over opposite shoulder	More distance	Not following through, lack of depth
Forehand Overhead Clear	Right hand	More distance and power	Snapping wrist Not extending elbow
	Left hand	More power and distance	Snapping wrist
	Reach up and contact shuttle high in front of body, like throwing something on roof		
	Whip!		
	Push from back to forward foot (Figure 4.2)	More power	Weight forward

continued

CLEARS, continued			
SKILL	**CUE**	**WHY**	**COMMON ERROR**
Drill 1: ***High/Clear Tip Drill*** So often beginners hit under the shuttle. Contact the shuttle high and in front of the body. Don't let the shuttle get behind you when you hit high clear. Take a step back so that you are hitting it well in front of you. If you swing and miss it, for example, it should fall against the front of your body and not over your head.			
Drill 2: ***1, 2, or 3 Feeders*** Feeders have at least 25 shuttlecocks: One player hits underhand clears, rotate; one player hits underhand and overhead clears, rotate. Spend lots of time hitting clears—3 or 4 days can be spent having students practice feeding and clears forehand, backhand, underhand, and overhead.			

FIGURE 4.2 Forehand Overhead Clear

SMASH—DRIVES—NET SHOTS

SKILL	CUE	WHY	COMMON ERROR
Forehand Smash (Figure 4.3)	Lean into the net		
	Contact shuttle high and in front of body	To hit shuttle down	Contacting shuttle behind head
	Pronate hand	Shuttle will go downward	Snapping wrists
	Pronate hand	Power	
	Wrist starts cocked, finishes in pronated position	Power	
	Whip action	Faster	
	Swing is half-moon with face of racquet pointing down at contact	Control	Swinging too long or too short
Forehand Drive	Pivot on racquet foot and move other foot toward shuttle		Feet are stationary
	Contact more to the side of body, like throwing a ball sidearm	Control and accuracy	Contact too high or too low

continued

FIGURE 4.3 Forehand Smash

SMASH—DRIVES—NET SHOTS, continued			
SKILL	**CUE**	**WHY**	**COMMON ERROR**
Backhand Drive	Same as forehand; change grip		
Net Shot (Finesse Shot) (Figure 4.4)	Loosen grip	More control	Firm grip
	Be gentle; slide racquet under shuttle		Swinging at shuttle
	Focus on palm of hand; lift shuttle over, use arm only, not racquet		Hitting hard
	Push/lift/nudge/caress		
Drill: ***1, 2, or 3 Feeders*** Feeders hit high clears; hitter smashes shuttle. Rotate hitters. Switch to backhand smashes. Then feeders feed to forehand and backhand. Partner smashes both sides.			
Drill: ***3 Feeders, 1 Hitter*** Each feeder needs 25–30 shuttles. All 3 feeders feed 1 hitter. Feeders mix up shots: long, short, high, low, side; hitter moves all over court. Rotate hitters. Great workout.			

FIGURE 4.4 Net Shot (Finesse Shot)

SERVING			
SKILL	**CUE**	**WHY**	**COMMON ERROR**
Long Singles Service	Bend knees and swing under and up		Side swing
	Contact out in front of body		Contact behind body
	Swing under shuttle		
	Follow-through straight up to hit face with biceps		No follow-through
Short Doubles Service (Figures 4.5 and 4.6)	Stand 12–18 inches behind T		
	Pinch shuttle at tip of feathers		
	Drop shuttle		
	Gently stroke the shuttle into opponent's court with backhand or forehand motion		
	Stand up straight		Leaning over holding the shuttle close to the floor
Serving Drill: Players serve to each other with short and long serves.	You want to be as tall as you can so the shuttle starts out high. You want shuttle to go on its downward path after it goes over the net.	You want player to hit up so that you and your partner have advantage on third shot; opponent can't attack if hit obtaining shot	
	The rules require that you strike the shuttle at your waist or below		
	The entire hand holding the racquet must be higher than the racquet head as you strike the shuttle upward over net		

continued

SERVING, continued			
SKILL	**CUE**	**WHY**	**COMMON ERROR**
Gamelike Drill: This drill can be done with clears, clears and smashes, or all the skills of badminton; good drill to use with large classes. Assign 3–4 players per court; 1 player hits, gets off court to back; partner comes on court and plays next shot. Rotate hits.	This drill allows each player to play the full court		

Note: The serve is a defensive shot, not an offensive shot as in tennis, for example. Remember the quote of the great doubles champion Don Paup: "The serve and return of serve are the two most important shots in any rally."

FIGURE 4.5 Service

FIGURE 4.6 Short Doubles Service

SINGLES RULES—SCORING—STRATEGIES

SKILL	CUE	WHY	COMMON ERROR
Scoring	Only the server can score points		
	1 point scored when opposing player fails to return shuttle back over net		
	1 point scored when shuttle comes back over the net and lands out of bounds		
	Server serves in right court when server's score is 0 or even		
	Server serves in left court when server's score is odd		
Service Boundaries	Tall and narrow man (Figure 4.7)		

continued

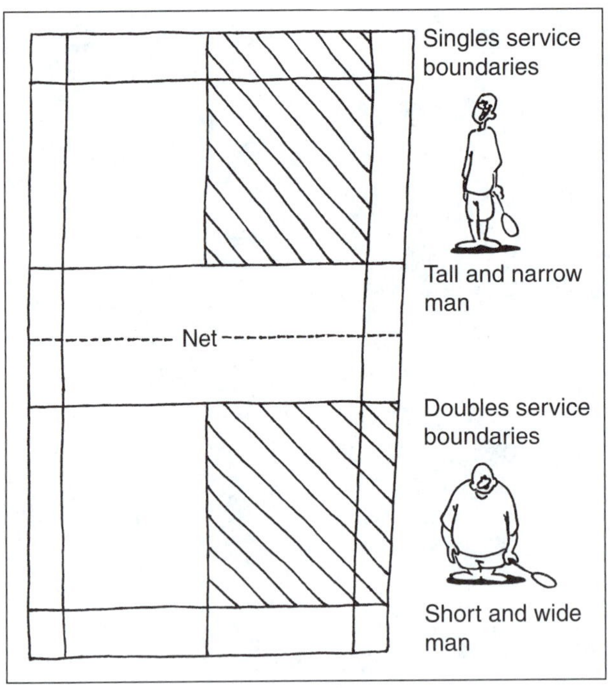

FIGURE 4.7 Service Boundaries for Singles and Doubles

SINGLES RULES—SCORING—STRATEGIES, continued			
SKILL	**CUE**	**WHY**	**COMMON ERROR**
Men's Singles	Played to 15 points		Forgetting to take the option to set when score is tied
Setting	14–14, play to 17		Starting score at 13 and playing to 17
	First player to 14 has option to play 17		Starting score at 14 and playing to 17
Match Play	Player who wins 2 out of 3 games wins the match		
Women's Singles	Played to 11 points		Forgetting to take the option to set when score is tied
Setting	10–10, play to 13 points		Starting score at 9 and playing to 12
	First player to reach 10 has option to play to 13		Starting score at 10 and playing to 12
Match Play	Player who wins 2 out of 3 games wins the match		
Strategies	Play opponent's weak side		Playing opponent's forehand side
	Mix up shots; be unpredictable		Using same shot
	Use deception, and disguise shots		
	Use clears to force opponent deep in court and on the move		Hitting shuttle to middle of court
	After hitting, get back to the Big T		
	Mix shots, then take advantage of the weak return with a well-placed, powerful smash	Make your opponent run to weaken his or her return	
	The patient, aggressive player wins points		

DOUBLES RULES—SCORING—STRATEGIES

SKILL	CUE	WHY	COMMON ERROR
Front/Back (Figure 4.8)	"Up/back" formation in attack mode after a smash or drop		
	Front player is halfway between service line and net		
	Back player is shadow to front player		
Side to Side (Figure 4.9)	If one partner moves to side of court, the other goes to the opposite side of court to cover court area		
	When defending or in trouble, use side position that is parallel to partner		
	Each player covers own property		
	Stay within property line		Crossing over line
Basic Guidelines	Support partner in every way possible		
	Always be ready to cover for partner		
	Don't get in each other's way; let partner take his or her own shots		

continued

FIGURE 4.8 Doubles Formation for Attack Mode after a Smash or Drop

FIGURE 4.9 Doubles Formation when Defending or in Trouble

DOUBLES RULES—SCORING—STRATEGIES, *continued*			
Basic Guidelines, *continued*	Call for "iffy" (in-between) shots (say "mine")		
	Whenever possible, send shots between opponents to confuse them		
Inning	A doubles team has an "inning," meaning both players are entitled to serve		
Starting Position	Start in right-hand court		
	One hand in first inning (first server)		
	Two hands in each inning after (two servers)		
	We like to use the term ABBA to help remember the order: A: Player A1 serves one hand, then B: Player B1 serves one hand, then B: Player B2 serves one hand, then A: Back to player A1 and then to player A2		
Server	Server alternates serving court each time point is made	AABB = Two hands in each inning after ABBA	
Receivers	Receivers do not change courts		
Scoring	Serve to score		
Points	15-point games; *see* Men's Singles, Setting on page 47		
Match	Win 2 out of 3 games		
Break	5-minute rest period between second and third games		
Doubles Service Area	Short and wide man (See Figure 4.7 on page 46)		

5

Baseball

INTRODUCTION

"There is no joy in Mudville: mighty Casey has struck out."
(Ernest Lawrence Thayer)

What the fans in joyless Mudville never knew about their mighty slugger Casey is that after striking out, Casey decided to ask his coach how to improve his batting skills. Casey's coaches now face the challenge of correcting Casey's swing and restoring joy to Mudville. Was there really anything wrong with Casey's swing, or was the pitcher just better that day?

Selecting critical errors and giving the right cue is not an easy task for the coach. The cues in this chapter were designed to help coaches analyze skills and provide effective cues. For example, the cue "See the ball hit the bat" helps the batter focus on the ball all the way into the hitting zone as the bat head makes contact with the ball.

SKILLS LISTED WITH CUES

This chapter presents cues for the following baseball skills: hitting, throwing, fielding ground balls and fly balls, bunting, pitching (fastball, curveball, slider, knuckleball, forkball, screwball), catching, and sliding (feet first, head first).

TIPS

1. Warm up with a fungo bat (lighter than a normal bat). This drill teaches quick hands, which increases bat speed. Warming up with heavy bats teaches your hands to drag the bat through the strike zone.
2. Run a couple of laps around the bases or the park before stretching out and warming up the arm. This activity warms the arm up a little faster and helps circulate the blood.

3. Start with short-distance throwing and move into a long toss. A long toss is defined as throwing the ball as far as possible but still keeping it on the line. The long toss is the only true way to increase arm strength, and it also feels good.
4. Using the fungo bat in a drill with Wiffle golf balls is ideal. "See the ball hit the bat" helps with a quick wrist to develop bat speed.
5. Regular bats can be used for batting tees and soft-toss drills.

EQUIPMENT TIPS

1. Gloves: infielders need short-pocket gloves for quick access and release, and outfielders need large-pocket gloves for fly balls and fielding ground balls on the run.
2. Bats: pick a bat that is comfortable in the hands; it should not be too heavy or long. The key to hitting is bat speed.
3. A fungo bat is used to hit infield balls. These bats are not made for hitting pitched balls. The bat will break when hitting a pitched ball.
4. Batting gloves protect the hands when hitting. They also provide protection under the mitt as well as protection for baserunning. The runner should hold the batting gloves in clenched fists to protect fingers when sliding.
5. Wiffle balls can be used for soft-toss drills. They can also be used for batting practice in a very small area if a cage is not available. A player can use Wiffle balls for batting practice before games. The use of Wiffle balls avoids damage to fences. Baseballs have a tendency to bend a chain-link fence.
6. Catcher equipment is needed for protection: shin guards, chest protector, helmet, cup, mask, and throat guard.
7. Baseball caps are critical to help block the sun.
8. Shoes with plastic cleats or spikes are recommended because they help with traction.

TEACHING IDEAS

1. *Batting drill stations:* To develop the necessary techniques and rhythm to hit a live pitch, many repetitions of a correct swing are necessary. The emphasis in these drills should be on hand position at setup, hand action during the swing, and hip rotation.
   a. *Soft-toss drill:* The batter hits into a fence or net. The partner kneels at a 45-degree angle from the batter, a short distance from the batter's front foot, and tosses underhand. The batter cocks the bat as the partner takes the ball back to tossing position and swings upon delivery.
   b. *Batting tee:* A tee is used. The ball is rotated to different positions to give the batter a variety of areas to hit.
   c. *Hip drill:* Place the bat behind the back, cradling it in the crook of the elbows. Now rotate back and forth and feel how the body weight is naturally transferred from back to front foot as the hips rotate. Make sure the back foot comes up at the heel (squash the bug) as the weight is transferred forward.

2. *Four-corners drill:* Four to 12 players on the four bases throw the ball around the bases. The goal is to catch the ball in the catching zone. (The catching zone is the top left-hand side toward the glove side, to the left of the heart for a right-handed player.) This drill teaches players to shuffle feet and have a quick ball exchange. Modifications of four-corners drill: catch, shuffle, throw; hop, chase. Go clockwise, then counterclockwise.

FYI

For further information and special help, consult the following resources.

PUBLICATIONS

Petrack, C. (1998). *Complete guide to outfield play.* Haworth, NJ: Harding Press.

Delmonico, R. (1996). *Offensive baseball drill.* Champaign, IL: Human Kinetics.

Delmonico, R. (1995). *Defensive baseball.* Chicago, IL: Masters Press.

WEBSITES

www.howtoplay.com/ht_p/baseball/essentials.html
www.educationworld.com/a_sites/sites082.shtml

BATTING

SKILL	CUE	WHY	COMMON ERROR
Hitting			
Stance (Figure 5.1a)	Stand sideways with eyes focused on pitcher		Standing forward, head tilt
	Feet slightly wider than shoulder width, knees slightly bent	Proper balance	Feet too far apart or too close together
	Weight over balls of feet, heels lightly touching the ground, more weight on back leg		Weight on heels
Arm Swing	Hitter should think "shoulder to shoulder" (start with chin on front shoulder; finish swing with chin on back shoulder)	Keeps the head in proper position; head should stay still	Moving head during the swing; head too tense
Hip Rotation (Figure 5.1b)	Back hip snaps or rotates at pitcher; drive body through ball; take photograph of pitcher with belly button		No hip rotation

continued

BATTING, continued			
SKILL	**CUE**	**WHY**	**COMMON ERROR**
	Throw hands through baseball; "slow feet, quick hands"		Using arms instead of wrists
Focus of Eyes	See the bat hit the ball	Gets the barrel of the bat to the ball and not the handle	Not seeing the ball hit bat
	Watch ball all the way into catcher's mitt	Helps the batter to see the ball all the way into the hitting zone	
Step	Step 3–6 inches (stride should be more of a glide)		Overstriding causes bat to drop during swing (jarring step)
			Also causes head to drop, which causes eyes to drop as well; obscures vision on the ball
	Short stride, quick swing		Hitter "steps and then hits"
Follow-Through (Figure 5.2 on page 54)	Top hand rolls over bottom hand; bat goes around the body on follow-through		
Recommended Progression	Teach cues in order listed; when first 3 are mastered, add others		

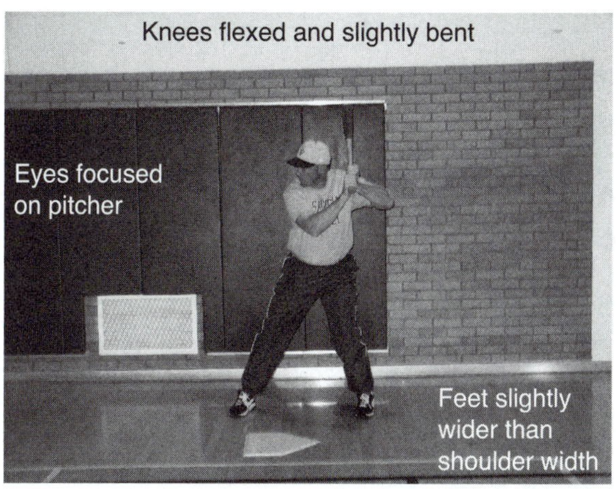

(a) Batter's Stance

(b) Hip Rotation

FIGURE 5.1 Hitting

HITTING—INEXPERIENCED BATTERS

SKILL	CUE	WHY	COMMON ERROR
Bunting	Pivot toward pitcher; square body to pitcher	Both eyes focused on the ball	Hitter or bunter does not get properly squared around in position to bunt
	Slide top hand up bat; keep bat head slightly above the handle; keep fingers behind bat or protect fingers from ball	Less chance to hit ball in air	Hands remain together (bat is not kept level if pitch is either high or low); wrapping hand around bat
	Catch ball with bat—imagine a net in the barrel of the bat; catch the ball in the net	Deadens the ball	Pushing bat at ball, swiping at ball
Checkpoint for Coaches	If the batter is not gripping, standing, or holding the bat correctly, coach could correct the player individually		Don't use these cues unless a player needs assistance; give one at a time
Grip	Hold bat in base of fingers (this allows wrist to roll freely and generates bat speed)	Enables wrists to turn freely during the swing	Bat held in palm of hand, squeezing bat slows the swing
	Align knuckles "Eight middle knuckles, all in a row"		
Closed Stance	Feet are shoulder width apart; then front foot is placed toward plate (helps untrained hitter step toward the pitcher)		Stepping back or stepping into the bucket

continued

FIGURE 5.2 Hitting (Follow-Through)

HITTING—INEXPERIENCED BATTERS, continued

SKILL	CUE	WHY	COMMON ERROR
Bat Position	Bat held armpit high and far enough away from the body that both fists of player could fit between the chest and bat		Bat held too close to shoulder
	Back elbow held away from body at about an 8:00 position. Front elbow should be in closer to body	Creates a shorter swing	Back elbow drops, creating an upswing and a fly-ball swing
Bat Angle	Straight up in air or up and angled slightly back over shoulder	Helps make a short, quick swing	Cradling bat around head; bat is pointing back toward pitcher

THROWING

SKILL	CUE	WHY	COMMON ERROR
Grip	Get a seam, either across the seams or with the seams	Makes ball spin backward, allowing it to travel farther and straighter	Not getting a seam; poor control of ball
	Hold ball with fingertips: first 2 fingers on top of ball, second 2 underneath to the side, thumb opposite side		Holding baseball in palm or placing more fingers on top of ball
Stance	Stand sideways; instep of back foot faces target		Standing facing the target
Throwing Action	Point glove-hand shoulder at target		Staying square to target (no shoulder or hip rotation is possible)
	Take a long step toward target		Stepping across body, no step at all, or a step that is too high
	Stretch arm way back		
	Make L shape with throwing arm		Taking the ball directly behind head with bent elbow
	Pull glove arm down, and replace glove arm with throwing arm		
	Whip the arm through; snap wrist		No wrist action; all arm
	Follow-through; wrist goes to opposite knee; slap knee		No follow-through

FIELDING—GROUND BALLS

SKILL	CUE	WHY	COMMON ERROR
Stance	Feet shoulder width apart, weight on balls of feet (right-handers lead slightly with left foot because the slight lead of the left foot means that less time is needed to rotate body to throw)	Proper balance	Weight on heels; feet too close or too far apart
	Create a triangle with both feet and glove; the glove is the apex (top) of the triangle		Glove inside or behind knees
	Bend at knees; bend slightly at waist		Bending at waist and not at knees
Catching Action	Field ball out in front		Trying to play ball behind the legs
	Keep glove close to ground		Starting with glove waist high and trying to go down at ball
	Keep the glove lower than the ball		
	Elbows inside knees act as shock absorber to cushion the impact of a ground ball	Creates soft hands	
	Put your nose on the ball; follow the ball into glove with eyes		Pulling head up; not seeing ball into glove for fear of being hit in the face
	Secure ball with both hands	Keep throwing hand close for quick release	Fielding ball with only the glove
	Read a hop; read the path of the baseball; try to field ball on big or long hop; after a big hop, ball will usually stay low		Letting ball dictate how to play it (letting ball play fielder)

FIELDING—FLY BALLS

SKILL	CUE	WHY	COMMON ERROR
Stance	Comfortable stance, weight on balls of feet	Running with weight on the heels makes it difficult to track a fly ball	Rigid, fight stance; weight on back of heels like a boxer
Catching Position	Position body underneath flight of baseball (the path should be coming down to the eyes)	Having to catch ball behind your head or below your waist	
Catching Action	Place glove slightly out from and above head; reach for the sky with fingers just before the ball arrives		Catching ball to side of body; fingers stretched out rather than up
	Always use both hands to secure ball		One-handed "showboat"
	Follow ball into glove with eyes		Not watching ball all the way into the glove

PITCHING

SKILL	CUE	WHY	COMMON ERROR
Delivery	Step directly toward home plate		Foot goes too far one way or the other
	Use normal throwing motion, nice and easy (loosey-goosey)	Don't try to throw across body	Overthrowing, trying to throw the ball too hard; avoid sidearming
	Simply play catch with catcher, throwing strikes		Trying to do too much; overthrowing and not throwing any strikes
	Comfortable, smooth delivery		No rhythm
	Follow-through throwing hand should come down and brush against the opposite knee		
Pitches *Fastball*	Grip with seams for a sink action; grip across seam for a rise		Wrong grip or simply grabbing ball
	Pressure on fingertips		No pressure points
	Smooth delivery		Rushed motion
	Wrist snap		No wrist action

continued

PITCHING, continued			
SKILL	**CUE**	**WHY**	**COMMON ERROR**
Pitches, *continued* *Curveball*	Grip with seams	Creates a spin on the baseball, causing it to spin or curve	Wrong grip
	Fastball motion		Motion too slow and obvious
	Reduce speed of ball		Too much speed; no rotation or spin
	Tickle ear		Not cocking wrist
	Pull down		Lazy arm action
	Snap fingers		Letting ball simply roll off fingers
Slider	Backward C		Wrong grip and placement of fingers
	Off center		Holding ball in center
	Fastball speed and motion		Slow or rushed motion
	Turn wrist over or turn doorknob		Throwing like a curveball, cocking wrist
	Second finger		First finger releases ball
Knuckleball	Fingernail grip	Lack of spin causes ball to float	Knuckles on seams
	Dig seams		Not enough pressure on seams
	Extend and push toward plate		Forcing the ball
	Stiff wrist		Snapping the wrist
Forkball	Make a fork shape with fingers	Causes the ball to dip or dive	Fingers not far enough apart
	Fingers outside seams		Fingers directly on seams
	Ball rolls away		Pressure on fingertips
	No wrist action or snap		Too much wrist
Screwball	Grip narrow seams	Causes the ball to spin and break opposite of curveball action	Simply grabbing baseball
	Overhand		Sidearm
	Inside out		Curveball motion
	Reverse snap		Not enough wrist action
	Thumb flip		No thumb

CATCHING

SKILL	CUE	WHY	COMMON ERROR
Catcher's Stance (Figure 5.3)	Feet outside shoulders, heels elevated	Balance	Kneeling
	Head up		Flinching; head down
	Elbows resting outside the knees		
	Place throwing arm behind back	Placing arm directly behind or to the side of the catcher's mitt is more likely to cause injury	
	Catch the ball using both hands; elbows act as shock absorbers		Relying solely on catcher's mitt
	Move to ball laterally. Allow the ball to get through the hitting zone.	Batter may make contact with mitt or hand, causing injury	Reaching for ball

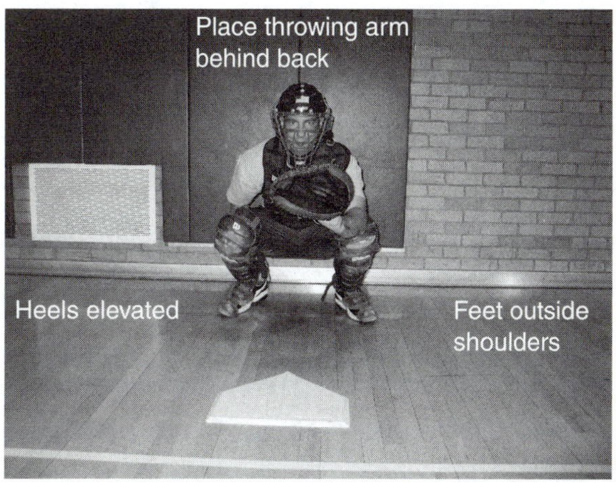

FIGURE 5.3 Catcher's Stance

SLIDING

SKILL	CUE	WHY	COMMON ERROR
Feet First	Sprint		Slowing up
	Slide early		Sliding too late (injuries)
	Sit down		Falling and hopping
	Curl leg under, making a figure 4		Sliding with both legs forward
	Keep hands in front of the body		
	Roller-coaster ride		Lying down completely
Head First	Sprint		Slowing down
	Sink		Upright and no balance
	Dive		Belly-flopping onto base
	Outstretched arms	Prevents injury	Hands and arms too close to body
	Balance and fingers up		
	Superman in flight		

6

Basketball

INTRODUCTION

Former Assistant Coach Al Brown from the University of Tennessee states, "You need to develop three fundamental skills—dribbling, passing, and shooting—to become a good basketball player." This chapter provides teaching cues and fundamental drills to practice these skills and others. The paramount thing for a teacher to remember in teaching basketball is to provide lots of opportunities for the students to touch the ball. When possible, lower baskets and have dunk contests and other fun activities for the students.

SKILLS LISTED WITH CUES

Cues are provided for stationary ball handling, dribbling, passing and catching, the set shot, shooting drills, right- and left-handed layups, basic ball handling, free throw, jump shot, rebounding, jumping and dunking, blocking out, the pick, offensive footwork, offensive one-on-one moves, spacing, defense, and out-of-bounds plays.

TIPS

1. Play a lot of games: half-court and full-court games.
2. Play dribble tag, relays, passing games, shooting contests (using right and left hands).
3. Be creative in your games. Use your imagination. Change and modify your rules (e.g., you must find a way to score without dribbling).
4. Time players on dribbling the length of the court, dribbling right- and left-handed.
5. Time the player on rebounding and throwing a baseball pass the length of the court.

6. Direct stretching, footwork, and ball handling at the beginning of each session before activity begins.
7. All jump balls go to the defense.

EQUIPMENT TIP

Have a lot of basketballs and baskets available.

TEACHING IDEAS

1. Every player should have a basketball. This is a must.
2. Practice should be 90 percent dribble, pass, shoot, and handling the ball.
3. Practice—practice—practice! How many hours are you willing to practice?
4. Use two basketballs per player to dribble or pass to a partner.
5. Know the feel for the ball and what the ball can do for you.
6. The best players shoot the ball up to 8 hours a day. Recruiters look for 90 percent ball-handling and shooting skills. Tell students that to be good they need the fundamentals: dribble, pass, and shoot.
7. When playing a game you must boil down teaching to the basic cues of the game, like placing your rebounder under the basket on the right-hand side of the basket. Why? Most of the balls go there.

Court Sprints

1. Diagonal sprint from under the basket on the baseline to the left hash mark to the right hash mark on the other side of the court to the other baseline; repeat.
2. Run forward from baseline to baseline.
3. Run backward from baseline to baseline.
4. Run from far baseline to far free-throw line forward, then backward, back to the baseline. Keep your balance by using your arms when running backward.
5. Conditioning your players must involve forward, backward, lateral, sprinting, and jumping gamelike movements. You can sprint while dribbling the ball.
6. Use half-court and full court for speed drills and change-of-speed crossover drills. Emphasize change of direction and change of speed. Keep head up. Ball-handling drill on the end line.

FYI

For further information and special help, consult the following organizations and resources.

ORGANIZATION

University of Tennessee Women's Intercollegiate Athletics, Basketball
Coach Pat Summitt
207 Thompson-Boling Arena
1600 Phillip Fulmer Way
Knoxville, TN 37996-4610

PUBLICATION

Krause, J. V., & Meyer, D. (1999). *Basketball skills and drills.* Champaign, IL: Human Kinetics.

WEBSITES

www.basketballworldinc.com
www.encarta.msn.com

STATIONARY BALL—BALL HANDLING

SKILL	CUE	WHY	COMMON ERROR
Hand Position Drill	Slap the ball with wide fingers	This will develop a feel for the ball and control of the ball	Palm on ball
Around the World	Move the ball around the waist; change directions; then move the ball around your head; then change directions quickly	To develop quick reaction time with hands and body awareness	Dropping the ball
Figure 8 Around Legs	Move ball in figure 8 formation around the knees and then change directions quickly		
Scissor Walk with Basketball (Crab Walk) (Figure 6.1)	Lunging down the court, move the basketball in and out of your legs, going from baseline to baseline and staying low	Promote basketball position and coordination in ball movement	Standing straight up

FIGURE 6.1 Scissor Walk with Basketball

FULL- AND HALF-COURT DRIBBLING DRILLS

SKILL	CUE	WHY	COMMON ERROR
Hand Placement on Ball When Dribbling	Thumb out, fingers spread wide, ball touching all 5 finger pads when dribbling; look up court	Develop feel for the ball	Fingers together
Hand Action	Yo-yo action with your hand on the ball; push ball hard toward floor	Develop feel for hand on ball and force in dribbling	Slapping the ball
	Waving action with your hand		Palm touches the ball
	Hand waving down at the ball		Dribble with both hands
	Note: Use left and right hands equally when practicing		
Eyes	Eyes looking up the court for open players and for opportunities to pass, shoot, or drive; see the defenders but don't look at them	To develop court awareness and player positions	Eyes looking down at the ball
Speed Drills *Change of speed, Crossover*	Emphasize change of direction and change of speed; keep head up	To promote ball-handling skills and ability	
Five-Trip Dribble (Single Ball)	Used to change direction on the court; protect ball with arm guard		
Speed Dribble	Quickly dribble down the court with right hand; dribble back with left hand	Control with speed	Bouncing ball too high
The Crossover	Take 3 dribbles with the right hand toward the sideline, lower the dribble and cross the ball over to the left hand at knee high, then dribble toward the other sideline; repeat; use the crossover down to the baseline and back to the other baseline. Make a zigzag pattern.	Develop change of direction skills	High dribble

continued

FULL- AND HALF-COURT DRIBBLING DRILLS, continued			
SKILL	**CUE**	**WHY**	**COMMON ERROR**
Five-Trip Dribble (Single Ball), *continued*			
Around the Back	Take 3 dribbles with the right hand toward the right sideline; bring the ball around your back to the other hand, then dribble toward the other sideline; go down and back		Holding ball too long in hand
Through the Legs	Take 3 dribbles with the right hand toward the right sideline; make sure the left foot is in front when you bounce the ball between your legs to change directions, then dribble with the left hand toward the left sideline; make sure your right foot is forward to change directions; go down and back		Stepping with the wrong foot
Reverse Spin	Take 3 dribbles toward the right sideline; keep ball in your right hand and quickly spin so your back shuts out your defender; switch the ball to the left hand, take 3 dribbles and reverse-spin again; go down and back; keep ball low on spin		Carrying the ball
Five-Trip Dribble (Two-Ball)	Used to change direction; keep rhythm with balls		
Speed Dribble (Figure 6.2)	Dribble 2 balls to half-court and back		
The Crossover	Repeat the single-ball crossover drill using 2 balls, to half-court and back	Helps improve confidence, creativity, and dribbling skills	
		Develop advanced skills in dribbling	

continued

FULL- AND HALF-COURT DRIBBLING DRILLS, *continued*			
SKILL	**CUE**	**WHY**	**COMMON ERROR**
Five-Trip Dribble (Two-Ball), *continued*			
Around the Back	Repeat single-ball drill with 2 balls		
Through the Legs	Repeat single-ball drill with 2 balls		
Reverse Spin	Repeat single-ball reverse-spin drill using 2 balls, to half-court and back; keep balls low		

FIGURE 6.2 Dribbling Two Balls, Ball Handling

PASSING AND CATCHING

SKILL	CUE	WHY	COMMON ERROR
Passing (Figure 6.3)			
Hand Position	Two thumbs down behind the ball	For proper spin	Thumbs up
Fingers	Spread fingers wide	For control	
Eyes	Eyes focused on your target	For accuracy	
Passing Action	Extend your arms like shooting horizontally, following through with thumbs down	For proper speed and accuracy	
	Palms out at finish		
Catching (Figure 6.4)			
Hand and Finger Position	Big hands, wide fingers	To develop receiving skills	
Catching Action	Reach out, pull the ball in, or suck the ball in like a vacuum; your nickname is "Hoover"	Prevent defense from stealing ball	
Eyes	Smother the ball with your eyes	To assure catching	

continued

FIGURE 6.3 Two-Hand Chest Pass

FIGURE 6.4 Catching the Pass

PASSING AND CATCHING, continued			
SKILL	**CUE**	**WHY**	**COMMON ERROR**
Passing and Catching Drills			
Partner Passing	Face each other using one ball; one-hand push pass with your right hand and then your left hand; follow through each time	Like shooting a basketball, only horizontally with right hand	
		To pass around a defender; right side/ left side	
Target passing	Throw to your partner's target (e.g., partner's shoulder, head, or hands); make a target on the wall when practicing by yourself	Like shooting a basketball, only horizontally with the left hand	
Chest Pass and Bounce Pass Simultaneously	Both partners have a ball; 1 partner makes 2-hand chest pass while the other partner makes bounce pass at the same time; then switch after awhile	Develop advanced skills in passing	
Pass with a Figure 8	Perform a figure 8 around your knees, then pass to your partner off the figure 8; keep the ball moving	Passing while on the move	
Behind-the-Back Passing	Standing slightly sideways, bring ball behind the back, pass to your partner; use your right hand, then your left hand; learn through error	Alternative pass for advanced players	
Baseball Pass	Throw (as a football quarterback passes a football) to your partner	For long-distance passing with accuracy	
	Start close to your partner, then keep taking steps farther back as needed to throw farther		
	Stretch arm back and make an L at the elbow		
	Release the ball at 2:00 on your pretend clock		

continued

PASSING AND CATCHING, continued			
SKILL	**CUE**	**WHY**	**COMMON ERROR**
One-Bounce Baseball Pass	Use strong then weak arms to throw your baseball passes with a bounce first	Alternative pass for advanced players	
	Step farther back as needed to throw longer passes		
Buzzer Beater Baseball Pass Length of the Floor	Dribble once, then throw downcourt to partner at the other end of court, counting to self . . . 3-2-1 BZZZZZ	Develop end-of-game confidence	
Two-Player Running and Passing Drills			
Dribbler and Trailer	Player 1 baseball passes to player 2, who is at half-court	To develop necessary skills in passing for advanced players	
Full Court	Player 2 passes to player 1, who drives to the basket		
Pass and Cut	Partner 1 stands at half-court		
Half-Court	Partner 2 stands on free-throw line extended at the wing spot		
	Partner 1 then passes to the wing and cuts hard inside to the basket, receiving the ball from partner 2 for a layup shot		
Three-Man Player Drills			
Side Center Side	Start with 3 lines, ball in middle line		
	Pass back and forth with no weave		
	Pass back and forth downcourt with 1 shooter		
	Perfect execution for the layup		

continued

PASSING AND CATCHING, continued			
SKILL	**CUE**	**WHY**	**COMMON ERROR**
Three-Man Weave	Start with 3 lines, ball in middle line	To include movement in passing as done in game situations	
	Running downcourt, middle passes to player on right side, who passes to the player coming toward her		
	Pass and go behind; follow your pass. Be ready to receive ball back quickly.		
	Person who receives the ball at key drives in for the layup		
	Use game speed; go all out		
Rebound Pass	Two players start in the paint, one outside the paint	To develop fast-break strategy	
	Teacher tosses the ball off the rim		
	Player rebounds		
	Everyone takes off downcourt with no dribble		
	Pass down the floor to closest player by the basket for the layup		
	Move the ball up the floor as quickly as possible for a quick layup		

SET SHOT

SKILL	CUE	WHY	COMMON ERROR
Setup	Shooting is the most important aspect of the game	To develop a knowledge base	
	Layups and free throws are 2 shots you must make; these are freebies		
	The best 3-point shot is a layup and a free throw, not the arch shot		
Shooting Hand	Air valve between index finger and middle finger	To develop proper position for successful shooting	
	Extend thumb along seam when shooting		
	Spread fingers Hand up; balance like a waiter's tray		Fingers close together Ball held in palm
(Figure 6.5)	Elbow makes an L with ball sitting on a pretend serving tray of finger pads		

continued

FIGURE 6.5 Setup

SET SHOT, continued			
SKILL	**CUE**	**WHY**	**COMMON ERROR**
Setup, *continued*			
Nonshooting Hand (Figure 6.5)	Hand faces side of ball; fingers only touch ball		
	Hand brushes ball		
Alignment	Arm, eye, and hand line up with nail hole in floor and with basket, like throwing a dart		Elbow points to side Pushing ball sideways Arm at 45° angle
Sight	Focus on 2 inches above the rim	You have to see what you're shooting for	
	"Basket looks like big bin and the basket gets bigger on a good night" (Michael Jordan)		
Legs	Slightly bend knees with buttocks out	Strength of shot comes from legs	Insufficient force from no use of legs
Footwork	Feet square to basket and balanced		
Shooting Action			
Fingers	Ball rolls off fingers for a nice, pretty backspin	To develop proper backspin	Ball is thrown

continued

(a) Side View

(b) Front View for Right-Handed Players

FIGURE 6.6 Set Shot—Finish Position

SET SHOT, continued			
SKILL	**CUE**	**WHY**	**COMMON ERROR**
Shooting Action, *continued*			
Wrist	Flip wrist, wave good-bye to ball		Inadequate wrist action
Shoot Over	Shoot up over a telephone booth	Important for arch development	Insufficient drive upward, loss of balance
Path of Ball	Make a rainbow; exaggerate the arch for your first couple of shots		Lack of follow-through and arch
Finish Position (Figures 6.6 and 6.7)			
Wrist	Gooseneck finish, thumb points at shoes	To ensure proper and consistent release	
	Freeze hand at the top		

FIGURE 6.7 Finish Position on Shot for Left-Handed Players

FUNDAMENTAL SHOOTING DRILLS

SKILL	CUE	WHY	COMMON ERROR
Fundamentals			
Right Hand and Left Hand	Start close to the basket shooting 5 on the right side 1-handed, then shooting 5 on the left side 1-handed	Develop confidence and form at close distances	
Shooting Practice with No Defender	Take 5 steps back from under the basket, shoot 5 right-handed and 5 left-handed	Develop consistency and accuracy	
	Take 5 steps back until you are at the free-throw line; shoot 5 with strong hand only		
Consecutive Free Throw	Consecutive free-throw shot with no dribble and a partner	Confidence	
	Find a rhythm		
Shooter Rebounds Free Throw	Shooter rebounds ball before it touches floor and passes back to partner for the shot; so shooter rebounds own shot and passes to partner on foul line	Shoot and follow shot	
	Left hand comes off ball with the shot; thus it is a 1-handed shot		
	You want to shoot without a defender because you make more shots when you're open; when you're defended you tend to pass and not shoot	Shoot when open; more shots are made	
Body Position for the Shot	Feet and hand must be in line with the basket	Extremely important for successful shooting	
Three-Man	You need a passer, a shooter, and a rebounder	Practice advanced skills	

continued

FUNDAMENTAL SHOOTING DRILLS, continued

SKILL	CUE	WHY	COMMON ERROR
Three-Man *continued*	Rebounder cannot let ball hit the floor before passing it to the passer. The passer bounce-passes it to the shooter along the free-throw line		
	Shoot from the right side of the court and then the left side of the court; then rotate		
	Rebounder to passer to shooter to rebounder		
Three-Man	Same formations as previously, only the shooter runs along the 3-point line; he shoots where he receives the pass		
Two-Man	Need a shooter and a rebounder		To develop individual shooting skills
	The shooter rebounds, passes to the partner, and plays defense on the shooter		
	Do not block the shot		
Three-Man Weave with a Bounce Pass	Get into 3 lines along the baseline, ball in the middle line		
	While running full court, pass the ball with a bounce pass to the right side; follow the pass and go behind		
	Expect the ball back		

LAYUPS

SKILL	CUE	WHY	COMMON ERROR
Right-Handed *The Approach*	Head up, eyes on top of square	The closer you are to the basket, the more likely you are to make it	
	Ball in outside hand with low approach		Shooting ball more likely to be blocked if approach is high
Release of Layup	Bring ball close to chin; chin ball, step, and push off foot with opposite shooting hand	Harder to block	
(Figure 6.8)	Extend arm, reach high (ball kisses backboard) Release ball at peak of reach		
Left-Handed *Footwork*	Step left, right, hop (jump)	Same as right hand	Jumping off wrong foot
Shooting Action (Figure 6.9)	Left hand shoots ball		Using wrong hand on wrong side

FIGURE 6.8 Right-Handed Layup

FIGURE 6.9 Left-Handed Layup

BASIC BALL HANDLING

SKILL	CUE	WHY	COMMON ERROR
Ready Position (Figure 6.10)	Triple threat	A position that allows player to execute all parts of the game	Not assuming the position
	Purpose: to fake out opponent with the option of shooting, passing, or dribbling		
Hand Position	Shooting position on ball		Hands not in shooting position; hands too close together
Holding Ball	Hold ball to side on hip		Ball held too high or too low
	Keep ball on hip—hold ball to side to pass, dribble, or step into shot		
	Elbows out		

FIGURE 6.10 Ready Position—Triple Threat

FREE THROW

SKILL	CUE	WHY	COMMON ERROR
Front Toe Stays on Line	Work off the center of free-throw line with front toe in direct line with rim	It lines up the player with the center of the basket	
	Place front toe directly on center of free-throw line; find the nail hole	Shooting is a straight-line function	
	Put the front toe on same place every time; toe on the line	Consistency	
Head Position	Put head down; head comes up with ball in one motion	Focuses eyes on target	
	Head level; eyes up		
Balance	Get balanced on free-throw line	Important to have weight properly distributed	
Routine	University of Tennessee uses player's choice—no dribble or 1, 2, or 3 dribbles	Develop consistency	
Body	Body makes a line with the basket—same place every time		
Leg Action	Bend your knees; the legs compel the shot	Consistency comes from the legs	
Back Foot	Feet shoulder width apart, then place back foot slightly back	Help maintain balance	
	Back foot does not have anything to do with shot		
Fundamental Drills	Repetition and competition: dribble 3, shoot	Develops confidence and consistency	
	Rebounder passes to shooter		
	Find a rhythm		
	Example: Partner shooting: shoot 5; person with the most shots made wins		

continued

FREE THROW, continued			
SKILL	**CUE**	**WHY**	**COMMON ERROR**
Fundamental Drills *continued*	Group free throw; everybody shoots 1 and runs for the missed shots		
	Speed or lightning shots with eyes closed (Michael Jordan drill)	Advanced skill players only	

JUMP SHOT			
SKILL	**CUE**	**WHY**	**COMMON ERROR**
Execution (Figure 6.11)	Jump above the defense, then shoot at the top of the jump; get high	Reduce blocked shots	
	Body in a coil all ready to jump	Develop consistency	

FIGURE 6.11 Jump Shot

REBOUNDING

SKILL	CUE	WHY	COMMON ERROR
Attacking Basket	Work on blocking out, then attacking the basket	To reduce chance of opponent getting ball	
One Player	Cover the weak side of basket (opposite side of shot)	70% of missed shots fall away from side shot on	
	Most shots go long off the back side		
	Rebounding involves contact		
	Move from side to side and back up into a player; keep contact		
	Be active, aggressive, and alert		
Two Players	Check the player without the ball: if he moves to the basket, take him; if not, attack the basket for the ball	To reduce chance of opponent getting ball	

JUMPING AND DUNKING

SKILL	CUE	WHY	COMMON ERROR
Jumping *Fundamentals*	Jump naturally	Forced movement reduces ability	
	Work on getting high; act like a bungee cord		
Dunking	Lower baskets for student to dunk on	Develop confidence and have fun	
	Do not hang on rims		
	Have lots of baskets to jump with		
	Use jump ropes		

BLOCKING OUT

SKILL	CUE	WHY	COMMON ERROR
Action of Body	Find with hands	Develop a routine to keep opponent from getting ball	
Turn Back to Opponent (Figure 6.12)	Put buttocks under opponent's hip or create a stable wall between opponent and ball		Not able to hold position
Hands (After Pivot)	Elbows out, palms wide; feel for opponent		

FIGURE 6.12 Blocking Out

THE PICK

SKILL	CUE	WHY	COMMON ERROR
Hustle	Earn your position	To avoid fouling	
Stance	Stand wide	Develop larger target; more effective	
	Weight on balls of feet		
Arms	Elbows bent and big		
Men	Hands clasped in front to protect sensitive parts of your body		
Women	Arms crossed against body to protect sensitive parts of your body		
Coming off the Pick (Figure 6.13)	Rub shoulder to shoulder	To shake off the defender with the pick	
	Right to right; left to left		

continued

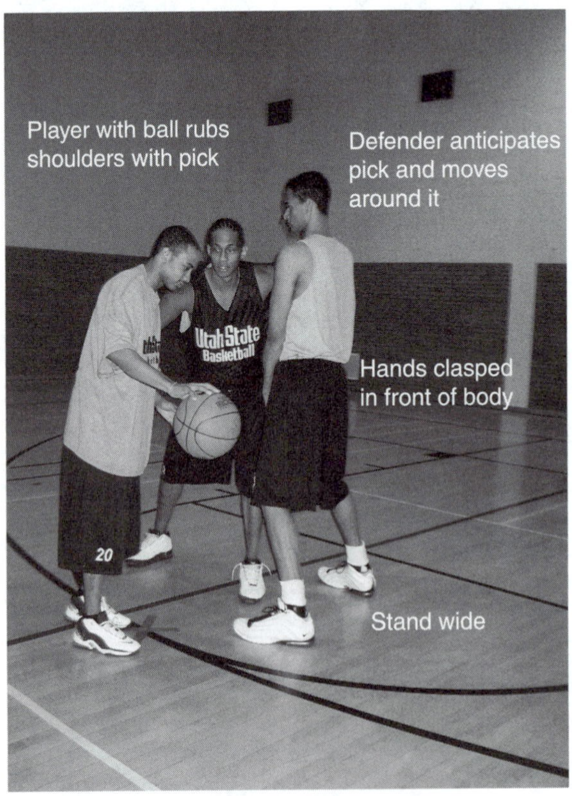

FIGURE 6.13 Player Coming Off the Pick

THE PICK, continued

SKILL	CUE	WHY	COMMON ERROR
Pick and Roll	After you pick, you pivot toward basket	Gives a player more opportunity to get open	
	Hand up high; ask for ball		
	Receive pass and go in for layup or shot		
Defender Going Through a Pick	Anticipate taking a hook step around player	To beat the defender to a position	

OFFENSIVE FOOTWORK

SKILL	CUE	WHY	COMMON ERROR
Technique	Ready and triple-threat position	To develop advanced skills	
	Two-step stop—emphasis on heel-toe (jump stop to be used for post people only)		
	Change of speed and direction		
	Fake shot and drive—left and right (without the ball)		

OFFENSIVE ONE-ON-ONE MOVES

SKILL	CUE	WHY	COMMON ERROR
Guards and Wings	Catch and shoot	To develop confidence and advanced skills	
	Catch and drive		
	Catch and reverse		
	Catch shot, fake, and drive		
	Catch, swing through, and drive		
	Catch, jab, and go (emphasis on heel-toe technique)		

continued

OFFENSIVE ONE-ON-ONE MOVES, continued			
SKILL	**CUE**	**WHY**	**COMMON ERROR**
Posts	Front pivot shot (both ways)		
	Front pivot crossover		
	Drop-step baseline/ power shot		
	Drop-step middle, drop hook, jump hook, or power shot		
	Step-back shot		
	Post people can also use perimeter drills		

SPACING			
SKILL	**CUE**	**WHY**	**COMMON ERROR**
Teach Spacing When Passing on Offense			
Spacing Creates Open Areas	The perfect passing distance is 15 feet	Put pressure on defense to react	
	Anything beyond 15 feet is a potential stolen pass		
	Teach students to play off each other to create efficient spacing		
	Use the free-throw line to gauge distance; use lines on the floor to gauge the distance of 15 feet		

DEFENSE			
SKILL	**CUE**	**WHY**	**COMMON ERROR**
Man-to-Man Defense	Force opponents from the middle to the sideline; force them to play on one side of the floor	So teammates will know where to help	
On-Ball Defense (Figure 6.14)	One hand mirrors the ball; the other hand is in the passing lane	Prepares defender to block pass or steal ball	

continued

FIGURE: 6.14 On-Ball Defense

FIGURE: 6.15 Off-Ball Defense—Two Passes Away

DEFENSE, continued			
SKILL	**CUE**	**WHY**	**COMMON ERROR**
Off-Ball Defense (Figure 6.15)	Deny defense is one hand always in the passing lane, palm facing ball	Develops a team defense concept	
	One eye on your player, the other eye on the ball one pass away		
	One eye on your player, one eye on the ball two passes away in pistol formation		

WHAT DOES ZONE DO?			
SKILL	**CUE**	**WHY**	**COMMON ERROR**
Zone Defense	Will win more games		
	Effective because teams can't shoot over the zone		
	Teams can't pass or play against stationary defense		
Zone Movement	Defense shifts with ball movement		
	Everybody knows where the ball is at all times, including those on the bench		

continued

WHAT DOES ZONE DO?, continued

SKILL	CUE	WHY	COMMON ERROR
The Key to a Zone	A key to zone defense: keep them out of the lanes and deny the passing lanes		
	Run an odd front when playing zone defense: If they have an offense set at a 1-2-2, you play a 2-3 zone defense; if they have 1 guard, you have 2 defenders on their point guard; if they run a 1-3-1 defense, you run a 2-3 offense (2-guard front and 3 low post)		
	The objective is to take the point guard out of the game; she runs the show		

OUT-OF-BOUNDS PLAYS

SKILL	CUE	WHY	COMMON ERROR
Box Set—Box 1	Player 1 takes the ball out of bounds		
	Players 3 and 4 run to right-side elbow of key and set a double pick for player 2, who rolls off pick to receive ball from 1 guard for layup; player 5 is decoy		
Line Formation—Stack	Player 1 takes ball out of bounds		
	Players 2, 3, 4, and 5 make a line outside of key under basket		
	Players 3 and 4 roll toward basket after pick for possible option		

continued

OUT-OF-BOUNDS PLAYS, continued			
SKILL	**CUE**	**WHY**	**COMMON ERROR**
Line Formation—Stack *continued*	Player 1 slaps ball, then teammates 2 and 4 split to the left, and teammates 3 and 5 split to the right		
	Player 1 passes to open player		
Box Set—Box 2	Player 1 takes ball out of bounds		
	Players 2 and 4 on left side of key		
	Players 3 and 5 on opposite side of key		
	Players 2 and 4 run across key to set picks for 3 and 5 away from ball, 2 and 4 set screen away from ball		
	3 and 5 come off screen		
	5 receives ball on ball side of floor, then passes to 3		
	3 passes to 2 on the wing		
	2 passes to 4 on the baseline for the shot		
	1 steps in bounds to rebound		
Out-of-Bounds Defense	Man-to-man formation		
	Player 1 is on ball		
	Player 2 guards opposing guard at top of key		
	Player 3 defends guard opposite player 2		
	Player 4 guards lower post, opposite side of ball; player 5 guards lower post, ball side		

7

Bowling

INTRODUCTION

"Strike!" The crashing of pins fills the air with excitement and anticipation of bowling the perfect game of 300. Families, friends, coworkers, and peers can all join in the fun of bowling. How does one learn to bowl? Many bowlers learn by trial and error. Teachers offering bowling in their curriculum could use the cues in this chapter to explain the skills of bowling, even when a bowling alley is not available. (How do you add bowling but not a bowling alley to your curriculum? See equipment tips.)

SKILLS LISTED WITH CUES

Teachers can use simple instructional cues in this chapter to teach the following bowling skills: grip, stance, arm action and leg action on approach and delivery, delivering a straight ball and hook ball, using the arrows for spares and placement of feet, and finding an eye target for spares, splits, and adjustments. Because scoring the game of bowling can be confusing and frustrating to the beginning bowler, we have added scoring cues.

We hope that these cues will help students be more comfortable with bowling and that they will seek real bowling opportunities. Friends can go bowling and experience success together.

ETIQUETTE FOR BOWLERS

1. Remain behind the foul line at all times.
2. Never walk in front of another bowler.
3. Give the bowler to your right the right-of-way.
4. Remain quiet while other students are bowling.
5. To avoid injuries, have students cradle the ball when walking with it.

EQUIPMENT TIPS FOR BOWLING IN GYMS

1. Gym floor.
2. Rubber bowling balls can be ordered, or round soccer Nerf balls can be used.
3. Pins can be made from 2-liter pop bottles or empty tennis ball cans, or white plastic pins can be ordered.
4. Scorecards can be obtained from a local bowling alley.
5. Long ropes can be used for lane dividers, or a gym wall can be one side of a lane.
6. Use colored tape for lane arrows and X's to mark the spots where the pins stand.

EQUIPMENT TIPS FOR BOWLING ALLEYS

1. Bowling shoes are used so dirt and other abrasive particles are not brought onto the lanes.
2. Go to a pro shop to get fitted for a ball.
3. Bowling shoes are designed with soles that allow the bowler to slide.

TEACHING IDEAS FOR BOWLING IN GYMS

1. Have students practice technique and scoring in gym. Have two lines back to back at center court. Pair up in partners (bowl to wall, take turns with balls).
2. Same drill as in 1, except bowl to 1 pin only, progress to 3 pins, 5 pins, and all 10 pins. Work on technique. Scoring options: Set one pin up; if they knock one pin down, award 1 point. Set three pins up; if they knock three pins down, score 1 point. Set five pins up; knock five pins down to score 1 point. Team competition: four on a team; set three pins up; count number of pins knocked down by team, have a 5-minute time limit. One student bowls; the other runs the ball down to partner; and the other two set up pins. Rotate after they finish their frame at bowling (Figure 7.1, page 90). Work on fitness and bowling skills.
3. Strength Activities: squeeze a tennis ball, do push-ups, swing a bowling ball.
4. Teach scoring with 10 pins in gym. Get bowling cards from local bowling alleys. Even teams of four. One student bowls, one student runs the ball down to bowler, one sets up pins, one keeps score; rotate after these students finish their frame at bowling. These drills and scoring system add fitness to the lesson, and the students enjoy the competition.

TEACHING IDEAS FOR BOWLING ALLEYS

1. Throw one frame to warm up if bowling alley permits it.
2. Handicapping is used in bowling to create parity between bowlers and stimulate greater competition. The following rules and formulas are used when computing a handicap.
   a. A minimum of nine games must be bowled before students can compute a handicap.
   b. Handicap = (200 − Average score) × 0.8
   c. Average score = total points ÷ number of games

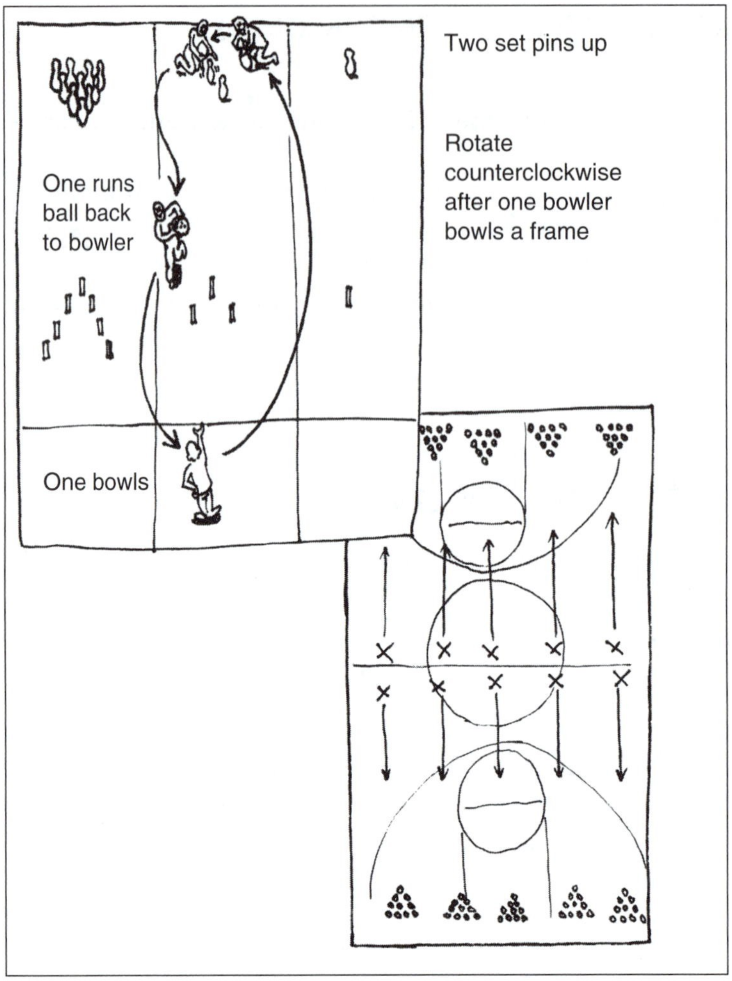

FIGURE 7.1 Gamelike Fitness Drill

d. The handicap is added to each player's total score at the end of a game during tournament play, as in the following example:

Joe bowls the following scores for nine games: 107, 113, 121, 115, 135, 101, 112, 115, 140

$$(107 + 113 + 121 + 115 + 135 + 101 + 112 + 115 + 140) \div 9 = 117.7$$

Joe's average number of pins per game is 117.7. To compute his handicap

$$(200 - 117.7) \times 0.8 = 65.84$$

Joe bowls against Frank in the tournament. Joe gets a final score of 132, and Frank's score is 159.

Joe's handicap is 66, and Frank's handicap is 63. The final scores are as follows:

Joe: 132 + 66 = 198

Frank: 159 + 63 = 222

Frank wins the tournament.

3. Bowling in a gym is fun. Tournaments can be set up. However, the best place to bowl is at a bowling alley.
4. Take a trip to a local bowling alley (funded by parents).

FYI

For further information and special help, consult the following organizations and resources.

ORGANIZATIONS

American Bowling Congress (ABC) coordinator at local bowling center.

Young American Bowling Alliance (YABA)
5301 South 76th Street
Greendale, WI 53129-1127
Phone: (414) 423-3384
Fax: (414) 421-3013

PUBLICATIONS

Blassingame, C., & Cross, T. S. (1994). *Success in bowling through practical fundamentals.* Champaign, IL: Kendall/Hunt.

Harrison, M., & Maxey, R. (1987). *Bowling.* Glenview, IL: Scott, Foresman.

WEBSITES

www.amug.org/~a249/pinboy.html
www.encarta.msn.com

BASIC GRIPS AND STANCE

SKILL	CUE	WHY	COMMON ERROR
Conventional	Thumb on top, handshake position		
	Thumbhole at 12:00, finger holes at 6:00		
	Grip ball with second groove of 2 middle fingers		Squeezing with thumb
	Ring finger and middle finger		
Fingertip	Cradle ball in opposite hand	Helps balance the ball	
	Grip ball with first groove of 2 middle fingers		Thumb in first Squeezing with thumb
Stance (Figure 7.2, page 92)	Erect, knees relaxed		Knees locked, shoulders not square to pins
	Stand tall		
	Ball supported by non-delivery hand	Helps balance the ball	Ball hanging from thumb and fingers
	Ball carried on palm of right hand		

continued

FIGURE 7.2 Bowling Stance—First Step

BASIC GRIPS AND STANCE, continued			
SKILL	**CUE**	**WHY**	**COMMON ERROR**
Stance, *continued*	Ball on right side at shirt-pocket level		Ball above or below shirt pocket
	Ball hides right shirt pocket (good place to start); find your comfort zone		
	Lower right shoulder	Helps put bowler on plane with bowling ball	
	Tilt body slightly to right		
	Feet slightly apart		
	Three boards between feet		
	Left foot slightly advanced		
	One-half foot length ahead		
	Eyes focus on aiming spot	More ball control by looking at spot or arrows	Looking at pins
	Look at second arrow from right	Ball will hit the pocket and blow out the pins	

APPROACH

SKILL	CUE	WHY	COMMON ERROR
Arm Action (Figure 7.3a)	First step and arms push away together		Stepping before pushing away
	Step away, push away		
	Extend ball arm straight forward to waist level		Pushing ball up or to the right too far
	Long reach but short step, like handing ball to friend		
	Use pendulum swing, like ball on end of string	Accuracy and speed	Applying too much force, changing direction of ball
	Ball falls downward and backward		
(Figure 7.3b)	Ball swings back, shoulder high	Power	Ball goes too high or arcs behind body
	Horizontal in front to horizontal in back		

continued

(a) Arm Action (Approach)

(b) Delivery

FIGURE 7.3 Straight Ball—Fourth Step

APPROACH, continued			
SKILL	**CUE**	**WHY**	**COMMON ERROR**
Arm Action, *continued*	Extend left arm outward for balance	Balance	
	Keep ball swinging, arms relaxed		Trying to throw ball too fast
	Gravity and inertia provide main force		
	Release ball as arm passes vertical; ball should land 3–4 feet beyond foul line	Will drop ball and cause it to bounce	Dropping ball or setting it down on boards
Drill: *When a bowler first starts to bowl* Roll the ball and see how the ball is moving. Look to see if it goes straight down or slides. Then the bowler can start playing with arrows, dots, etc. Once you get the ball performing the way you want, you can move on.			
Leg Action	First step very short	Short steps = control	First step too long
	Each step is a little longer and faster		
	Second step medium		
	Third step long		
(Figure 7.4)	Fourth step longest	Longer steps = power	
	First step and push away together		Feet finishing before arm swing
	Keep ball swinging and feet walking		
	Second and third steps with down and backswing		
	Fourth step with forward swing and delivery		

continued

FIGURE 7.4 Straight Ball—Fourth Step (Follow-Through)

APPROACH, continued			
SKILL	**CUE**	**WHY**	**COMMON ERROR**
How to Avoid Ball Bouncing	Bend at knees	Smooth ball delivery and higher scores	Straight legs
	Release knee high		
	Lean forward at waist		Standing up
Coordination	Push, step, swing, roll		Taking 2–3 steps
Drill: Take a white locker-room towel or towels used to wipe hands in bowling. Fold towel and place by foul line. Make sure ball goes over towel—prevents the bowler from dropping the ball.			

DELIVERY

SKILL	CUE	WHY	COMMON ERROR
Straight Ball (Figure 7.3b)	Wrist straight and firm		Arm rotation right or left
	Thumb at 12:00		
	Release ball as arm passes vertical and starts upward		Dropping or setting ball on approach before foul line
	Trajectory like airplane, landing 3–4 feet beyond foul line		Holding ball too long causes you to loft ball
(Figure 7.4)	Follow-through in straight upward swing		Stopping arm action on release of ball
	Arm points in direction you want ball to go		
	Shoulders stay square (parallel) to foul line		Body rotates clockwise on ball of foot
Hook Ball	Cup the palm		
	Thumb at 10:30		
	Hand stays behind ball		Hand on side of ball
	Thumb comes out first (ball spins counterclockwise)	Control of backspin	Spins like a top
	Deliver ball with finger only		
	On release, flip the fingers and shake hands	Spins the ball	
	Release with the V form		
	Follow-through in straight upward swing	Power and accuracy	
Leg Action	Lower the body during third and fourth steps		Bouncy up-and-down action
	Bend knees to smoothly lower body at end of approach		
	Decelerate fourth step		Loss of balance from too quick a stop
	Left foot steps and slides to a stop		

continued

DELIVERY, *continued*			
SKILL	**CUE**	**WHY**	**COMMON ERROR**
Leg Action, *continued*	Keep back foot in contact with floor		Poor timing results in picking up back foot and clockwise body rotation
	Don't spin out		
	Left knee and foot point toward pins		Body rotation
	Keep facing target		

USE OF ARROWS			
SKILL	**CUE**	**WHY**	**COMMON ERROR**
Using Arrows	Easier to hit a target 15 feet away than one 60 feet away		Looking at pins
	Focus eyes and attention on aiming points (arrows)		
Three Basic Positions			
Strike	Second arrow from right (10 boards in from right edge)	More control of ball to hit correct pin	
Right-Side Spare	Third arrow from left (15 boards in from left)		
Left-Side Spare	Third arrow from right (15 boards in from right)		
Aim of Eyes (Strike)	Second arrow from right (10 boards in from right side)		Bowling down center of lane
Placement of Feet (Strike)	Left toe on second dot board from right		
	Third dot from right at foul line		

continued

USE OF ARROWS, continued			
SKILL	**CUE**	**WHY**	**COMMON ERROR**
Use of Arrows (Spare)	Use 1 of 3 basic positions; move start position 1 board left to move ball contact 3 boards right; move feet 1 board right to move ball contact 3 boards left	More control of ball to hit correct pin	
	1-inch change in starting position equals 3-inch change in ball contact point		
Aim of Eyes (Spare)	Left-side spares (7 pin, etc.): same starting position as strike ball—aim over third arrow from right		Bowling down left side of lane
	Right-side spares (10 pin): third arrow from right		
Placement of Feet (Spare)	Left-side spares: same as strike starting position; make slight adjustments right or left to change ball contact point		
	Left toe on second dot from right		
	Right-side spares: left foot 4 boards in from far left edge of lane		
Splits	Use same arrows as spares; adjust starting position slightly right or left to change contact point of ball	More control of ball	
Adjustments			
Leaving Spares	Are you hitting your target on arrow? If no, hit target.	More control of ball hitting correct pins	Not hitting target on arrow

SCORING

SKILL	CUE	WHY	COMMON ERROR
Open Frame	Count pins you knock over		
	Pin count		
Spares (Figure 7.5)	Score 10, plus pin count from next ball		
	Maximum 20 points		
Strikes (Figure 7.5)	Score 10, plus pin count from next two balls		
	Maximum 30 points		
Tenth Frame	You can score bonus points in the tenth frame by bowling a spare or a strike		
Open	Score like a regular frame		
Strike	Bowl 2 more balls		
Spare (Figure 7.5)	Bowl 1 more ball; 10 points plus score from first ball; for example: 8 points plus spare = 18		
Strike Plus Spare	Bowl 3 balls; add 20 points to total score after ninth frame		
Three Strikes	Bowl 3-ball maximum; add 30 points to total after ninth frame		
	To score a 300 game you must get 3 strikes in the last frame		
	Note: When scoring, mark a spare with a slash (/) and a strike with an X.		

Enclosed are blank score sheets (see Figure 7.6, page 100).

For helpful bowling hints, see Figure 7.7, page 101.

How to Mark Score

Spare (/) Count 10 plus what you knock down on next ball.
Strike (X) Count 10 plus what you knock down on next two balls.
Immediately after each ball bowled, mark results in proper frame box.

1	2	3	4	5	6	7	8	9	10
7 /	X	6 2	X	X	0 /	3 3	X	X	X X 6
20	38	46	66	86	99	105	135	165	191

FIGURE 7.5 How to Mark Score

Bowling Game Score Sheet

Name	HDCP	1	2	3	4	5	6	7	8	9	10	Total
1												
Name	**HDCP**	1	2	3	4	5	6	7	8	9	10	Total
2												
Name	**HDCP**	1	2	3	4	5	6	7	8	9	10	Total
3												
Name	**HDCP**	1	2	3	4	5	6	7	8	9	10	Total
4												

Bowling Game Score Sheet

Name	HDCP	1	2	3	4	5	6	7	8	9	10	Total
1												
Name	**HDCP**	1	2	3	4	5	6	7	8	9	10	Total
2												
Name	**HDCP**	1	2	3	4	5	6	7	8	9	10	Total
3												
Name	**HDCP**	1	2	3	4	5	6	7	8	9	10	Total
4												

Bowling Game Score Sheet

Name	HDCP	1	2	3	4	5	6	7	8	9	10	Total
1												
Name	**HDCP**	1	2	3	4	5	6	7	8	9	10	Total
2												
Name	**HDCP**	1	2	3	4	5	6	7	8	9	10	Total
3												
Name	**HDCP**	1	2	3	4	5	6	7	8	9	10	Total
4												

FIGURE 7.6 Bowling Game Score Sheet

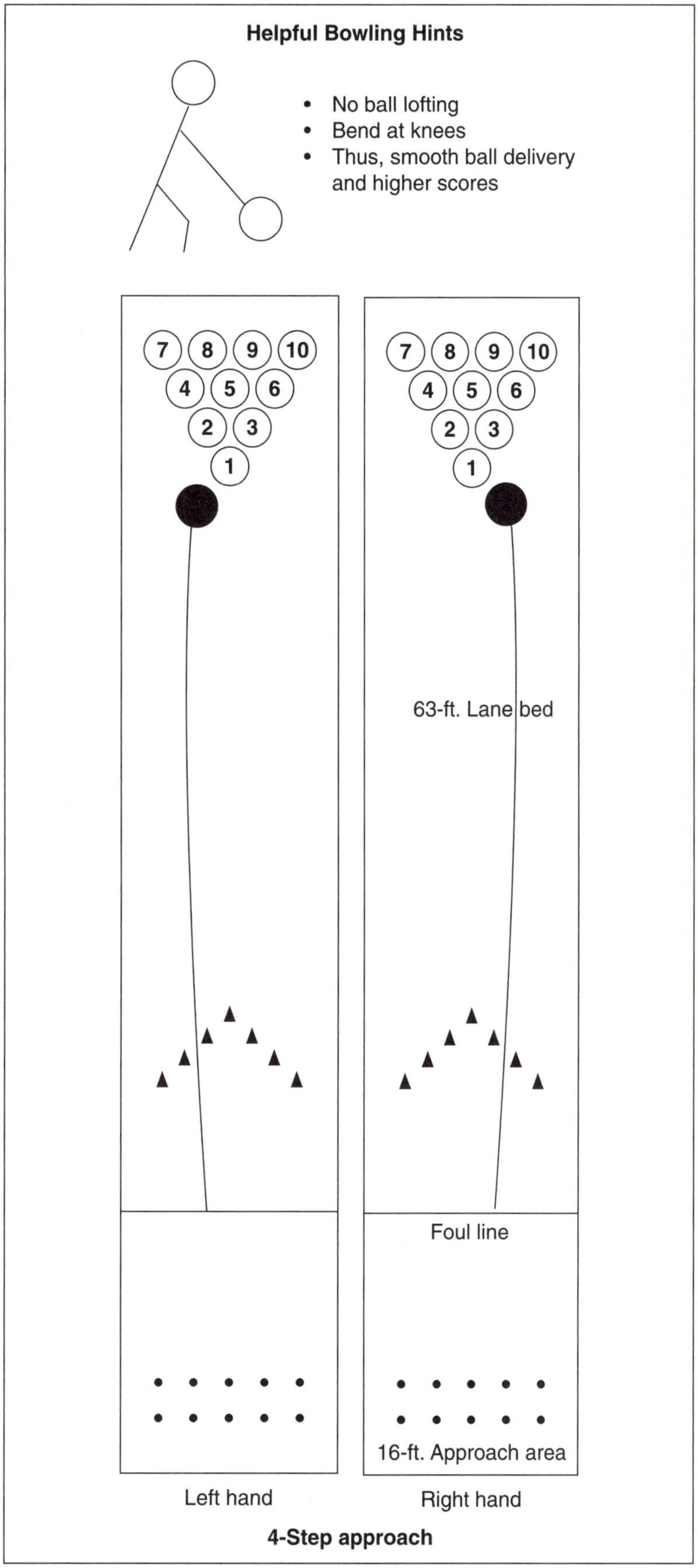

FIGURE 7.7 Helpful Bowling Hints

8

Cycling—Mountain Biking

INTRODUCTION

Mountain biking has become an increasingly popular activity since its beginning in the early 1980s (see Figure 8.1). It is a great aerobic workout and at times requires anaerobic power as well. It can challenge your technical riding ability depending on where you ride, and it's also a lot of fun. However, to make it the most fun, bikers should take precautions to prevent personal injury, injury to other trail users (bikers, hikers, and equestrians), and damage to the bicycle or trail.

Mountain biking requires a variety of skills to cope with obstacles such as rocks, logs, switchbacks, creeks, ditches, holes, tire ruts, animal crossings, washouts, shale, and the like. The cues in this chapter are intended to help the biker ride safely, learn correct biking techniques, have more fun, and experience success more quickly.

One of the most important safety features in mountain biking is a helmet. Wearing a helmet will minimize the risk of serious head injury. Following are two examples where a helmet saved a rider from serious injury and perhaps even death.

One accident involved a friend of mine, Curt, who was riding a trail on his way to work at a hospital. He slid off the trail, and as he landed, he hit his head, shoulder, and ribs. He separated his shoulder and broke a couple of ribs, and his helmet had a huge crack in it. Had he not been wearing his helmet, it would have been his head with the crack in it. Curt happens to be a pediatric anesthesiologist, and he sees many children admitted to the hospital with head injuries because they weren't wearing a helmet when riding a bicycle.

The other instance in which a helmet saved the person from injury was perhaps even more serious than Curt's accident. A young woman was pulling her child in a carrier behind her bike. She was crossing a busy street during morning rush hour and was hit by a car. The wheel of the car ran over her head. Had she not been wearing a helmet, she would most likely have died.

FIGURE 8.1 Have Fun on the Trail

Fortunately, her child was unharmed, and the woman's helmet kept her alive. Some people may think helmets look silly or that it's too big a hassle to put one on, but a helmet can save your life.

SKILLS LISTED WITH CUES

Included in this chapter are cues for the following techniques: buying the correct size bike, body position (feet/seat/upper body position), body position while climbing/descending, bunny hop, braking (to stop fast, to corner in loose terrain, to ride in rough terrain), pedaling and shifting under a load, riding down curbs, riding up curbs, cleaning the bike, and rules of the trail.

TIPS

1. Statistics show that in most bicycle accidents, the rider, for some reason, simply falls off the bicycle. The remainder of bicycle accidents are collisions with automobiles, fixed objects, and other bicyclists.
2. Check brakes and pads. There shouldn't be so much play in brakes that you have to completely squeeze them before they'll work. Check quick releases; make sure they are tight (by the way, that's what holds the wheels on).
3. Check all cables (frayed cables could cause a serious accident).
4. Check bottom bracket. Grab the crank arms, not the pedal, and move them from side to side. If there is any play, the bike needs adjustment. This procedure should be repeated with the wheels. Any play in these needs to be eliminated immediately.

5. Check lock on front brake. Rock it forward and back. If there is any play in the head set, get it adjusted immediately, or a repair can be expensive.
6. Every bike, no matter how much it is ridden, needs a checkup every year. If something is wrong with your bike, get it checked more often.
7. Check wear and tear on drivetrain: chain/crank set/cassette.

EQUIPMENT TIPS (Figure 8.2)

1. The first and most important equipment needed is the *helmet*. Different brands fit different heads. The author recommends a Bell helmet (see FYI). The biggest problem with wearing a helmet is getting the correct fit. Find one that is the correct size for your head, and then use the supplied pads to make it fit comfortably without any pressure spots. It should be about a finger's width up from your eyebrows and fit squarely on your head. Buckle up the helmet and tighten the strap so that moderate forces won't allow it to slide more than about an inch. You can test the fit by grasping the helmet and moving it from side to side and front to back. It should be tight enough so that you can feel the strap slightly pressing your throat as you swallow. Some helmets have a lower retention system that cradles the lower rear portion of your head. This is the best type of helmet for mountain biking because it creates a more secure fit and will keep the helmet from rattling on a rough trail or dislodging when you have a big crash.
2. Lightweight biking components are suggested.
3. Gears are a matter of personal preference and riding terrain. Counsel with local bike dealers for area specifications.
4. Padded biking gloves are best because they provide safety and cushioning during a ride and during a wreck (the palms usually hit first in a wreck); they also provide better friction between hand and grip, especially when hands are moist. Gloves will also keep your hands from getting too sweaty, sore, blistered, or cold.
5. Take two water bottles or a water backpack. Precaution: hydrate well even when you don't feel like drinking. Bikers are not aware of how much water they lose.

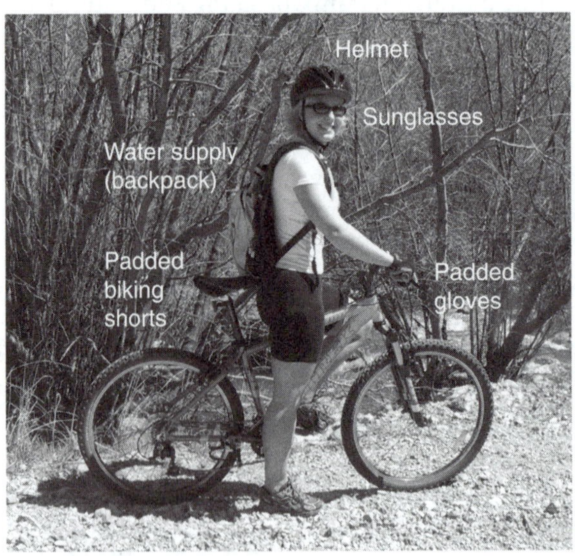

FIGURE 8.2 Equipment Tips

6. Snacks can include hard candies to keep mouth moist. Cut fruit and other foods into bite-size pieces and put in plastic sandwich bags. Carry "gorp" on long rides: raisins, peanuts, M&M's, and so on. Milky Way and 3 Musketeers bars are high in carbohydrates (two-thirds of their calories).
7. Take juice or fruit drinks in aluminum-foil packets.
8. Binoculars improve view and enjoyment of outdoors.
9. Take a lightweight jacket.
10. Padded biking shorts are optional. They not only increase comfort but also improve circulation.
11. On every ride, the following items should be carried in your backpack or bag: tire repair kit and chain breaker, spare tube, portable air pump, patch kit, tire levers, and spare change for phone calls or a cell phone.
12. Toe clips (or clipless pedals) are optional but highly recommended. They will keep the foot in the proper position on the pedal and will allow force to be applied while both pushing down and pulling up on the same pedal, a motion known as pedaling in circles (see the body position cue for riding uphill). Toe clips are helpful especially when climbing hills and doing bunny hops.
13. Sunglasses will be helpful when it is sunny, and they will also help keep bugs, rocks, and dirt from entering the eyes. If it isn't sunny, a pair of clear sport glasses will help protect your eyes from debris.
14. Suspension is a feature that adds a lot of comfort to your riding. Having front and/or rear suspension helps absorb the bumps and provides a smoother ride, making your arms and body less tired.
15. Bar ends on your handlebars allow for a change in hand position as a rest from the traditional grip, and they make it easier to lean forward when riding up hills.

RULES OF THE TRAIL

1. *Ride on open trails only.* Respect trail and road closures, private property, and requirements for permits and authorizations.
2. *Leave no trace.* Don't ride when ground will be marred, such as on certain soils after it has rained. Never ride off trail or skid tires. Never discard any object; pack out more than you pack in.
3. *Control your bicycle.* Inattention for even a second can cause disaster. Excessive speed frightens and injures people.
4. *Always yield.* Make your approach well known in advance to hikers, horseback riders, and other bikers. A friendly greeting is considerate and appreciated. Stop and walk when horses are present.
5. *Never spook animals.* Give them extra room and time to adjust to you; running livestock and disturbing wild animals are serious offenses. Leave ranch and farm gates as you find them, or as marked.
6. *Plan ahead.* Know your equipment, your ability, and the area in which you are riding, and prepare accordingly. Be self-sufficient. Keep your bike in good repair. Carry necessary supplies.

TEACHING IDEAS

1. Start in a parking lot and have students become familiar with the bike and its gears. Practice shifting; get the feel of what makes pedaling easier and

harder. Practice turns and braking; then move to wide, flat dirt roads and then to a wide dirt hill with a gradual incline.

2. Practice braking techniques: apply rear brake first. Practice on dirt roads so that when students ride on the trail, it is not a drastic transition.
3. Practice smooth transitions while shifting and especially while shifting under a load, such as when ascending a hill.
4. Technical riding: provide rocks or cones and have students ride between them. Make different trails. This drill lets riders know when they hit a rock or cone, or when they do it right. This drill will teach where the front and rear wheels are on the trail.
5. Practice braking downhill as well as riding downhill.
6. Technical skills can be practiced all the time.
7. Once students get the feel of the bike on these terrains, you can move to rougher terrains and sharper turns, with hills and other different situations.
8. Practice these basic skills on varying types of terrain.

FYI

For further information and special help, consult the following organizations and resources.

ORGANIZATIONS

U.S. Cycling Federation
One Olympic Plaza
Colorado Springs, CO 80909
Phone: (719) 578-4581
Fax: (719) 578-4956
Website: www.usacycling.org

Provides rules of the trail and a free 40-page book especially for newcomers who want to get started right on a bike.

Bicycling Magazine
New Rider Network
Box 6075
Emmaus, PA 18098

Provides information regarding helmets.

Bell Sports Customer Service
1924 County Road 3000 N.
Rantoul, IL 61866
Phone: (800) 456-Bell
Fax: (217) 893-9154

1. Bell will replace your helmet (starting at $20.00) if you write and describe the crash.
2. With this information, Bell can do research on actual crashes.
3. A Bell helmet has many air vents, permitting hot air to be replaced by cool air while riding. This ventilation reduces the risk of heat exhaustion.
4. A Bell helmet goes down lower and protects the occipital lobe of the brain, which is responsible for sight and other critical functions.

PUBLICATION

Sloane, E. (1988). *The complete book of cycling.* New York: Simon & Schuster.

WEBSITE

www.bicyclesource.com

BIKE SIZE

SKILL	CUE	WHY	COMMON ERROR
Legs (Figure 8.3)	Straddle bike		Bike is too big. When riding up steep hill, front wheel comes up. Bike also corners poorly.
	Pull bike to crotch; front tire should be 2 inches off ground		A bike that is too small can be uncomfortable because you bend over too far
Seat Height	At bottom of stroke knees are slightly bent	More efficient	Too high; knees are hyperextended, or hip rocking occurs

FIGURE 8.3 Fitting Bike

BODY POSITION

SKILL	CUE	WHY	COMMON ERROR
Feet	Ball of foot over axle of pedal	More efficient	Foot too far forward, pedal under arch
Seat Position	Position seat so that when knees and legs are at 3:00 and 9:00, seat is slightly behind ball of foot and pedal axle		
Upper Body	About 60% of body weight should be over rear wheel and 40% over front wheel		

UPHILL—DOWNHILL—ROUGH TERRAIN RIDING

SKILL	CUE	WHY	COMMON ERROR
Riding Uphill (Figure 8.4)	Balance weight 60–70% over back wheel and 30–40% over front wheel to keep traction in back	More efficient	Not enough weight on front wheel will cause front wheel to come off ground

continued

FIGURE 8.4 Body Position for Riding Uphill

UPHILL—DOWNHILL—ROUGH TERRAIN RIDING, continued			
SKILL	**CUE**	**WHY**	**COMMON ERROR**
Riding Uphill, *continued*	Shift weight to middle	To keep front wheel down so that you do not lose traction in loose dirt	
	Pedal in circles, using both a pulling and pushing action on each pedal	Less injury	Using only a pushing action
Riding Downhill (Figure 8.5)	Move back on seat and down	Won't crash	Sitting too far forward on seat causes flying over handlebars
	Hold seat with upper thigh		
	Watch ahead; pick a path	Won't fly over handlebars	

continued

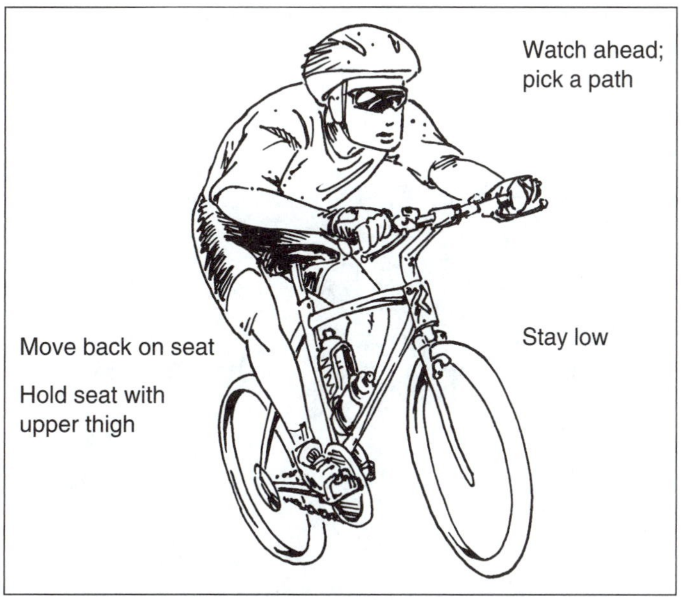

FIGURE 8.5 Body Position for Riding Downhill

UPHILL—DOWNHILL—ROUGH TERRAIN RIDING, continued			
SKILL	**CUE**	**WHY**	**COMMON ERROR**
Riding in Rough Terrain (Figure 8.6)	Power through corner		
	Keep rear wheel behind you	More control of bike	
	Relax; go with the flow		Too stiff; cannot let knees, elbows, body flow to absorb bumps
	Stutter-step; get dominant foot in front toe position		
	Be like a shock absorber		
	Soak up the bumps with knees and arms like a sponge	More efficient	
	Let bike float over things		
	Straddle saddle; stand on pedals		
	Avoid hitting obstacles with pedal	Won't crash	

FIGURE 8.6 Riding in Rough Terrain

PEDALING—BRAKING—SHIFTING

SKILL	CUE	WHY	COMMON ERROR
Pedaling	Mountain cadence at a spin of about 80 rpm	Don't get tired as fast	Usually too slow, which lugs your motor
	Ride smarter, not harder		
Braking			
To Stop Fast	Scoot buttocks back	Very efficient in stop	Sitting too far forward, weight shifts forward
	Pedal at 3:00 and 9:00 position		
	Squeeze both brakes		Squeezing one brake
	Keep both wheels on the ground		Squeezing both brakes when body position is too far forward
	Keep tires from skidding		
To Corner in Loose Terrain	Control slide of rear wheel for faster sharp cornering		Failing to make corner, slowing way down, losing control of front wheel, and turning too hard
	Move weight to inside		
	Pedal through corner		
Shifting Under a Load	Anticipate shift	Easier to shift when gears are under-loaded	Waiting before cadence slows before shifting
	Shift front gear first; fine-tune with smaller gears		
	Give pedals a hard push for half-stroke; then ease off and shift		Not easing off pedal prior to shifting

CURBS/OBSTACLES			
SKILL	**CUE**	**WHY**	**COMMON ERROR**
Riding Down Curbs/ Obstacles	Make sure there is enough speed to maintain forward motion		Going too slow
	Stand up on pedals with both knees slightly bent		Sitting
	Balance weight over pedals		Weight too far forward may cause you to go over the top of handlebars
	Keep handlebars straight		Turning handlebars
	Let front tire roll off curb; back wheel will follow		
	Slightly bend elbows and knees to absorb shock		Keeping extremities stiff
Riding Up Curbs/ Obstacles	Go fast enough to maintain forward motion		Going too slow
	Stand up on pedals		Sitting
	When you're about 3–6 inches from curb, pull up on handlebars to lift front wheels onto curb		Either pulling up too soon or waiting too long
	When front wheel has landed, lean forward slightly to get weight off back of bike		Keeping weight back
	Continue to pedal through so back tire just rides right up curb		Stopping pedaling and freaking out
Bunny Hop	Use for jumping over large rocks and branches in the trail		
	Go fast enough to maintain forward motion		Going too slow

continued

CURBS/OBSTACLES, continued			
SKILL	**CUE**	**WHY**	**COMMON ERROR**
Bunny Hop, *continued*	Stand up on pedals with knees slightly bent		Sitting
	Just before reaching the object, bend knees and elbows so back is nearly parallel with ground		Keeping extremities stiff
	Pull up on your handlebars as if you were riding up a curb		Not pulling soon enough
	When the wheel is in the air, push the handlebars out forward and down as you leap, or spring with your legs (this will bring the back wheel up)		
	Your front wheel actually goes through an arc motion as you pull up on the handlebars and then push forward and down		No arc motion

CLEANING THE BIKE			
SKILL	**CUE**	**WHY**	**COMMON ERROR**
Drivetrain	Remove dirt and grease; use oil-based lubricants	Water causes rust and ruins gears	Using water
Cleaning Steps	Turn bike upside down, balance on handlebars to clean		Resting bike on kickstand
Spraying	Spray oil-based lubricant on chain in back cassette while turning pedals backward		Turning pedals forward
	Continue to spray for 3–5 seconds		Spraying longer than 5 seconds
	Have chain in middle of back gears when spraying		Chain on either end

continued

CLEANING THE BIKE, continued			
SKILL	**CUE**	**WHY**	**COMMON ERROR**
Cleaning Steps, *continued*			
After Spraying	Grab a rag and place it around bottom part of chain in between the two cassettes		
	Continue pedaling backward; change rag to a clean spot; continue pedaling		Pedaling forward
	Change rag until no more dirt or grease comes off on rag		Using dirty rag
	Take rag and run it between gears, trying to remove any excess dirt		
Finish Coat	After removing all dirt and grease, apply a finish coat of dry lube; both are dry-lube-based and will protect chain from collecting dirt while riding		Not applying a finish coat
Spray	Spray dry-lube-based finish coat for one to two complete backward pedal rotations		
Check Chain	Even though a chain looks clean, it usually is not		Not cleaning chain often enough

9

Cycling—Road Biking

INTRODUCTION

Accomplished riders become highly skilled through countless hours aboard a bike, for there is no substitute for time and mileage. Most have also had some coaching, both formal and informal, which has honed their skills at all levels, especially early in their experience. Remember, cycling isn't fun if you're not in shape or if you lack technique.

Oftentimes cycling skills are learned by trial and error. For example, you purchase a new road bike, strap yourself in for the first time, and feel a little uncomfortable with the new situation. You take the bike for a spin and find yourself faced with narrow roads, sand and gravel on roads, hills, different terrain, traffic, corners, new gears, trying to drink from a water bottle, and so on, not to mention rude drivers. Cyclists could benefit from cues to help them feel more successful with techniques and to master the different situations. Following the rules of the road is key to increasing safety when riding a bicycle in motor vehicle traffic.

SKILLS LISTED WITH CUES

The ideas and cues contained in this chapter are concerned with methods of learning to cycle properly, including buying the correct size of bike, developing correct body position on the bike, pedaling for effective energy transfer (pedaling action, revolutions per minute, and riding in a straight line), cornering (braking, anticipating turns, sharp corners), climbing hills, and the transition from climbing to descending a hill.

TIP

Practice bunny hops, corners, and turning.

EQUIPMENT TIPS (Figure 9.1)

1. Purchase road bikes that weigh less than 24 pounds.
2. The first road bike should cost about $700 to $900.
3. Clipless pedals are easier to twist out of (twist sideways) than strapped pedals and are more energy efficient.
4. It is harder to get feet out of strapped pedals. Coast to 5 mph; practice pulling feet out of pedals. Caution: the rider will tip over sideways if the foot is not pulled out in time. Adjust pedal tension as needed.
5. Purchase riding shoes that are comfortable and have stiff soles. The bottom of the foot is like a platform that gives you more energy transfer.

TEACHING IDEAS

1. Stretch before and after riding, especially the hamstrings, quadriceps, and calf muscles.
2. Start slowly and progress. As your miles increase, increase the number of days. Add another day—up to five or six days a week. Take Wednesday and Sunday off. Learn to listen to your body.
3. Each rider is different when he or she starts putting in mileage. Ride for fun! Ride more days rather than taking one long ride.
4. Technical skills: practice bunny hopping in a parking lot. Use lines in a parking lot to hop the bike or jump with both wheels over an obstacle.

FIGURE 9.1 Equipment Tips

Lift up on the handlebars; jump over the line or bunny hop over the line by raising both wheels. This drill helps the rider when faced with an unexpected pothole or other obstacle in the road. Learn to ride with a group; doing so improves technical skills and enhances intensity of the workouts.

5. There are two types of spinning drills—muscle and spinning cadence. Always spin at a constant cadence.
6. Spin to win! Try to keep the same pace on long rides. For example, if you are laboring and spinning too slowly, drop from 8th gear to 6th gear for a 10-speed bike, and 16th gear to 12th gear for a 20-speed bike. Spinning faster causes less pressure on the legs, but the rider maintains the same speed.
7. Practice positioning as you ride down hills. Tuck down and stay behind the handle bar.
8. Practice sprinting: come up out of the saddle into a standing position, hands hanging on to brake hoods and handlebars. Rock bike side to side, keep the wheels in line, and stay in a straight line or hold your line. Avoid zigzagging the wheels.
9. Hydrate your body before and after each ride.

FYI

For further information and special help, consult the following organizations and resources.

ORGANIZATIONS

U.S. Cycling Federation
One Olympic Plaza
Colorado Springs, CO 80909
Phone: (719) 578-4581
Fax: (719) 578-4956
Website: www.usacycling.org

Provides a free 40-page book especially for newcomers.

Bicycling Magazine
New Rider Network
Box 6075
Emmaus, PA 18098

Bell Helmets (see FYI, Chapter 8)

PUBLICATIONS

Burke, E. (1986). *The science of cycling.* Champaign, IL: Human Kinetics.
Doughty, T. (1983). *The complete book of competitive cycling.* New York: Simon & Schuster.

WEBSITE

www.bicyclesource.com

BIKE SIZE

SKILL	CUE	WHY	COMMON ERROR
Selecting a Bike	Proper bike size is critical when purchasing a bike		
	Stand straddling bike with 2–3 inches of crotch clearance		No clearance or too high: 3–4 inches off ground
	Get fitted by qualified bike shop		

BODY POSITION

SKILL	CUE	WHY	COMMON ERROR
Become More Aerodynamic (Figure 9.2)	Decrease frontal area; keep back flat	Faster, more efficient on bike	Body is big, like a sail
	Get prone with elbows and knees in		
	Wear tight clothing		Wearing baggy clothing
	It takes practice to become comfortable; work 5–10 minutes at a time in biking position		Not holding position
	Hands should hold bar lightly		White knuckles, gripping too tight, wasting energy
	Bend at waist		Back vertical
	Eyes glance ahead		People do not look ahead, and they run into things or the head stays down

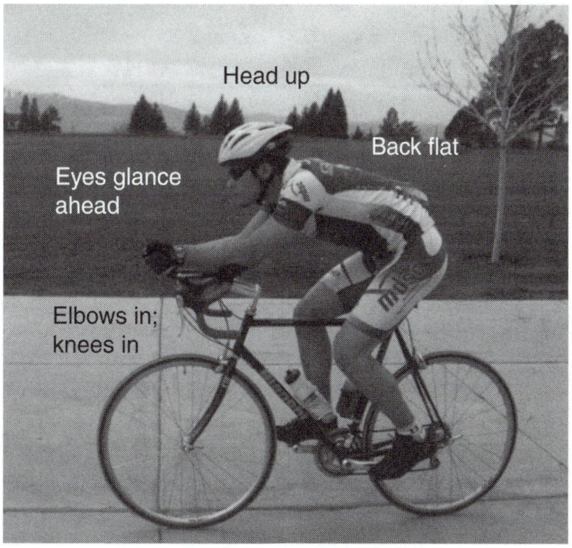

FIGURE 9.2 Correct Body Position on Bike

PEDALING FOR EFFECTIVE ENERGY TRANSFER			
SKILL	**CUE**	**WHY**	**COMMON ERROR**
Pedaling Action	Spin; pedal in circles, not squares	More efficient; less energy used	Mashing and stomping pedals
	Downstroke motion, like scraping mud off your shoes		Pushing hard at bottom of stroke will not do any good, just attempts to lengthen crank action
	Backstroke motion: pick up your feet		Many riders only push on downstroke and fail to apply pressure to pedals all the way around the circle
			Dead time at 6:00 or bottom of pedal stroke
Revolutions per Minute (rpm)	80 rpm: adults 90–120 rpm: racers		Pedaling too slow; lugging motor; hard on your knees
Riding in a Straight Line	Keep eyes on road 10–15 yards ahead	Prevent crashing	Not looking ahead causes one leg to fight the other and creates a rocking or a bouncing motion that depletes energy
			Keeping eyes focused on front wheel
	Ride straight		Wobbling

CORNERING			
SKILL	**CUE**	**WHY**	**COMMON ERROR**
Braking	Assess the speed and do most braking entering corner or curve	Prevents crashing	Applying brakes while leaning through a corner or curve will cause handling problems
Anticipating Turn	Start wide and head for inner tip or point of turn	More efficient and faster	Not turning until well into the corner, which slows you down and can be dangerous
	Visualize the line or path you will travel through the curve and follow it		Following a jerky, changing path
	Lean bike and carve your line through the turn		
(Figure 9.3)	Keep outside pedal down; stand on it to lower center of gravity	Prevent crashing	Leaning too far into curve, hitting ground with inside pedal; crash
Sharp Corner	Raise inside pedal to top of pedal stroke	Prevents pedal from making contact with ground and crashing	Making sparks while cornering with pedal
			Dragging pedal

FIGURE 9.3 Cornering

CLIMBING

SKILL	CUE	WHY	COMMON ERROR
Breathing	Breathe from stomach, like blowing into an instrument	Exchange of O_2 better helps cardiac functions	Breathing in chest; short, gasping breaths
Sitting Climb	Push butt into saddle and push back on handlebars (squeeze saddle with butt like a leg press)		
	Scoot back on seat; sit hunkered down; helps to use your buttocks muscles more		Sitting on seat too hard and not standing on pedal
	Choose easy gear	Easier to go up hills	Gear too tight
	Pull up on bars, so you can push harder on the pedals; like giving yourself more weight on a scale		
	50 rpm minimum; spin if you can, uphill		Low rpm makes poor recovery
	Get into *your* rhythm		Trying to match someone else's pace
Standing Climb (Figure 9.4, page 122)	Stand, lean forward, pull up and down on bars, and rock the bike		
	Make sure your line stays straight		
Transition from Climbing to Descending	Accelerate near top of hill, pick up speed fast	Faster	Trying to recover at top of hill
			Decelerating at crest of hill
	Recovery occurs after descending speed is reached		

DESCENDING			
SKILL	**CUE**	**WHY**	**COMMON ERROR**
Position for Fast, Steep Descent	When you cannot pedal fast enough, you spin out	Faster	
Grip	Hands on end of handlebars		Grip the handlebars near the stem, hands right next to each other
Body Position (Figure 9.5)	Back flat, feet at 3:00 and 9:00 position	More streamlined, less air current; faster	Chest up
	Weight on the pedals, knees in		Weight on arms, knees out

FIGURE 9.4 Standing Climb

FIGURE 9.5 Body Position for Descending

RULES OF THE ROAD

SKILL	CUE	WHY	COMMON ERROR
Ride on the Right	Always ride on right; go with flow of traffic		Riding in middle of road; going against traffic
	Be predictable; maintain a straight line; change direction without swerving	Prevents crashing	Swerving back and forth
Hand Signals	Use hand signal when turning, same as motorist; when making a right turn, use your right arm to point		Not using hand signal when turning
Stay Alert	Obey all traffic laws Pay attention	Prevents crashing	Breaking traffic rules Wearing headphones
	Use your eyes and ears as warning devices alerting you to potential hazards		
	Assert yourself		Letting vehicles creep by, forcing biker into parked cars or curb
	Ride defensively		
	Expect a car to pull out from side street or turn left in front of you; if you anticipate the worst, it will rarely happen		Daydreaming
What to Wear	Be visible, wear bright colors, and put reflectors and reflective tape on your bicycle	Prevents crashing	Wearing light colors in daytime
			Wearing dark clothing at night
			Not putting reflective tape on bicycles
Warning Signal from Cyclist	Shout: it's the quickest way to let motorists know you're putting them in danger or to warn inattentive pedestrians you are approaching		Not giving a warning signal
Feet Strapped or Connected to Pedal	Loosen strap, twist foot out of pedal		Leaving foot strapped or not twisting foot out of pedal

EATING AND DRINKING WHILE RIDING

SKILL	CUE	WHY	COMMON ERROR
Rule of Thumb	Drink before you're thirsty and eat before you're hungry		Not drinking or eating before ride; eating too much
Hot, Humid Weather	Take a big swig from water bottle every 15 minutes		Not drinking during ride
Most Popular Food	One banana provides 105 calories of carbohydrates and replaces potassium, an important element lost via sweating		
Storing Food	Best place: rear pocket of jersey		
5–20 Miles; Less than 90 Minutes	Eat a pre-ride meal with lots of carbohydrates		Eating too much and not waiting 30 minutes for food to digest
15–50 Miles; 45 Minutes–3 Hours			
Avoid Bonking	Do not allow glycogen stores to become depleted; this happens when ride is 2 hours or longer; drink sports drinks		Not eating premeals or snacks
Avoid Dehydration	Loss of body fluids results in fatigue; carry sports drink, 1 bottle		Not drinking water or sports drinks
	Carry water, 1 or more bottles depending on distance		
50–100 Miles; Over 4 Hours	Eat lots of carbohydrate-rich foods in days preceding the event		Failing on long rides due to poor eating habits
Premeal	Eat a big meal a couple of hours before the big ride		Not eating a premeal
Snack during Ride	Bananas; sandwiches with jam, honey, apple butter, and so on		
	Nibble through ride		Eating too much at once
Water during Ride	Four water bottles		Three or fewer water bottles

10

Field Hockey

INTRODUCTION

Field hockey is one of the oldest organized team sports played in the United States. It is a team game, played on artificial turf or grass, in which players use a curved stick and try to drive a hard-core ball into the opposing team's goal. The tactics are similar to soccer, a more commonly played game in the United States.

Modern field hockey evolved in England in the early nineteenth century. Originally the game was played exclusively by men. Today the game is played by both men and women on six continents. More than 70 countries are members of the International Hockey Federation. In the United States and Canada, field hockey is primarily considered a women's sport.

Field hockey was introduced in the United States in 1901 by Constance Applebee, an English field hockey player. Field hockey became an Olympic event for men in 1928, and an Olympic event for women in 1980.

SKILLS LISTED WITH CUES

We provide cues for the following skills: grip, dribbling (moving with the ball), push pass, receiving, hitting and shooting, aerials (flick throw, low lift), and defense skills—dodging, marking, covering, tackling, and goaltending.

TIPS

1. Players should first learn the skills of running with the ball.
2. Passing and receiving skills should be taught second.

EQUIPMENT TIPS

1. Shin guards and mouth guards are mandatory at the high school level.
2. Recently made hockey sticks have smaller toes that make stick control easier.
3. Cleats (plastic) should be used on grass; turf shoes should be used on artificial surfaces.

TEACHING IDEAS

1. Running with the ball (dribbling) is the first skill that should be taught. It is best taught with competitive relays using obstacles and with small games where everyone has a ball and is moving the ball constantly.
2. Passing and receiving should be taught second and together. You cannot pass to a teammate unless the teammate receives.
3. Hitting should be taught only after the preceding skills have been mastered to some degree. In early games, hitting should not be allowed.
4. Field hockey can be played in physical education class and should be played in small groups (4–7 players on each side). STX markets a field hockey training stick that is very useful in physical education classes.
5. A full game consists of two 30-minute halves with 11 players on each side, including a goalie, and various combinations of players depending on their skills. The most traditional lineup for field hockey would be 5 attackers, 3 halfbacks, 2 fullbacks, and 1 goalkeeper. Many other player lineups are used (4, 3, 2, 1, 1; 3, 3, 3, 1, 1; etc.). At the introductory level of play, smaller games should be incorporated into the teaching session. Small games open up the space, provide more opportunity to play the ball, and make tactics easier to master and see.
6. Training sessions should follow this format:
   - Light jog
   - Stretching
   - Running skills for better movement
   - Ball-control skills
   - Technical skills (passing combos, two-against-one concepts, etc.)
   - Games, cooldown, stretching

FIVE BASIC RULES FOR FIELD HOCKEY

1. No body or excessive stick-to-stick contact allowed.	Violation: Penalty shot
2. Players must keep both hands on their sticks.	Violation: Penalty shot
3. Stick and ball must be at or below waist height at all times (when running, hitting a ball, or following through).	Violation: Penalty shot
4. Do not kick or advance the ball with any part of the body.	Violation: Change of ball
5. Play should be continuous; no stalling.	Violation: Change of ball

Field Hockey Official Rules allow only the left side (flat) of stick to be used to hit and advance the ball.

Note: Players and coaches will invent variations of the suggested game to suit age and skill levels.

GAME STRATEGIES

1. Play the ball, not the opponent. All players must be free to move as in soccer and basketball.
2. Note that the spirit of Intro STX is not strength or size but teamwork, stickwork, and fair play.
3. Keep it simple and have fun!
4. Have extra game balls ready to put into play.

SAFETY

1. Close supervision is essential to the success of a school Intro STX program.
2. The "no-contact" rules and use of the specified game ball are important to a safe game.

INDOOR FIELD HOCKEY RULES

(Played on basketball court)

1. Same five basic rules as outdoor field hockey.
2. Use basketball key area for crease area.
3. Honor the crease. Shots at goal must be taken outside of designated crease area.
4. Shoot to score. Scoring is possible only when attacking team has ball over the center line.
5. Penalty shot is taken behind the center line. It's the law!
6. No body or excessive stick-to-stick contact.
7. Honor the crease. No players allowed in designated crease area at any time.
8. Toe the line: offside if 6 players on each team; only 4 offensive players are allowed on offensive side at a time.

FYI

For further information and special help, consult the following organization and resource.

ORGANIZATION

United States Field Hockey Association (USFHA)
One Olympic Plaza
Colorado Springs, CO 80909
Phone: (856) 231-1199

1. The USFHA offers learning packs (sticks and balls).
2. Its youth development committee aids in the development of field hockey in the United States.

WEBSITE

www.usfieldhockey.com

GRIP

SKILL	CUE	WHY	COMMON ERROR
Position	Lay the stick parallel to feet	Ball control	Hands together
	Point to the right		Pointing to left
	Pick up with left hand		Picking up with right hand
	Right hand halfway down stick		Left hand halfway down stick
	Hold stick firmly but comfortably		Holding stick too loosely
Left Hand	Left hand is the holding hand/turns stick		
Right Hand	Right hand is the pulling and pushing hand		

DRIBBLING

SKILL	CUE	WHY	COMMON ERROR
Moving with the Ball (Figure 10.1)	Ball "glued" to stick	Able to control ball	Ball too far in front of stick
	Use small taps for grass play		Hitting, not tapping
	Keep ball outside and ahead of right foot for grass play		Right foot behind ball
	Keep ball on the right side at 3:00 position for turf play	Must have full field vision	Wasting dribbles
Strategy	To run with ball		

PASSING AND RECEIVING

SKILL	CUE	WHY	COMMON ERROR
Push Pass (Figure 10.2)	Push ball with stick		Wide backswing
	Stick on ball; no contact noise		Stick off ball, tapping or hitting ball
	Firm right hand	Ball control	Relaxed right hand
	Left wrist pulls stick back		Stiff left wrist
	Short, accurate passing		
Strategy	No time to hit ball or shoot		
Receiving	Angle stick slightly forward to deflect ball down	To trap ball	
	Stop ball on stick		Bouncing off stick

FIGURE 10.1 The Dribble

FIGURE 10.2 The Push Pass

HITTING AND SHOOTING

SKILL	CUE	WHY	COMMON ERROR
Hitting (Figure 10.3)			
Grip	Slide right hand up stick	Better ball speed	Forgetting to slide hand up
	Bring hands together on top		Hands too far apart
	Contact ball opposite left foot		Contacting ball off same foot
Driving Action	Hip-to-hip swing, like a pendulum		Bending wrists
	Toe of stick up on backswing and up on follow-through	Affects direction and control	Toe facing grass
	Right hand guides stick in direction of pass		Hand not guiding stick
	Left arm pulls		
	Bend elbow slightly for a relaxed swing	More consistency and control of ball	Bent left arm
Strategy	Used for passing and shooting		
Shooting	Variations	To beat defender	
	Follow shot	To get rebound	
	Must be in circle	Rule	
	Shots must be on ground or not dangerous	To control danger	

FIGURE 10.3 Hitting

AERIALS

SKILL	CUE	WHY	COMMON ERROR
Flick Throw	Throwing action	Shot variations are important to throw off opponent's reaction time and ability to steal ball	
	Face ball—head, body low		
	Ball between feet (positioning varies) and away from body		
	Toe of stick is extension of hand		
Low Lift	Shovel ball into air, low and gentle		
	Lift the ball up, throwing action		
	Face ball		
	Raise ball slightly—or high, depending on what you are trying to do		
Strategy	Used for shooting at close range, penalty strokes, lifting ball to cover a big distance		
	Used for lifting ball over a defender's stick		

DEFENSE

SKILL	CUE	WHY	COMMON ERROR
Footwork	Balance	To be able to change directions quickly	
	Drop		
	Approach attacker with control and balance		
	Break down steps		
	Stay in front space		
	Stick defense at 10:00–2:00 position		

continued

DEFENSE, continued			
SKILL	**CUE**	**WHY**	**COMMON ERROR**
Dodges	Get out of the way!		Backing into the defender
	Execute dodge outside of defense playing distance		Anticipating too late or too early
	Execute dodge right off dribble	Must be able to beat defender with the ball	Stalling
	Accelerate by defender; cut in behind defender		Constant speed and direction
			Crash! Head-on collision
Techniques	1. Pull to the right, accelerate 2. Pull to the left, accelerate 3. Spin and accelerate; must move away from defender		Backing into the defender Backing into the defender Backing into the defender
Pressuring Defender *Marking*	Stay between your goal and offensive player	To keep attacker from scoring	Not anticipating soon enough or focusing on defenders
	"Face to face" with your opponent at all times		Tumbling with backside to opponent, losing concentration
Covering *Supporting Defender*	Either mark dangerous space or take next dangerous attacker	Take away attacker's options	
Covering Defender	Make decisions on dangerous space; decide to make attacks or cover space		
Tackling	Body low, frontal body position	To maintain balance	
	Hands and arms away from the body, body in low position; slide stick in, tackle at 5:00 position		
	Block ball hand quickly; move away with ball		

continued

DEFENSE, continued			
SKILL	**CUE**	**WHY**	**COMMON ERROR**
Goaltending	Stop ball by making a V with ankles—keep knees together	Easier transition to attack	Feet and knees apart
			Standing straight
	Move by sliding feet across goal mouth		Picking up feet
	Always clear ball to sides		Clearing ball in front of cage
	Stop ball before clearing for better control of direction		Hitting ball before clearing
	Can use either side or tip of boot when clearing		Not focusing on ball

11

Fitness Equipment Work-Out

INTRODUCTION

The list of positive health benefits derived from physical fitness is astounding. Physical fitness reduces the risk for type 2 diabetes (Hu et al., 2003), decreases the risk of certain cancers (Lee, 2003), reduces the risk of heart disease (Lee et al., 2001), decreases the risk of osteoporosis (Nelson et al., 1994), and is effective in treating and preventing depression (Dunn et al., 2005), among other positive benefits. Even with all this documentation, only a small percentage of the U.S. population is physically fit enough to enjoy these benefits. Imagine how much healthier we could be if physical fitness was a priority.

The components of health-related physical fitness include cardiorespiratory endurance, body composition, and musculoskeletal fitness, which include flexibility, muscular strength, and muscular endurance (Neiman, 2007). Based on health benefits, cardiorespiratory endurance is arguably the most important component. It is defined as the ability of the body (the circulatory and respiratory systems as well as the muscles) to utilize oxygen to fuel physical activity. Body composition is the amount of fat and lean tissue in the body. Flexibility is defined as the capacity of the joints to move through their full range of motion. Muscular strength is the amount of force a muscle exerts, and muscular endurance is the ability of a muscle to withstand fatigue (Neiman, 2007).

The purpose of this chapter is to review available workout equipment (besides free weights, which are covered in Chapter 22) that will enhance the components of health-related physical fitness. The most important thing to remember when trying to improve physical fitness is for the individual to choose something that he or she can enjoy and incorporate into their lifestyle. While this chapter focuses on workout equipment, numerous chapters in this book focus on fitness-enhancing activities from biking (Chapters 8 and 9) to yoga and Pilates (Chapter 30).

To be successful and continue being active for a lifetime, you must choose something you enjoy—the choices are seemingly endless. Another important aspect of improving fitness is to start out slowly and tailor the activity to suit your fitness level. If you have not been active at all, you may need to start out slowly. The body is an incredible machine; but unlike mechanical machines, it improves when you "run" it. A car engine wears out faster the more it is used, but our bodies adapt to the stress of physical activity and will work better and be more healthy as we become more active.

SKILLS LISTED WITH CUES

Cues are provided for the following exercises using fitness equipment: cable weights for upper body (bench press), cable weights for a variety of exercises (Cable Cross), treadmill walking or running, upright cycling, recumbent cycling, Incline Trainer walking, and elliptical training.

TIPS FOR STRENGTH DEVELOPMENT EQUIPMENT

1. Warm up before lifting.
2. Each muscle group should be exercised 1–3 times per week.
3. Start out with low resistance and high repetitions (10–12); if strength increases are desired, increase the resistance and decrease the repetitions gradually.
4. Perform the lift with a slow, controlled movement, breathing in as the targeted muscle group lengthens and breathing out as the muscle group shortens.
5. The greater the extent of muscle fatigue during resistance training, the greater the resulting increases in strength.
6. Strength-training machines should be adjusted to fit the student. Pivot points on machines should correspond with the articulating joint. Cable machines should be positioned so the direction of force is opposite the desired travel direction. Seats can often be adjusted up and down to put the student in the proper exercise position relative to the articulation of the machine.

TIPS FOR CARDIOVASCULAR DEVELOPMENT EQUIPMENT

1. Warm up slowly for 3–5 minutes.
2. Cardiorespiratory training should take place 3–4 times per week.
3. Exercise at a level that is somewhat difficult. A proper level will allow the students to speak a full sentence without inhaling between words.
4. Exercise equipment has adjustments to make the apparatus fit a broad range of students. The seat should be adjusted up or down so that the knee is slightly bent (15° of flexion) when the pedal is in the bottom position. The seat should be adjusted fore and aft so that the knee is directly over the pedal spindle when the pedals are horizontal.

TEACHING IDEAS

1. For motivational purposes, have students chart their progress.
2. Provide resistance-training pictures to help the students learn the lifts, and provide anatomical charts to help the students learn the muscle groups used in different lifts.

3. Monitor heart rate to demonstrate to the students the physiological changes that occur as they increase their cardiorespiratory fitness.

(See Chapter 22 for strength-training cues that include progression, safety, and other concepts.)

TRAINING ON CARDIORESPIRATORY EQUIPMENT

The overload principle applies to cardiorespiratory equipment, just as it does with strength-training equipment. Overload is accomplished on a treadmill by increasing the speed and/or grade and by increasing the resistance and the revolutions per minute (rpm) on cycle and elliptical trainers.

SAFETY

1. Be sure there is adequate range of motion for all exercises.
2. Keep other students away from exercise equipment that is in use. There are many moving parts that may present a hazard to unsupervised students.

FYI

For further information, consult the following organizations.

ORGANIZATIONS

National Strength & Conditioning Association
1995 N. Union Boulevard
Colorado Springs, CO 80909
Phone: (800) 815-6826 or (719) 632-6722
Fax: (719) 632-6367
E-mail: nsca@nsca-lift.org
Website: www.nsca-lift.org

Freemotion Fitness
A subsidiary of ICON Health & Fitness
1096 Elkton Drive
Suite 600
Colorado Springs, CO 80907
Phone: (719) 533-2928
Fax: (719) 533-2949
E-mail: freemotionfitness@freemotionfitness.com
Website: www.freemotionfitness.com

PUBLICATIONS

Dunn, A. L., Trivedi, M. H., Kampert, J. B., Clark, C. G., & Chambliss, H. O. (2005). Exercise treatment for depression: Efficacy and dose response. *American Journal of Preventive Medicine, 28*, 1–8.

Hu, F. B., Li, T. Y., Colditz, G. A., Willett, W. C., & Manson, J. E. (2003). Television watching and other sedentary behaviors in relation to risk of obesity and type 2 diabetes mellitus in women. *Journal of the American Medical Association, 289*, 1785–1791.

Lee, I.-M. (2003). Physical activity and cancer prevention: Data from epidemiologic studies. *Medicine & Science in Sports & Exercise, 35*, 1823–1827.

Lee, I.-M., Rexrode, K. M., Cook, N. R., Manson, J. E., & Buring, J. E. (2001). Physical activity and coronary heart disease in women: Is

"no pain, no gain" passé? *Journal of the American Medical Association, 285*, 1447–1454.
Nelson, M. E., Fiatarone, M. A., Morganti, C. M., Trice, I., Greenberg, R. A., & Evans, W. J. (1994). Effects of high-intensity strength training on multiple risk factors for osteoporotic fractures: A randomized controlled trial. *Journal of the American Medical Association, 272*, 1909–1914.
Nieman, D. C. (2007). *Exercise testing and prescription: A health-related approach* (6th ed.). Boston: McGraw-Hill.

CABLE BENCH PRESS

SKILL	CUE	WHY	COMMON ERROR
Hand Position (Figure 11.1)	Secure, yet relaxed grip	More control	Grip too tight
Feet Position	Feet flat on ground	Better balance	Weight on heels or toes
Back Position	Back flat against bench	Lessens back strain	Back hunched
Execution	Slow, controlled movement	Develops each muscle group to maximize capacity	Too fast and jerky

FIGURE 11.1 Cable Bench Press

There are too many ways to use the Cable Cross to outline as part of this chapter, so the cues will not be specific to certain exercises.

CABLE CROSS			
SKILL	**CUE**	**WHY**	**COMMON ERROR**
Hand Position (Figure 11.2)	Secure, yet relaxed grip	More control	Grip too tight
Feet Position	Have feet far enough apart to be balanced	For balance	Feet too close together

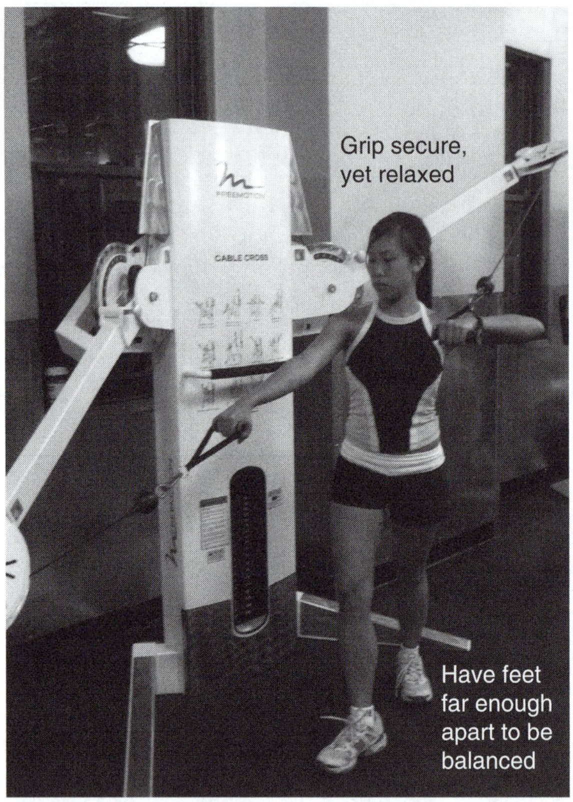

FIGURE 11.2 Cable Cross

TREADMILL

SKILL	CUE	WHY	COMMON ERROR
Focus (Figure 11.3)	Look forward toward console; pull chin in	Helps maintain balance	Looking down or to the side
Hand Position	Beginners should hold rails	Safety: could trip or fall off	Letting go of rail
Walking Stride	Stride normally; ball of foot strikes first	No breaking motion	Striking on heel first
Running Stride	Land lightly on treadmill	Reduces stress on joints	Heavy, noisy foot strikes
Back Position	Back straight	More efficiency in the running stride	Back hunched over
Arms	Left thumb moves toward the left side of the face and down to the left side of the buttocks, and the right thumb moves similarly on the right side of the body. Arms should stay at 90°.	Fast pace	Cross body with arms
	Brush hips	Slow pace	

continued

FIGURE 11.3 Running on Treadmill

TREADMILL, continued			
SKILL	**CUE**	**WHY**	**COMMON ERROR**
Safety	Use safety key	More efficient with energy	
	Teachers should limit max speed	Helps improve posture	
	Do not stop		

UPRIGHT CYCLE			
SKILL	**CUE**	**WHY**	**COMMON ERROR**
Hand Position (Figure 11.4)	Light hands on handles	Avoids strain on shoulders and back	Too much pressure on handles
Feet Position	Ball of foot on pedal spindle	More power and control	Heel on pedal
Leg Position	Knees in line with hips and feet	More efficiency, less strain on knees	Knees bent out
Movement	Pedal in circles; "scrape off mud" at bottom of pedal stroke	More power; uses more muscles	Stopping the feet at bottom of pedal stroke and not pulling up
Back Position	Straight back	Helps with breathing	Hunched over

FIGURE 11.4 Upright Cycle

RECUMBENT CYCLE			
SKILL	**CUE**	**WHY**	**COMMON ERROR**
Hand Position (Figure 11.5)	Light grip	Conserve energy; less strain on back and shoulders	Tight grip
Feet Position	Ball of foot on pedal	More power, more efficient pedaling	Heel of foot on pedal
Back Position	Flat against seat	Works core	Lean forward
Execution	Pedal circles	More efficient	Pedal slow
Leg Position	Knees in line with hips and feet	More efficient	Knees out of alignment with hips and feet

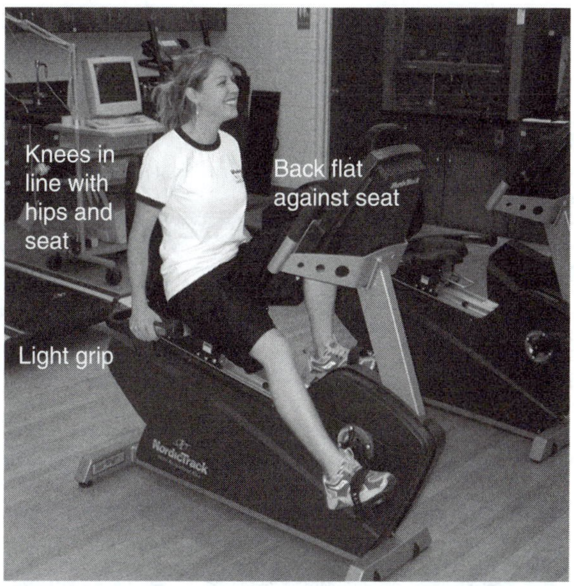

FIGURE 11.5 Recumbent Cycle

INCLINE TRAINER			
SKILL	**CUE**	**WHY**	**COMMON ERROR**
Arm Position	Elbows 90°	More efficient; conserves energy	Arms straight
Back Position (Figure 11.6)	Back straight	More energy	Lean forward
Feet Position	Step on balls of feet	To strike under hip	Heels striking
Back Position	Straight; be tall	To work core better	Hunched
Execution	Short, high steps	More control	Long steps
Arms/Hands	Brush shorts	Slower pace	Elbows out
	Left arm moves toward the left side of the face, and the right arm moves toward the right side of the face (cheek to cheek)	Faster pace	Elbows out

FIGURE 11.6 Incline Trainer

ELLIPTICAL TRAINER

SKILL	CUE	WHY	COMMON ERROR
Hand Position (Figure 11.7)	Hold lightly	Conserves energy	Holding too light
	Hold reciprocating arms	More energy expended	Not holding arms
	Hold T handle	Reduce upper body involvement	
Focus	Can look around; forward is better	More control; will not fall off	Not focusing on what you are doing
	Can have heel come off pedal	More comfortable	
Back Position	Straight	Works core	Back hunched
Leg Position	Knees and hips in the same plane	More efficient	Moving hips and knees off plane
Execution	Comfortable walking stride	To enjoy the machine	Too fast
	Keep weight from shifting	More efficient	Shifting weight from side to side
	Adjust resistance to maintain 60–80 rpm	Seems to be most comfortable	

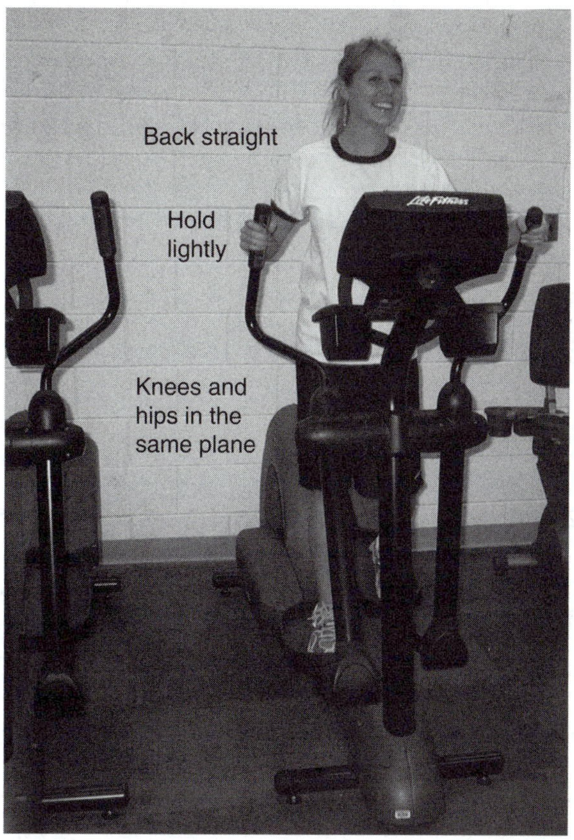

FIGURE 11.7 Elliptical Trainer

12

Floor Hockey

INTRODUCTION

Floor hockey is a fast sport because of its transitions, the fact that players are constantly moving from offense to defense, and the speed of the puck or ball. You can substitute players during play without waiting for a whistle. Students have more playing time. Floor hockey develops cardiovascular endurance, core strength, reaction time, hand-eye coordination, foot speed, and agility. Floor hockey also works on skills that transfer to other sports, such as soccer and lacrosse.

Floor hockey is a sport that can be played successfully by all students. There is a role for every student, regardless of physical stature. Each student's personality plays a major role in the cohesion of the team.

SKILL LISTED WITH CUES

This chapter focuses on cues for the following skills: stance, grip, stick position, forehand passing, backhand passing, forehand receiving, backhand receiving, shooting, and goaltending.

EQUIPMENT TIPS

1. Sticks that have a plastic or wood shaft should be used.
2. A plastic puck is recommended for safety reasons because it is easy to control and harder to lift. A plastic ball also works well.
3. PVC nets are recommended for safety and durability instead of metal nets.
4. Safety equipment for all players includes helmet with face mask, gloves, shin guards that cover from the ankles to the top of the knee, and a mouth guard.
5. The goalie needs a helmet with face mask, catcher and blocker gloves, and shin guards.
6. Colored vests should be worn to identify the teams.

TEACHING IDEAS

1. Teach the players to keep the sticks on the floor at all times. This prevents high sticks, which can cause injury. If a player breaks the *sticks on the floor* rule during a game, that player sits out for 2 minutes, just like in ice hockey. The team plays one player short for the duration of the penalty.
2. Teach the players to watch out for each other. They should avoid hitting another player's ankles, tangling up sticks, or causing a player to fall.
3. Make sure players are in a good hockey stance, stick on floor, knees slightly bent, like making a triangle with stick and feet. Emphasize good posture while in the sitting position: head over shoulders, shoulders over hips, hips over heels.
4. When teaching passing and shooting, make sure to teach the transfer of weight from the back leg to the forward leg. This increases the power of the shot and helps with the accuracy of the follow-through.
5. When teaching passing and shooting, emphasize the wrist rollover during the follow-through. When these moves are executed properly, the blade of the stick faces down toward the floor. The stick should point to the target and be a foot or so off the floor.

TEACHING PROGRESSIONS

1. When practicing accuracy, have the students stand 10 to 15 feet from a wall. Each student will pick a spot on the wall or have a target at which to aim, for example, a cone. Having a target helps the student focus on rolling the wrist over and pointing toward the target with the stick.
2. Have students stand 20 feet apart with a partner. Work on passing and receiving skills. When students can do this with control, move the partners closer together and have them speed up the passes. The goal of this drill is to improve passing accuracy, receiving speed, and the releasing of a pass.
3. Hang a vest in the upper corners of the goal and/or place cones on the floor in the lower corners. Have three to four students stand in a semicircle. Have each student shoot for the vests. This improves shot accuracy, speed, and power (Figure 12.1).

MINI-GAMES

Play games of 3 on 3, 4 on 4, or 5 on 5. Set up several mini-games using the width of a basketball court. If a team scores 3 points, it stays on the court, and the opponents step off the court. The next team of three comes onto the court

FIGURE 12.1 Shooting Drill

and plays a new game. These games keep the players moving. You can also play these games with goalies at each end.

FLOOR HOCKEY RULES AND GAME

1. Typically, there are 6 players per team, with only 4 on offense (past center line).
2. Due to the physical nature of the game, it is important to abide by a set of rules. Enforcing these rules keeps the sport safe and the game in control.
3. If a player breaks a rule, send him to the 2-minute penalty box.
4. Slashing (using a stick to strike another player) is a violation.
5. Tripping (using a stick, knee, foot, arm, hand, or elbow to cause an opponent to trip or fall) is a violation.
6. High-sticking is carrying the stick above the shoulders.
7. Interference with the progress of an opponent who is not in possession of the puck or ball is a violation.
8. Unsportsmanlike conduct, such as overly violent behavior, swearing, teasing, fighting, and so forth, is a violation.
9. Cross-checking—when a player has both hands on her stick (off the ground) and uses the stick to shove another player—is a violation.
10. See Chapter 10, Indoor Field Hockey Rules.

FYI

For further information and special help, consult the following organization and resources.

ORGANIZATION

Olympic training ground for the Amateur Hockey Association of the United States.

USA Hockey
4965 East Fountain Boulevard
Colorado Springs, CO 80910
Fax: (719) 599-5994

PUBLICATION

Ice hockey books have more drills, rules, and information.

HOCKEY STANCE			
SKILL	**CUE**	**WHY**	**COMMON ERROR**
Feet (Figure 12.2)	Slightly wider than shoulder width, flat and firm on floor	Stability, balance, ready to move forward, backward, or laterally	
Knees	Slightly bent, but not over toes	Stability, balance, ready to move forward, backward, or laterally	
Hips	Slightly back	Core stability and balance	
		Helps to keep knees from going over toes	
Stomach/Back	Keep stomach muscles tight and back straight	For core stability	
Head	Head up; looking forward over entire floor	Allows you to see entire floor and what is happening	
Holding Stick	Arms in front, holding stick straight out, forming a triangle with feet and stick	Stability, balance, ready for pass	
	Stick blade flat on ground 2–3 feet in front of feet	More surface area on ground to hit puck	

Emphasize These Cues

1. Feet firm on floor
2. Hips slightly back
3. Back straight, head up
4. Stick flat on floor; form a triangle with feet

FIGURE 12.2 Hockey Stance

GRIPS			
SKILL	**CUE**	**WHY**	**COMMON ERROR**
Right-Hand Shot	Left hand on top; right hand halfway down shaft	Right hand is power hand	Hands too close together and grip too tight
Left-Hand Shot	Right hand on top; left hand halfway down shaft	Left hand is power hand	
Top Hand	Form a "V" with thumb and index finger; place at the top of shaft		
Bottom Hand	Form a "V" with thumb and index finger; place about halfway down shaft	Good control of stick; able to utilize more power	
Knuckles of Each Hand	Knuckles of each hand will face opposite direction of each other	Good control; hand halfway down the shaft utilizes flex in stick for harder and faster shot	

STICK HANDLING			
SKILL	**CUE**	**WHY**	**COMMON ERROR**
Stick Position	Hold stick in front of body, forming a triangle with feet and blade	Balance, stability, ready for puck pass	
	Blade should be flat on floor 2–3 feet in front of feet		
Stick-Handling Stance			
Stance	Good hockey stance		
Head	Head up; see puck in peripheral vision	Can see the rest of floor and action going on	
Stick Motion	Blade travels parallel to foot line	Control of puck	
	Blade rotates toward puck at about 45° angle		
	Blade "cups" puck and pulls it forward and backward	Control of puck	
Wrists	Wrists roll toward puck when you catch it	Control of puck	

Emphasize These Cues

1. Keep puck between feet (stick on outside of puck); thus, you have to pick up blade and place on other side of puck. Do this while rolling wrists to get 45-degree angle.
2. Use soft hands; there should be noise from the puck hitting the stick.

FOREHAND PASSING

SKILL	CUE	WHY	COMMON ERROR
Stance	Good hockey stance		
Puck Position (Figure 12.3, page 150)	Puck starts at heel of blade and behind back foot	Gives proper spin on puck; control	
	Travels forward to toe of blade and then off blade		
	Puck travels parallel to foot line	Accuracy, power, and speed of pass	
Stick	Puck stays on floor	Accuracy, ease of receiving pass	
	Sweep puck parallel to foot line		
	Puck is released from blade slightly in front of front foot		
	Hands on top of stick and halfway down shaft		
	Blade "cups" puck throughout motion		
	Blade should end up 1–2 feet above floor, with blade pointing toward floor		
Head and Eyes	Look at puck position on blade; look at target; look at puck position; pass		
Wrists	Follow puck path to its receiver	Improves follow-through, keeps pass down	
	As you sweep puck forward, roll wrist forward toward target	Puts proper spin on puck, keeps puck down	

FIGURE 12.3 Passing and Shooting Position

Emphasize These Cues

1. Weight on back foot (see Figure 12.4a)
2. Puck starts at heel of blade
3. Blade sweeps puck forward, with a cupping motion
4. See target, then puck, and pass
5. Roll wrist toward target

BACKHAND PASSING

SKILL	CUE	WHY	COMMON ERROR
Backhand Passing	This motion is the same as the forehand pass; reverse the motion		
	Puck starts on back foot		
	Weight on back foot		
	Transfer weight to front foot		

FOREHAND RECEIVING

SKILL	CUE	WHY	COMMON ERROR
Stance (Figure 12.4b)	Good hockey stance		
Head and Eyes	Watch puck come all the way into blade until you have control of puck	Ensures you receive puck and maintain control	
Stick Position	Stick path parallel to foot line	Control	
	Blade flat on floor, slightly in front of foot	Greater area on floor to receive pass, more time to catch pass	
	When puck reaches blade, pull blade backward to absorb pass		
	Blade travels all the way back to back foot	Control	
	Blade "cups" puck as it moves backward	Control	
Puck Position	Initial catch is on toe of blade (front third of blade)	Control; also allows for immediate pass or shot because puck is in proper position	
	As you absorb puck, it should travel forward with heel of blade		
Wrist Position	Wrists roll forward for incoming pass, as stick and hands absorb the pass	Control; soft hands to help absorb pass; wrists in position to immediately pass or shoot	

(a) Passing to a Partner

(b) Receiving a Pass

FIGURE 12.4

Emphasize These Cues

1. Hockey stance
2. Watch puck into stick blade
3. Absorb puck with blade in a reverse sweeping motion
4. Roll wrist forward when puck meets blade

BACKHAND RECEIVING

SKILL	CUE	WHY	COMMON ERROR
Backhand Receiving	This motion is the same for a forehand or backhand pass reception; reverse motion		
	As puck approaches, weight should be on front foot; as you absorb puck with stick and hands, transfer weight to back foot	This makes you ready to immediately pass again or shoot	

SHOOTING

SKILL	CUE	WHY	COMMON ERROR
Forehand Wrist Shot (Figure 12.5)	Bottom hand on stick should slide 2–3 inches further down		
	Weight transfer is very important; drive off back leg	Use of legs and hips aids speed and power of shot	
	Sweeping motion of stick should be faster than a pass		
	Bend knees a little more	To add in weight transfer while keeping good hockey stance	

continued

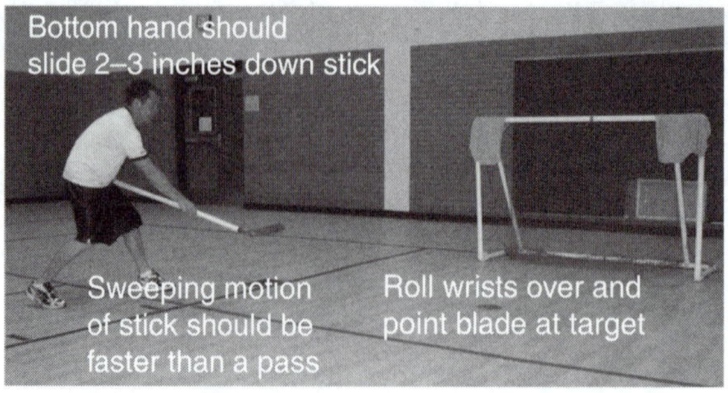

FIGURE 12.5 Shooting

SHOOTING, continued			
SKILL	**CUE**	**WHY**	**COMMON ERROR**
Forehand Wrist Shot, *continued*	Roll wrists over and point blade at target		
	Height of follow-through affects height of shot		
Backhand Wrist Shot	Same cues as for forehand wrist shot, reverse motion		
	Momentum from weight transfer should "pull" shooter onto the front foot only		

Emphasize These Cues

1. Good stance
2. Lower hand slides 2 to 3 inches down shaft
3. Transfer weight from back foot to front foot
4. Roll wrists over and point blade at target

GOALTENDING			
SKILL	**CUE**	**WHY**	**COMMON ERROR**
Stance (Figure 12.6, page 154)	Head over shoulders, shoulders over hips, hips over ankles, feet shoulder width apart, bend knees at 45° angle	Having good posture allows quick reaction time to stop the ball or puck	
Hand Position	Hold open catching hand off to the side, waist level	Having the open hand off to the side takes up more space, protecting the net even more	
		It also keeps the hand ready to respond quicker	
	The opposite hand holds the stick so the blade is on the ground in front and makes triangle with feet	Having the stick on the ground in front of the feet provides a barrier between the feet so that the puck does not get past	
	Blade flat on the ground	It also protects more surface area of the net	

Emphasize These Cues

1. Hockey stance
2. Catching hand open, waist-high, and off to side
3. Stick blade flat on floor, making a triangle with feet

FIGURE 12.6 Goalie Stance

Note

1. The goaltender is the last line of defense. The goaltender has one major goal: to stop the puck. The most effective way of goaltending is to take up as much area of the goal plane as possible. The goaltender's body and the stick help to take up this area.
2. To avoid muscle pulls and strains, always make sure that the goaltenders and players are properly stretched before any activity begins. Goaltenders need to be flexible because the position requires a quick reflex time, which could cause injury if the player is not warmed up properly.
3. Before beginning the game, let the goaltender's team take practice shots, from a distance, at the goaltender. This drill serves the important role of getting the goaltender's reflex time prepared for scrimmage, as well as warming up the rest of the team.

13

Football

INTRODUCTION

When teaching flag football, keep the rules as close to those of the regular game as possible. The students can relate to our national pastime more easily. Football is a huge part of our society. The students will be able to enjoy the game with their family or friends because they will know the skills, rules, and some common plays.

SKILLS LISTED WITH CUES

The cues in this chapter cover the following skills: throwing, catching, punting, catching a punt, snapping the ball, quarterback steps, lateral pass, handoffs (right and left side), tuck away after catch, running down the sideline, blocking, and in, out, and post running routes.

EQUIPMENT TIPS

1. New webbed footballs have an easy web grip. Two sizes are available: 6-inch and mini-footballs. Nerf multicolor footballs and Zwirl footballs are easy to grip and throw, or you may use smaller leather footballs. Avoid using large, regulation-size leather balls, as they are difficult to throw and catch. See the FYI section on page 157 for information on ordering these fun balls.
2. Order a variety of colored vests: red, yellow, green, orange, purple, and blue.
3. Flags with Velcro belts: This avoids the question of whether the player was down.
4. Flip scorecards: If players can see a scorecard, it will add motivation to the game.
5. For those who play recreation and league football, use a helmet, pads, and rubber cleats.

TEACHING IDEAS

Divide students into pairs: a highly skilled student with one with fewer skills. Have them practice the skills together. The highly skilled student can give tips to the other one.

TEACHING PROGRESSIONS

1. Practice throwing a football with the right and left hands.
2. Practice kicking a football with the right foot and the left foot. Play Philadelphia Football (similar to ultimate frisbee [see Chapter 28] except played with a football).
3. Practice catching a punted ball with a partner. Challenge the pair to catch 10, 15, or 20 balls.
4. Practice plays with three players. One is the center, one is the quarterback, and one is the receiver. Rotate positions after three thrown balls. Teach the quarterback steps and centering skills. Add a defender and teach the defensive skill of backpedaling and mirroring the offensive player.
5. Play 4 on 4 (passing plays only).
6. Practice handoffs and a lateral pass. Play 3 on 3 mini-games with running plays only.
7. Practice a combination of passing and running plays.
8. Let the teams make up their own play patterns and play 4 on 4 games.

MINI-GAMES

1. Philadelphia Football.
2. Mini-games of 2 on 2 and 3 on 3: these games can be played to practice in, out, and post plays, with a defender on each player.

MODIFIED FLAG FOOTBALL RULES

1. Six to eight players on a team.
2. Football field, using 40 to 50 yards for each mini-game.
3. Kick off from the 20-yard line.
4. Each team has four plays to make a touchdown. Why? Players don't have to worry about keeping track of the line of scrimmage.
5. Score the game just like a regulation football game.

   6 points for a touchdown

   1 point for a run-in after the touchdown

   2 points for a pass-in after the touchdown

   2 points for a safety. A safety occurs when the defensive team pulls the flag off an offensive player who is in their offensive end zone (safety zone is 3 yards).
6. Any offensive player on the line can catch the pass.
7. There is a 3-yard neutral zone. The students take three steps back from the line of scrimmage. The line of scrimmage is where the football lies.
8. A lateral pass is the same as in regulation football. The pass must be thrown behind the quarterback or to the side. There are no forward lateral passes.

9. The quarterback must be behind the line of scrimmage in order to throw a forward pass.
10. In this game, no one is standing around. Everyone is moving and having fun practicing all the skills. If you have a class of 32 students, you could organize 4 mini-games, with 4 players on each team.

FYI

For further information and special help, consult the following organizations and resources.

ORGANIZATIONS

Innovative footballs: Tech Tac web footballs and others
Sportime
One Sport Way
Atlanta, GA 30340
Phone orders: (800) 283-5700
Fax orders: (800) 845-1535
Website: www.sportime.com

WEBSITES

www.goflagfootball.com
A rule book is available at this site, which includes passes, the field, equipment, clock, kicks, handling, deflagging, scoring a tie game, substitutions, interference, unfair and unsportsmanslike conduct, fouls and penalties, and a glossary of terms.

www.afafootball.com

THROWING			
SKILL	**CUE**	**WHY**	**COMMON ERROR**
Grip	Grab top of ball like holding a soda can or a fish's head	More surface area on ball, better control	Grabbing middle of ball
	Put 3–4 fingers on the laces, depending on the size of your hand	Better grip	Grabbing all laces or not enough
	Finger pads hold laces	Better release	Palm holding ball
Throwing Action (Figure 13.1)	Stretch arm way back; make an L shape	For better control and to throw the ball farther	Dropping the throwing elbow
Stance and Leg Action	Short to medium step	To get rid of the football fast	Overstriding, high stepping, or taking no steps
Release Point	Release at 2:00 with right hand; left hand, 10:00	Ball will go at correct angle	Releasing too early or too late
	Football points upward	Arch on ball	
Follow-Through Action	Turn palm out on follow-through; ball comes off index finger, thumb finishes down	Ball will fly through the air in a spiral motion	

FIGURE 13.1 Throwing

CATCHING

SKILL	CUE	WHY	COMMON ERROR
Hand Action (Figure 13.2)	Big hands; reach out; shape hands like a diamond	Won't bounce off chest	Hands too close
	Catch ball in diamond	Ball fits best	Catching with chest
(Figure 13.3)	Soft hands	Cushion	Too stiff
Eyes	Pull ball into chest; watch ball into chest	Helps to avoid dropping ball	
Tuck the Ball	Catch with hands, turn ball downward against forearm, tuck ball under armpit	Protect ball	Carry ball with hand only

FIGURE 13.2 Catching Above Waist

FIGURE 13.3 Catching Below Waist

KICKING A PUNT

SKILL	CUE	WHY	COMMON ERROR
Punting (Figure 13.4)	Hold ball with two hands away from body	Ball is more stable	One-hand hold
	Support foot is planted when ball is released	Better stability	
	Pull kicking leg back	More power to send the ball far	
	Drop the ball from waist level	Less chance for error	Dropping from chest or using toss drop
	Swing leg under body	More effective technique	
	Ball makes contact with shoelaces and below knee	More surface area on which to contact ball	Knee bent with contact
	Toes pointed	To get a spiral	
Follow-Through (Figure 13.5)	Kick high, like a scissors kick	Gives more distance to ball	

FIGURE 13.4 Punting Stance

FIGURE 13.5 Punting Follow-Through

CATCHING A PUNT

SKILL	CUE	WHY	COMMON ERROR
Elbows (Figure 13.6)	5-point (hand-hand-elbow-elbow-bottom of sternum)	Big area for ball to land	Open arms
	Make a cage with arms about 2–3 inches apart	More surface area to catch ball	Arm and hands parallel to ground
	Fingers pointing to sky	Does not hurt the fingers	Curling fingers into a fist
	Palms toward face	Place for ball to go	Palms facing together
	Elbows to stomach	Keep ball from coming out	Elbows out, ball slides through
Action of Catching	Pull ball toward chest	Ball won't drop to ground	Ball hits too high off chest

FIGURE 13.6 Catching a Punted Ball

SNAPPING BALL FROM THE SIDE

SKILL	CUE	WHY	COMMON ERROR
Foot Position to the Ball	Feet behind ball	*Rule:* Feet behind the ball on line of scrimmage	One foot by the ball
Hand Position on the Ball	Hold top of ball with an eagle claw	More surface area on the ball, more control of ball	Grabbing just one end of the ball
Hiking Action with the Arm	Straight arm to the quarterback	More accuracy with this method	Raising arm results in shorter toss
	Put the ball into the quarterback's hands; focus on hands	Gives you a focus on the target	Not watching where ball is tossed
		More concentration and better accuracy	

QUARTERBACK DROPBACK

SKILL	CUE	WHY	COMMON ERROR
Foot Action	After receiving the snap, turn to side and sidestep	These steps help the quarterback have a fast reaction time	Staying forward and throwing
	Grapevine		
	Slide-slide		
	Plant your back foot and throw	The player has better control of the ball at the time of the throw	Throwing off of front foot

LATERAL PASS

SKILL	CUE	WHY	COMMON ERROR
Hand Position	Hold ball with both hands	Better control	
	Wide fingers on ball	More surface area on the ball, better control	
Throwing Action (Figures 13.7 and 13.8)	Underhand throw	Helps to avoid dropping ball	
	Arms straight	More accuracy	Bending at elbow
Pitch	Lead the runner	So they can keep running with the ball	Ball is thrown behind runner
	Step to runner	Direct the ball	Not stepping
	Flip wrist with thumb finishing downward	Make the ball go end over end	Push ball
Rule	Lateral pass has to go behind or to the side	A forward pass is illegal	Ball going forward is a forward pass

FIGURE 13.7 Lateral Pass

FIGURE 13.8 Pitch

HANDOFFS

SKILL	CUE	WHY	COMMON ERROR
To Right Side of Quarterback			
Receiver Arm Position	Inside elbow up with thumb pointing down	Better target area for ball to go in	
	Outside elbow down	Ball is carried with outside arm	Carrying ball with inside arm
	Arms are parallel to each other	Big target	Arms too close to each other
Quarterback Action	Put the ball between the receiver's arms	Target place	
Receiver Action	Squeeze the ball	Ball won't fall out	
To Left Side of Quarterback (Figure 13.9, page 164)			
Receiver Arm Position	Inside elbow up	The ball fits in the pocket better	
	Outside elbow down		
	Arms are parallel to each other	Elbow is not in the way	
Quarterback Action	Put the ball between the receiver's arms	Target place	
Receiver Action	Squeeze the ball	Ball won't fall out	

BALL-CARRYING TECHNIQUES

SKILL	CUE	WHY	COMMON ERROR
Tuck Away After Catch	Tuck ball into 4 REEF pressure points:	Ball won't get loose	Ball not on 1 of 4 pressure points
Arm Action (Figure 13.10)	1. Rib cage (stuff ball into rib cage)	Ball protected	Carrying like a loaf of bread
	2. Elbow (tuck elbow in)	Holds the ball in place	Carrying with elbow on top of ball
	3. Eagle claw (spread fingers over point of ball with index finger over tip of ball)	Large surface area means more control of the ball	
	4. Forearm (covers ball)	Holds ball against the body, so the ball won't bounce out	
Running Down Sideline	SOAP (Switch Outside Arm Position): outside arm on top when switching	Use inside arm to push away defenders	Carrying ball on the inside
Ball Position	Running to the right sideline, carry ball in right hand	If ball gets knocked out, it will roll out of bounds	
	Running to the left sideline, carry ball in left hand	If ball gets knocked out, it will roll out of bounds	

FIGURE 13.9 Handoff

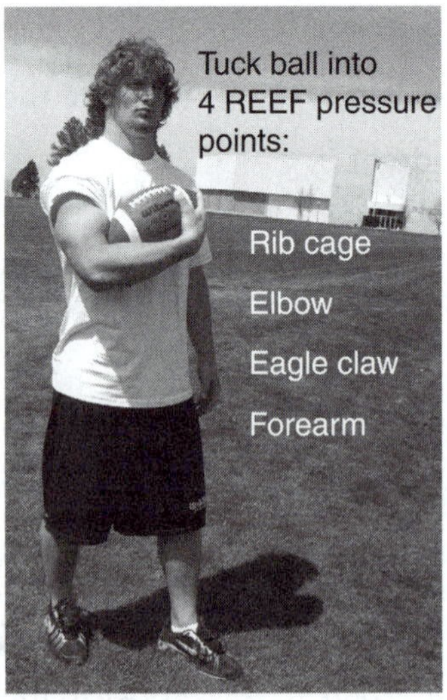

FIGURE 13.10 Tuck Away Ball

BLOCKING

SKILL	CUE	WHY	COMMON ERROR
Stance	Comfortable squat position on the balls of your feet, as if you are sitting on a chair	Good leverage	Putting weight on heels
Arm Action	Arms crossed in front of body, ready to contact the defender	Quicker reaction time	Too much weight on hands
			Stopping feet and lunging
	Feet shoulder width apart	Good base	Feet too wide or too narrow
Strategy	Keep the opponent away from the ball carrier	Keeps you on the opponent	Not keeping with opponent
Body Force	Push with your upper body, using your legs for strength and balance	Legal position on the block	Using any other parts for blocking

BASIC RECEIVER ROUTES

SKILL	CUE	WHY	COMMON ERROR
In Route (Figure 13.11, page 166)	Run straight, plant outside foot	To fake opponent	
	Cut to middle: run a straight line to middle; find an open area between defenders	Get to ball faster and run away from opponent	Rounding out the route
	Big hands for target for the quarterback	More target area for the quarterback to see and the receiver to catch the ball	Chest catch
Out Route (Figure 13.11, page 166)	Run straight, plant inside foot, and cut to the outside; run toward the sidelines; find an open area between defenders	To fake opponent	
	Run a straight line	Get to ball faster	
	Big hands, for the quarterback to have a target	More target area for the quarterback to see, and the receiver has more surface area in which to catch the ball	

continued

FIGURE 13.11 In Route (Opposite for Out Route)

BASIC RECEIVER ROUTES, continued			
SKILL	**CUE**	**WHY**	**COMMON ERROR**
Post Route	Run straight for 10–12 yards, then cut to one of the goalposts	Fakes defender	Run too flat
Stop Route	Run straight	The defender will not know in what direction you will be going	
	Stop as if you had come to a stop sign	The defender will be slow to react to your sudden movement	Take too much time to stop
	Turn around, with your arms and hands ready to receive the ball	Provides a good target to receive the ball	Turning away from quarterback
Fly Route	Run straight until you pass the defender	The defender will not know where you are going	
	Don't stop	Run away from the defender	

14

Golf

INTRODUCTION

The game of golf is the fastest-growing sport in the world. For a student who has played a satisfying round, it is easy to see why it has become so popular. Golf may be the hardest skill game played today, and it definitely cannot be learned quickly. Three things need to happen with each shot. The golfer must (1) hit the target, (2) hit the ball the correct yardage, and (3) hit the "sweet spot" on the club face or hit the ball squarely on the club face. It takes most recreational golfers years to learn the game, even when they are naturally gifted athletes. Keeping this fact in mind, teachers should remember to be patient with students, while instructing and encouraging those with a real interest in golf to play as much as possible.

Three to five demonstrations of a golf stroke, associated with one cue phrase, will simplify the learning process and make the skill and stroke more beginner-friendly. Stay with one or two cues until the students are comfortable moving on. Tiger Woods' book, *How I Play Golf,* is a great resource for cues. As one golf pro said, "It's not what you say but it's what the student hears."

SKILLS LISTED WITH CUES

This chapter presents teaching cues for the following golf skills: three different grips, approach to the ball, and the basic swing for iron shots. Once the students have mastered these skills, additional cues provide information for golf shots, which include specifics for wood shots, putting, and chipping. Also provided are cues on how to handle sand shots, shots on a windy day, and different golf lies, including downhill, uphill, and low shots. These particular cues are designed for beginning, right-handed golfers, but they can be adapted for left-handed golfers. Through the use of these cues, you and your students can be more successful golfers!

TIPS

1. Type the cues on 3″ × 5″ note cards, laminate and hole-punch the cards, and place them in your bag for quick reference on different shots.
2. It is essential to grasp and ingrain the fundamentals of golf: grip, stance, backswing, through swing, and finish.
3. Good equipment and good fundamentals of golf equal good golf.
4. Core exercises and stretching are critical to a good golf swing; Tiger Woods' book, *How I Play Golf,* covers these areas well.

EQUIPMENT TIPS

1. Ball differences: Premium golf balls (Titleist Pro V1 and Pro V1x, Nike One Platinum and Black, Bridgestone 330 and 330 S, Callaway HX Tour 56, and Srixon 2-UR and 2-URS) do not travel as far as many of the other golf balls, but they have a higher spin rate, which is an advantage in controlling the ball. These balls can cost more than $40.00 per dozen, and the balls that cost less than half of that are adequate for most golfers.
2. Standard set of clubs: 1, 3, and 5 woods; 3, 4, 5, 6, 7, 8, and 9 irons; pitching wedge, sand wedge, and putter; and utility clubs: hybrids that can replace long irons; 2 iron; 4 and 7 wood; and lob wedge.
3. Go to a professional to be fitted for proper club length, proper flex of shaft, and proper lie.
4. Golf shoes with soft spikes help the golfer stay on the ground and prevent slipping. Golf sandals are popular, but bee stings are common; you might want to wear socks.
5. Artificial-turf doormats can be used to hit the ball indoors. These mats protect the floor.

TEACHING PROGRESSION

Professionals often suggest it is best to learn the game starting from the green. Putt first, move to the chip shot, pitch, sand shot, swing fairway woods, driver, and then teach students how to handle problem shots. It is important to learn the mental aspect of the game while learning its physical aspects. The proper mental approach to golf can make a huge difference in a player's success and enjoyment.

TEACHING IDEAS

1. Choose clubs beginners can have success with. Clubs that are fairly easy to hit with include 5, 6, and 7 irons. These clubs can be used to help ingrain the swing. When a player begins to feel comfortable with the irons, progress to the woods.
2. The driving range is a place for beginners to practice the skills of golf. Beginners can become easily frustrated on a golf course. When the beginner can get the ball up in the air with consistency, it's time to play a round of golf.
3. Putting and chipping are the least difficult skills to learn; however, many hours of practice are required to keep the feel for the ball and maintain these skills.

4. Golf is easy to make complex! The simpler we can make it, the better. Stay away from complicated language. Progress happens when staying with the fundamental skills and basic swing.
5. When keeping score in golf, *par* is a set number of hits that the golfer is expected to meet within a certain distance. Par is based on distance to the hole:
    - Par 3 distance: 60–250 yards
    - Par 4 distance: 250–475 yards
    - Par 5 distance: over 475 yards

    If the hole is a par 3, the ball should be on the green in 1 stroke and 2 putts.

    If the hole is a par 4, the ball should be on the green in 2 strokes and 2 putts.

    If the hole is a par 5, the ball should be on the green in 3 strokes and 2 putts.

    Here are some possible situations that might occur on a par 3 distance:
    - Hole in one: the golfer puts the ball in the hole in 1 stroke.
    - Birdie: the golfer puts the ball in the hole in 2 strokes.
    - Par: the golfer puts the ball in the hole in 3 strokes.
    - Bogie: the golfer puts the ball in the hole in 4 strokes.
    - Double bogie: the golfer puts the ball in the hole in 5 strokes.

    The scorecard will indicate if the hole is a par 3, 4, or 5 (see Figure 14.1). The scorecard will show the number of the hole, the par of the hole, and yardage for the hole for ladies' and men's distances. The number of strokes it takes the golfer to put the ball in the hole is recorded on the scorecard in the appropriate box of the "Hole No." column. There are 9-hole or 18-hole golf courses. The total score at the end of 9 or 18 holes is the golfer's final score.
6. Setting up a nine-hole golf course on a football field or large grass field is an excellent way to teach scoring and provide a gamelike experience (Figure 14.2, page 170). Equipment and procedures include the following:
    - Scorecard designed by teacher or picked up at a local golf course
    - Pencils
    - Jump rope and cones to mark tee box
    - For holes use soccer corner flags, or attach flags to dowel sticks and stand the sticks in orange cones with holes in top. Place the flag in the center of a hula hoop. Object of game is to hit ball in hula hoop.

Blue Tees	480	150	565	220	330	395	560	290	362
White Tees	469	135	527	161	289	389	541	287	357
Hole No.	1	2	3	4	5	6	7	8	9
Par (Men's/Ladies')	5	3	5	3	4	4	5	4	4
Red Tees	459	117	467	139	236	389	499	287	357

FIGURE 14.1 Example of a Golf Scorecard for Nine-Hole Course

FIGURE 14.2 Ideas for Modified Golf Equipment and Golf Course

- Regulation clubs, white Wiffle balls, and tees
- Set up nine holes that match the pars on the score card.
- Use a shotgun tournament start (several players start on each hole and begin on a signal). Have three or four students on each hole. Give each group a 5 iron, a 7 iron, a 9 iron, a scorecard, and a pencil. On the whistle, everybody starts to play.
- Students can play games where the teams take the best score on each hole (best-ball tournaments) and other types of contests. Have fun golfing!

7. Have a contest to see who can hit the ball closest to the hole. Tee shots are made from the top of a hill (if hills are not available, tee off level ground) (Figure 14.3).
   - Set up a tee box area and a par 3 hole at the bottom of a small hill.
   - Place a hula hoop about 50 yards out from the tee box with a soccer goal marker or flagstick inside the hoop.
   - Place a blue plastic tarp in front of the hole for a water hazard.
   - Provide 7, 8, and 9 irons for the students to use.

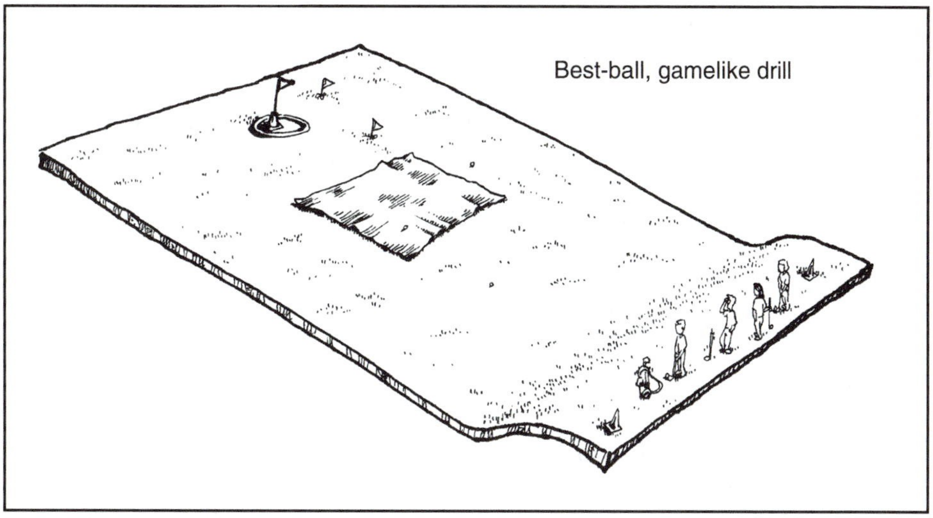

FIGURE 14.3 Early Bird Special Golf Activity

- Each student tries to get her or his shot closest to the large flagstick. When a student does, a teacher, teacher's aide, or student can mark the spot with a small flagstick.
- Closest ball to the hole wins the early bird special.

8. If you don't keep practicing golf, it's easy to lose your skills. Stay with it.
9. To maximize the chance to improve, golfers should spend one-third of their time putting and chipping, one-third of their time hitting range balls, and one-third of their time on the course playing.
10. Try to organize a field trip to the golf course, and have students work on each area just listed. Have the golf pro talk about course etiquette and rules.

FYI

For further information and special help, consult the following organization and resources.

ORGANIZATION

Hook a Kid on Golf
2611 Old Okeechobee Road
West Palm Beach, FL 33409

GOLF PROS

Contact the Professional Golf Association (PGA) professionals at local golf courses.

Dan Roskelly
PGA Head Professional
Logan Golf and Country Club
Logan, UT 84322

PUBLICATIONS

Fronske, H., Wilson, R., & Strand, B. (1996, November/December). Teaching golf creatively. *Strategies, 10*(2), 32–37.

George, J. D. (2004). *Let's golf.* San Francisco: Benjamin Cummings.

Hogan, B. (1990). *Five lessons: The modern fundamentals of golf.* New York: Simon & Schuster.

Mack, G., & Casstevons, P. (2001). *Mind gym.* Chicago, IL: McGraw-Hill Contemporary Books.

Woods, T. (2001). *Tiger Woods: How I play golf.* New York: Warner Brothers.

WEBSITES

www.golf101.com

www.golfmaestro.net

www.nationalgolfer.com/productions/golf_instruction/butch-harman.ultimate_golf.htm

www.nationalgolfer.com/products/golf_instruction/demo_flicks_on_golf.htm

www.pga.com (includes video instructional lessons)

GRIPS

SKILL	CUE	WHY	COMMON ERROR
Overlap (Strongest)	Little finger of right hand rests on index and middle finger		Gripping too tightly with right thumb
	Last 3 fingers on left hand and middle 2 fingers of right hand are the grippers	Control of club	Gripping top of club—instinct is to grip with thumb and index finger
	Fingers are welded together like Siamese twins		
Hand Position	The V of thumb and index finger of each hand points to right shoulder		
Interlocking	Little finger interlocks with index finger		Little fingers not interlocking
Baseball	No unity between hands; right hand is strong hand of grip	Control of club and more power	Hands too far apart
	Hold club like a baseball bat		

APPROACH

SKILL	CUE	WHY	COMMON ERROR
Stance	Stand tall, wide shoulders		Standing straight up; legs stiff or straight
Arms	Arms hang comfortably		Elbows locked
	Knees flexed ever so slightly	Can turn back and through the ball	
	Bent over at hips comfortably but not too far		
Focus of Eyes	Look through the lower part of eyes		Eyes and head tilting down
	Keep chin up through swing	Left shoulders turn under chin	Chin hitting front shoulder during swing
Head	Head needs to be still		

BASIC SWING

SKILL	CUE	WHY	COMMON ERROR
Backswing Position	Right elbow points down and away from side	Helps keep club face square and club on line	Elbow up or too close to body
	Left elbow wide and straight	By pushing your left arm away from head as far as you can there is more time to accelerate speed and power on downswing	Left elbow bent
	Wide at the top; the longer and wider you make your backswing, the better the swing		Both elbows bent
	Club shaft is parallel to target at top of swing	Helps for a perfect path and plane line through the face of club	
Head Position on Completion of the Swing	Head stays still until trailing shoulder forces it up	More speed and power through the swing	Keeping head down all the way through swing; don't get as much power

BASIC SWING—THREE KEYS

SKILL	CUE	WHY	COMMON ERROR
Swing Key 1 Low and Wide	Arms wide on the takeaway	Foundation of a wide swing arc	Downswing too steep or choppy
	Low, wide, straight		
	Back takeaway		
	Get the feeling of swinging your left forearm more across your chest rather than up		
Swing Key 2	Keep your right knee as quiet as possible while you turn your shoulders		
	A controlled turn is a tight turn		
	Keep right knee in same position as address		
	Push left hip 2 inches to left		Weight gathered on right foot
	80% of weight on right leg; 20% of weight on left leg	More power from weight transfer; ball will go longer	80% on left leg, 20% on right leg
			Not transferring weight to back leg
	Coil		
Swing Key 3	Rip it		Open club face at impact
	Right forearm rotates over the left		90% of balls slice or go to right
	Let the right forearm rotate over the left as aggressively as you can until the ball stops going right; rip it		
	"You finish more around your body than up."		

SLICE

SKILL	CUE	WHY	COMMON ERROR
Slice	80–90% of balls slice	Club face open at impact	
		Forearms rotate too much on takeaway	
		Left wrist is cupped at top of backswing	
		Swing path too much from inside	
How to Correct Slice	You want a flat wrist and square club face at top of backswing		
	Have quicker hands and restrict forearm rotation on backswing		
	Have partner or use mirror to check angle		

HOOK

SKILL	CUE	WHY	COMMON ERROR
Hook		Club face closed at impact	
		Lack of body rotation on through swing	
		Chin buried in the chest	
		Wrist bowed at top of swing	
How to Correct Hook	Flat wrist		
	Maintain triangle		
	Stay connected		

WOOD SHOTS

SKILL	CUE	WHY	COMMON ERROR
Stance (Figure 14.4a)	Front foot lines up with ball		Ball lined up with back foot or middle of stance
Tee Ball	Top half of ball should be above club face		Ball teed up too high or low
(Figure 14.4b)	Inside of feet line up with outside points of shoulders	You get more motion in your upper body	
Swing	Tickle grass on backswing		Wood face comes up too soon
	Emphasize low and wide backswing		Hurrying the takeaway swing
	Turn left shoulder under chin		
	Drive tack through ball		
	Sweep the ball off tee		Hitting at down angle
	Keep club head traveling fairly low to ground after impact	Will promote solid contact	
Follow-Through	Belt buckle faces hole		
	Right knee points to target		Left hip faces hole
Focus of Eyes	Head stays still until trailing shoulder forces it up		Raising head too soon or too late

(a) Stance

(b) Ball Placement

FIGURE 14.4 Wood Shot

PUTTING			
SKILL	**CUE**	**WHY**	**COMMON ERROR**
Grip	Hold the putter lightly	Able to feel weight of putter head at other end	Hold too tightly
	On 1–10 pressure scale, hold it at 5 or less		
Stance	Stand fairly tall	Easy to see path of ball	Hunched over
		Allows for better shoulder swing	
Eyes	Position eyes directly over ball	Keeps you in line with hole	Eyes too far forward or back
	Eyes parallel to line of putt		
Putting Action (Figure 14.5)	Same length back and through	More control of ball	Short—too much acceleration at contact
	Shoulders and arm do most of work	Control of ball	
	Left arm and putter act as one	Avoids angles of putter head	
	Keep a steady head and sternum	Keeps putting path stable and true	Head moves right to left
	No peeking	Solid contact	Peeking

continued

PUTTING DRILLS

1. Putt with your eyes closed.
2. Always have a routine. Tiger Woods gives an example in his book.
3. Putting is largely about touch to get a feel for speed. The stroke should be easy, smooth, and natural.
4. Start close when putting (the same philosophy as warm-up shooting a basketball). Gradually work yourself back from the hole, putting close shots and then longer shots.

FIGURE 14.5 Arm Swing for Putting

PUTTING, continued			
SKILL	**CUE**	**WHY**	**COMMON ERROR**
Have a Routine	Always have the same routine when you putt	Puts you in a great form physically and mentally	Routine or process too quick
	Perform it exactly the same way every time		

CHIPPING			
SKILL	**CUE**	**WHY**	**COMMON ERROR**
Grip	Hold down on club	Extra control	
Club	Use 7 or 8 iron	More control—ball does not go as high; more accurate	
Posture	Open stance	See the hole path better	Hunching down on ball
	Chin high		
	Back straight		
Hand position	Set hands slightly ahead of the ball		
Tilt	Lean a little toward target	Promotes a downward blow	
Ball Position	Position ball slightly back of center	Promotes a downward blow	
Read the Shot	See the shot before you hit it		
	Choose a spot you want the ball to land		
	Form a mental picture of the ball traveling there		
Swing Action	Hit down on back of ball	Loft of club will give it height	Stabbing at ball
	Accelerate smoothly		
	Keep eyes focused on back of ball through contact; see grass where ball was		
	Return arm to position at address		

PITCH SHOT

SKILL	CUE	WHY	COMMON ERROR
Address and Club Use	Choose a lofted club—sand wedge		
	Open your stance, aligning your feet left of target lane		Closed stance
	Open club face to increase loft		Closed club face
	Play the ball forward off your left toe		Play ball back off your right toe
Action Cues	Mini version of the full swing		
	Hips turn slightly back and through	To accommodate the motion of your shoulders, arms, and hands	
	Let the club do the work		
	Slide club head under the ball		
	Accelerate through the swing		Allow club head to stop
End of Swing	Club face should be aiming at the sky	Proves that the loft of the club face has been maintained	

30-YARD PUNCH

SKILL	CUE	WHY	COMMON ERROR
Short Punch from About 30 Yards	Position ball back of center	Helps golfer hit down on the ball	
	Narrow stance; feet between the width of the shoulders		
Backswing	Start the backswing low and wide		
	Left arm fully extended		
	Turn shoulders and hips		
	Simply unturn your hips and let them guide the shoulders, arms, and hands through the downswing		
	A low, abbreviated finish	Prove big muscles have directed the motion	Arms and hands directed the motion

SAND SHOT

SKILL	CUE	WHY	COMMON ERROR
Stance	Be careful not to ground club	Stroke penalty	Placing club face in sand
Feet (Figure 14.6a)	Dig feet into the sand; open face at address	Solid stance	Failing to dig feet into sand, closed face
Stance and Club Alignment	Open stance and club face; weaken left hand	Don't want club face to rotate to closed position	Closed club face; tight grip easier
	Align feet, hips, and shoulders left of target	Preprogramming and out-to-in swing	
	Aim club face to right	Increases loft of the club face in order to hit high and soft	
	Play ball off left heel	Promotes a higher trajectory	
		Slides club through sand easier	

continued

(**a**) Feet Position

(**b**) Swing Technique

FIGURE 14.6 Sand Shot

SAND SHOT, continued			
SKILL	**CUE**	**WHY**	**COMMON ERROR**
Swing	"Easy does it" about technique		Too much strength
	Swing hands back to about shoulder height; easy rhythms		
	Cock wrist firmly	Hardy shot with little movement in hips or legs	Too much hip with leg movement
(Figure 14.6b)	Slide through the ball		Chopping at ball
	Accelerate through the ball		Fastest speed of club 6 inches beyond contact
Want the Ball to Run After It Hits Green	Hit 3 inches behind ball	Ball comes out without any backspin	Stopping in sand
			Taking no sand
Hit Ball High, Stop Quickly	Hit 1 inch or less behind ball	Ball stops with more backspin	Hitting no sand
			Ball gets away from you
Buried Ball in Sand	Make a deeper divot	This will allow ball to get up in the air	
	Swing down firmly; punch		
	Not much follow-through		

WIND SHOT			
SKILL	**CUE**	**WHY**	**COMMON ERROR**
Wind Shot	Wider stance; flex knees more		
	Play ball off back of foot for a low shot just right of center		Playing ball off front foot or middle of stance
	Decrease club number; for example, change from a 5 iron to a 3 iron	More control of ball will go farther in the wind	Using a club number that is too high
	Shorten wide swing, keep hands low; easier swing		Hard, heavy swing
	Take a thin divot		
	Finish low to hit ball low		

HILL SHOT			
SKILL	**CUE**	**WHY**	**COMMON ERROR**
Golf Ball Lies Downhill (Figure 14.7a)	Play ball off front foot	Where the club face hits ball first for accurate contact of ball	
	Use 1 less club (5 to 6 iron)	Ball goes longer; ball travels farther	Playing ball in a straddle stance or off front foot
	Keep shoulders parallel to the ground like airplane wings		Leaning forward
Beginner	Aim at target line		Aiming straight
Intermediate	Wrists break earlier to close club face		
Golf Ball Lies Uphill (Figure 14.7b)	Play ball off low foot	Where club face hits ground first for accurate contact of ball	
	Play ball off back foot		Playing ball in a straddle stance or off back foot

continued

(**a**) Downhill

(**b**) Uphill

FIGURE 14.7 Hill Shot

HILL SHOT, continued			
SKILL	**CUE**	**WHY**	**COMMON ERROR**
Golf Ball Lies Uphill, *continued*	Keep shoulders parallel to the ground like airplane wings	Leaning forward	
Beginner	Use 1 more club	Ball will go higher	Aiming straight
Intermediate	Wrists break later to keep club face open longer		

LOW BALLS			
SKILL	**CUE**	**WHY**	**COMMON ERROR**
Feet	Play ball off back foot	More control of ball	Playing ball in a straddle stance or off front foot
	Widen stance		
	Flex knee more		
	Choose more club		
Club Face	Square the club face		Open or very closed club face
Swing	Short, wide swing	Ball will stay low	No follow-through
	Keep hands low		

15

In-Line Skating

INTRODUCTION

In-line skating is an enjoyable new sport that can be introduced to people of all ages. Students from elementary, middle, and high schools can enjoy and learn about in-line skating. Many students already participate in in-line skating, and this activity can easily be added to any physical education class.

In-line skating can be incorporated into a physical education program under National Association for Sport and Physical Education (NASPE) standards. Skate in School is a program developed by NASPE and Roller Blade, Inc., that comes with ready-to-use lesson plans and affordable equipment (skates, helmets, and protective gear).

SKILLS LISTED WITH CUES

Cues are presented for the following basic skills: standing up, ready position, falling, V-walk, using the ABT brake, striding, turning, using edges, stopping, and swizzling.

EQUIPMENT TIPS

1. Each student *must* wear a helmet and knee, wrist, and elbow pads. You wouldn't play football without a helmet and padding—ouch! Wearing protective equipment helps prevent injury.
2. Organization of the equipment is important.
   - Mark all of the equipment with permanent markers.
   - Mark skates with the size on the back of each skate. Skates should be stored as pairs on some type of shelving.
   - Mark all protective gear and helmets with S, M, L, or XL.
   - Keep equipment by type or by size. You can use large buckets—one each for knee pads, elbow pads, and wrist pads—or you can use mesh bags that hold one of each type of equipment, all the same size. Choose the method that works for you. You may want to experiment to find out which is better.

3. After each day's use, the equipment should be cleaned with a spray disinfectant and stored in a well-ventilated area to allow drying.
4. On the first day of class, go over rules and talk about the physical benefits of skating, the importance of protective gear, and the proper techniques for getting and putting away the equipment.
5. Depending on the type of skates and brake pads, you can skate in the gym (with indoor skates) or on a flat, smooth surface outside. For indoor use, you need a nonmarking brake pad, like the ones Roller Blade, Inc. uses in its program.
6. All equipment should be maintained on a regular basis.
7. Skating in water or sand can damage bearings and hurt skate performance. Stick to dry surfaces.

TEACHING IDEAS

1. Always discuss the importance of protective gear. Don't scare students, but remind them that a broken wrist or concussion is worse than a messed-up hairdo.
2. Talk to students about the physical benefits of in-line skating.
3. Discuss with students the importance of control. If control is maintained, falling should not occur often. Each student's level of control may be different.
4. Students should be reminded to keep their body weight low and slightly forward, with knees bent, most of the time.
5. Discuss the skating area, and use boundary markers and cones when possible. Also, establish traffic patterns for safety.
6. Start nervous beginners on floor mats to ease falls and build confidence.
7. Have students assist each other verbally, but not physically.
8. Avoid hills and declines when starting out. Start on a flat surface—parking lot, tennis court, or basketball court.

TEACHING PROGRESSION

1. Rules and procedures
2. Protective gear and skates
3. Standing up
4. Ready position
5. Falling
6. Stopping
7. Rolling and stopping
8. V-walk/stroking
9. V-walk, roll, and basic stop
10. Stride
11. ABT brake
12. Turns
13. Edges
14. Slalom
15. Forward swizzle
16. Backward swizzle

MINI-GAMES

1. *Practice—practice—practice:* Balance on one skate at a time. This helps one to stop better. Skate width of gym and stop. Repeat until skill is mastered. The goal of this activity is for students to practice stopping techniques.
2. *Musical Braking:* Students skate to popular music on a circular course. Periodically, the music is turned off for 3 to 5 seconds. The goal of the activity is for every student to come to a complete, controlled stop before the music is turned on again.
3. *Skating Pins:* Students skate in lanes up and down a flat area. A "wall" of bowling pins is placed at each end, and a line is placed approximately 2 to 3 feet in front of the pins. The goal of the activity is for students to perform the basic stop between the line and pins without knocking over any pins.
4. *Slalom Races:* Divide the class into teams of four. Set up a slalom course. In relay fashion, have the teams race through the slalom course, turn around the last cone, and race back to tag the next person in line. Every cone that is knocked down adds 1 second to the overall team score.
5. *Student Routines:* Put the students in groups of 4 to 6. Have the students develop a skating routine to music of their choice. (Be sure the music is appropriate beforehand.) The students need to include at least four different skating skills in the routine. Have students present their routines to the class.

FYI

For further information, consult the following organization.

ORGANIZATION

National Association for Sport and Physical Education (NASPE)
1900 Association Drive
Reston, VA 20191
Phone: (800) 213-7193, ext. 410

STANDING—READY POSITION

SKILL	CUE	WHY	COMMON ERROR
Standing Up	Start on both knees	Beginning skaters need to understand the most efficient way to get up, conserve energy, and not get frustrated	
	Lift non-brake knee and place wheels on ground		
	Place both hands on knees		
	Push up slowly		
	Position skates in a V (heels together)		
Ready Position (Figure 15.1)	Position skates in a V (heels together)	This position is needed to begin all movements	
	Ankles, knees, and hips flexed		
	Weight forward and low		
	Arms forward and in front of knees		
	Put hands on knees to regain balance if falling backward		

FIGURE 15.1 Ready Position

FALLING—V-WALK—STOPPING

SKILL	CUE	WHY	COMMON ERROR
Falling (Figure 15.2)	Drop to all fours (knees, then hands, using plastic part of wrist guard)	Students need to understand that falling forward is the safest way to fall	
V-Walk	Ready position	Basic step for movement	
	Shift weight from one foot to the other	Students are in control of their speed	
	While shifting weight, point toes out like a V		
ABT Brake (Heel Brake)	Weight on non-brake leg		Failing to lift toe in ABT
	Put brake leg forward		Keeping all wheels on the ground
	Slightly lift toe	Great for beginners	
	Press calf against back of skate		
	Shoulder and arms should be forward		

continued

FIGURE 15.2 Falling

FALLING—V-WALK—STOPPING, continued			
SKILL	**CUE**	**WHY**	**COMMON ERROR**
Standard Brake (Figure 15.3)	Scissor brake foot forward		
	Lift toe and press heel into the pad		
T-Stop Brake (Figure 15.4)	Glide and coast on both skates	Not all students have brakes	
	Lift back braking foot and place behind front coasting foot in T position	Effective for more experienced skaters	
	Apply pressure and ease skate to stop		

FIGURE 15.3 Stopping Standard Brake

FIGURE 15.4 T-Stop Braking

STRIDING—TURNING—USE OF EDGES

SKILL	CUE	WHY	COMMON ERROR
Stride	Ready Position	Short strokes increase power	
	V-walk	Don't twist body while gliding	Twisting body while gliding
	Right foot stroke, push forward; lift left foot off the ground, coast		
	Left foot stroke, push forward; lift right foot off the ground, coast	Keep nose, knees, and toes in forward position	
	Repeat, shifting weight back and forth	Take wide strides	
	Note: There is minimal time that both skates are on the ground	Students experience smooth timing	
Turns (for right turns; opposite for left turns)	Look to the right	Don't lean hips out; rather, have upper body lean and leave hips aligned over skates	
	Rotate upper body to right		
	Turn hips and knees to right		
	Skates about 6 inches apart		
	Lean to each side		
Use of Edges	One skate on outside edge	Allows smooth turning	
	One skate on inside edge		
	Roll forward by pressing on edges		

TURNING AND SWIZZLING

SKILL	CUE	WHY	COMMON ERROR
Parallel Turn	Stride/coast, keeping feet under shoulders and parallel	Use with more experienced skaters	
	Point shoulder to left; skates will follow, using one outside and one inside. Make the right leg lead with the outside edge	Students who feel comfortable on skates will experience success with these skills	
	Lean into the outside edge		
Forward Swizzle	V position	These skills allow the students to move in multiple directions and combine a number of skills	
	Bend knees, lean forward		
	Turn toes inward		
	Push heels out		
	Feet are about shoulder width apart		
	Then bring feet together		
	Repeat		
Backward Swizzle	Same movement backward		
	Start with toes together (backward V)		
	Put pressure on the inside edges of both feet		
	Turn toes inward toward edge		
	Push heels out		
	Grab heels, pulling them back in (like gripping)		
	Bring feet together		
	Turn toes inward and lean		

BRAKING			
SKILL	**CUE**	**WHY**	**COMMON ERROR**
ABT Brake	Put weight on non-brake leg		
	Slide brake foot forward		
	Press calf against cuff of boot and depress brake		
	Keep shoulders forward		
Standard Brake	Scissor brake foot forward		
	Lift toe and press heel into the pad		
T-Stop Brake	Glide and coast on both skates		
	Lift braking foot and place in back of coasting foot in T position		
	Apply pressure and ease skate to stop		

16

Lacrosse

INTRODUCTION

"A unique combination of speed, skill, agility, grace, endurance, finesse and historical significance, lacrosse may just be, according to basketball inventor James Naismith, 'the best of all possible field games'" (Lacrosse Foundation, 1994).

Lacrosse is considered to be America's first sport since it originated with the North American Indians and was adapted by the Canadians. With a history spanning over a century, modern lacrosse is one of the fastest-growing team sports in the United States. No sport has grown faster at the high school level over the last 10 years. Men's professional indoor and outdoor lacrosse leagues also are very popular and have brought the game to national attention.

Lacrosse is played with a stick, the crosse, which the player uses to throw, catch, and scoop the ball. When these skills are mastered, the rest of the game flows. The sport of lacrosse is a combination of basketball, soccer, and hockey. Anyone can enjoy lacrosse, since physical size is not important to being successful at the sport. The game focuses on coordination and agility, not brute strength. Lacrosse is a fast-moving and exciting game with rapid scoring. Fast transitions and quick, precise passes and dodges are common in both men's and women's lacrosse.

Men's and women's lacrosse evolved from the same original game, but today they are played under different rules. Women's rules limit stick contact, do not allow body contact, and therefore require little protective equipment. Men's lacrosse rules allow some stick and body contact, although violence is not allowed—nor is it in keeping with the culture of the game. Here is a summary of rule differences between men's and women's lacrosse:

- Field dimensions are different (see Figures 16.1 and 16.2, pages 194–195), as well as restraining lines.
- Women play with 11 field players and a goalie; men play with 10 and a goalie.
- Men's game allows some stick-to-body contact and body-to-body contact within 5 feet of the ball.
- Women's game allows only stick-to-stick contact within strict guidelines and no body contact at any time.

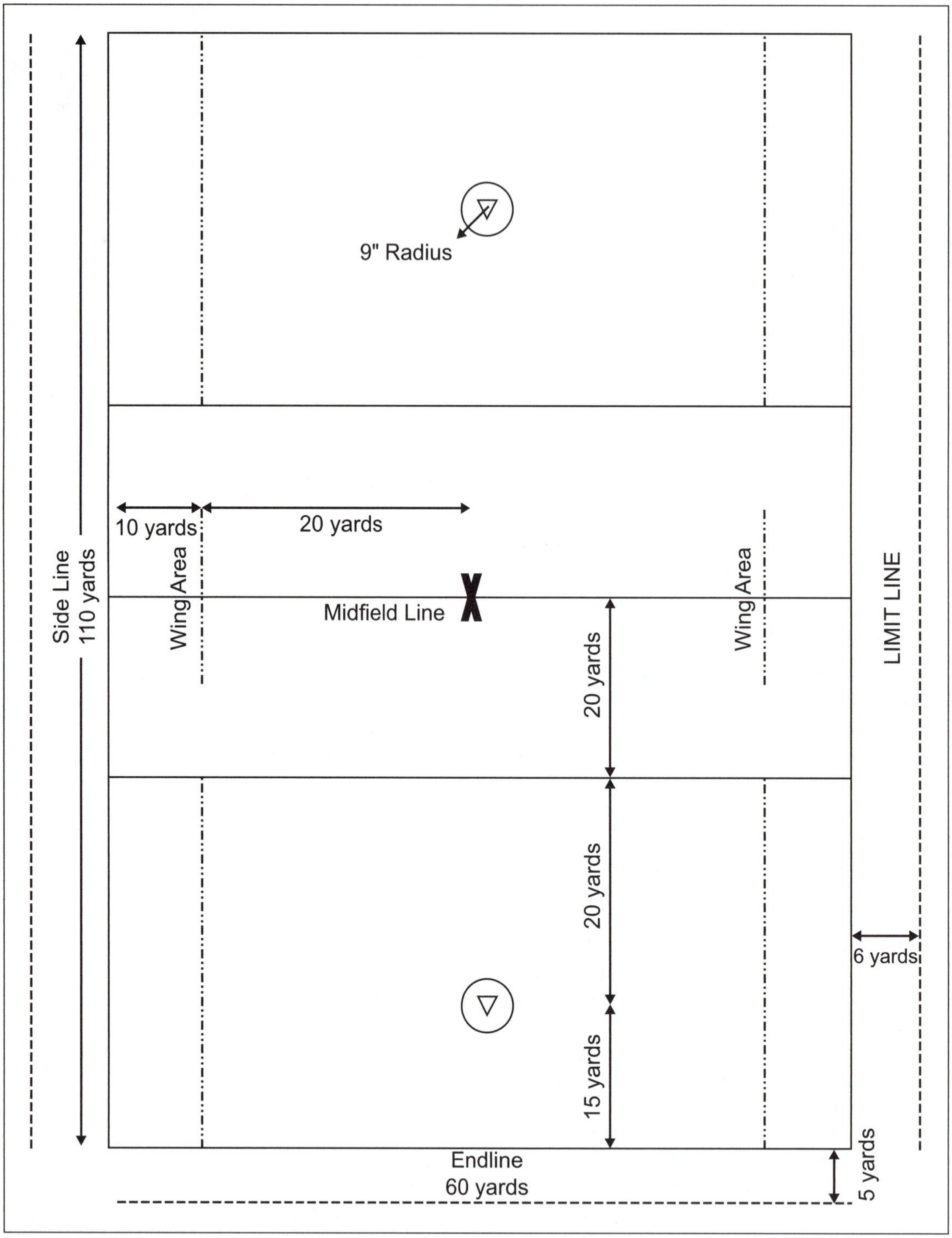

FIGURE 16.1 Men's Lacrosse Field

- Men wear helmet, shoulder pads, mouth guard, and protective gloves.
- Women wear eye protection and a mouth guard.
- Stick pockets may be deeper in the men's game than the women's.

Variations of lacrosse can be added to a curriculum with minimal expense and with such benefits as improved eye-hand coordination, aerobic and anaerobic fitness, muscular coordination, mental toughness, and competitiveness.

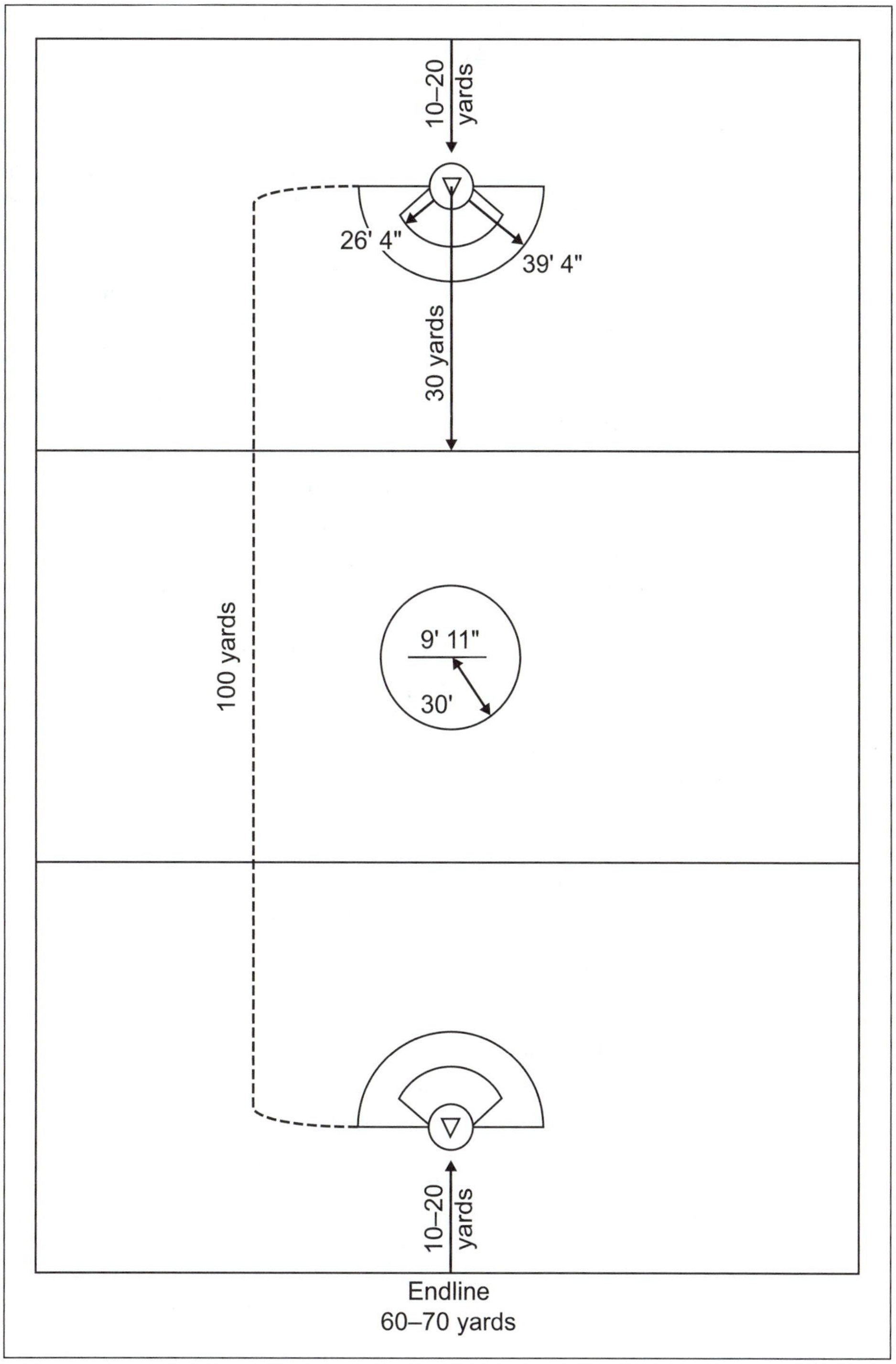

FIGURE 16.2 Women's Lacrosse Field

SKILLS LISTED WITH CUES

The tips and cues presented in this chapter are based on co-ed, noncontact play, using soft lacrosse equipment. The skills, however, are directly transferable to the traditional men's and women's games.

If students enjoy the basic skills and tactics of lacrosse learned in their physical education class, they may become acquainted with the standard game of lacrosse—including regulation equipment, protective gear, and rules—by seeking out local playing opportunities. The knowledge and skills gained in physical education class will help them succeed.

TIPS

1. A good drill for catching and throwing is called "wall ball." Find a straight wall. Using the stick and a ball, practice throwing the ball against the wall. Catch the ball in the pocket with the stick. Follow the throwing, catching, and cradling cues. Spending hours throwing the ball against the wall will lead to mastery of these skills. Pick spots on the wall to aim for, or tape an imaginary goal outline to the wall. This will improve shooting, passing, and catching. The goal cage is 6 feet × 6 feet. This drill can also be done in a gym.
2. Cradling is a critical skill that prevents the player from losing the ball when moving. Have students run at full speed down field with just a ball in their stick, not cradling; then have them cradle as they run down the field. This exercise will reinforce the need for cradling.
3. Body position for passing and catching the ball is important for balance, fluidity of motion, and quick transition to other areas of the game. The ready position consists of a relaxed body with knees slightly bent, holding stick in throwing-ready position. (See cue for ready position.)
4. Ground ball position: bending at the waist and knees and having your butt down is critical. Keep head up using peripheral vision to locate and scoop the ball. This allows the player to have visual contact with his or her own team and opposing players.
5. Develop ambidextrous skills. Perform each skill, alternating right hand and left hand on top.
6. Throwing tip: when developing stick-handling skills, it is important to emphasize wrist and hand flexibility and strength. After instructing the fundamentals of grip and throwing motion, have players practice throwing and catching while in a kneeling position. This isolates the upper body and helps focus on the importance of hand and wrist flexibility.

EQUIPMENT TIPS

The recommended equipment for teaching lacrosse in the physical education classroom is known as "soft lacrosse" equipment. Soft lacrosse sticks are not gender-specific and differ from men's and women's lacrosse sticks. Soft lacrosse utilizes a larger, softer ball. The US Lacrosse Sports Science and Safety Committee has determined that no protective equipment is necessary to be worn when utilizing soft lacrosse balls or sticks.

Should teachers choose to use standard lacrosse sticks and balls, which is *not* recommended for physical education play, the following statement has been issued by US Lacrosse:

> Any clinic, class, or competitive lacrosse program offered using sticks and/or balls other than the "soft lacrosse" equipment (oversize plastic head and oversized, soft, hollow ball) *must* adhere to players' use of *all equipment required* by either the boys' or the girls' lacrosse rules (found at www.uslacrosse.org), depending on which set of rules is chosen for play. Programs using "soft lacrosse" sticks and balls should use the non-contact, "soft lacrosse" rules and may opt to use a form of protective eyewear or other protective safety equipment.

1. Indoor soccer goals, hockey goals, or plastic garbage cans can be used for physical education classes. Soccer balls and volleyballs can be used to

teach the tactical skills of the game. Tennis balls may be used as an alternative to lacrosse balls.

2. Men's equipment differs from women's equipment:
   - Men's equipment: Helmet with face mask, shoulder pads, arm guards, gloves, lacrosse stick, lacrosse ball, mouth guard, two goals 6 feet × 6 feet, field 110 yards by 60 yards
   - Women's equipment: Stick, ball, eye protection, mouth guard, gloves optional, two goals 6 feet × 6 feet, field 120 yards by 70 yards

TEACHING IDEAS

1. Lacrosse can be played in physical education classes in teams of 5–7 players, each using a smaller goal such as an indoor soccer goal or a plastic garbage can. Lay the can down and throw the ball into the can. This sharpens the shooting skills. The field can be reduced to size available. This provides opportunity for multiple games involving the greatest number of players.
2. Scrimmage once a week with interested students for at least two periods of 15 minutes each on a regulation field. Regulation play requires 10 players for men's lacrosse (1 goalie, 3 defenders, 3 midfielders, 3 attack men) and 12 players for women's lacrosse (1 goalie, 3 defenders, 5 midfielders, 3 attackers).
3. Physical education teachers can teach the tactical skills of lacrosse with a soccer ball or volleyball carried in the hands of a player (instead of a stick). In this scenario, teachers do not need to purchase equipment but can teach the game and rules of lacrosse and present an alternative enjoyable experience.

FYI

For further information and special help, consult the following organization.

ORGANIZATION

US Lacrosse
113 W. University Parkway
Baltimore, MD 21210
Phone: (410) 235-6882
Fax: (410) 366-6735
Email: info@uslacrosse.org
Website: www.uslacrosse.org

Materials available:

1. US Lacrosse Physical Education Curriculum
2. Coaches' Education Program Level 1 outline courses
3. Physical education and youth equipment grants
4. New Team Assistance programs
5. Online store with educational books, videos, and DVDs
6. Men's and women's rules, sports science and safety studies, equipment specs, connections to your local chapter, the latest in lacrosse news

WEBSITE

Lacrosse Foundation (1994). www.uslacrosse.org

THROWING			
SKILL	**CUE**	**WHY**	**COMMON ERROR**
Grip	Soft hands; opposing grip (bottom hand palm down, top hand palm up)	Stick mobility, agility with stick	
Top Hand	Dominant hand on top, about 6 inches from head	Dominant hand on top provides most success for beginners	
	Shaft should lie across fingers of top hand, which curl around shaft		
	Keep handle in fingers and off palm of hand		Death grip on stick; no gap between palm and shaft of stick
Bottom Hand	Gently grips butt end of stick	Provides stability and support; moves in synch with the top hand	Bottom hand not moving in tandem with top hand—windshield wiper action
Throwing Ready Position (Figure 16.3)	Arms up and away	Top hand/arm moves up and behind body at ear level—just like an overhand throw of a baseball, softball, or football; bottom hand points toward target	Elbow of top hand/arm will be tight against body instead of up
	Point with opposite shoulder	Body perpendicular to target by pointing non-throwing shoulder at target.	
Throwing Motion/ Release (Figure 16.4)	Push/pull	Top hand pushes while bottom hand pulls to create a lever action	Dropping stick below the shoulders or throwing sidearm; too much push with the top and not enough pull with bottom (will look like punching) will send ball into the ground
	Step	Like push/pull, step with opposite foot (just like throwing a ball)	Stepping with same side foot; no step
	Follow through	Trunk rotates through toward target	Not following through to target

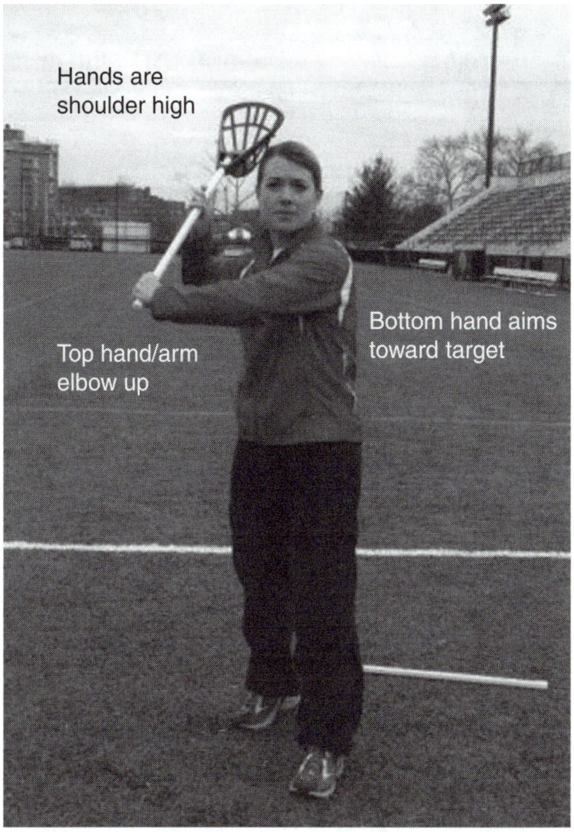

FIGURE 16.3 Throwing Ready Position

FIGURE 16.4 Throwing Motion/Release

CATCHING, CRADLING, AND SCOOPING

SKILL	CUE	WHY	COMMON ERROR
Catching	"Ask" for the ball (hold stick out as a target)—should be upright in front of body and shoulder at a 45° angle	Gives thrower a target, exposes largest surface of stick for ball	Not providing a target
	Give/soft hands—As ball enters stick, player should give softly by moving the stick in the direction the ball is traveling, as if cushioning an egg or a water balloon	Ball will bounce out of stick if stick is rigid	Ball bounces out of stick—student not giving, or timing the give of the stick incorrectly
	Triple threat—catch motion should finish with stick in the box by shoulder and ear	From this position, the player may either pass, cradle, or shoot	Basket catching—player lowers stick and catches ball as if it were falling into a basket

continued

CATCHING, CRADLING, AND SCOOPING, continued			
SKILL	**CUE**	**WHY**	**COMMON ERROR**
Cradling (Two-Handed)	Opposing grip (bottom hand palm down, top hand palm up)		
(Figure 16.5)	Soft grip—shaft should lie across fingers of top hand, which curl around shaft; bottom hand gently grips butt end of stick		Death grip on stick; no gap between palm and shaft of stick
	Stick in box—head of stick almost upright near shoulder and ear, facing outward		Stick hanging horizontal or below shoulders

continued

FIGURE 16.5 Cradling Grip

CATCHING, CRADLING, AND SCOOPING, continued			
SKILL	**CUE**	**WHY**	**COMMON ERROR**
Cradling (Two-Handed), *continued*	Use top hand to turn the stick head in a semicircular motion, creating centrifugal force of the ball against the pocket. While top hand curls in and out, the bottom hand should allow the shaft to rotate in the fingers.	The two-handed cradle is used by men's and women's lacrosse players to maintain possession and set up faces and dodges. The more adept a player is with the two-handed cradle, the more effective he or she will be in maneuvering with the ball.	Bottom hand out of synch with top hand—causes a windshield wiper effect and ball will fall out of stick
	"Rock the baby" (to describe both hands working together), "swing the bucket" (top hand motion), "rev the motorcycle" (bottom hand motion)	Keep ball in the pocket with centrifugal force—smooth motion	Jerky wrist movements cause the ball to be lost
Scooping (Picking Up Ground Balls) (Figure 16.6)	Stick parallel to the ground—lower arms, bend at the knees, get butt down	Necessary to attain proper positioning	Student bends at waist instead of knees

continued

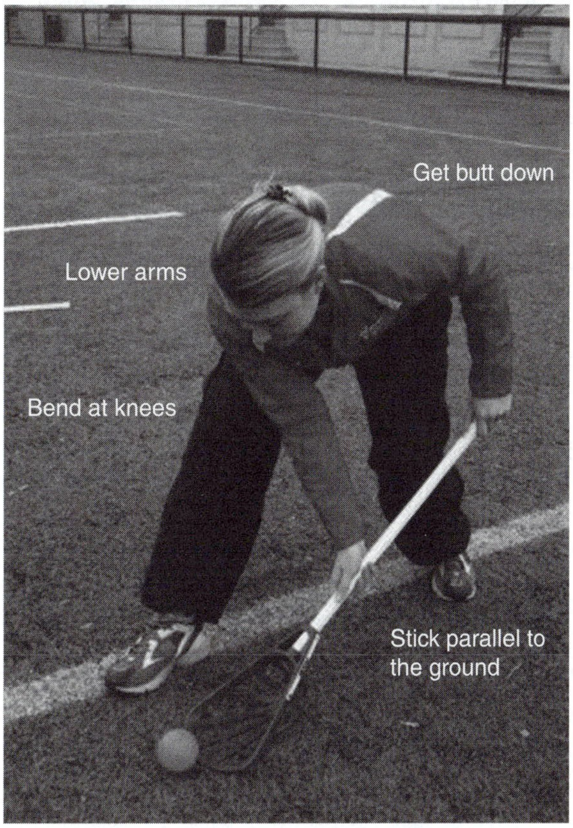

FIGURE 16.6 Scooping Up Ground Balls

CATCHING, CRADLING, AND SCOOPING, continued			
SKILL	**CUE**	**WHY**	**COMMON ERROR**
Scooping (Picking Up Ground Balls), *continued*	Head of the ball		
	Step with same side foot as top hand, even with ball		Step is too far behind or in front of ball
	"Scrape your knuckles"—push stick under and through ball by pushing bottom hand through	Need to force stick under ball	Student shoves ball along ground as if "vacuuming"
	"Kiss your stick"—raise head of stick to vertical position in front of face	Important for stick protection	Student hangs stick out in front (easy to check in the traditional game, though not allowed in physical education classes)
	Run through the scoop; begin cradling immediately	Move out of traffic to make a safe pass	
	Talk, talk, talk—three things need to be communicated each time a ball hits the ground:		
	1. "Ball down!"	Lets teammates know a loose-ball situation exists	
	2. "Ball!" Communicates your intention to pick up the ball	This allows teammates to concentrate on getting into position or boxing out other players within 5 yards of the ball. Also prevents the situation of multiple players from the same team fighting for the ball.	
	3. "Release!" Announces you have the ball	Allows teammates to stop blocking opponents and move into position to support the pass	

INDIVIDUAL OFFENSIVE PLAY

SKILL	CUE	WHY	COMMON ERROR
Off-Ball Movement: Cutting	Cutting—purpose is to create space, occupy defender, break free to receive a pass	Off-ball movement is essential; quick and even slower, organized motion will create holes in the defense and opportunities for the offense	Standing around watching ball as a spectator
	Watch his cut—when opponent's eyes are off you, make a move		Not being aware if opponent is watching you
	Backdoor cut—cutting behind the opponent		
	Cut away and then cut to—take defender away from ball, then cut back toward ball carrier to receive pass	Moving toward the ball and bringing defender into the area of the ball	
	Catch, clear out, or else you clog—three things can happen when a teammate approaches you with a ball: 1. Catch—you cut successfully, get free, make the catch. 2. Clear—you cut successfully but are not the recipient of the pass; move on to make space for the ball carrier or another cutter. 3. Clog—you cut successfully, but don't do either 1 or 2; you will impede the ball carrier's progress by clogging the space.	Sometimes players are forced to leave their man to cover a more dangerous threat. Calling for a slide signals that the other defenders each need to drop in and cover the next open person left by the movement (sliding) of defenders.	Not communicating when player is leaving an attacker

continued

INDIVIDUAL OFFENSIVE PLAY, continued			
SKILL	**CUE**	**WHY**	**COMMON ERROR**
With the Ball *Dodging*	Key principles: deception, change of direction, change of speed, quick feet		No change of speed or acceleration through dodge—steady pace
	Protect opponent off—get body between stick and opponent		Hanging stick out, presenting stick to defender when setting up dodge
	Seal opponent off—get back on a straight opponent as soon as possible (north-south)	Does not allow for easy recovery by opponent beaten by dodge	Finishing dodge parallel or in front of defender instead of behind defender on north-south line
Face Dodge	Shake and bake—dodge performed facing defender; fake to cradling side, pull stick to opposite side, protect stick with body, bring back to cradle side when past defender		Weak fake to strong side doesn't pull defender off balance
Roll Dodge	Fake to one side, plant foot, roll off defender		Ending the roll in front of or beside defender instead of behind
Tips	Be creative! Try combining moves from the roll and face dodges		
	Switch hands—try switching hands to protect the stick on the dodge or to create new dodges		

TEAM DEFENSIVE STRATEGY

SKILL	CUE	WHY	COMMON ERROR
Man-to-Man Defense: Individual Positioning	Good defensive stance—knees bent, weight slightly forward on balls of feet not heels, shuffling feet (similar to basketball)	Quick footwork is essential to reacting and dictating where the offense is going	Standing upright, off-balance, lunging after opponent
	Mirror the stick—your stick should mirror the movement of your opponent	Puts defender in position to block, intercept, or force a bad pass	Stick drops to waist and is ineffective
	Goal-side positioning—keep your body between your man and the goal	This strategy slows the attacker down, or forces the attacker away from the goal (similar to basketball)	Letting attacker have a line to the goal
	Stay with your man—maintain a stick length between you and your man		Leaving man to cover another—this leaves your man open for an easy pass
	Slide! Move from your man to a more dangerous open man	Sometimes players are forced to leave their man to cover a more dangerous threat. Calling for a slide is a signal that the other defenders each need to drop in and cover the next open person left by the movement (sliding) of defenders.	Not communicating when player is leaving an attacker
	Help! Indicates you have lost your man and another teammate must pick him up		
	Stick up—if your man does not have the ball, stick should be up in the potential passing lane	Increases chance to block or intercept a pass, makes you seem "bigger"	"Lazy sticks"—arms hanging down around waist
Tips	Communication is essential for good defense		

GOALKEEPING

SKILL	CUE	WHY	COMMON ERROR
Leading the Team Defense	Goalie controls defense like a soccer goalie: *talk*	Goalies must communicate where the ball is at all times as well as instructing defenders when and where to move	Lack of communication
	Calls all the passes and movement of the ball; wherever the ball goes, goalie calls the movement ("ball top right"; "ball top left")		Concentration and focus elsewhere
	Goalie needs to have confidence and has to maintain motivation of the team		Getting down on a teammate
	Goalie needs to be always up, mentally tough	Lacrosse is a high-scoring game. Goalies need to know how to bounce back so they can make the next save.	Becoming discouraged
Playing the Ball	Goalie needs to step to ball		Not stepping out to meet the ball when possible
	Position body between the opponent who has the ball and the goal		

17

Pickleball

INTRODUCTION

Pickleball is a combination of tennis, badminton, and table tennis that is played on a doubles badminton court (20 feet × 44 feet) with a perforated plastic ball and wooden paddles. The doubles badminton court on the gymnasium floor can be converted to a picklebill court simply by attaching the nets to the volleyball/badminton net standards at a height of 3 feet. Pickleball can also be played on the inside singles lines on the tennis court. Pickleball is an ideal lead-up game for teaching tennis and racquet skills.

The strategies of the game include lobbing, overhead slamming, passing drive shots from the baseline, and fast volley exchanges at the net. The game is played by two or four people; a fifth person can be designated to be the scorekeeper, which helps accommodate large PE classes and provides the opportunity for that student to learn the official rules of the game. Many teachers have emphasized how pickleball has been effective in developing the students' reflexes and eye-hand coordination skills along with quickness and agility. Pickleball is a success-oriented game because after the player strikes the ball, the perforations slow the ball down in midflight, thereby promoting longer rallies and providing an equalizing factor for differences in strength, skill, and athletic ability. Many teachers are adding pickleball to their curricula because students can become successful with the game the first time they try it.

Pickleball is played mainly during the fall and winter months and is a good unit to present before tennis because many of the teaching cues are similar. For example, two cues used for the forehand stroke for tennis and picklebill are "Hold your arm in a cast" and "Finish on edge." The only major adjustment would be to the longer tennis racquet. We have found that students who become successful with the game of pickleball are not as intimidated when learning the game of tennis. Another way to introduce pickleball is to start with a tennis unit, then add pickleball, and finish with a tennis unit.

FIGURE 17.1 Rainy Day

SKILLS LISTED WITH CUES

The cues for pickleball skills include the ready position, forehand and backhand swing (grip, stance, and stroke), lob and drive serves, volley and drop shots, top-spin, backspin, and the overhead smash. Also provided are cues for singles and doubles boundaries and scoring, along with singles and doubles strategies.

TIP

A pickleball unit can be presented before or after a tennis unit, or on rainy days during a tennis unit. Teachers need not cancel a tennis class at any level because of inclement weather if their school has a gym (Figure 17.1).

EQUIPMENT TIPS

1. Pickleball court (Figure 17.2).
2. Pickleball, ball—a specially designed Wiffle ball with a 3-inch maximum diameter (Figure 17.3, page 210).
3. Solid wood paddles. The ball contacting the wood paddle has a tendency to stay on the paddle longer, giving the player the advantage with direct shots on the court. Plastic on plastic tends to spray all over the place and will not stay on the surface of the racket as long. Players have a harder time controlling the shots, and fewer rallies occur. Longer rallies are the result of good equipment.

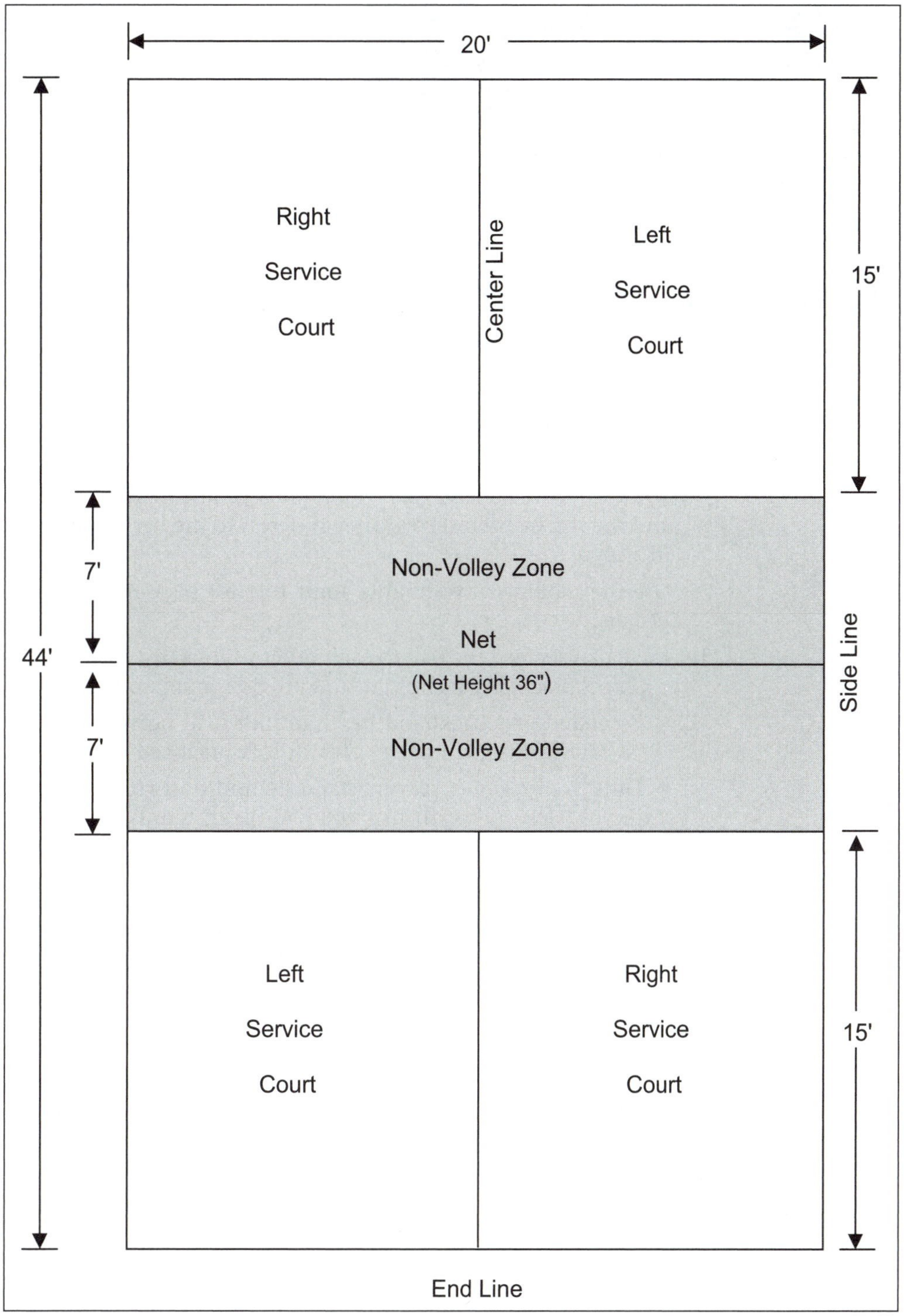

FIGURE 17.2 Pickleball Court

4. The length of the paddle makes a difference in performance because it is light in weight and short (see Figure 17.3, page 210). Players can feel more control with the racquet, especially with backhand shots (see Figures 17.4 and 17.5 on page 213).

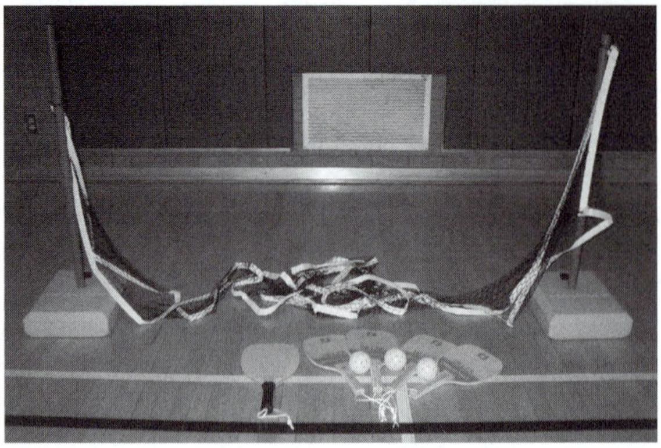

FIGURE 17.3 Pickleball Equipment

TEACHING IDEAS

1. For large beginning classes, have players hit the ball against the wall 10 times. This exercise gives them practice hitting forehands, backhands, and the like by themselves. They progress to the net when they can hit 10 in a row.
2. Use the modified two-bounce-limit rule for beginning classes or less fit players.
3. Have players feed the ball to each other using half-court. This method encourages practicing technique and provides numerous practice trials.
   - Forehand and backhand baseline shot drill provides forehand and backhand stroke practice. This drill is practiced at the baseline.
   - Dink volley game: players stand behind non-volley zone and hit drives back and forth like volley drills in tennis.
   - Hit offensive and defensive lob shots with a partner.
   - Overhead smash drill with a partner.
4. Volley the ball in the air with a partner. Your goal is to see how many times you can hit the ball back and forth while keeping the ball in the air. This drill is good for eye-hand coordination.
5. Score on every serve. The side-out rule can be modified so that a point is scored on every serve. One player serves for a total of 5 serves, then the opponent serves for 5 serves until one player scores 10 points. If time permits, one player serves 10 serves, then the opponent serves 10 serves until one player scores 11 points. Different numbers of serves can be substituted.
6. Provide challenge drills, modified games, games, or tournaments set up before class. These "early bird specials" encourage the students to come early (Strand, Reeder, Scantling, & Johnson, 1997).
7. Rally Game:

   A. This is a game to help with the transition from hitting a ball that is tossed to actually playing pickleball. It is an extremely versatile formation for a large class and allows each student to maximize the amount of practice with minimal waiting time. It can be set up for any size class; the actual arrangement depends on the class size and the number of courts. The students can rotate on just one court, or the game can be organized so that students rotate up and down all of the courts. Either way, it is a fun game for students because they get some competition with many repetitions. It makes better use of the space because the court is divided and two rallies occur at the same time.

B. Following is an example of how to set up the Rally Game with 30 students and 6 courts. Five players are assigned to each court, with 1 player waiting at the net off the court and 2 players on each end of the court behind the baseline. The court is divided along the center line, so that two rallies occur simultaneously. The students play 1 point and then rotate to their left. Players keep track of their own points and continue to play for 5–10 minutes. If you incorporate a rotation with all of the courts, after the 5–10 minutes have ended the players with the highest points on courts 2–5 go up, and the players with the lowest points go down. Then on court 1 the player with the lowest points goes to court 2, and the one with the highest points on court 6 goes to court 5. Now there should be 5 per court, and each player starts at 0 to begin a new game.

Options:

- There are many variations of this basic setup to practice other aspects of pickleball.
- Start the two players on one end at the net just outside the non-volley zone.
- Have all of the players at the net outside the non-volley zone.
- Have the students play as a doubles team with all back, one team up to net, or both teams up to net.
- Dictate that one end of the court has to hit lobs, drop shots, only forehands, or only backhands.

FYI

For further information and special help, consult the following organization and resource.

ORGANIZATION

Provides a free catalog on request. A rule book, 9-minute videotape for the game of pickleball, textbook, and equipment (paddles, balls, nets, standards, and sets) are also available at this address.

Douglas Smith, President
Pickle-Ball, Inc.
4700 9th Ave Northwest
Seattle, WA 98107
Phone: (206) 632-0119 or (800) 377-9915
Fax: (206) 632-0126
E-mail: info@pickleball.com
Website: www.pickleball.com

PUBLICATION

Curtis, J. (1998). *Pickleball for player and teacher* (3rd ed.). Englewood, CO: Morton.

READY POSITION

SKILL	CUE	WHY	COMMON ERROR
Stance	Knees bent		Knees locked
	Weight on balls of feet	Ready to react faster	Weight on heels
	Square to net		Not square with net
Move to Swing	Pivot and step for both forehand and backhand strokes	More control to hit ball in sweet spot of paddle	
	Turn shoulders—gets paddle back early		

FOREHAND STROKE

SKILL	CUE	WHY	COMMON ERROR
Grip	Index knuckle on ¾—like tennis grip	Puts paddle in best position to make contact with ball	Choking the paddle; holding too tight
			Extending first finger behind paddle head
Stance	Pivot and step	Gets player ready to hit	Legs not moving; body is parallel to net
Stroke (Figure 17.4)	Shoulder turn for early racquet preparation		
	Arm in cast; firm wrists		Bending wrists or arm
	Swing low to high	More power on ball; gives ball topspin	Scooping ball
	Wait for ball to drop		
	Hit ball in front of left hip	More control	Finishing with paddle flat
Pickleball Drills: Have partner toss ball to partner: Toss, hit forehand Lots of balls Switch			

FIGURE 17.4 Forehand Stroke

FIGURE 17.5 Backhand Stroke

BACKHAND STROKE

SKILL	CUE	WHY	COMMON ERROR
Grip	Knuckle on 2— like tennis grip		Failing to turn paddle
Stance	Pivot and step; get paddle back early	Gets player ready to hit	Not taking paddle back soon enough
Stroke (Figure 17.5)	Swing low to high	Gives ball power and topspin on ball	
	Wait for ball to drop		
	Hit ball knee-high	Better accuracy	Face of paddle tilted too far up or down
Drill: Have partner toss balls to backhand; Lots of balls Toss and hit Switch places Have partner toss 1 forehand, 1 backhand; switch			

SERVING

SKILL	CUE	WHY	COMMON ERROR
Lob (Figure 17.6)			
Foot Placement	One foot in front of baseline, other foot in back of baseline		Both feet behind baseline
Toss	Drop the ball, then swing the paddle		Throwing ball up or not dropping the ball
Swing (Figure 17.7)	Like pitching horseshoes		
	Follow-through straight up to hit face with biceps		Follow-through too low
	Finish like Statue of Liberty		

continued

FIGURE 17.6 Serving Position

FIGURE 17.7 Lob Serve

SERVING, continued			
SKILL	**CUE**	**WHY**	**COMMON ERROR**
Drive (Figure 17.8)			
Foot Placement	One foot in front of baseline, other foot in back of baseline		Both feet behind baseline
Toss	Ball held waist high and out in front		Ball held too high or too low
	Paddle is held behind you, waist high		
	Wrist in cocked position		
Swing	Drop the ball, then swing		Contacting the ball late
	Arm stiff, like a board, at contact		
Follow-Through	Paddle finishes on edge, shoulder level		
Drills: Partners serve lots of balls—to each other Partners serve Play the rally out			

FIGURE 17.8 Drive Serve

FOREHAND/BACKHAND VOLLEY SHOT

SKILL	CUE	WHY	COMMON ERROR
Ready Position	One foot behind non-volley zone	Rule	Both feet in front of non-volley zone (illegal)
	Paddle at eye level	React faster	Paddle held too low
Grip	Knuckle on 2		
Legs and Swing Action (Figure 17.9)	Step and make a short swing		
	Little or no backswing	More control	Too much backswing
	Slight turn of shoulders		Turning shoulders too much
	Meet ball in front of you	Better accuracy to place the ball	Letting ball come to you
	Keep paddle in peripheral vision		

continued

FIGURE 17.9 Forehand Volley

FOREHAND/BACKHAND VOLLEY SHOT, continued

SKILL	CUE	WHY	COMMON ERROR
Follow-Through	Contact ball in center of paddle		Contacting ball on paddle edge
	Make a short swing		Swinging too hard
	Limit follow-through		Too long a follow-through
Strategy	Play just behind non-volley zone	Rule	
Drill: Feeders toss ball to partner behind non-volley zone; switch; feeder hits forehand/backhand volley to partner; switch			

DROP SHOT

SKILL	CUE	WHY	COMMON ERROR
Swing	Graze shorts with paddle		Contact to side and front of body
	Slide paddle under ball		
	Love tap/soft touch	More control, softer touch to ball	Hitting too hard
Contact	Open-face paddle to give ball underspin		Closing paddle face
	Push, lift, nudge, caress		Fakes opponent because of spin and short
Follow-Through	Look in mirror at finish		Paddle is on edge
Strategy	Swing like a ground stroke when opponent is playing deep		Swinging like a drop shot
Drill: Feeders hit forehand to partner, then hit backhand; switch			

TOPSPINS AND BACKSPINS

SKILL	CUE	WHY	COMMON ERROR
Topspin	Swing racket from low to high	Puts topspin on the ball	Swinging paddle level
	Like making a candy cane at end of swing		Finishing with paddle on edge
Backspin	Paddle swings high to low	Puts backspin on ball	Swinging paddle level
	Shave the ball like shaving your face		Finishing with paddle on edge
	Cut flat under ball		
Drill: Try backspins against wall; then have partner toss to forehand and then to backhand; then have a rally; try to use topspin and backspin naturally	Follow through with racquet flat to the net		Stops at contact of ball

SMASH

SKILL	CUE	WHY	COMMON ERROR
Position (Figure 17.10)	Get in back of ball		Too far in front of ball
Contact with Ball	Contact ball in front of body	Better accuracy to get ball down	Contact ball behind head
	Paddle face tilted toward floor		Paddle face tilted toward wall
Follow-Through	Like a volleyball smash		No follow-through
	Recover quickly to ready position		Off balance; can't recover to hit opponent's passing shot
Drill: Have 3 people hitting balls, 1-2-3; hit ball in air, partner returns ball in smash			

FIGURE 17.10 Smash

SINGLES

SKILL	CUE	WHY	COMMON ERROR
Boundaries (see Figure 17.2, page 209)			
Court	20 feet × 44 feet		
Non-Volley Zone	7 feet on each side of net		
Scoring	Can score a point only when serving		
	When score is zero or even, serve in right court		
	When score is odd, serve in left court		

continued

SINGLES, continued			
SKILL	**CUE**	**WHY**	**COMMON ERROR**
Scoring, *continued*	Ball must bounce once in receiver's court as well as once in the server's court on the return: "bounce, bounce"		Volleying the ball before it has bounced once on each side of the net
	Play to 11, win by 2 points		
Strategies	Hit ball deep into opponent's court		Hitting ball in middle of court
	Hit most balls to opponent's weak side (usually backhand)		Hitting ball to player's forehand
	Hit ball to side to cause opponent to move		Hitting ball in middle of court
Server	Vary the serves—deep corners at opponents, hard, soft, etc.		
Receiver	Return ball to opponent's deep court		
Playing	Deep shots to sides		
	Weak sides when possible		
	Wait for errors; then attack net		
	Short volleys followed by deep lob to keep opponent off balance		
	Right at receiver		
	Mix up shots		Using same shot
Drills: After all skills have been taught, use this drill with 3 feeders and 1 hitter: Feeder 1 hits ball to forehand; feeder 2 hits ball backhand; feeder 3 hits short shot. Then feeders mix up shots. Hitters are to move all over court; rotate hitters every few minutes.			

DOUBLES			
SKILL	**CUE**	**WHY**	**COMMON ERROR**
Boundaries of Court (see Figure 17.2, page 209)			
Court	20 feet × 44 feet		
Non-Volley Zone	7 feet on each side of net		
Service Court	6 feet × 6 feet		
Scoring	Server must have 1 foot behind baseline without touching the line		
	Serve across the net diagonally		
	Must clear non-volley zone		
	Ball must bounce once in receiver's court as well as once in the server's court: "bounce, bounce"		
	First service: team A, 1 player serves		
	Second service: both players on team B serve; then both team A players serve		
	Server switches courts with teammate if point is scored by server		
	Service always starts in the right-hand court		
Strategies	To mix up drive and lob serves		Using same serve
	Accuracy is key over power		Trying to kill shots
Front/Back	Shadow your partner; attack the net		Not following your partner
Side to Side	Don't cross the property line; each one is responsible for ball in own side of court		Playing teammate's ball
	When ball goes close to middle line, call it		Not calling balls
	Communicate		

18

Racquetball

INTRODUCTION

Racquetball is a game of geometric angles that requires agility, speed, and accuracy. One of the great things about racquetball is never having to chase the ball. Racquetball allows the player to practice shots and court movements without an opponent.

Players should work on their forehand and backhand strokes first. Other strokes, such as the ceiling shot, can be developed from the successful use of these strokes.

When learning the forehand and backhand strokes, many players want to hit the ball hard and fast, but hitting too hard causes the player to lose control. Practicing technique and accuracy will help the player progress to the ultimate goal of hitting the ball harder and faster with better control.

Learning to track the ball is another skill players need to develop. A player must watch the angle of the ball coming off the wall to anticipate the next shot. Experience is the best teacher.

SKILLS LISTED WITH CUES

Included in this chapter are cues for the ready position and grips, forehand and backhand strokes, drive and lob serves, corner and ceiling shots, strategy of service return, singles-game scoring and strategy, and cutthroat rules.

TIPS

1. Always wear proper eye protection approved by the American Amateur Racquetball Association (AARA), no matter what your level of skill is. The ball can travel 80 to 100 miles an hour.
2. Adequately warm up and stretch before and after games.
3. If out of position or unsure, play defensively.
4. Concentrate on proper footwork (i.e., body parallel to side wall for proper forehand).

EQUIPMENT TIPS

1. Use of proper racquet weight and string tension will prevent shoulder and arm pain.
2. Proper eye protection (AARA approved) is required.
3. Proper shoes that provide ankle support and gripping.
4. Be sure racquet grip fits hand.

TEACHING IDEAS

1. Use the modified no-bounce-limit rule when starting with younger students and beginners. The player may allow the ball to bounce as many times as desired before hitting it.
2. Use the modified two-bounce-limit rule for older students, junior racquetball leagues, beginning classes, or players who are not physically fit.
3. Stop and hit. Step, drop, and hit. Set up off front wall, step, here also and hit. Continual rally, step, and hit.
4. Play with scoring on each rally. Both server and receiver can score points.
5. One player tosses ball to rebound off wall; the other player hits the ball. This drill can be done with forehand and backhand strokes.

FYI

For further information and special help, consult the following organization and resources.

ORGANIZATION

Jim Hiser
American Amateur Racquetball Association (AARA)
1685 West Uintah
Colorado Springs, CO 80904-2921
Phone: (719) 635-5396
Fax: (719) 635-0685
E-mail: racquetball@usra.org
Website: www.usra.org

Materials available:

1. Videos
2. Training materials
3. Racquetball magazine
4. Clothing

It's not always necessary to join a health club to play racquetball. Facilities are available for use at a nominal fee.

PUBLICATIONS

Edwards, L. (1992). *Racquetball.* Scottsdale, AZ: Gorsuch Scarisbrick.
Norton, C., & Bryant, J. E. (2003). *Beginning racquetball.* Belmont, CA: Brooks/Cole.

READY POSITION AND GRIPS

SKILL	CUE	WHY	COMMON ERROR
Ready Position	Knees bent	Ready to move	Standing upright
	Weight on inside of soles of feet in order to push in either direction		Weight on heels
	Forearms on table	Able to move easily to forehand or backhand position	Arms (racquet) to side of body
Forehand Grip	V shape, top of bevel		Gripping too tightly
			Choking up on grip
	Index finger positioned to pull trigger; squeeze trigger finger at impact		Incorrect placement of index finger
	Butt end of racket in palm of hand (for more wrist action)	Creates power	
Backhand Grip	Rotate V one bevel toward thumb	Allows for a more natural arm motion, reducing injuries and creating power	Failing to rotate grip from forehand to backhand
	Turn clockwise		

FOREHAND STROKE

SKILL	CUE	WHY	COMMON ERROR
Hit Prep (Figure 18.1a)	Shoulders parallel to side wall		Hitting with body facing front wall
	Set racket first, then step, and then pivot		
	Elbow above shoulder	More power; less arm strain	Rushed and incomplete backswing
Execution (Figure 18.1a)	Like skipping a rock	Low, straight shot	No wrist snap
	Shoulders dictate aim of ball; shoulders parallel, hit parallel	Accuracy	Dropping front shoulder; lifting back shoulder
	Okay to contact ball at knee height; ankle is best	The more parallel to the floor and the lower the contact point, the less bounce	Hitting ball at peak of bounce or ascent
	Wait for it to descend		

continued

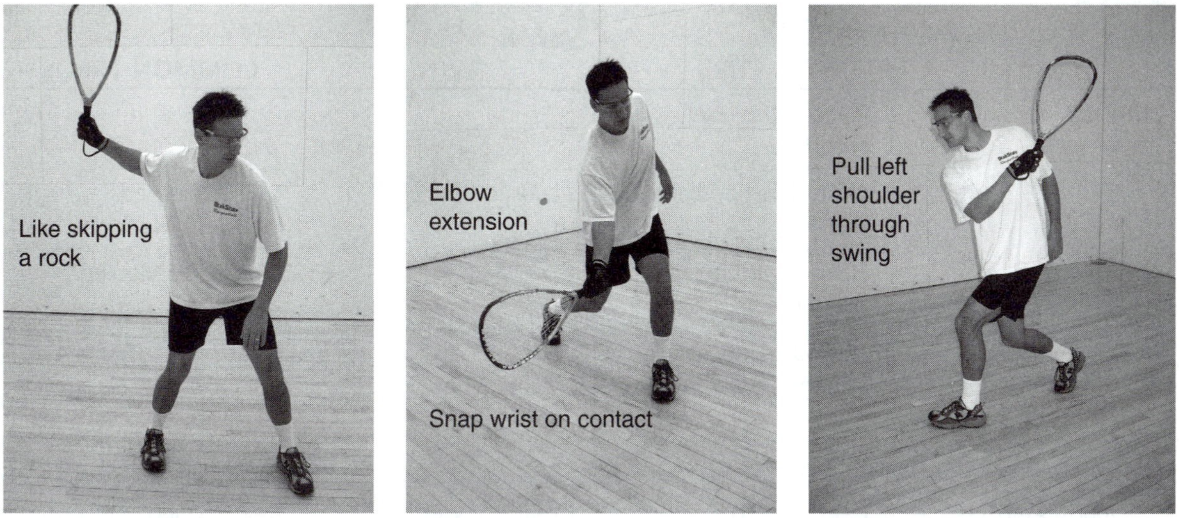

(**a**) Execution (**b**) Contact (**c**) Follow-Through

FIGURE 18.1 Forehand

FOREHAND STROKE, continued			
SKILL	**CUE**	**WHY**	**COMMON ERROR**
Execution, *continued*	Step into hit		Ball too high on front wall; racquet face tilted up
	Shift weight from back to front		
	Hit ball off front foot or close to front foot, depending on shot		
	Watch ball hit strings	Accuracy	Watching target, not ball
(Figure 18.1b)	Elbow extension plus snap wrist on contact	Power	Wrist in a cast
	Follow-through	Accuracy/power	No follow-through
		Less arm strain	
Opposite Arm (Figure 18.1c)	Pull left shoulder through swing	Power	Left arm hanging at side
	Hit and move to center of court	Ready to retrieve opponent's next shot	Standing still, not moving after shot

BACKHAND STROKE

SKILL	CUE	WHY	COMMON ERROR
Hit Prep	Pivot—step—set racquet		
	Shoulders parallel to side wall	Accuracy	Shoulders perpendicular to side wall
(Figure 18.2a)	Elbow pointing to ground		Elbow too close to body
	Hitting elbow about 4 inches away from body		
	Wrist cocked		Wrist not cocked
Opposite Arm	Elbow pulling racquet back	Create power on release	Keeping left hand on racquet
Execution	Shift weight back to front	Body movement creates power	No weight transfer
(Figure 18.2b)	Okay to contact ball at knee height; ankle is best	Low, level shot = less bounce	Hitting ball too high
(Figure 18.2c)	Push belly button to front wall	Power	No hip rotation
	Wait for ball to descend		
	Snap wrist, like backhanding someone	Power	Arm in a cast
	Drive through with hitting shoulder		
	Watch ball hit strings	Accuracy	Watching target or opponent, not ball

continued

(a) Preparation (b) Execution (c) Follow-Through

FIGURE 18.2 Backhand

BACKHAND STROKE, continued

SKILL	CUE	WHY	COMMON ERROR
Execution, *continued*	Hit ball off front foot	Accuracy	Hitting ball into floor; hitting off back foot
	Shoulder parallel to floor through swing	Accuracy; shoulders dictate direction of ball	Swinging upward or dropping shoulder and skipping ball
	Follow-through at shoulder level		
	Racquet in "back-scratch position" (allows for more wrist snap in follow-through)		Open stance
	Hit and move to center of court	Ready for opponent's next shot	Hitting and standing still

SERVING

SKILL	CUE	WHY	COMMON ERROR
Drive	Visualize bull's-eye on front wall 1–2 feet up	Serve accuracy	Not having a target
Ball Drop	Contact ball between calf and knee		
	Drop ball to allow extension and follow-through or consistent drop	Correct, natural swing	Ball drops too close to body (jamming player)
	Drop—step—drive—move—follow ball		
Bull's–Eye	Should be ⅓ of distance between ball drop and side wall—not more than 1 foot from ground	Aim serve toward the corner—more difficult for opponent to reach	Hitting ball too high
	Hit and move toward center of court	Ready for opponent's return	Inconsistent movement
			Not moving to center after hitting
	Watch ball and know where opponent is		Not knowing where opponent is and not watching the ball

continued

SERVING, continued			
SKILL	**CUE**	**WHY**	**COMMON ERROR**
Lob	Firm wrist	Accuracy	Wrist snap
	Elbow extended	Not too much power	
	Like pitching horseshoes		Hitting ball
	Soft touch		
	Like pushing ball instead of hitting ball		
	Contact ball between waist and shoulder		
	High follow-through	Accuracy	No follow-through
	Pull arm to opposite shoulder		
High	Soft touch	Accuracy	Hitting ball too hard
	Contact on rise 15 to 18 feet—graze side		
Half	10 to 12 feet—approach opponent at shoulder height	Difficult for opponent to make offensive shot	No follow-through
	Pull arm to opposite shoulder		
	Hit and move to center of court; gain position	Ready for opponent's next shot	Not moving after serve

CORNER AND CEILING SHOTS			
SKILL	**CUE**	**WHY**	**COMMON ERROR**
Corner Shot (Offensive Shot)	Pinch in corner	Use when opponent is deep in court—ball stays in front court	Hitting too far from corner and too high
	Low shot		
	Pinch—ball hits side wall and then front wall, or vice versa		
	Near side corner	Hit low on front wall so that it bounces twice before reaching the other side wall (otherwise the ball will pop up off the other side wall)	

continued

CORNER AND CEILING SHOTS, *continued*			
SKILL	**CUE**	**WHY**	**COMMON ERROR**
Corner Shot (Offensive Shot), *continued*	Eyes focus on ball 1–2 feet from front		Eyes wandering
	Hit ball hard	Creates a spin and keeps ball in front court	Can't pinch ball if not hit hard enough
Ceiling Shot (Defensive Shot)	Forehand lob to ceiling		
(Use when not in position to make an offensive shot)	Volleyball overhand server motion	Accuracy	
	Aim to hit ceiling about 3 feet from front wall, depending on speed of ball	Should land about 4 feet from back wall and less than 4 feet high on back wall—very difficult for opponent to get an offensive shot	Hitting front wall first

SERVICE RETURN			
SKILL	**CUE**	**WHY**	**COMMON ERROR**
Strategy *Beginner*	Keep ball and self in center court		No plan
	Consistency; try to read ball and play		
Intermediate	Control rally with return of serve		On the defense, not offense
	Read serve and place ball to control rally		
Advanced	End rally with return of serve		
	Read serve and place ball to end rally		

SINGLES GAME

SKILL	CUE	WHY	COMMON ERROR
Scoring			
Server (Figure 18.3)	Server must stand in the service zone to serve		

continued

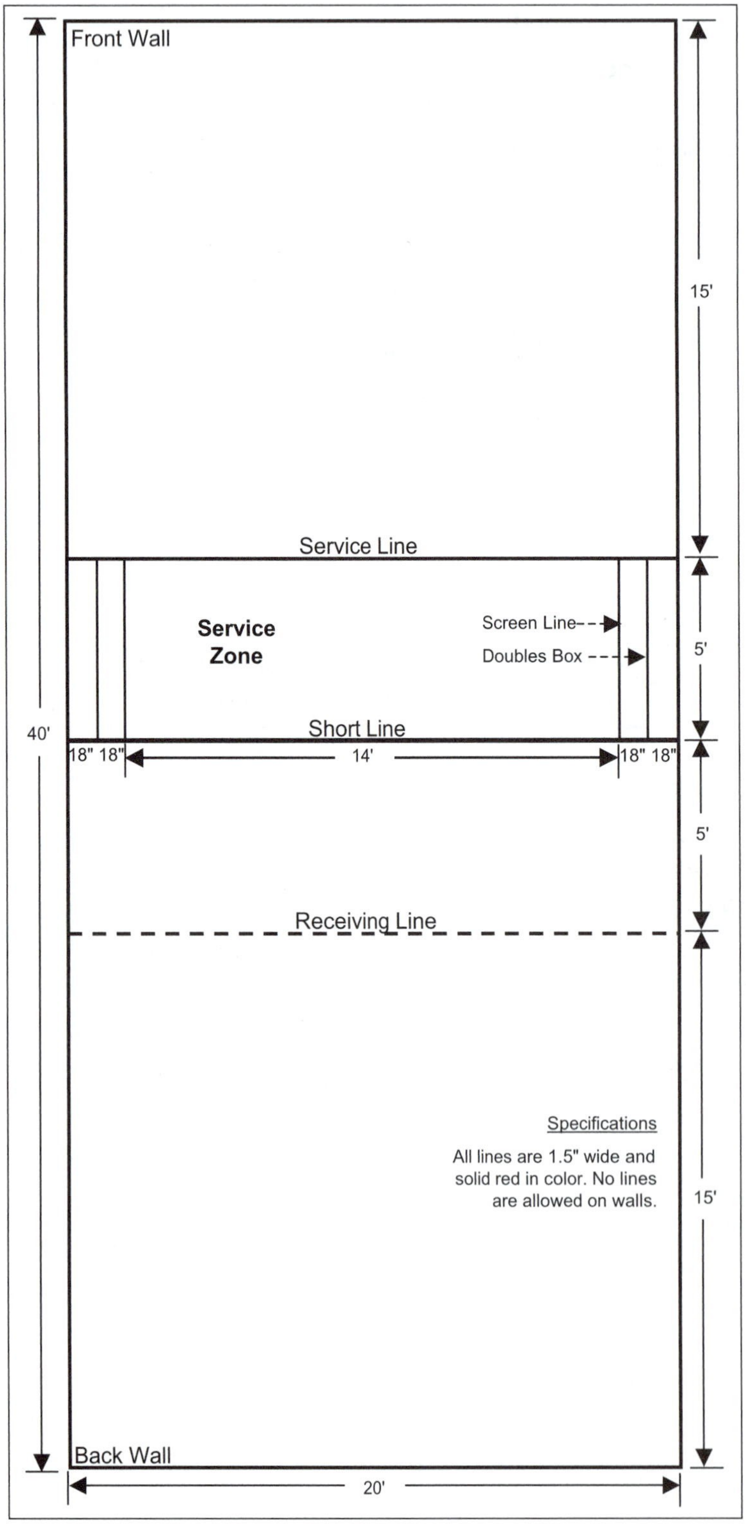

FIGURE 18.3 Racquetball Court

SINGLES GAME, continued			
SKILL	**CUE**	**WHY**	**COMMON ERROR**
Scoring *Server, continued*	The server must bounce the ball and then hit the ball to the front wall		
	The server must hit the ball behind the second line to start play		
	Only the server can score points		The receiver scores points
	Servers permitted 2 serves		Servers permitted only 1 serve
Receiver	If the receiver wins the rally, the receiver gains the serve and the opportunity to score		
Winning Score	The first player to win 15 points		
	There is no deuce game, overtime, or requirement to win by 2 points		
Match Play	First player to win 2 games		
Each Player Wins One Game	If both players win 1 game, play the next game to 11 points		
	The first player to reach 11 points wins the match		
	Serve in tiebreaker goes to player who scored the most points in the previous 2 games		
Strategy	Hit ball away from the opponent		
	If opponent is up close, hit far/passing shot		
	If opponent is back in court, use a dink shot/ pinch shot		
	Mix up shots		
	Mix up serves		
	Mix up sides of court where you stand to serve		

RACQUETBALL SERVICE RULES

Single-Fault Serves

1. Short serve: A serve that, after hitting the front wall, does not cross the short serve line before bouncing on the floor.
2. Long serve: A serve that, after hitting the front wall, hits the back wall before bouncing on the floor.
3. Three-wall serve: A serve that, after hitting the front wall, hits both side walls before bouncing on the floor.
4. Ceiling serve: A serve that, after hitting the front wall, hits the ceiling before bouncing on the floor.

Double-Fault (Side Out) Serves

1. Two consecutive single-fault serves.
2. Any serve that does not hit the front wall first. This includes hitting the front wall and another wall simultaneously (e.g., it bounces off a side wall, the floor, or the ceiling before hitting the front wall).
3. A serve that strikes the server or any part of the server's clothing or equipment.
4. Any serve that leaves the area of the court (e.g., through the observation window).

CUTTHROAT

SKILL	CUE	WHY	COMMON ERROR
Rules	Cutthroat is played with 3 players; a server plays against 2 receivers		
Server	Server has 2 serves		1 serve
	Serve has to hit behind second line		First line
	Must alternate hitting between server and 2 opponents		All 3 players hit
Receivers	When the server loses the rally, another player earns the serve		
Rotation	Rotate clockwise: player 1 trades with player 2; player 2 with player 3; player 3 with Player 1	Eliminates one player having to play against another's strong side every time he or she serves	Rotate randomly or in a circle

continued

CUTTHROAT, continued			
SKILL	**CUE**	**WHY**	**COMMON ERROR**
Rules, *Rotation*	Previous server trades with next server. The other player keeps his position. Player 1 trades with player 2, and player 3 remains. Next, player 2 trades with player 3, and player 1 remains. Then, player 3 trades with player 1, and player 2 remains. Repeat.		
	After each serve, player goes to the opposite corner of previous position		
Scoring	Only server can score points		
	Serve against the 2 opponents		Receivers can score if they win rally
Strategies	Hit ball farthest away from opponent		
	Go to middle of court after you serve or hit to be ready for the next ball		
Serving Rules	The ball may hit only 1 side wall and must strike the front wall first on the serve		A serve that hits the front wall and then either the back wall or ceiling is a fault
Receiving Rules	The ball must bounce behind the second line before the receiver may return the ball		
After the Ball Passes the Short Line	The receiver must return the ball to the front wall before it bounces on the floor twice		
	The return may hit any number of walls first as long as it hits the front wall before it hits the floor		

19

Recreational Walking, Running, and Hiking

INTRODUCTION TO RECREATIONAL WALKING

Walking for recreation and health has become one of the most popular physical activities enjoyed by adults (Select Marketing Groups of America, 2000). Everyone knows how to walk, it doesn't require any special equipment, it can be accomplished anywhere, and it is a social activity that can be done with a friend or a group. Many people prefer walking over running because it is less strenuous, but they can still get health benefits from their activity. Research has shown that adults who participate in moderately intense activity (such as brisk walking) on most days of the week can significantly reduce their risk for heart disease, breast cancer, and other health maladies (U.S. Department of Health and Human Services, 1998).

Since walking is such a popular activity for adults, it is important that walking for exercise be taught in the schools so that students learn to value walking as a health-enhancing activity. Physical educators should include some instruction on walking for exercise and give their students an opportunity to walk and be social in their classes. This kind of instruction can teach students that walking and talking together can be valuable and that they don't always have to work at high intensity levels to gain health benefits.

Lately, pedometers have become a popular tool for monitoring physical activity and are especially useful for monitoring walking. Pedometers are small devices (about the size of a pager) that are worn on the waistband of pants or shorts. They measure vertical movement and can keep track of steps, time, distance, and kilocalories expended (depending on the model purchased). Pedometers are inexpensive, easy to wear, and easy to read and understand.

WALKING SKILLS

Walking cues are given on the following pages, along with instructions for how to use a pedometer. Additionally, a few introductory pedometer activities are described and some references are given to explain where pedometers can be purchased at a reasonable price.

WALKING CUES

Encourage good posture when teaching walking. Arms should be bent, the head up, and the shoulders back. Walking is an even rhythm, and one foot is always in contact with the ground.

1. Head up, eyes forward, pull chin in
2. Swing arms
3. Shoulders back, tummy flat, chest out
4. Heel to toe

PEDOMETERS

A major objective of physical education is to teach students how they can be physically active both in and out of physical education (PE) class. Walking is a highly beneficial physical activity, and pedometers are a simple way to monitor that activity (see Figure 19.1). Pedometers even measure activity time and step count.

How Pedometers Work

Pedometers have a spring-loaded lever that registers a step count whenever there is vertical movement. Each vertical movement is counted as a step. While not all vertical movement is an actual step, all vertical movement can still be considered activity (standing up, sitting down, etc.). You should be careful to teach students that not every step count is an actual step. Help them understand that the number of step counts recorded can give them an estimate of how active they have been for a given time period.

How to Wear a Pedometer

Proper placement of the pedometer is important for the most accurate recording of steps. Pedometers are worn on the waistband of shorts or pants. They should be worn at the waistline, on the front side of the body, and be located directly above the knee (either right or left is fine). Pedometers should not be worn on the side of the body.

FIGURE 19.1 Pedometer

How Many Step Counts Are Enough?

It is important to teach students that step counts are personal. Not everyone will have the same number of step counts. The goal is to encourage physical activity. Some students will accumulate many thousands of steps in a day, while others will accumulate only a few thousand steps. The Presidential Active Lifestyle award (President's Council on Physical Fitness and Sports, 2001) recommends that young people accumulate 11,000 to 13,000 steps per day. While this standard will give you an idea of how many steps they need to earn an award, it is unrealistic to suggest that students who on a normal day might accumulate only 3,000 to 4,000 steps should set a goal of 11,000 to 13,000 steps. Externally imposed goals may seem unattainable for some students. Personal goal setting should be the objective. Allow students to take a few days to get a baseline of how active they currently are. Once they have a baseline, they can then set personal goals for improvement. A realistic goal for personal improvement might be to add the equivalent of a 30-minute walk to their goal (30-minute walk = 3,000 to 4,000 steps, depending on pace). Regardless of the number of steps students are taking, making them aware of their activity levels and helping them improve should be the ultimate objective.

Ideas for Introducing the Pedometer to Students

The following are a few simple activities that will introduce pedometers to students. These activities can be done during the PE class and are designed to help students understand how pedometers work and how they measure physical activity.

Sprint 2/Jog 2/Walk 2

Students set the pedometers to zero. Have them sprint two laps around the gym and stop immediately when they get back to check how many steps they took. Let them catch their breath. Have them jog two laps around the gym and check their steps. Let them catch their breath. Then have them walk two laps around the gym and check their steps. Ask the following questions: Which activity gave you the most steps? Why? Is it better to sprint, jog, or walk? Why? Remember that the focus is that all activity is good for health, whether you are walking, jogging, or sprinting.

Develop a Personal Fitness Routine

Have students pair up; challenge each pair to accumulate a total of 1,200 steps together. While one person does a strength (e.g., push-ups, sit-ups) or flexibility (stretching) exercise, the other person does an aerobic exercise (e.g., walking, jogging, locomotor movements) for 30 to 60 seconds. After 30 to 60 seconds, have them switch roles and continue working. Every 30 to 60 seconds, they switch roles until they have accumulated 1,200 steps between them. The goal is to teach students to work together while learning that fitness is fun and step counts are personal. One partner may get 700 steps while the other gets 500 steps, and that's OK! *Note:* It might be more motivating to have music that stops every 30 to 60 seconds, with about 5 seconds in between, playing while students are working.

Get in Sync

Have students select a partner. Encourage them to move in sync with their partner so that at the end of the movement they have the same number (or close to it) of steps. The team with the smallest difference between steps wins. The objective of this activity is to get the students to move in a synchronized way with a partner. Direct them to do walking, jogging, skipping A's, running A's, basketball slide, carioca, or other movements.

Lowest Count Wins

The purpose of this activity is to teach students that they can exercise without accumulating steps and learn to analyze different movements. Pair students up. The partners must come up with movements that accumulate the least number of steps possible. Partners with the lowest counts win. They must do something in the following three areas:

1. Ten repetitions of an upper-body strength exercise with correct form (offer students choices)
2. Travel across the floor to the other side of the gym
3. Ten repetitions of a lower-body strength exercise with correct form (offer students choices)

Change Placement

The purpose of this activity is to find creative ways to get the pedometer to count movements that it traditionally does not count. Encourage students to try the following activities and to come up with a way to get the pedometer to accurately count the movement for sit-ups, push-ups, arm circles, bicycle legs, and any dynamic stretch or core exercise.

How Much Do Pedometers Cost, and Where Can I Purchase Them?

The cost of pedometers varies depending on the manufacturer and the features. All pedometers have the ability to monitor step counts. Many models have features such as date and time, stopwatch, miles completed, kilocalories expended, and amount of time spent in activity. Prices generally range between $15 and $40. Educators who are buying multiple pedometers for their school may receive better pricing from vendors. A good resource for affordable pedometers is Walk4Life. See the FYI section for the website address.

Remember that the ultimate goal of recreational walking and using pedometers is to encourage active lifestyles. Walking is a highly beneficial activity that is overlooked in most PE programs. Teachers need not spend a lot of time on this unit, but including some instruction on the value of walking for healthy living is important. The resources in the FYI section will help educators develop appropriate activities for walking and using the pedometer.

FYI

For further information and special help, consult the following resources.

PUBLICATIONS FOR WALKING AND PEDOMETERS

Mize, M., & Decker, J. (2002). *Walking games and activities.* Champaign, IL: Human Kinetics.

Pangrazi, R. P., Beighle, A., & Sidman, C. L. (2003). *Pedometer power: 67 lessons for K–12.* Champaign, IL: Human Kinetics.

President's Council on Physical Fitness and Sports. (2001). *The President's challenge physical activity and fitness awards program.* Bloomington, IN: President's Council on Physical Fitness and Sports.
Select Marketing Groups of America. (2000). *The superstudy of sports participation* [print]. American Sports Data. www.sgma.com/research/marketplace/superstudy_sports_participation.html
Strand, B., Reeder, S., Scantling, E., & Johnson, M. (1997). *Fitness education: Teaching concepts-based fitness in schools.* Scottsdale, AZ: Gorsuch Scarisbrick.
U.S. Department of Health and Human Services. (1998). *Physical activity and health: A Report of the Surgeon General.* Atlanta, GA: Centers for Disease Control and Prevention.

WEBSITES FOR PEDOMETERS

Walk4Life
www.walk4life.com

INTRODUCTION TO RECREATIONAL RUNNING

By far the most popular forms of cardiorespiratory training in the United States are jogging and running. More than 17 million Americans jog or run to develop cardiovascular endurance. Why do Americans participate in these activities? They require no special skills, expensive equipment, or unusual facility, and they can be performed alone (Strand, Reeder, Scantling, & Johnson, 1997).

Another great reason to run is the way it makes you feel when you're done: the brain is clear, the body is physically refreshed, and the feeling stays with you for hours. The key to running injury-free is to wear a good pair of running shoes. Once you have good shoes, it only takes the first step and you're off to a new adventure, experiencing fresh air and different surroundings and letting go of the stress. Start today.

One advantage running has over walking is that a runner can cover a greater distance in a shorter period of time and thus can burn more calories. Jogging is defined as slow running at a comfortable pace at 8 to 12 minutes per mile. Running is defined as a faster pace of under 8 minutes per mile (Strand et al., 1997).

RECREATIONAL RUNNING SKILLS LISTED WITH CUES

In this chapter cues have been structured for the following: runner's cues, uphill running, downhill running (short, steep hills; gradual hills), building striders, striders, race course preparation, prerace routine, start of race, racing strategy, post-performance routines, and senior high school mileage.

TIPS

1. Have your runners hydrate well before, during, and after jogs, runs, and races.
2. It has been suggested that side-ache can be related to weak conditioning, weak abdominals, shallow breathing, a large meal before exercise, and dehydration or excessive exercise intensity. Pain may be relieved by holding the right arm over the head and stretching the side. This condition is not serious, just uncomfortable to the runner (Strand et al., 1997).

3. An important concept in running is that of pacing. In general, pacing means being able to run at a steady pace for a given length of time. Beginning runners have a tendency to start off too fast when given a certain distance to run. Soon they are walking because they have not been able to maintain the speed and have moved into anaerobic training. Teachers need to teach pacing in a jogging class and let students experience what it feels like to run at a steady state for various intensity levels for various lengths of time (Strand et al., 1997).
4. Have runners wear pedometers.

EQUIPMENT TIPS

1. Get a good pair of running shoes. Spend $50 or more and buy a brand-name running shoe. Make sure the shoe is comfortable.
2. Have water and towels available.
3. Wear clothing that is breathable.
4. Dress in layers for cold weather.

TEACHING IDEAS

1. Teachers sometimes get too caught up in the mechanics of running. If they would block out the upper body and see what the legs are doing, they would often find that the runner has good mechanics from the waist down. The runner is doing what feels good to her or him. Remember that the runner is propelled along the ground with the legs, not the arms, head, or hands. Arms are for balance. Reasons that runners may not have perfect mechanics might be a leg length discrepancy, spine curvature, or individual structural difference (people are wired differently). You are fooling around with nature when trying to make major changes in the mechanics of runners. The more they run, the more they will develop an efficient and economical running style. Relaxation and running economy are the keys. It also helps to inherit good genes.
2. Prepare an activity in which students are required to walk or run at a certain pace. Have them check their heart rates. Switch the pace during the workout and see if they can hold that pace. Have students talk about what happened during their run. Did they go too fast or slow when they started? What happened when they tried to keep a steady pace? For more running activities, read *Fitness Education* (Strand et al., 1997).
3. *Training for the beginning jogger* (Strand et al., 1997):
   a. Jog for 15 to 25 minutes; distance will vary from 1.5 to 3 miles; stretch.
   b. Jog for 20 to 30 minutes; distance will vary from 2 to 3.5 miles; stretch.
   c. Jog for 25 to 35 minutes; distance will vary from 2.5 to 4 miles; stretch.
4. *Training for joggers developing into runners* (Strand et al., 1997):
   a. Warm up with a 10- to 12-minute jog.
      Workout: four 800-meter runs, jog, rest 5 minutes between repetitions, stretch 5 to 15 minutes.
   b. Warm up with a 10- to 12-minute jog.
      Workout: six 400-meter runs, jog, rest 5 minutes between repetitions, stretch 5 minutes.

c. Warm up with a 10- to 12-minute jog.

   Workout: six 600-meter runs, jog, rest 5 minutes between repetitions, stretch 5 minutes.

5. *Training for fun runs, 5k, 10k, and up:*

   a. *Warm-up ritual/routine:* Jog about 1 mile with flat shoes, stretch out approximately 10 minutes, jog about 1 mile, building striders (2–4). Make the warm-up similar to race pre-performance ritual/routine.

   b. *Two workouts per day:* Start with daily early morning runs about 2 to 3 miles during training session at 70 to 80 percent of runner's top speed.

   c. *M–W–F afternoon workouts:* A hard workout might include Monday: long hard run; Wednesday: gradual uphill distance run; and Friday: fartlek training on a grass "hilly" park.

      T–Th–S: Easy workouts to finish running mileage for week's total.

   d. *Hard and easy weeks:* 10 to 15 miles one week, 20 to 25 miles the next week. Gradually build up mileage. Avoid overtraining as it causes injuries.

FYI

For further information and special help, consult the following organizations.

ORGANIZATIONS FOR RUNNING

Road Runners Club of America (RRCA)—National Association of Nonprofit Running Clubs
1150 South Washington Street, Suite 250
Alexandria, VA 22314-4493
Phone: (703) 836-0558
Fax: (703) 836-4430
E-mail: rrcaoffice@aol.com
Website: www.rrca.org

1. Provides information on local clubs.
2. Dedicated to promoting long-distance running as a competitive sport and as a healthful exercise.
3. Mission to represent and promote the common interests of its member clubs.
4. Running clubs join the RRCA for a modest annual fee and receive a range of programs and services in return. Services include nonprofit tax-exempt status, liability insurance, equipment insurance, and more.
5. Provides running books, videos, a curriculum guide for teachers and coaches, and a program guide for parents and children.

American Running Association
4405 East-West Highway, Suite 405
Bethesda, MD 20814
Phone: (800) 776-2732, (301) 913-9517
Fax: (301) 913-9520
E-mail: run@americanrunning.org
Website: www.americanrunning.org

RUNNER'S CUES

SKILL	CUE	WHY	COMMON ERROR
Relaxation (Figure 19.2)	Work on drills to relax face, jaw, neck, shoulders, arms, and hands	Conserves energy; smoother running technique	Tensing face, neck, jaws, shoulders, arms, hands
	Repeat the word "relax" or other predetermined cues		
Breathing (Figure 19.3)	Belly breathing	Avoids side-aches caused by breathing too fast and high in chest	Side-aches caused by breathing too fast and high in chest
	Pouch stomach out as you breathe in	Side aches also caused by starting too fast when not trained to do so	

FIGURE 19.2 Distance Running Relaxation Cues

FIGURE 19.3 Distance Running Cues

HILL RUNNING			
SKILL	**CUE**	**WHY**	**COMMON ERROR**
Uphill (Figure 19.4)	Short, quick steps	Prevents overstriding	Overstriding
	Quickly get feet back to touching ground	Faster	
	Compact stride contained within oneself		
	Run on forefoot		
	May lean forward depending on steepness of hill		
	Maintain the hill and power over the crest of the hill	Prevents slowing down at the top of the hill and losing momentum	Slowing down at the top of the hill
Downhill *Short, Steep Hills*	Brake to avoid falling and/or gaining too much speed		Gaining too much speed
	Use a heel-first running stride		
	Shorter braking stride		Overstriding
	Short, quick steps		
	Bring arms out further away from body	For balance	Arms too close to body
	Power down the hill with shorter, steeper hills	Prevents falling	

continued

FIGURE 19.4 Running Uphill

HILL RUNNING, continued

SKILL	CUE	WHY	COMMON ERROR
Gradual Hills	Make body perpendicular to hill		Overstriding
	Keep hips forward		
	Swing out arms away from body	For balance	
	Place foot under center of gravity	More efficient running technique	
	Let gravity work with you		
	Maintain body balance		

STRIDERS

SKILL	CUE	WHY	COMMON ERROR
Building Strider			
1–50 Meters	Start from jog; go into a good pace by 50 meters	Warm up for the race	Sprinting too soon
50–80 Meters	Accelerate to 80% of full speed	Get the muscles ready to race	Accelerating over 80% of full speed
80–100 Meters	Smooth transition to acceleration and then to deceleration		Decelerating too quickly
Strider			
Distance 50–100 Meters	Begin slowly, but by 50 meters athlete is at 80% speed		Athlete is over 80% speed

RACE COURSE PREPARATION

SKILL	CUE	WHY	COMMON ERROR
Knowing the Course	Go over course before race		Not taking time to go over course; arriving too late
	Walk or run course alone	Helps them focus	Running the course with team instead of individually; good for team unity, but all may not focus on course
	Have a tentative plan		
	Know where crucial hills and blind spots are on course		Daydreaming during course

PRERACE ROUTINES/RITUALS

SKILL	CUE	WHY	COMMON ERROR
Prerace	When countdown starts for the athlete, do not interfere	If the coach's job has been done well, there is no need for last-minute coaching	Pep talks to teams and individuals just before race
	Athlete knows what is expected early in week		
	40–60 minute warm-up before competition. Example: Athlete finds quiet spot; makes rest-room stop; jogs about 1 mile; stretches alone; makes restroom stop; puts on spike shoes or racing flats; jogs; 2–6 building striders; walks or jogs 5 minutes		
	A shorter warm-up is needed		
Hot Day Warm-Up	Hydrate well all day		
	Warm up in shade if possible		
	A longer warm-up is needed		
Cold Day Warm-Up	Don't forget to hydrate	Keeps body in top performance; prevents energy loss; gets the muscles ready to go	

RACING

SKILL	CUE	WHY	COMMON ERROR
Start	Both arms down		Both arms up
	Dominant leg back	More powerful start	Weakest leg back
	Most weight on back foot		Weight even or too much on front leg
Leg action	Push off back foot first	Faster start; legs will be in correct running stride	Forgetting to push with back leg first
Arm action	Arms come up	To protect yourself at the crowded start	Left arm forward and left leg forward
Strategy *Beginning of a Race*	Begin race significantly fast in order to gain good position	Gives you a jump start	Getting behind at start
	Maintain good early position		Going out too fast for too long
	Be near front		
	Control breathing		High, quick breathing
	Find key people position		
	Fast and relaxed		
	"I feel strong"		
	Draw into oneself, the sport, and opponent		Responding to harassment by spectators
Tactics during a Race (Figure 19.5, page 246)	Catch someone and pass 'em	Provides a specific goal on which the runner focuses	Not focusing on a runner or group of runners ahead of you to pass
	Catch someone and beat 'em	Keeps the mind alert	
	Don't get into no-man's land	Other runners motivate and support you for maximum potential; less likely to give up	Not staying with the pack or another runner
	Don't run alone; stay with group		
	Focus on the runner in front of you by imagining that you are connected with a rope and are slowly being pulled in		

continued

FIGURE 19.5 Tactics during a Race

RACING, continued			
SKILL	**CUE**	**WHY**	**COMMON ERROR**
Tactics during a Race, *continued*	Accelerate and pass runners after a turn, over a hill, or through trees	Discourages other runners	Don't attack or charge up hills; it's not energy efficient
	Blind spots are effective for 20–50 yards when runners cannot be seen		
	Use of groups is helpful to break opposing groups (extended acceleration of 100–200 yards)		
Finish Line	Run through the line	A better time	A racer might pass you
Postperformance Ritual	Flexibility exercises, static stretches	Blood is circulating in muscles to get a better stretch	Overtraining runners
	Jogging, easy running (no acceleration, flat terrain, training shoes)	A cooldown helps recovery; gets rid of lactic acid wastes	Could injure legs by overtraining tired muscles

MILEAGE			
SKILL	**CUE**	**WHY**	**COMMON ERROR**
High School Distance Races	2–3 miles		Overtraining runners
	Cross-country distance is 3 miles (5 kilometers)		School schedules often require 2 competitions per week. If this is done all season, it may be too much racing.
			Injuries from lack of proper adaptation time

INTRODUCTION TO RECREATIONAL HIKING

It's often thought that hikers are just outdoorsy types. After all, it takes real passion to spend all day trudging to the top of a mountain, only to turn around and come back. However, hiking comes with both physical and mental benefits that can be reaped even from a short evening hike on a local nature trail.

Since you have to walk in order to hike, the health benefits of hiking are comparable to those of walking. Research has shown that "walking may help reduce the risk of age-related conditions like heart disease, insulin resistance and type 2 diabetes, as well as stroke, high blood pressure and metabolic syndrome" (Upton, 2005, p. 1). Other studies have also shown that adults who walk for 2½ to 4 hours a week "tend to have less than half the prevalence of elevated serum cholesterol as those who do not walk or exercise regularly" (Greenberg, 2004, p. 404).

So, why hike? If there are so many healthy reasons to walk, why not just stick close to home with smooth sidewalks and civilization? Hiking on uneven surfaces may improve balance and blood pressure even more than simply walking on smooth surfaces will. Consider this study from Oregon Health Sciences University: "Participants (all over 60 years old) significantly improved their blood pressure when they walked on cobblestones for half-hour a day compared to those walking on smooth surfaces for three times a week" (Upton, 2005, p. 6). The research was influenced because the study participants used cobblestone walking paths that the Chinese say stimulate acupressure points on the feet (Upton, 2005, p. 6).

Hiking provides a wide variety of trails and different terrain for any level of hiker. Hiking uphill and downhill can build muscles and strengthen bones ("Hike for good health," 2002, p. 9). The incline of hiking provides a greater cardiovascular workout than walking does. In addition, hiking allows the participant to enjoy nature's fresh air and sunshine, a good source of vitamin D—just remember to wear sunscreen!

Hiking is also a great way to relieve stress. Wherever the hiker goes, there are beautiful surroundings. Hiking can be quiet, peaceful, and renewing; being able to view the beauty of this earth can bring peace to a person's life. Taking a trail that leads to the top of a peak, ridge, or just an overlook leaves the mind and body with a great sense of accomplishment after reaching the destination.

HIKING SKILLS LISTED WITH CUES

The cues contained in this chapter are concerned with methods of hiking properly, including using correct hiking equipment, treating blisters, hiking downhill, hiking uphill, and hiking down steep terrain.

EQUIPMENT TIPS

1. The most important item is sturdy hiking shoes. Shoes don't need to be the top-of-the-line Gore-Tex backpacking boots, but they should have good tread, be broken in (to prevent blisters), and be comfortable.
2. Wear socks that wick away moisture. Wigwam has a Gore-Tex sock. Anything with Gore-Tex will bump up price by 100 percent or more.
3. The company Under Armour offers underwear, T-shirts, and compression shorts that wick moisture and prevent chaffing. They are made from 86 percent nylon and 14 percent elastane.
4. Shirts and pants with nylon that wick moisture away and/or have a UVA rating of 30 percent are ideal. The higher the UVA rating is, the higher the cost of the item will be. Have short- and long-sleeved T-shirts as well as short and long pants available.
5. Sunscreen, hat, and sunglasses are essential for hiking outdoors.
6. A hiking stick helps with balance.
7. Most hiking trails don't have drinkable water, so bring your own. How much depends on the individual person, the location of the hiking area, and how long the hiker plans to be hiking. "Rangers at Grand Canyon National Park recommend 2 gallons per person for a full day of hot-weather hiking . . . in cooler climes, you may be able to hike on less than 1 gallon a day. The important thing is that you pay attention: to your body, to your thirst, to your environment, to your map" (Berger, 1997, p. 162). Most short hikes will take a couple of hours, so a whole gallon isn't necessary; a more general rule to follow is drinking 1 liter per hour. Water can easily be dumped, so to be safe, always bring more than you think you will need (Sinclair, 2004, pp. 31–33). There are water bottles with filters—these cost anywhere from $20 to $50 a bottle. You can fill the bottle with water from a stream safely for 40 to 50 times before you have to purchase a new filter. Replacement filters cost less than $10.
8. It is wise to check the weather of the area where you plan to hike before the trek.
9. Get a map or trail guide of the hiking area as well as a compass. Getting lost is no fun and can easily be prevented by carrying a map and taking frequent inventory of the surrounding area as you progress. For most hiking areas, there are several guidebooks with decent maps in them. For even greater detail, topographical maps can be purchased at the forest station in a hiking area.

TEACHING IDEAS

1. Have your hikers hydrate well before, during, and after hikes.
2. Prevent blisters by making sure shoes fit properly. Make sure hikers keep their feet as dry as possible.
3. Go on shorter hikes until shoes break in and fit the feet of the hikers. If necessary, have hikers wear two pairs of socks.

4. If hikers feel an irritation in shoes, have them stop and take care of it. If they wait, the irritation can develop into a huge blister.
5. Have hikers carry a first-aid kit with antiseptic (such as Neosporin), zinc oxide ointment, and moleskin or second skin for blister care and treatment.
6. If a hiker gets a blister, have him treat it by doing the following:
   a. If the blister has not opened yet, tell the hiker not to open it to drain it. Putting needles or other objects into the blister only introduces the possibility of infection, whereas the closed blister is sterile.
   b. If the blister has popped and drained on its own, have the hiker cut away the dead skin. Do not peel it away, as this can lead to peeling away live skin.
   c. Make sure the hiker cleans the wound with soap and warm water. He should also use an antiseptic and cover the wound with an antibiotic.
   d. If the hiker is in a clean environment, the wound can be left open to dry out. If the hiker continues to be active, he should cover the blister up with moleskin or second skin to help keep it clean. Both items are available at local pharmacies.
   e. The best thing to do is rest and let the blister heal. The more active one is, the more chance there is of infection. If the hiker thinks the blister is infected and notices red streaks or the area getting hot, he should see a physician.

FYI

For further information and special help, consult the following organizations and resources.

WEBSITES FOR HIKING

American Hiking Society
www.americanhiking.org

Hiker's Corner—Hiking and Backpacking Gear
www.hikerscorner.com

Hiking.biz
www.hiking.biz

LifeTips—Hiking
www.hiking.lifetips.com

PUBLICATIONS

Berger, K. (1997). *Everyday wisdom: 1,001 expert tips for hikers.* Emmaus, PA: Backpacker.

Greenberg, J. S., Dintiman, G. B., & Oakes, B. M. (2004). *Physical fitness and wellness.* Champaign, IL: Human Kinetics.

"Hike for good health." (October 2002). *Consumer Reports on Health, 14,* 9.

"Mental Health: 10 ways to keep your brain in top shape." (October–November 2003). *Massage and Bodywork, 18,* 168.

Sinclair, J. (2004). *Cache trails.* Logan, UT: Bridgerland Audubon Society.

Upton, J. (September 2005). "Walk yourself well: EN's step-by-step guide to good health." *Environmental Nutrition, 28,* 1 and 6.

Williams, M. (May 26, 2006). Personal Interview. Athletic Trainer, Utah State University, Logan, Utah.

HIKING PREP

SKILL	CUE	WHY	COMMON ERROR
Measure a Hiking Stick	Bend elbow with arm parallel to ground; stick should reach hand	Stick is appropriate in height	Using stick that is too short
Preventing Blisters	Wear shoes that are broken in	Prevents blisters	Wearing sandals, tennis shoes, or street shoes that are flat on the bottom; wearing hiking shoes that aren't broken in
	Stop when you feel rubbing		Not stopping—blister gets worse
(Figure 19.6)	Carry first-aid kit	To treat blisters and other injuries	Not packing a first-aid kit

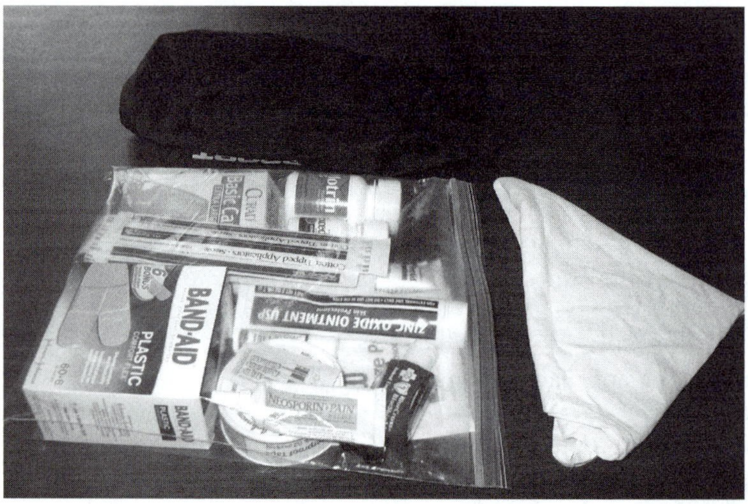

FIGURE 19.6 Carry First-Aid Kit to Treat Blisters and Other Injuries

WHILE HIKING			
SKILL	**CUE**	**WHY**	**COMMON ERROR**
Hiking Terrain (Figure 19.7)	Hike on uneven surfaces	Burns more calories; promotes better balance	
Hydrating the Body (Figure 19.8)	Drink plenty of water	Prevent heat exhaustion and heat stroke	Not bringing enough water or running out of water
Resting (Figure 19.8)	Take frequent rests	To conserve energy for a longer hike	Hiking too fast or for too long without rest
Keeping Balance (Figure 19.9, page 252)	Use a hiking stick	Provides balance; takes pressure off body back and legs, especially when packs are heavy and terrain is steep and rough	Not using a hiking stick
Relaxation (Figure 19.10, page 252)	Pause to enjoy the natural scenery	Provides sense of accomplishment; decreases stress	Being tense
	Breathe in the fresh air	Increases blood flow to the brain	

FIGURE 19.7 Hiking Terrain

FIGURE 19.8 Drinking and Resting

FIGURE 19.9 Keeping Balance

FIGURE 19.10 Relaxation

CLIMBING

SKILL	CUE	WHY	COMMON ERROR
Hiking Uphill (Figure 19.11)	Step on balls of feet	Conserve energy	Weight on heels

DESCENDING

SKILL	CUE	WHY	COMMON ERROR
Hiking Downhill	Short, quick steps	Balance weight transfer; conserves energy	Taking long strides
	Bend knees	Absorb the momentum	Straight legs
	Use hiking stick	For balance	No stick
	Look down	So you do not trip on objects on trail	Looking up

continued

FIGURE 19.11 Hiking Uphill

FIGURE 19.12 Hiking Down Steep Terrain

DESCENDING, continued

SKILL	CUE	WHY	COMMON ERROR
Hiking Down Steep Terrain (Figure 19.12)	Side-step	Prevents falling forward	Feet forward going downhill
	Lean toward hill	Prevents falling downhilll	Lean out away from hill
	Bend knees; back straight—be tall	Keep balance	Straight legs
	Pole on downhill side	Keep balance	

TREATMENT OF BLISTERS

SKILL	CUE	WHY	COMMON ERROR
How to Treat Blisters	Keep blister covered	Prevents infection—protects the area	Popping blisters causes infection
	Apply ointment with cotton swab	Prevents infection	Not carrying ointment in pack
	Apply large bandage to cover area, or apply moleskin	Protects and pads area	

20

Soccer

INTRODUCTION

Soccer is a game that everyone can play, a game that keeps you fit and challenges you to the max. Soccer has been around for centuries and is played in every country of the world. It has been termed the Sport of the World, and rightly so. In most countries, it is more commonly known as *football*, and here in the United States it is known as *soccer.* What makes it so exciting is the challenge of a whole team trying to score. Soccer is a simple game, one that all students will enjoy.

SKILLS LISTED WITH CUES

The following soccer skills are included in this chapter: ball control and ball control drills; the dribble and dribbling drills; passing and two-player passing; chipping and two- to three-player chipping drills; the long-pass and two-player drills; trapping and trapping drills; kicking-shooting and kicking-shooting drills; heading; throw-in; goalkeeping; goaltending; defense; and offense.

EQUIPMENT TIPS

The first thing you need to consider is proper equipment:

1. A 12-inch ball is appropriate for students 12 years and older.
2. One ball for every two to four students is recommended to practice skills. The students can work in small groups, with no standing in line waiting for a turn. This maximizes student involvement.
3. Students should wear comfortable clothes that are appropriate for hot weather.
4. Comfortable shoes (no sandals): cleats are not needed at this level of play. Decide whether cleated shoes will be allowed in class. Be aware that some toes may get stepped on. However, cleated shoes are recommended for recreational soccer teams.

5. Shin guards are important in preventing injury to the anterior compartment of the shin (this anterior compartment is susceptible to injury because there is very little room for tissue and blood). It is recommended that all students have shin guards, especially for games.
6. The field of play can be an actual soccer field or an open, grassy area at the school or a nearby park.
7. Use cones to outline the field. Flags can be substituted for goals. Half cones are great to use in drills. You can make a set of goals 3 feet high × 3 feet wide out of PVC pipe.
8. Use colored vests to divide students into teams.

TEACHING IDEAS

1. Include warm-up with every class practice. A proper warm-up involves moderate physical activity, such as jogging or a game of keep-away with the soccer ball. This, along with proper stretching, decreases the likelihood of injury.
   - Warm-up
   - Elevation of heart rate
   - Breaking a sweat is important
   - Ideas for warm-ups: running and dynamic stretching
2. Safety concerns:
   - Emphasize the importance of playing with control and being aware of others' personal space. Use mini-games to reduce the number of players in a game situation.
   - Be prepared for accidents. Have a first-aid kit available and a first-aid plan.
   - Have plenty of water available during the activity, especially on a hot day.
   - Avoid playing during the heat of the day when possible.
   - Ensure no wearing of jewelry, shirts tucked in, and proper clothing for weather conditions.
   - Have proper warm-up and cooldown periods to prevent possible muscle injuries.

MINI-GAMES

1. Play games of 3 on 3, 4 on 4, and 5 on 5.
2. Scoring options in these games: ball goes over endline, 1 point; ball goes through two cones, 1 point.

FYI

For further information and special help, consult the following organizations.

ORGANIZATIONS

American Youth Soccer Organization
12501 S. Isis Avenue
Hawthorne, CA 90250
Phone: (310) 643-6455
Fax: (310) 643-5310
Website: www.soccer.org

U.S. Soccer Federation
1801–1811 South Prairie Avenue
Chicago, IL 60616
Phone: (312) 808-1300
Fax: (312) 808-1301
Website: www.ussoccer.com

Women's United Soccer Association
6205 Peachtree Dunwoody Rd, 15th Floor
Atlanta, GA 30328
Website: www.wusa.com

Major League Soccer
420 5th Avenue, 7th Floor
New York, NY 10018
Phone: (212) 450-1200
Fax: (212) 450-1300
Website: www.mlsnet.com

U.S. Youth Soccer
9220 World Cup Way
Frisco, TX 75034
Phone: (800) 476-2237
Website: www.usyouthsoccer.org

BALL CONTROL/BALL CONTROL DRILLS

SKILL	CUE	WHY	COMMON ERROR
Ball Control			
Knowing the Ball	Kicking the ball	To get familiar with the ball and how it works	
Kicking Top of Ball	Ball goes down (ball stays low)	Keeps ball low and in control	
Kicking Middle of Ball	Ball goes straight		
Kicking Bottom of Ball (Figure 20.1)	Ball goes up (like a pop-up in softball)	For chipping and defensive clears	
Kicking Left Side of Ball	Ball goes right		
Kicking Right Side of Ball	Ball goes left		
Ball Control Drills			
Juggling the Ball: Try to keep the ball in the air, using only the feet, as long as you can. Goal is 2 balls, then 3, then 4. Players who can do between 5 and 10 have good ball control.		Increases ball touches, familiarity with the ball, thus increasing ball control skills	
Experimenting with Ball (Partner Drill): Players strike the ball on the 5 surfaces listed above		Again, just getting familiar with all the different surfaces	

FIGURE 20.1 Ball Control

DRIBBLE/DRIBBLE DRILLS

SKILL	CUE	WHY	COMMON ERROR
Dribble Technique	Caress ball in stride	If you push the ball too far ahead, a defender can easily steal it away	
Dribble Ball with Different Surfaces of Foot (Figure 20.2)	Inside, outside, sole, or laces		
	Close control; keep ball close	Keeps ball close and under control, which makes it much more difficult for the defender to gain possession	
	Push firmly		
	Head up; pull chin back		
	Arms out; elbows bent for balance		
Action of Dribble	Depending on the situation, change pace and direction		

continued

FIGURE 20.2 Dribble

DRIBBLE/DRIBBLE DRILLS, continued

SKILL	CUE	WHY	COMMON ERROR
Dribble Drills Using 6 or 7 cones for each small group, have students dribble through cones in a weaving pattern		Learn how to keep control of the ball while dribbling; cones help players control the ball. The goal is for the player to stay close to the cones while dribbling.	
Races			

PASSING/PASSING DRILLS

SKILL	CUE	WHY	COMMON ERROR
Passing			
Push Pass	Pendulum swing with the foot (like on a grandfather's clock)	For easy, quick passes to a teammate	
Foot Position	Ankle firm		
Inside	Strike ball with instep of foot		
Outside	Strike ball with outside of foot		
Laces	Strike ball with laces, not the toe	Don't toe ball, because there is no accuracy	
Striking the Ball Action	Knee over ball	To have more control so the ball won't go flying up in the air	
2-Player Passing Drills *5- to 10-Yard Passes:* Pass back and forth to partner, using different surfaces of foot		Gain familiarity with the technique of the push pass	
		Kicking with right and left foot gives you an edge over the average player, who can't pass with both feet	
Passing Accuracy: Player 1 stands with legs shoulder width apart; player 2 tries to pass the ball through partner's legs; switch positions		Gain accuracy with the push pass	

CHIPPING/CHIPPING DRILLS

SKILL	CUE	WHY	COMMON ERROR
Chipping the Ball			
Eyes	Focus on the bottom part of the ball	Clears the ball out of the defense, or for a pass over the opposing team to one of your teammates	
Approach	Approach the ball straight on		
Action	It's a quick, hard stab under the ball (like a shovel)		
	Bring your knee toward your chest		
Chipping Drills *2-Player Drills:* 1. Practice chipping to each other from 10–20 yards apart			
2. Accuracy: Mark off an area 5–10 feet square using cones (the distance from each box is variable). Two players stand in the coned area and chip to their partner.			
3-Player Drill: Player 1 passes the ball to player 2, who passes ball to player 3, and player 3 tries to chip the ball over player 2 to player 1. Rotate players so that each player goes to the position spot they passed to (player 1 goes to player 2's spot, player 2 goes to player 3's spot, and player 3 goes to player 1's spot). Repeat.			

LONG PASS/LONG-PASS DRILLS

SKILL	CUE	WHY	COMMON ERROR
Long Pass		Used for crosses and shooting	
Ankle	Ankles firm (no floppy feet)		Stronger, more controlled pass
	Take a slightly angled approach		
Nonkicking Foot	Place it next to the ball	Helps create greater velocity in kicking foot	
	Toe is pointing at target, so ball will go to target		
Kicking Foot	Strike the ball with laces and inside of foot	More foot surface is on the ball; better control	
Used for Corner Kicks and Clears	Follow through with the foot pointed and leg toward the target		
	Strike the ball where the ball touches the grass; keep your ankle locked when striking; your leg kicks up and into the ball with a good follow-through		
2-Player Drills *At Least 20 Yards Apart:* Player 1 passes to player 2; pass back and forth; have players take a step backward each time they do a successful pass at that distance			

TRAPPING/TRAPPING DRILLS			
SKILL	**CUE**	**WHY**	**COMMON ERROR**
Trapping			To gain quick possession of uncontrolled ball
Trap	Absorb ball and soften the hit by moving your body away slowly	Controls the ball, brings it right to your feet	
Different Surfaces	Cushion the ball; stop the ball as if catching an egg		
Foot	Trap ball with soft feet		
Thigh (Figure 20.3)	Trap ball with upper front of thigh		
Chest (Figure 20.4)	Trap ball with breastbone		
Head	Trap ball with forehead		
Receiving the Pass	Present the trapping surface to the ball; take the pace off the ball by withdrawing the body part as soon as the ball is received		
Trapping Drills *Each Player Has a Ball:* Have the player throw the ball up in the air, and practice using the different surfaces to trap the ball		Helps player practice the skills of trapping	

FIGURE 20.3 Thigh Trap

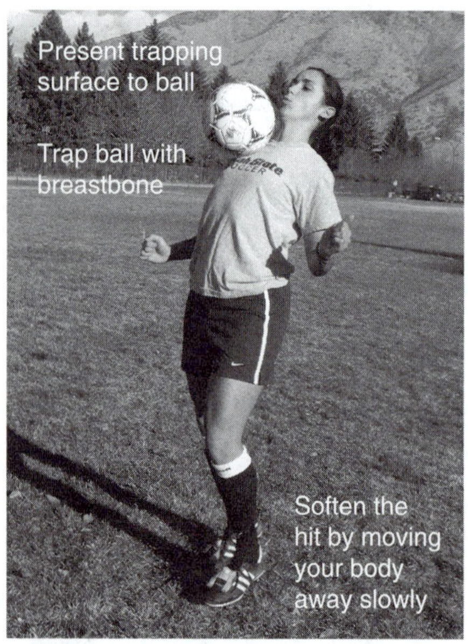

FIGURE 20.4 Chest Trap

KICKING-SHOOTING AND KICKING-SHOOTING DRILLS

SKILL	CUE	WHY	COMMON ERROR
The Kick (a striking action executed with the feet—e.g., the long-pass kick, corner kick, goal kicks)	Body is stationary and leg is straight, with little flex at the knee; there is minimal movement of the arms and the trunk; concentrate on the ball; hold arms out for balance		
The Shot			
Nonkicking Foot	Place the nonkicking foot alongside the ball, toes pointing at the target	Ball goes where the toes point	
Leg	Like firing a cannonball. Pull back the kicking leg; have it pointing at the target.		
Kicking Foot	After shooting, follow through. After the follow-through, land on the kicking foot (not the nonkicking foot).	Puts more power and control in the stroke	
Ankle (of Kicking Foot)	Ankle is firm; toes are pointing down		
Head	Keep head down and chest over the ball	To keep the ball low	Head up
Kicking/Shooting Drills Each player has a ball and faces the goal; have each player practice shooting on the goal (no goalie is needed). To prevent injury, don't retrieve balls until all have been shot.			

HEADING

SKILL	CUE	WHY	COMMON ERROR
Head	Strike ball with top of forehead (where the hairline meets the forehead)	It doesn't hurt when heading on the hairline; more control	
Eyes	Keep eyes open—watch the ball meet your forehead		Close eyes
Upper Body	Draw upper body back (pull shoulders back)	It will provide more power in the header	
Chin	Pull chin in		
Follow-Through	You strike the ball—do not let the ball hit you		No power in the header if you let it hit you
Torso	Snap the upper body forward to meet the ball (whip the body through the ball)	Most of the power comes from here	
Offensive Header	Head downward toward goal	Use offensive header for passing and shooting	
Defensive Header	Head upward	Used to clear the danger area	

THROW-INS

SKILL	CUE	WHY	COMMON ERROR
Throw-Ins	When the ball crosses the touchline into out-of-bounds, it is thrown back onto the field (which is the only time a field player may touch the ball with the hands), stand where the ball crossed the line and throw from behind the head (USSF rules)		

continued

THROW-INS, continued			
SKILL	**CUE**	**WHY**	**COMMON ERROR**
The Throw (Figures 20.5 and 20.6)	Face the field		
	Use both hands		
	Start behind the head, and throw over the head (follow through with both hands)		
	Keep both feet behind the touchline; both feet must stay on the ground		
	Arms throw outward		
Follow-Through (Figure 20.7)	Body snaps through the throw	More power in the throw	
Short and Close Throw	Snap (arms snap down, hands and palms down)		
High and Low Throw	Snap up! Throw up and over		

FIGURE 20.5 Soccer Throw-In (Hand/Arm Position, Side View)

FIGURE 20.6 Soccer Throw-In (Hand/Arm Position, Front View)

FIGURE 20.7 Soccer Throw-In (Follow-Through)

GOALKEEPING

SKILL	CUE	WHY	COMMON ERROR
Receiving	Goalie calls for the ball		
Low Balls	Scoop into body with hands outstretched, fingers spread; wrap it up		
Hand Positions for Catching in Air	Big hands		
The "M"	Palms up, pinkies together; used to receive low balls		
"Hershey Kiss" or Triangle	Palms out, pointer fingers touching; thumbs create a "Hershey Kiss" or triangle	So ball will not slip through fingers	
Punching	Clear the ball away from the goal, using a flat surface on the hand	Used for high balls hit over the top of the goal; used when diving to hit the ball away from the goal	
Diving (Figures 20.8 and 20.9)	Lunge and cover lots of area with body		
	When diving, land on the outer part of the thigh, hip, and side of the upper body; don't land on the knees		
	Reach out with hands		
	Catch the ball and pull it in		
Distributing Ball	Balls can be distributed by punting, rolling, or throwing		

FIGURE 20.8 Goalie Dive

FIGURE 20.9 Goalie Dive Landing

GOALTENDING

SKILL	CUE	WHY	COMMON ERROR
Throwing (10–20 yards)	Twisting action will limit bounce for player receiving		No spin on release makes ball bounce and difficult to receive
Rolling (10 yards or less)	Rolling a bowling ball	To make it easier for player receiving	Holding ball too loose
	Underhand pitch in softball		Too short a follow-through will not allow ball to reach target
	Roll in front of or directly to player's feet		Releasing ball too high causes it to bounce and be hard to control

DEFENSE

SKILL	CUE	WHY	COMMON ERROR
Tactics	Team gets compact	To give attackers very little room to play in	Team is spread out in front of goal, creating space for attackers to exploit
	Players in front of goal will be close together, closing down goal-scoring options for attackers		Defense posture is loose, allowing goal-scoring opportunities
	*Stagger the defense for depth and support		Players are caught in a straight line across the field, allowing for penetration with a single pass
	*Delay opposition as far away from goal as possible to allow players to recover		Team in possession allowed to freely advance forward
	†Players closest to ball must provide immediate pressure		Closest individual defender does not delay attacker

*Important when the defense brings the ball up; supports the offensive attack

†Important in an attacking situation on defense

continued

DEFENSE, continued			
SKILL	**CUE**	**WHY**	**COMMON ERROR**
Tactics, *continued*	†Keep playing space narrow for opponents by channeling toward touchline or supporting defenders		Defending with body square to attacker allows for options to the sides or through legs
	†Keep balance of team organized through communication		Confusion and disarray in defense through lack of communication
	If ball cannot be won directly from challenge, clear ball away from danger area either upfield or over touchline	Players in their defensive third of the field attempt to advance ball under extreme pressure and lose possession, possibly creating goal-scoring opportunity for opponent	
	*Once ball has been recovered, offense begins immediately	While defense is on its heels	Slow transition from defending to attacking
	Results can be achieved through man-to-man marking, zonal marking, or a combination		
Objectives	Regain possession		
	Deny penetration		
	Slow down attack		
	Stop shots		
Stance	Bend knees slightly; bend elbows (ready for action); eyes on the ball and the opponent		
Tips	Keep on the goal side of your opponent		
	Be first to the ball		
	Defend the ball, not the player		

*Important when the defense brings the ball up; supports the offensive attack

†Important in an attacking situation on defense

OFFENSE

SKILL	CUE	WHY	COMMON ERROR
Tactics	*Offense begins immediately when ball has been won	To have many options that the defenders must contend with	Delay in transition may result in loss of possession
	*All players are involved in offense from point of recovery		Player fails to move into offense, limiting options
	*Create options by utilizing width of field (spread the field out)		Attacking players squeezing in toward center of field closes down space for players in possession
	†Quickly move ball into defensive half through quick, short, crisp passes to open players, directly to forward target, or by dribbling	To open up more space for the attackers to play in	Delay in advancing ball allows defense to recover
	†Forward movement of offensive players not in possession creates dribbling or passing opportunities for player with ball		Lack of movement provides few options for player with ball
	Vary focus and method of attack		Team becomes predictable and easy to defend
	Creativity and imagination in final offensive third of field are vital to creating chances for scoring		Lack of imagination and creativity stifles attack
	†Taking risk in front of opponents' goal is encouraged as loss of possession does not create immediate danger	The ultimate objective in soccer is to score goals; therefore, always attempt to end attack with a shot or goal	Without taking risk in front of defensive team's goal, scoring will become difficult

continued

*Important when offense begins an attack

†Important when offense is attacking and trying to score

OFFENSE, continued			
SKILL	**CUE**	**WHY**	**COMMON ERROR**
Tactics, *continued*			Teams that play so as not to lose rather than to win develop players who find the game to be dull and boring
Dribbling	Keep head up; look for a pass		Body forward and erect
Off the Ball	Get on the goal side of the opponent		
	Penetrate the defense		
	Move into empty space, always creating chances		

21

Softball, Fast-Pitch and Slow-Pitch

INTRODUCTION

"Safe!" yells the umpire, as the runner slides into home. The crowd goes wild as the home team wins the tournament.

One of softball's unique features is that it is a hometown game that pulls a community together. Recreation departments accommodate people of different ages and provide opportunities for them to join youth, coed, female, and male leagues. Nearly every town, small or large, has a ball diamond where residents gather to enjoy the cool evenings and chat with neighbors while watching the game. Opportunities to teach softball skills begin in middle school and continue through high school and college.

SKILLS LISTED WITH CUES

Softball requires a variety of skills: throwing, catching, windmill pitching, hitting, sacrifice bunting, baserunning, runner-on-base techniques, the catcher, sliding (straight-in slide), and slow-pitch skills. The use of these organized cues and progressions can be very beneficial.

TIPS

1. Going over players' positions before the season begins creates harmony and team success. Explain the mental and physical expectations of each player and her or his role on the team. For example, a player's responsibility might be sitting on the bench, warming up ready to hit or run, or perhaps to play second or third base if an infielder is injured or is not having a good game. A team member who plays second base in one game may play shortstop or be a defensive replacement in the next game. This approach develops a team concept, team cohesion, and a sense of personal responsibility to and for the team. If a player makes an error, have him or her focus on the next play. Direct the energy into a positive focus. Pick up a rock, pretend the rock is the error, and toss it—get rid of it.

2. Make practice fun and competitive! At the beginning of practice have a verbal cue, for example, "blue." When they hear the cue "blue," the players stop and do what the coach explained they would do at the beginning of practice. The coach can have a variety of motivational ideas or conditioning exercises to give to the players. For example, perform 5 sprints, 10 sit-ups, 15 push-ups, or some other exercise; give a high five to a player standing next to you; run together and laugh; tell a player something positive; or call a player's name, and have that player tell the team what they are going to do. At completion continue practice where the coach left off of the blue drill. Change off with hitting one day and defense the next day.
3. Vary practice so drills don't become monotonous.
4. Use of batting tees provides instant feedback and helps correct batting errors more quickly. Pitching machines build confidence in batting. Live pitching allows for game-like preparation and competition.

EQUIPMENT TIPS

1. Outfielder's glove is longer for more range; infielder's glove is shorter for more quickness. Use a batting glove under the glove to help pad it.
2. Batting gloves also can be used to protect the hand when diving back to base or sliding into base or when hitting for bat grip.
3. Boys, girls, women, and men should use a bat light enough to control and swing for quickness. Start with a 22-ounce bat for young girls and boys and go up to a 25- to 28-ounce bat for college-age athletes.
4. Sliding shorts, knee and elbow pads, and sweat bands are especially good for sliding drills to avoid scratches and abrasions.
5. Steel cleats add quickness and agility for defense, running base paths, and preparation for sliding.
6. Make sure equipment is comfortable and functional.

TEACHING IDEAS

1. Warm up arm: First throw short distances (emphasize correct throwing technique); then move to longer distances.
   a. *Progression drill:* Have a partner throw 10 ground balls to the backhand side, 10 on the glove-hand side, and 10 ground balls that need to be charged so that ground-ball technique is emphasized as well as defensive movement.
   b. *Short-hop drill:* Have a partner throw ball at receiver's feet or glove when in a defensive position, so the player can't catch it in the air.
   c. *Short underhand or overhand lob drill:* Correct technique, close and long pop-ups; 10 short hops: always catch with two hands; 10 pop-ups: call pop-ups, move feet, communicate "mine," move with glove tucked.
2. Quick-hands partners drill: Catch the ball with two hands, rotate the glove to see the ball, grip it, and get rid of it as quickly as possible. The goal is to see who can get rid of the ball the fastest while keeping the fundamentals in mind.
3. Soft-toss drill against a fence: Partner stands on bench or chair and drops ball straight down. Hitter works on quick hands and ball contact.
4. Beach-ball drill: Put a beach ball between knees, which forces the batter to stay closed with hitting. If one knee opens, ball drops—gives direct feedback.

5. Bingo drill: Place a batting tee and ball at home plate; place another batting tee and ball directly in front of the first tee. The batter's goal is to hit the first ball off the tee into the other ball straight in front of it. Yell "Bingo" if the goal is accomplished. This drill helps timing, batting stride, quick hands, and knowing where the batter should be contacting the ball.
6. Throw ball to fielders, progress to side/side, up and back, hitting ball with bat.
7. Lateral drill: All players line up at third-base position; coach hits ball to first player in line. That player fields the ball and then throws home; moves to the shortstop position and fields ball, throws home; moves to second-base position, fields ball, and throws home; moves to first-base position, fields ball, throws home. That player stops at first base and waits until last fielder goes. The fielders in line repeat the same drill. Everyone goes back around. All players in line encourage the fielder who is up.
8. Baserunning and defensive strategy drills are best taught without batting to permit more offensive and defensive plays (repetitions).
9. Give players opportunities to play all positions.

FYI

For further information and special help, consult the following organizations and resources.

ORGANIZATIONS

Fast Pitch World
P.O. Box 1190
St. Charles, IL 60174
Phone: (800) 591-1222

1. Equipment, notebooks, techniques, rules, and umpire information
2. Video: 12 fast-pitch USA videos
3. *Fast Pitch World Magazine*

All junior high, high school, and college coaches are welcome to become members of the National Fastpitch Coaches Association.

National Fastpitch Coaches Association (NFCA)
100 GT Thames Drive, Suite D
Starkville, MS 39759
Phone: (662) 320-2155
Fax: (662) 320-2283

PUBLICATION

Kneer, M. E., & McCord, C. L. (1995). *Softball: Slow and fast pitch.* Dubuque, IA: Brown and Benchmark.

VIDEOS

Baseball World's *Defensive Drill Video* with Tom Emanski.
A proven training program that improves arm strength, running speed, practice organization, infield/outfield skills, quickness, and agility.

Simple Hitting for Youth Coaches, Parents and Players.
Presented by the Rob Andrews Baseball Camps (former MLB player), Concord, CA.

THROWING			
SKILL	**CUE**	**WHY**	**COMMON ERROR**
Grip	Hold ball in pads of 2 fingers	Ball control	Gripping the ball in palm
	Grip ball lightly	To avoid tensing muscles	Gripping too lightly
Stance	Stand sideways	Allows rotation of body during throw	Standing forward
	Point glove-hand shoulder at target as well as glove	Pointing glove helps you to know where the ball is being thrown	
Throwing Action (Figure 21.1)	Take a long step toward target		Not stepping; stepping too high; stepping across the body
	Keep knees bent		
	Take arm straight down and stretch it way back		Bringing ball behind head
	Make an L with throwing arm		
	Wrist snap	Puts the "zing" on the ball	Keeping weight on back foot
	Follow through with throwing hand to opposite knee		
Focus of Eyes	Both eyes focus on target	Look where you want the ball to go	Looking anywhere else or at path of ball

FIGURE 21.1 Throwing the Ball

FIELDING A GROUND BALL

SKILL	CUE	WHY	COMMON ERROR
Glove (Figure 21.2)	Put fingers of glove in dirt	So balls don't go under the glove	Glove too high
	Keep glove hand palm up, throwing hand with palm down as a shield (aka Venus flytrap)	Protects from bad hops hitting your face	
	Keep glove in front of body	Won't lose track of the ball	Glove off to side of body or behind oneself
Body	Keep body square to ball		Body too high off the ground and stiff
	Keep a good stance	Maintains balance	
	Keep buttocks down, like sitting on a stool	Allows for position readjustment if needed	Standing tall
	Stay behind ball		
	Keep knees flexed		
	Head down, chin down		Pulling head
	Eyes on ball		
Action	Call for the ball		
	Give target with both hands	Tells where you want the ball thrown	
	Reach out with hands, pull ball in		Hands too close to body
	Give with ball		Not pulling ball in
	Spread fingers over ball		
	Catch with both hands	Decreases the chance of balls popping out	
Focus of Eyes	Watch ball go into glove or fingers		Taking eyes off ball; not tracking the ball

FIGURE 21.2 Catching and Fielding a Ground Ball

FIELDING FLY BALLS

SKILL	CUE	WHY	COMMON ERROR
Glove	Out in front of body		Palm up or glove to side
	Raise glove toward ball		Glove down
Body	Square to ball		Side to ball
	Point fingers upward, thumbs together		Fingers down, hands apart
	Fingers toward sky; thumbs touch		
	Stay behind ball but keep your momentum forward	Forward momentum puts more power behind your throw	Not getting behind ball
	Block out sun	Don't lose the flight of the ball	
	Get feet in throwing position after catch		
Action	Soft glove		
	Give with catch		Arms stiff
	Cover ball with throwing hand	Balls don't pop out	Catching with one hand
	Catch ball with both hands		
Focus of Eyes	See ball all the way into glove		Looking away too soon in haste to make throw

FIELDING

SKILL	CUE	WHY	COMMON ERROR
Hard Hit	Catch ball as if it were an egg (aka soft hands)		Body stiff and hands hard
	Give with ball; funnel into waist		
	Glove down		
	If you can, get in front of ball	Getting in front of ball gets you in better position to throw afterward	
Slow Hit	Get behind ball		
	Charge slow balls		Waiting for ball
	Scoop ball as if with a shovel, but keep glove down		

continued

FIELDING, continued

SKILL	CUE	WHY	COMMON ERROR
Rolling Ball	Pick and throw on the run	Saves time for speedier runners	Using the glove to "pick" and then throwing
	Use hand to pick and throw if there's little time		
Focus of Eyes	See ball all the way into glove	Don't lose path of ball	Looking away or looking at runner
Chin	Keep head down with chin on chest as you go down	Head down, chin down decreases chance of getting hit in throat, face, or chin	Pulling head up too soon
Throwing Hand	Place above glove hand like a Venus flytrap for protection		Hand prevents bad hops from hitting one's face

WINDMILL PITCH

SKILL	CUE	WHY	COMMON ERROR
Stance	Square to target	Proper presentation of ball	Perpendicular to target
	Keep front heel and back toe on rubber		No contact with rubber
Grip	3-finger grip (thumb and 3 fingers)	Ball control	Holding ball in palm of hand
	Hold ball in fingers, without palm touching ball		
	Keep ball in glove or hand, waist high		Ball too high or too low
			Ball not in glove
Arm Swing (Figure 21.3, page 278)	Raise hand above head		Bringing arm to side
	Momentum should go back to front		
	Back-circle to release point		
Release (Figure 21.4, page 278)	Release ball at hip	Pitch's path is level	Releasing in front or behind hip
	Keep weight back		
	Turn belt buckle to target	Hips give the power behind the ball	Letting arm do all the work

continued

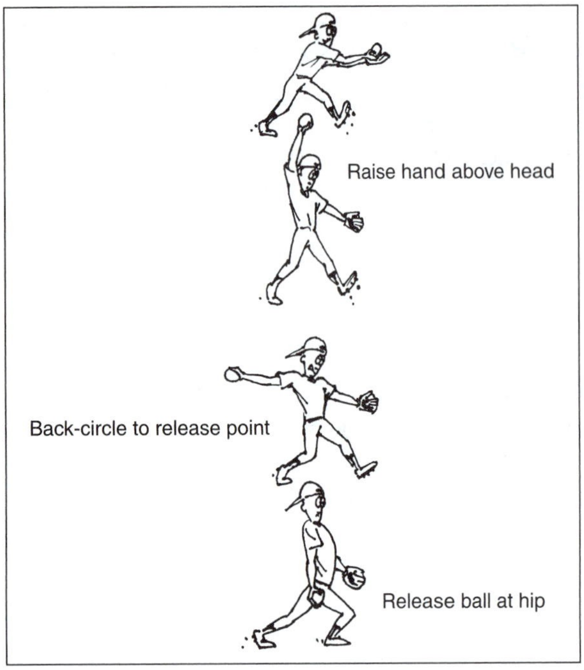

FIGURE 21.3 Arm Swing for Windmill Pitch

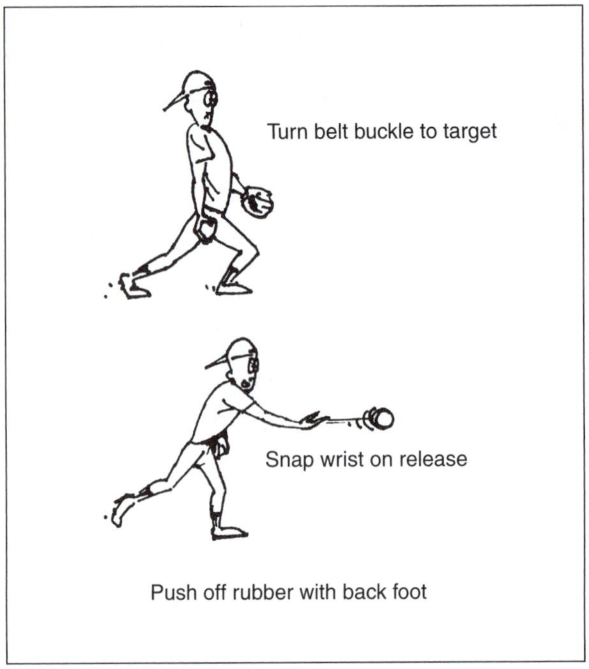

FIGURE 21.4 Release for Windmill Pitch

WINDMILL PITCH, continued			
SKILL	**CUE**	**WHY**	**COMMON ERROR**
Release, *continued*	Make sure to rotate hips		
	Snap wrist on release	Wrist snaps put the spin on the ball	Keep wrist stiff
	Keeping wrist relaxed		
	Follow-through after wrist snap		Bending elbow as hand finishes up by head
	Point toe at catcher	Push-off puts final momentum on ball	Not striding directly at plate
	Push off rubber with back foot		

HITTING

SKILL	CUE	WHY	COMMON ERROR
Stance	Stand sideways	Allows rotation of hips and shoulders	Standing forward
	Feet slightly wider apart than shoulder width		Feet too far apart or too close together
	Weight over balls of feet		Weight on heels
	Heels lightly touching the ground		
	More weight on back leg (80%/20%)	Weight back decreases the chances of lunging toward the ball; more power to hit ball	Weight on left leg during the swing
	Front shoulder slightly lower		
Arm Swing	Hitter should think "shoulder to shoulder" (start swing with chin on front shoulder; finish swing with chin on back shoulder), aka "Ike to Mike"		Moving head during the swing Head too tense
Hip Rotation	Snap or rotate back hip at pitcher, drive body through ball; take photograph of pitcher with belly button	Rotating hips provide the power; keeping 80% on back leg gives more power	No rotating hip
	Throw hands through softball: "Slow feet, quick hands"		Using arms instead of wrists
Focus of Eyes	Watch ball all the way into catcher's mitt	Middle-ball contact is solid contact	Not seeing ball hit bat
	Watch spin and delivery of ball	Pitch detection	
Step	Step 3–6 inches (stride should be more of a glide)		Overstriding causes bat to drop during swing (jarring step)
	"Step to hit"		Hitter "steps and then hits"
	Step toward catcher with weight on ball of foot	So your upper body doesn't fly open	Stepping "in the bucket"
	Keep front shoulder level		

continued

HITTING, continued

SKILL	CUE	WHY	COMMON ERROR
Follow-Through	Top hand rolls over bottom hand; bat goes all the way around the body		
	Take your right palm to the pitcher; draw a straight line through your chest with left thumb	Leads to quicker hands	
Teaching Progressions	Teach cues in order given (first 3); then add others as needed		Give cues in 3's to avoid information overload
	Remember the 4 basic steps to hitting: 1. Coil weight on back leg 2. Stride 3. Pivot 4. Pop		

HITTING FOR INEXPERIENCED BATTERS

SKILL	CUE	WHY	COMMON ERROR
Checkpoints for Coaches	If the batter is not gripping, standing, or holding the bat correctly, coach could correct the player individually	Personal feedback is always more beneficial	Don't use these cues unless a player needs assistance; give 1 at a time
Grip	Hold bat in base of fingers (this technique allows wrist to roll freely and generates bat speed)	Holding bat in palm of hand; squeezing too hard	Loose grip allows for greater wrist rotation/ extension and relaxes forearms
	Align knuckles		
Closed Stance	Place feet shoulder width apart; then move front foot toward plate (helps untrained hitter step toward pitcher)	Keeps hips in control	Stepping back Flying open
Bat Position	Bat held armpit high and far enough away from the body that both of the player's fists could fit between chest and fists	Bat up allows you to stay above the ball	

continued

HITTING FOR INEXPERIENCED BATTERS, continued			
SKILL	**CUE**	**WHY**	**COMMON ERROR**
Checkpoints for Coaches *Bat Position, continued*	Front elbow should resemble an L shape		
	Back elbow held away from body (aka "the box")		Holding bat too close to shoulder
Bat Angle	Straight up in air or up and angled slightly over back shoulder		Cradling bat around head; bat pointing back toward pitcher

SACRIFICE BUNT			
SKILL	**CUE**	**WHY**	**COMMON ERROR**
Grip	Grip bat lightly with thumb and 2 fingers		
	Pinch the bat		
Action	Pivot with back foot toward pitcher; square body to pitcher	Presents the bunt	Keeping side toward pitcher
	Bend knees	Allows hitter to go up or down with pitch rather than one's bat	Legs straight
	Slide top hand up to the bat trademark; keep bat at a 45° angle	45° angle helps to push ball to ground and not in the air when contacted	Not keeping bat at 45°
	Place bat in front of plate at top of strike zone	Increases the likelihood of ball being fair	Keeping bat behind body
	See ball all the way in	Easier to make contact	Take eyes off ball
Contact	Play catch with ball	Softens bunt, deadens ball, allows for ball/ bunt placement	Dropping bat to ball
	Give with the ball (aka soft hands)		Swinging at a ball
			Going for a pitch out of a strike zone
	Bunt strikes!!!		

BASERUNNING

SKILL	CUE	WHY	COMMON ERROR
Running to First	Push off with back leg	Legs provide your power	Swinging arms wildly
	Run through base, then brake down	So momentum doesn't slow	Pointing toes out
	Dig dig dig		Shortening or lengthening stride
	Full acceleration		
	Run with form and run relaxed		Leaping at base, which leads to injury
Extra Base	Make loop midway to base	So you are in position to advance to the next base	Looking at base Cutting too early or late
	Hit inside of base	Shortens base path	Hitting outside of base
	Round bag hard and jog back if necessary		Looping too wide
	Always look for the extra bag	Aggressive baserunning is the difference between winning and losing	

RUNNER ON BASE

SKILL	CUE	WHY	COMMON ERROR
Ready Position	Square body to next base		Keeping body perpendicular
	Take stagger start	Allows for better push-off from base	Keeping feet together
	Keep right foot a stride behind base		
	Push off left foot, stride with right		
Break	Find the pitcher's rhythm	Helps to establish when to lead off	
	Start stride at top of pitcher's windup	Gives you a good jump	Leaving before pitch is released; however, early is better than late
	Push off at release or a little sooner		
	Rock 'n' go, back-front	Adds to your momentum	
Approach	Pump arms with stride	To run faster	Little arm action
	Round base and look for coach	To see if you are supposed to advance	Not looking for coach

THE CATCHER

SKILL	CUE	WHY	COMMON ERROR
Stance	Crouch over balls of feet	Proper stance allows for good reaction time, especially on toes	Body held erect with weight over heels or down on knees
	Align right toe with left heel, toes out (slightly staggered stance)		
	Keep weight over balls of feet		
	Keep knees flexed, butt down		
Glove	Hold glove out as target in front of body	Big glove target gives pitcher an idea where you want the ball	Holding glove to one side or the other and not far enough in front of body
	Relax hands; give steady, big target		Arms and hands stiff
	Runner on: Keep bare hand alongside (slightly behind) glove. No runner on: Keep bare hand behind back.	Hand by glove with runner on increases the transition time from receiving to throwing	
Receiving	Pitch above waist: Fingers up		
	Pitch below waist: Fingers down		
	Frame pitch by catching outside of ball	Framing increases your strikes-to-ball ratio	
	Block ball in dirt with body while pulling head down		Trying to catch ball in dirt
	Relax hands and draw body in	Relaxed hands give with the ball, which means fewer bobbled balls	Arms and hands stiff; unable to cushion ball
	Keep weight on the balls of feet		Being caught on your heels
	Move body over to get in front of and receive inside or outside pitches	Decrease the chances of passed balls	Standing still and trying to reach to one side or other to catch, which leads to passed balls
	Let ball come to you; don't reach		

continued

THE CATCHER, continued			
SKILL	**CUE**	**WHY**	**COMMON ERROR**
Throwing	Get up quickly but keep body low; explode forward, drive with legs	Body low keeps ball on direct path to target	Sitting on heels and not getting into throwing position
		Body low is quicker and puts more power behind throw	Standing straight up, which leads to many overthrows
	Push off ball of back foot, step directly toward target with front foot	Fewer overthrows	Looking at the runner or covering person
	Keep eyes directly on final target		
	Trust your throw!		

STRAIGHT-IN SLIDE			
SKILL	**CUE**	**WHY**	**COMMON ERROR**
Approach	Inside corner of base on infield side of base (ball is in outfield)	Sliding to the corners of bags positions you to avoid the tag	Sliding straight into plate, which may injure lower extremities
		It is the difference between safe and out	
	Outside corner of base on outfield side of base (ball is in infield)		
Sliding Action (Figure 21.5)			
Leg Action	Lead with top leg straight, bottom leg bent under (looks like a number 4)	Number 4 with legs increases your momentum toward the base	Not getting bottom leg bent under, resulting in slides upon the knee; not fun
	Slide on outside of calf, thigh, and buttocks		
Torso Action	Sit down		Sitting straight up
	Lean back; relax back	Leaning back keeps your slide momentum forward	Body tense
Arms	Touchdown signal	Arms above head (prevents injuries)	Dragging arms and hands slows slide, so keep them up

continued

FIGURE 21.5

STRAIGHT-IN SLIDE, continued			
SKILL	**CUE**	**WHY**	**COMMON ERROR**
Sliding Action, *continued*			
Head Position	Back with closed fists	Eyes on play lets you know where the ball is, for you may not need to slide	Keeping head up, resulting in a tag in face or head
	Eyes on play		
Base Contact	Lead with heel, like stopping a scooter or slide, sole up	Soles up decreases the likelihood of injury and doesn't slow movement toward the base	Soles down and getting cleats stuck in dirt
	Straight leg, but don't hyperextend		Straight leg doesn't give when base is contacted

SLOW-PITCH SOFTBALL DIFFERENCES

1. There are 10 or 11 players rather than 9 players as in fast-pitch.
2. Tenth player extra on defense, called short fielder or rover, plays anywhere on the field.
3. Eleventh player, extra hitter (EH), may not be used on defense. Not allowed in coed slow-pitch.
4. Leading off and stealing bases are not allowed.
5. Bunting is not allowed.
6. Batting requires a lot of patience if you are used to fast-pitch. Basically wait longer for the ball, let the ball come to you, and don't reach for the pitch.
7. Pitched ball must travel through an arc between 6 and 12 feet high.

SLOW-PITCH STRATEGIES

1. Pitch the ball so it is as close to 12 feet high as possible when coming close to the batter.
2. Make the ball drop quickly as it crosses the plate. Placing a forward, backward, or sideward spin on the pitch is also a commonly used legal strategy. One foot must be in contact with the pitching plate when the pitch is released.

SLOW-PITCH SKILLS

SKILL	CUE	WHY	COMMON ERROR
Underhand Slow Pitch			
Grip	Like throwing a ball normally		Gripping the ball too tightly
Setup	Ball in front of chest	Allows for proper presentation of ball	
	Both feet parallel on mound		
	Feet not quite shoulder width apart		
Arm Action	Pendulum swing	Allows for the pitch's momentum	
Stepping Action	Step with foot opposite to throwing arm	Enhances ball arc, spin, and momentum	
Releasing the Ball	Release ball out in front of you at belt height		
Batting			
Batting Action	The key to slow-pitch batting is waiting for the ball	Let the ball travel to you until it is in your power zone; then explode!	Swinging too soon
	Be patient; be relaxed		Swinging too soon
	Focus eyes on ball spin	To detect the ball's movement and inside or outside pitch recognition	Eyes wandering
	Swing level	Level contact equals solid, line-drive contact	Reaching too high
			Trying to hit the ball like a golf swing

22

Strength Training with Free Weights

INTRODUCTION

"In the early 1900s Alan Calvert developed adjustable barbells with weighted plates that could be added or removed to change the resistance. In more than 80 years few changes have altered his basic design" (Allsen, Harrison, & Vance, 1983, p. 129).

Free weights have an advantage over machines in that they require the participant to balance the weights when lifting, using more muscles and training all muscle groups. When using free weights, the student progresses more quickly than when using machines, although there are different safety concerns. Many bodybuilders prefer free weights.

The use of weights in adolescent strength training is an important part of each person's development. The training of adolescents should involve the use of dumbbells and training bars to teach correct techniques and form. There is no need to use heavy weights at this young age, but teaching proper mechanics is important. We start kids playing sports early; why not teach kids strength training under proper supervision? To include weight lifting in the curriculum, teachers need to have the appropriate equipment and be able to offer a weight-lifting program for at least 6 weeks (the time it takes for the body to adapt to the regimen). By using a different lift for the same muscle group, the student can continue to progress.

The purpose of strength training is to achieve your potential. The benefits include increased muscle mass, increased strength and power, increased personal and sport performance, increased self-efficacy, and conquering personal challenges.

SKILLS LISTED WITH CUES

We provide cues for the following free-weight lifts: squat, bench press, power snatch, and power clean, as well as safety guidelines. Also provided are guidelines for core exercises: push-ups, sit-ups, and dips.

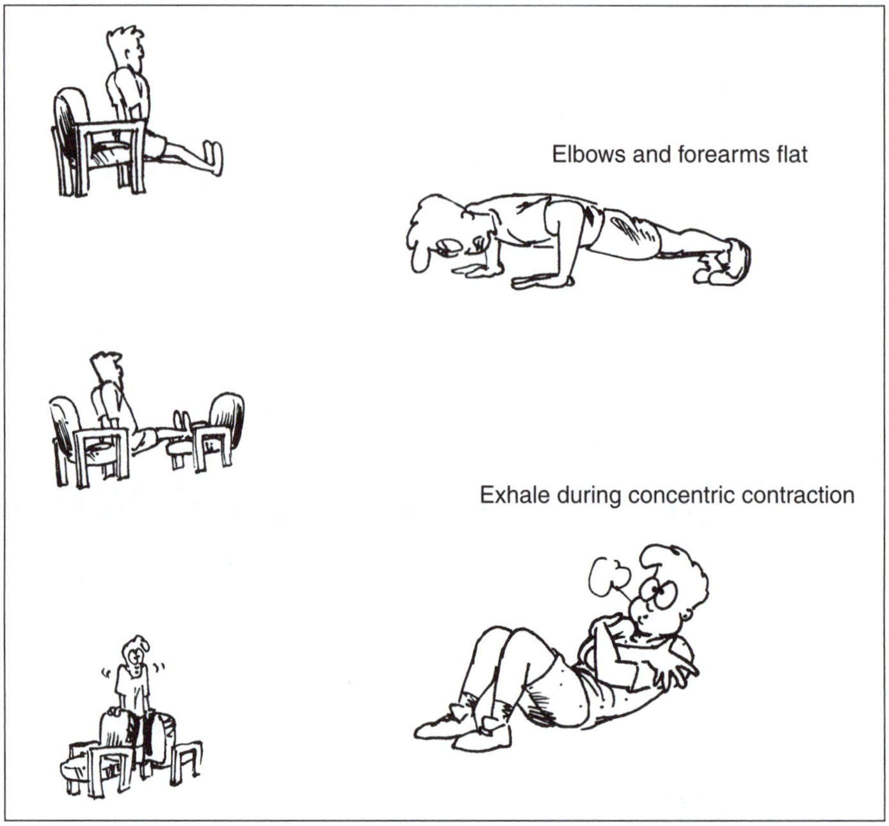

FIGURE 22.1 Push-Ups, Sit-Ups, and Dips Develop Rapid Strength Gains

TIPS

1. Each muscle group should be exercised two or three days a week.
2. Stretch before and after lifting.
3. Complete the full range of motion during any lift. Don't do partial or half movements.
4. Lifting weights should be a controlled movement. Avoid jerking movements. The positive move (concentric) is usually faster than the negative move (eccentric).
5. Push-ups (modified or regulation), sit-ups, abdominal curls, and dips are great strength exercises that develop the core and that can be done any time, any place (Figure 22.1).
6. Core training is essential to being a well-rounded athlete and should be done during each lift session. It can be done every day.

EQUIPMENT TIPS

1. Use two sturdy chairs or benches to perform modified dips.
2. Use mats, carpet squares, or grass to perform sit-ups and abdominal curls.
3. Stability balls should be used in core training.

TEACHING IDEAS

1. Have students chart their progress. Class or individual charts can be used. Students are motivated by seeing their progress.

2. Provide weight-lifting picture charts in weight rooms for students to refer to. These pictures can help teach correct weight-lifting techniques.
3. Always train with a partner, and train with one who has comparable strength. The partner spots the weight for the weight lifter. This method saves time because the partners don't have to keep changing the weight on the bar.

CORE EXERCISES

What is the core? Why is it important to develop the core? The whole body is a pillar—head over shoulders, shoulders over hips, and hips over feet. The center and the most important part of the pillar is the *core*, consisting of the area between the bottom of the rib cage and bottom of thigh both front and back. Development of the core is critical because it involves the center of all motion. Developing the core muscles can help improve performance in every sport. There are a variety of exercises to develop the core, including push-ups, abdominal work, and back extensions. While performing each exercise in a lifting session, the athlete should focus on his or her core while completing the lift.

Push-Ups

Start with 10 push-ups per day; work up to 50 to 300 a day.

1. Regulation
2. Modified with knees
3. All fours and lift one hand or leg

Push-up workout: Try three sets of 5 push-ups, working up to three sets of 10–15–20–25.

Push-ups should be done during rest; this helps strengthen the core. Add medicine balls and specialty ball when student is strong enough to perform push-ups on the floor.

Push-Up Progression with Medicine Balls and Specialty Balls

1. Push-ups
2. Push-ups with one foot 2 inches off the ground
3. Push-ups with knee to chest
4. Push-ups with medicine ball
5. Push-ups with medicine ball with one foot 2 inches off the ground
6. Push-ups with medicine ball with knee to chest
7. Push-ups specialty balls
8. Push-ups specialty balls with one foot 2 inches off the ground
9. Push-ups specialty balls with knee to chest

Students should start with holding push-ups for 10 seconds. Gradually work up to 45 seconds, then to 1 minute. The next progression is to perform three sets of push-ups for 45 seconds up to 1 minute.

Next, move to knee-to-chest push-ups. Same progression as above.

Sit-Ups

Sit-ups work abdominal muscles. Start with 10 per day; work up to 50 to 1,000 a day done three to five days per week. Variations:

1. Arms crossed in front.
2. Arms at side come up and touch toes.
3. Crunches with legs up, bent, twisting side to side.
4. Rowing.
5. Back extensions: Lie face down on ground with arms straight out to side; raise chest off ground.

Sit-up workout: Try three sets of 5 sit-ups, working up to three sets of 10–15–20–25.

Students need to be able to perform sit-up exercises on the floor before moving on to sit-ups with a medicine ball and/or specialty ball.

Sit-Up Progression with Medicine Balls and Specialty Balls

1. Sit-ups
2. Sit-ups with medicine ball
3. Sit-ups with specialty ball

Students should work up to three sets of 25 crunches, then move on to sit-ups with a medicine ball and/or specialty ball. The student should start at 10 seconds on the medicine ball and/or specialty ball. Gradually work up to 45 seconds to 1 minute. Perform three sets.

Dips

Dips work shoulders, forearms, and back of upper arms. Variations:

1. Place palms on end of bench, feet on ground, and dip.
2. Place palms on end of chair, feet on another chair; dip down.
3. Use dip bars in weight room.

Dip workout: Dips take a little more strength. Start with one set of 5 to 10 and work up to three sets of 15 to 20.

Rapid strength gains take place with lots of push-ups, sit-ups, and dips. You can perform these three strength exercises almost anywhere.

TRAINING

The overload principle involves continually subjecting the muscle to more stress than it is accustomed to. As a result, the body will adapt to reasonable amounts of stress. Excessive stress will cause the body to break down, leading to injury. The components of overload include load, repetition, rest, and frequency.

1. *Load* refers to intensity and the amount of resistance or weight being used during an exercise.
2. *Repetition* refers to the number of times an exercise is performed during a set.
3. *Rest* refers to the amount of time between sets. The greater the load or the higher the number of repetitions, the greater the amount of rest required between sets.
4. *Frequency* is the number of training sessions per week.

Recommendations for Beginners

1. Load: 50 percent of maximum
2. Repetition: performance lift 8 to 12 times, between two and four sets (usually three sets)
3. Rest: 2 minutes between sets
4. Frequency: two to three times per week
   - Two times a week will maintain strength; three times a week will increase strength
   - Power (speed and strength): 3 to 8 repetitions
   - Bulk mass: 1 to 6 repetitions
   - Endurance: 10 to 15 repetitions
   - Pyramid: ascending in weight, then descending back down
   - Super sets: pairing one lift with another; for example, a back squat with a pull-up
   - Plyometrics: bounding, sprinting, jumping.

Safety

Breathing

1. Exhale while exerting the greatest force.
2. Inhale while moving the weight into position.
3. Holding your breath causes a decrease in blood volume returning to the heart and impairs the volume and level of oxidated blood returning to the brain. It also affects blood pressure. You may get dizzy or faint. *Never hold your breath!*
4. While not holding your breath, you must hold your core tight. Squeeze your abdominal cavity while performing the required lift. This is an important safety factor during strength training.

Clothing

1. Sport shoes provide good support.
2. For serious lifters, weight-lifting belts protect the back when squatting or pulling.
3. Spotters.
4. Collars.
5. Grips—pronated: bench; supinated: curl; mixed: dead lift.

CONCEPTS OF STRENGTH TRAINING

1. Train specially for your sport.
2. Train all year round.
3. Get in shape gradually.
4. Listen to your body.
5. Train first for volume (more reps) and later for intensity (heavier weight).
6. Cycle the volume and intensity of your workouts.
7. Do not overtrain.
8. Train your mind.
9. Become a student of your sport or activity.
10. Always warm up and cool down when lifting.

FYI

For further information and special help, consult the following organization.

ORGANIZATION

National Strength & Conditioning Association
1995 N. Union Boulevard
Colorado Springs, CO 80909
Phone: (800) 815-6826 or (719) 632-6722
Fax: (719) 632-6367
E-mail: nsca@nsca-lift.org
Website: www.nsca-lift.org

PUBLICATION

Allsen, P. E., Harrison, J. M., & Vance, B. (1993). *Fitness for life: An individualized approach* (5th ed). Madison, WI: WCB Brown Benchmark.

PUSH-UPS

SKILL	CUE	WHY	COMMON ERROR
Push-Ups			
Regular	Flat back	Maintains posture	Arched back
	Arms in line with shoulders	Shoulder provides distributed base of support	Arms and hands too wide
	Align head with body	Maintains posture	Busy head
	Fill core set with air		Core collapses
	Draw air in like sucking through a straw		Breathing too fast
	Maintain pressure through the palms	Develops strength in all parts of body	Hands too far out
With One Foot 2 Inches Off the Ground	Hips square	Maintains posture	Hips arched or sunk
	Raise one foot 2 inches off the floor	Develops strength	Hips turn or rotate off balance
	Back flat—head aligned with body	Distributes weight equally	Back arched or humped
Knee to Chest	Pull knee to chest	Develop more strength	Body collapsed; not enough strength
	Toe up		Toe down
	Back flat	Better posture to distribute weight	Arched back
	Head aligned with body		Head down or up

PUSH-UPS WITH MEDICINE BALL AND/OR SPECIALTY BALL

SKILL	CUE	WHY	COMMON ERROR
Push-Ups with Medicine Ball (Figure 22.2)	Push through the ball	More power	
	Back flat	Better balance and distributes weight equally	Back arched
	Balls of feet press into the floor		Foot comes off floor
With One Foot 2 Inches Off the Ground (Figure 22.3)	Push through the ball	More power	
	Lift foot 2 inches off the ground	More power	No strength to lift foot; off balance
	Back flat—head aligned with body	Better posture to distribute weight	Arched back
Knee to Chest (Figure 22.4, page 294)	Push through the ball	More power	Not pushing
	Pull knee to chest	More power	No strength to bring knee to chest
	Back flat—head aligned with body	Better balance and distribution of weight	Body arched or humped

continued

FIGURE 22.2 Push-Ups with Medicine Ball

FIGURE 22.3 Push-Ups with Medicine Ball (with One Foot Raised 2 Inches Off the Ground)

PUSH-UPS WITH MEDICINE BALL AND/OR SPECIALTY BALL, continued			
SKILL	**CUE**	**WHY**	**COMMON ERROR**
Push-Ups with Specialty Ball (Figure 22.5)	Pressure through the ball	More power	No pressure applied to ball
	Push balls of feet through the floor	Better balance	Lift feet off ground
	Arms straight	More power	Arms bent
With One Foot 2 Inches Off the Ground (Figure 22.6)	Keep arms straight	More power	Arms bent
	Lift one foot 2 inches off the ground	More power	No strength to lift foot
	Back flat—head aligned with body	Better distribution of weight for developing the total core	Body arched or humped
Knee to Chest (Figure 22.7)	Pull knee to chest	More power	Brings knee up a short distance
	Toe up	Better posture	Toe down
	Straight arms	More power	Bent arms

FIGURE 22.4 Push-Ups with Medicine Ball (Knee to Chest)

FIGURE 22.5 Push-Ups with Specialty Ball

FIGURE 22.6 Push-Ups with Specialty Ball (with One Foot Raised 2 Inches Off the Ground)

FIGURE 22.7 Push-Ups with Specialty Ball (Knee to Chest)

SIT-UPS

SKILL	CUE	WHY	COMMON ERROR
Sit-Ups	Heels firm against floor	Better posture	Don't use momentum to get up
	Crunch torso	More power	Whipping head up
	Head aligned with shoulders		Pull head up

SIT-UPS WITH MEDICINE BALL AND/OR SPECIALTY BALL

SKILL	CUE	WHY	COMMON ERROR
Sit-Ups with Medicine Ball (Figure 22.8, page 296)	Legs straight	More power	Legs bent
	Ball touches toes	More power	Too weak to bring ball up
	Arms straight	More power	Arms bent
Sit-Ups with Specialty Ball (Figure 22.9, page 296)	Feet firm on ground	To support body	Feet come off ground
	Back in contact with ball all the time	Develop more strength	Back comes off the ball
	Hands cross chest—crunch		

FIGURE 22.8 Sit-Ups with Medicine Ball

FIGURE 22.9 Sit-Ups with Specialty Ball

BENCH PRESS

SKILL	CUE	WHY	COMMON ERROR
Grip	Grip couple of inches wider than shoulder width	Try to minimize sport movement	Too wide, too narrow
Feet Position	Feet flat on ground	Safety; always have balance	
Back Position	Back flat on bench	Raising buttocks can lead to back strains	Raising buttocks while lifting
Execution	Lightly touch chest when lowering bar	Slow, continuous movement	Bouncing bar off chest
		Always control weight; less stress on shoulders	
	Lift should be smooth		If weight wobbles, too much weight
	Chest puffs out		Chest caves in
Incline Bench Press	Same as bench press except bring bar down to lightly touch collarbone		Bringing bar down too low
Decline Bench Press	Same as bench press except execution		
	Bring bar down to lightly touch the lower part of the chest		Bringing bar down too high on chest

GENERAL RULES

SKILL	CUE	WHY	COMMON ERROR
Safety Guidelines (Figure 22.10)	Have spotter		
	Use collars		
	Control bar at all times		
	Inhale during eccentric contraction and exhale during concentric contraction		
	Always keep a tight core, sucking belly button to spine		
Weight Belt	We do not emphasize the use of a weight belt. It takes away from the development of core strength. Some students will put them on when weight gets too heavy—85% and above.		

FIGURE 22.10 Safety Guidelines

POWER CLEAN

SKILL	CUE	WHY	COMMON ERROR
Stance	Feet shoulder width apart	Use athletic stance as much as possible	Feet too wide
	Knees slightly bent	Again, athletic position	Knees too straight
	Chest over knees		
	Tight back	Suck belly button to spine	Rounded back
Grip	Just outside of knees		
Execution	Same as power snatch until catch (see next table)		Elbows not getting high enough
	Rotate elbows under bar		Bar is away from body
	Drop body and catch bar on clavicle and front deltoids		

POWER SNATCH

SKILL	CUE	WHY	COMMON ERROR
Stance	Feet shoulder width apart	Use athletic stance as much as possible	Feet too wide
	Knees slightly bent	Again, athletic position	Knees too straight
	Chest over knees		
	Tight back	Suck belly button to spine	Rounded back
Grip	Super-wide grip (as if carrying a wide table by yourself); form wide V		
Execution	Drive with legs (jumping in the air)		Performing slowly
	Explode hips when bar reaches knees		
	Pull bar high with elbows high and close to body (like putting on your pants)	Everything must go vertical	Bar away from body
	Drop under bar (hold world over head)	Drive heels in ground Catch in athletic stance, same as start	No drop
	Lock elbows and stand	Drop under weight to catch properly	

SQUAT			
SKILL	**CUE**	**WHY**	**COMMON ERROR**
Abdominals	Abdominals held in tightly	Important for safety	Being lazy
Stance	Feet shoulder width apart, slightly pointed out	Always train with an athletic stance	Feet parallel
Execution	Eyes at noon	Keep you from falling over	Looking down or looking up too high (at the ceiling)
	Back straight and shoulders upright and tall		Rounding the back and bending over too much at the waist
	Weight on heels (water skier taking off or sitting down in chair)	Keep stress on muscles, not patella of the knee	Weight on toes with heels off ground
	Knees stay behind toes	Same as above	Knees going beyond toes
	Femurs parallel to floor and knees at a 90° angle	To maximize on all muscles and prevent stress on knees	Going too low

23

Swimming

INTRODUCTION

The swimming and safety cues incorporated in this chapter provide instructors with a variety of creative ideas that students of all ages are able to visualize and incorporate into their swimming and safety skills. For example, when teaching the prone float, you might instruct the students to pretend they are "Superheroes looking over the city." Other feedback about this cue might be "Look to see if someone is in trouble." Questions could include "How is the person doing down there?" or "Can you see the crooks?" When these cues are used, students' imaginations are stimulated, and critical swimming skills are learned. When teachers use their imaginations with the cues and elaborate on them, the class becomes interesting and fun.

We have designed some vivid swimming cues to help the swimmer envision the arm stroke, kick, and coordination patterns. For example, making an inverted heart for the breaststroke or an hourglass for the butterfly stroke helps the student learn to perform a difficult arm movement more quickly and efficiently.

Other cues are designed to help refine and polish the strokes—for example, "Thumb brushes side of leg on the finish of the front crawl arm stroke" or "Hand rests on top of leg to finish the arm stroke on the sidestroke." These refinement cues should be used when the swimmer has mastered major arm, kick, and coordination patterns.

Learning correct swimming strokes through the use of cues helps the student feel more comfortable and efficient in the water, which could lead to a lifetime of fitness and recreational activities.

The fundamentals of swimming skills such as floats, etc. are found in *Teaching Cues for Basic Sport Skills for Elementary and Middle School Students* (Fronske, 2002).

SKILLS LISTED WITH CUES

Swimming strokes include the front crawl, back crawl, butterfly, sidestroke, breaststroke, elementary backstroke, trudgen, trudgen crawl, and double trudgen.

Swimming skills include the rotary kick, treading water, front and back open turns, swimming underwater, breaststroke and butterfly turns, speed turns, surface dives, and diving.

TIPS

1. Type the cue on a 3" × 5" note card, laminate it, and float the card on the water while teaching.
2. Punch a hole in the note card, put string through the hole, and tie a knot. Put string around instructor's neck. The note card won't float away from the swim instructor.
3. For laminating the note card, use clear contact paper, heavy plastic bag, and clear postal tape.

EQUIPMENT TIPS

1. Goggles help beginning swimmers enjoy the water and open their eyes underwater; they also prevent the eyes from burning when a person swims laps.
2. Kickboards.

TEACHING IDEAS

1. The following is a suggested teaching progression for the five basic swimming strokes: front crawl, back crawl, elementary backstroke, breaststroke, and sidestroke. The sidestroke should be taught after the whip kick has been mastered because of negative transfer with the scissors kick.
2. Front crawl: If students have erratic breathing habits or body twists, have them breathe on the opposite side. This tactic helps them relearn correct breathing patterns.
3. Sidestroke: Have students learn sidestroke on both sides.
4. Breaststroke coordination: When teaching the breaststroke to beginners, have students practice only one stroke. Stop until they master the one stroke; then add two strokes, three strokes, and so on. This method helps develop coordination and gliding for the stroke.
5. Wet base (modified game): A new water game played like baseball in the water. Instructions for the game follow.

   Equipment
   1 kickboard used for the bat
   1 lightweight plastic 8-inch ball
   4 hula hoops used for the bases
   4 ten-pound weights to keep hula hoops secure (optional)

   Rules

   1. Batter stands in shallow end of pool, bats to deep end of pool; pitcher pitches ball underhand, no more than three pitches.
   2. Bat like baseball, swim underwater through hoop to first base, then to second base, and so on. Award one point for making it back to home plate.

3. A ball that goes out on deck is a foul ball.
4. Outs are made just as in baseball.
5. Two teams, 4 to 10 players per team.

FYI

For further information and special help, consult the following organizations and resources.

ORGANIZATIONS

Your local American Red Cross

National Headquarters of the American Red Cross
430 17th Street Northwest
Washington, DC 20006
Phone: (202) 737-8300
Website: www.redcross.org/hss

U.S. Swimming, Inc.
One Olympic Plaza
Colorado Springs, CO 80909
Phone: (719) 578-4578
Fax: (719) 578-4669
Website: www.USASwimming.org

PUBLICATIONS

American Red Cross. (2004). *Swimming and water safety.* Washington, DC: American Red Cross.

American Red Cross. (1992a). *Swimming and diving.* St. Louis: Mosby.

American Red Cross. (1992b). *Water safety instructor's manual.* St. Louis: Mosby Life.

American Red Cross. (1993). *CPR for the professional rescuer.* St. Louis: Mosby.

American Red Cross. (2001). *Lifeguard training.* Boston: Staywell.

American Red Cross. (2003). *Lifeguard management.* Boston: Staywell.

Counsilman, J. E. (1977). *Competitive swimming manual for coaches and swimmers.* Bloomington, IN: Author.

Counsilman, J. E., & Counsilman, B. E. (1994). *The new science of swimming.* Englewood Cliffs, NJ: Prentice-Hall.

FRONT CRAWL

SKILL	CUE	WHY	COMMON ERROR
Body Position	Be a superhero	More streamlined through the water	Hips and shoulders sway
		No wave drag to slow you down	
Head Position	Water level at crown of head	More efficient in the water	Head too far under the water
		Best for streamlined body position	Head too high (creates a drag)
Arm Pull	Use an S pull	Creates power	Straight arm pull
	Thumb to middle of leg		Head-first recovery
Arm Recovery (Figure 23.1)	High elbow recovery	More energy efficient	Dragging elbow in water
		Prevents elbow drag in water, which slows you down	
	Drag thumb lightly along the water		Straight arm recovery
			Hand is higher than elbow during recovery

continued

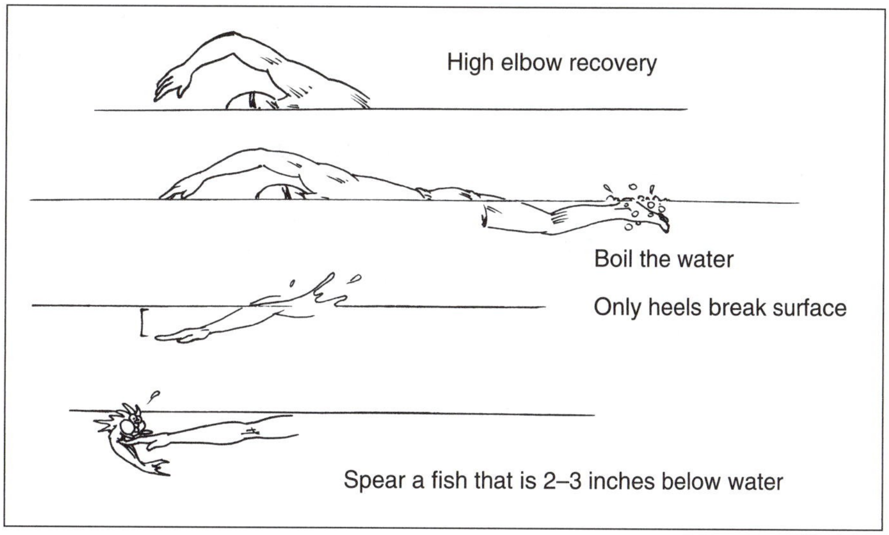

FIGURE 23.1 Front Crawl

FRONT CRAWL, continued			
SKILL	**CUE**	**WHY**	**COMMON ERROR**
Hand Entry	Spear a fish that is 2–3 inches below the water and in front of you	Gets the arm in position for greater pull under the water	Palm enters the water first
	Hand entry sideways	More speed because it cuts through the water more efficiently (more streamlined)	
		More water to pull creates more power in the stroke	
	Try to make a spear with arm; reach with arm		Hand starts to pull too soon
Leg Action	Point toes like a diver	Reduces wave drag to swim faster; more streamlined	If feet are flexed stiff, swimmer does not move forward; can even go backward in the water
	Kick heels to the surface	Less wave drag	
	Feet relaxed, like throwing a fishing line		
	Kick generated from large muscles of buttocks and thigh give more power		
Breathing	Follow the elbow back; look through window	Creates way for air, efficient breath	Head too far under the water (causes exaggerated roll)
		Keeps body streamlined	
	Roll chin to shoulder	Less wave drag	
	Rotate body on skewer	Less drag	
	Hum while face is in water	More efficient air exchange	Water gets in mouth
	Exhale through nose	Avoids getting water in mouth	

BACK CRAWL

SKILL	CUE	WHY	COMMON ERROR
Body Position	Iron rod down back	Less wave drag	Hips and shoulders sway
	Eyes look at toes splashing water		
Head Position	Lie down, as if head is on a pillow, water touching ears	Less wave drag	Head is too far back, eyes looking at the ceiling
Hand Recovery (Figure 23.2)	Thumb leads coming out of the water as if a string is pulling the thumb up	Specific goal for swimmer to heed	Fingers lead coming out of the water
	Thumbs up, making the OK sign	More streamlined; more efficient to cut through the water	
Shoulder Recovery	Lead with shoulder; straight arm	More streamlined	Arms are bent
	Raise hand to ask question	More efficient for best power position	
	Graze your ear with your arm		
	Skim the ear		
Hand Entry	Pinkie finger always leads going into the water	More efficient	Arms enter too far out to the side of the body
	Palms facing away	Less splash	Hand or elbow enters first
Arm Pull	Make a question mark with each arm pull	Creates power to move body forward	Straight arm pull
		Less stress on shoulders	

continued

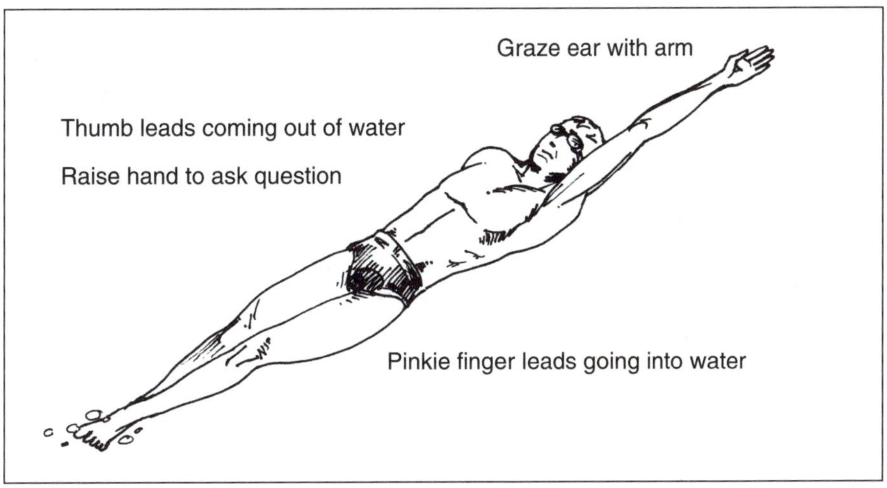

FIGURE 23.2 Back Crawl

BACK CRAWL, continued

SKILL	CUE	WHY	COMMON ERROR
Leg Action	Point toes like a diver	More streamlined; move through the water faster	Flexed, stiff feet; swimmer does not move forward well; knees and heels break the surface of the water
	Kick toes to the surface	More efficient	
	Make water boil	Less drag	
Body Rotation	Hip to sky	Keep body streamlined	
	Rotate body on skewer	More efficient	

BUTTERFLY STROKE

SKILL	CUE	WHY	COMMON ERROR
Arm Pull	Draw an hourglass with high elbow pull	More power	Straight arm pull
	Push arms; explode out of the back of stroke; touch thigh with thumb		
	Stay low		
Arm Recovery	Elbow is being pulled by string upward	Gets arms ready for power phase More efficient stroke	Elbows stay in water on recovery
	Thumbs drag along the water to keep elbows high		Arms drag along the water
	Pinkies exit first		
Hand Entry	Catch the water with hands		
Leg Action	Legs are together, like a mermaid	Gets legs in position for power phase	Legs too far apart
	2 strong kicks		Whip kick or frog kick
	Make kick like a metronome		
Coordination	Lead with head	Better coordination of stroke	
	As hands enter in front, chest is down, buttocks up		

continued

BUTTERFLY STROKE, continued			
SKILL	**CUE**	**WHY**	**COMMON ERROR**
Breathing	Keep chin near the water when breathing	Easier to take the breath	
Body Roll	Body roll through a relatively narrow band of water at the surface	Body is streamlined to move through water	
	No deeper than 1–2 feet	More efficient	

SIDESTROKE			
SKILL	**CUE**	**WHY**	**COMMON ERROR**
Body Position	Lay head on arm	Keeps body streamlined to move through water more efficiently	Ear and head too far above the water
	Lower ear is in water		Lying on stomach
Arm Pull	Tie a big knot	Creates best power from the arms	Both hands start above head
	Pick an apple from a tree and put it in your pocket	Keeps upper body above the water	
Arm Recovery	Rest the top hand on the top leg during glide	Keeps body stream-lined and aerodynamic to move through the water	Top arm pushes too far past the leg
Leg Action	Draw both heels toward buttocks	Legs in best power position	Whip or frog kick used
	Tuck the knees, flex the top foot, and point the bottom foot		
	Do the splits	Gets body ready for power phase	Legs too close together when trying to make the splits; legs go up and down, not sideways
	Splits done sideways		
	Legs do not pass each other when kick is finished	Keeps swimmer on side and streamlined	Legs pass each other on the kick
	Avoid up-and-down splits; close legs like scissors	More efficient	
Coordination	Stay streamlined	Rest	
	Count to 3 on glide		
	Stay parallel with side	Keeps body aero-dynamic in water	Roll or lie on stomach

BREASTSTROKE			
SKILL	**CUE**	**WHY**	**COMMON ERROR**
Body Position	Arch back to bring shoulders out of water		Body vertical in water
Head Position	Eyes focused on wall	Streamlined to move through the water more efficiently	
	Crown at water level		Hair submerged in water
Arm Pull/Arm Recovery	Make a small upside-down heart; start at the point of the heart, trace it with hand, then split it in half with hands	Creates power in the stroke	Heart shape is too wide or long
Arm Glide	Fully extend arms and count to 3 before starting to pull	Creates better aerodynamics	Starting to pull too soon
Leg Action (Whip Kick)	Kick buttocks with heels	More power	Knees too far apart
	Try being knock-kneed		Frog kick
	Knees a fist apart		
	Keep knees closer together than ankles		
	Draw circles with heels		Knees outside ankles
	Push feet/squeeze legs		
Breathing	Lift chin, not head, to breathe	Easier to breathe	Head too far out of water
Coordination	Pull, breathe, kick, glide	Saying these words helps you coordinate the stroke	Gliding when arms are at waist

ELEMENTARY BACKSTROKE

SKILL	CUE	WHY	COMMON ERROR
Body Position	Ears in the water	Helps streamline body to move through water more efficiently	Head too far out of water
	Arms down at sides		
Arm Recovery	Tickle sides with thumbs all the way to the armpit	Creates more pull for power	Hands do not come to armpits, half stroke
Arm Pull	Palms out	More power	Hands and arms come too far above head
	Make a T		
	Make a snow angel	Creates more pull for power	
Leg Action (Whip Kick)	Drop feet straight down	Requires less energy	Buttocks drop, knees bend to chest
	Make penguin feet	When knees come up, body sinks	
	Try being knock-kneed	Gets legs in position for power phase	Knees are outside of ankles
	Feet outside knees	Action with feet faster	
		More power	
	Upper legs form a table		Knees come out of water
	Draw heels toward buttocks		
	Try drawing circles with your heels	Action phase more powerful	Scissors kick with 1 or both legs
	Push feet, then squeeze legs		
Coordination	Recover the arms first, kick and pull, then glide		Arms and legs start at the same time

TRUDGEN STROKES

SKILL	CUE	WHY	COMMON ERROR
Trudgen	Front crawl with scissors kick		Breathing on both sides
	Roll hips to side	Creates power	Whip kick, staying on stomach
	Scissors kick when breathing	Help with timing to breathe	Kicking when head is in water
Trudgen Crawl	Front crawl with scissors kick and flutter kick		
	Roll hip to side		Hips flat
	Scissors kick when breathing; flutter kick when face is in water	Create more power in the stroke	Forgetting to flutter kick
	Breathe on one side		Breathing on both sides
Double Trudgen	Front crawl with no flutter kick		
	Scissors kick—scissors kick	Creates more power	Kicking on only one side
	Roll hip to each side when performing a scissors kick on each arm stroke		Not rolling hips
	Breathe on one side only		Breathing on both sides
	Head stays in water on one arm stroke and 1 scissors kick; keep head in water	Helps with the coordination of the stroke	Turning head right and left
	Try to keep arms moving and in sequence with each scissors kick		

SWIMMING SKILLS

SKILL	CUE	WHY	COMMON ERROR
Rotary Kick (Figure 23.3)	Sit on horse, back straight		Standing straight up
	1 foot rotates clockwise, the other foot counterclockwise		Legs going same direction
	Eggbeater		
	"Wax on! Wax off!" with your feet (as in the *Karate Kid* movie; same motion, but use feet)		
Tread Water	Look over fence		
Arms	Figure 8 with hands, palms up, palms down; or like spreading butter with sides of hands		Hands pushing down
Legs	Scissors/breaststroke/rotary		
Body Position	Relaxed		Body too rigid, not relaxed
			Too much energy, too tight

continued

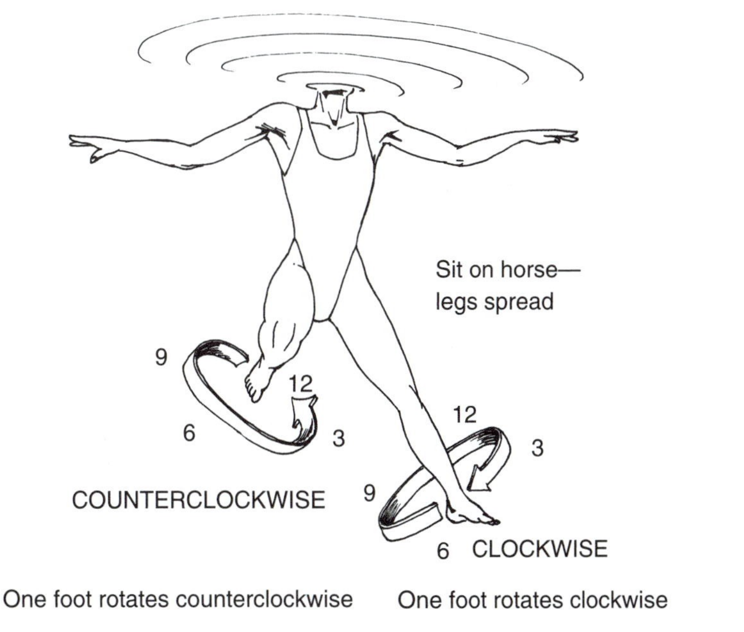

FIGURE 23.3 Rotary Kick

SWIMMING SKILLS, continued			
SKILL	**CUE**	**WHY**	**COMMON ERROR**
Front Open Turn	Drop 1 shoulder, meet hands above head		Grab wall with both hands
	Knees tuck against wall; submerge in water		Not tucking
	Spring off wall		Not pushing
	Stay submerged	More streamlined	Staying on top of water, not submerging
Back Open Turn	Drop 1 shoulder, meet hands above head		Arms by side
	Spring off wall		Not tucking
	Be a torpedo	Creates power	No power
Sidestroke Arms and Coordination	See sidestroke cues		
Swimming Underwater	Be a submarine	Body is streamlined	Swimming on top of water
	Scrape a big bowl with hands	More power; more efficient pull	Straight arm pull
Butterfly Arm Stroke and Coordination	See butterfly stroke cues, pages 306–307		
Breaststroke Turn	Drop shoulder, hands meet above head; submerge	Gets body underwater for more efficiency	Shoulders level
	Superhero looking over city underwater	More streamlined	
Sidestroke Turn	Touch wall with leading arm		Touching wall with both arms
	Drop one shoulder		
	Spring off wall		
Speed Turn and Pull Out for Breaststroke	Drop 1 shoulder, meet hands above head	Gets body in streamline position	
	Spring off wall		Not tucking
Arms	Draw lightbulb to thighs (feel water move down legs to toes)	More power	Shallow pull
Legs	Whip kick and stretch	More power	Kicking too quickly after pull

continued

SWIMMING SKILLS, continued			
SKILL	**CUE**	**WHY**	**COMMON ERROR**
Flip Turn for Front Crawl	Front somersault (1 stroke from edge of pool)	Gets body in ready position to be more efficient during turn	Body stays flat, too far from or too close to wall
	Bend at waist; be a hinge		
	Put buttocks in air		Not tucking
	Throw legs out of water	More power	
	Find wall with feet		Finding wall with buttocks; too close to wall, finding gutter instead
	Put footprints on wall	More power to push off	
Flip Turn for Backstroke	Turn on stomach 1 stroke from edge	Won't run into wall	
	Do a front flip turn		
	Push off on back like a torpedo, arms above head	Creates better control and power in push off	
Pike Surface Dive	Swim with continuous motion into pike; pull water up; drive your head down	Creates momentum to get body down	No power into pike
	Hands touch toes		Body stays flat
	Be a hinge or break like a pencil at hips		Stay in bent position
	Shoot legs up or put pencil back together as you dive down	Creates energy to get down to bottom of pool	
Tuck Surface Dive	Swim front crawl with continuous motion		No power put into swim
	Drive your head down; pull water up	Creates momentum to get body down fast	
	Swim and roll into ball or cannonball		Head remains up
	Cannonball explodes, shoot feet up in air	Gets body in a straight position to go down	

continued

SWIMMING SKILLS, continued			
SKILL	**CUE**	**WHY**	**COMMON ERROR**
Feet-First Surface Dive			
Arm Action	Start in T position		Starting with hands at side
	Perform jumping-jack action with arms	Gives body momentum	Keeping arms down at sides
	Arms and hands push down like a jumping-jack and push back up like a jumping-jack; or push arms back up like a referee's signal for touchdown	More power to get down Keeps body streamlined	

DIVING

SKILL	CUE	WHY	COMMON ERROR
Safety Rules	Dive in deep water (9 feet or more)	To prevent serious permanent injury	Diving in less than 9 feet of water can cause spinal or head injuries
Side-of-Pool Dive			
Kneeling Position	Kneel on 1 knee; grip pool edge with other foot	If head is up, you will flop in the water	Kneeling on two knees
	Head between arms and fingers pointing to water		Hands and arms moving to front of body
	Focus on target on bottom, 4 feet out; or surface 1–2 feet from side		Not focusing on target (causes a belly flop)
Action of Dive	Lean forward, try to touch water		Jumping in water with head lifted
	Push with front foot		Somersaulting in
	Keep hips up and dive over barrel	Keeps diver from falling into water	Hips down
	Straighten legs		Legs bent
	Push downward in water with hands	Breaks water with hands, not head	Pushing upward
		Does not hurt the head	

continued

DIVING, continued			
SKILL	**CUE**	**WHY**	**COMMON ERROR**
Side-of-Pool Dive, *continued*			
Compact Dive	1 foot forward, 1 foot back		Staying on knee
	Kneel and rise		Staying on knee
	Head between arms, point fingers at water		Head not between arms
	Hips up, stretch, and touch surface of water	Reaching for water gets body into position to go head first	Hips down, hands in air
	Lose balance, push off toward water	Gets students going in head first	
	Ankles together on water entry		Legs apart
Stride Dive	Walking stance		Legs together
	Front toes grab edge		Foot is not at edge
	Head between arms		Head is up
	Bend at the waist like breaking a pencil		Body is straight
	Kick back leg up, hips up	Correct body angle for water entry	Not kicking leg
	Once body is underwater, point fingers to surface of water		Fingers pointed down
Long, Shallow Dive	Push and stretch		Falling in or plopping in
	Spear into the water		Pointing fingers to bottom of pool
	Over the barrel and through the hoop		
	Hands enter through doughnut hole	Helps divers dive out, not deep	
	Go through the tunnel just below surface of water		

continued

DIVING, continued			
SKILL	**CUE**	**WHY**	**COMMON ERROR**
Diving from the Board	Hips up, arms stretched, fall forward; focus on target in water		Hips down
Approach Hurdle	Lift knee like a tabletop or a stork position	Gets diver up in the air	Keeping knee down
	Arms back, like pushing ski poles		
	Arms up to touchdown position		Arms staying down
Jump Off Board	Use approach hurdle position		One or 2 steps in approaching hurdle
	Arms back like a back arm circle	Gives diver power to get up—not out	
	Land on both feet and push off board	Balance and control	
Jump, Tuck Position	Use approach hurdle position		
	Jump off board		
	Lift knees to chest in fetal position; straighten back up in spear position		Not getting in a tuck position
Tuck Dive	Use approach hurdle position		
	Jump in tuck position		
	Lift hips		Hips down
	Drive heels into ceiling	Keeps body straight at entry point	
	Push hands into water, above head		Hands down
Pike Dive	Use approach hurdle position		
	Hips up	Power	Hips down
	Break the pencil		Bending at hips
	Fingers to toes	Gets in pike	
	Drive heels into ceiling	Keeps body straight at entry point	

24

Team Handball

INTRODUCTION

Although it is a popular Olympic sport for men and women throughout the world, team handball is an emerging sport in the United States, where it often suffers from an identity crisis. Most of the world calls the game "handball," but in the United States there is already another sport with that name. When most Americans hear "team handball" mentioned, they mistakenly envision a game like racquetball, played on a court and involving hitting a small black ball with both hands. Without a doubt, team handball is *not off the wall!*

Team handball is a dynamic sport that is fun to play and exciting to watch. Natural athletic skills such as running, jumping, throwing, and catching provide the action for the game. Players and spectators alike enjoy the fast, continuous play, body contact, and goalie action. First-time spectators describe team handball as soccer with your hands, but they also notice elements that remind them of basketball, water polo, and ice hockey.

Team handball is played between two teams, each with six court players and a goalie, on a court larger than a basketball court. The object of the game is to throw a cantaloupe-sized ball into the opponent's 2-meter × 3-meter goal and defend one's own goal from attack. A regulation game is played in 30-minute halves with no time-outs. A coin toss determines which team starts the game with a throw-off. From that point, the action is continuous. The clock stops only for injury or at the referee's discretion. A successful scoring attempt results in the award of one point. Goals scored per game typically range from the upper teens to mid-twenties.

A semicircular line 6 meters from the goal marks the goal area. Only the goalie occupies this area, and both attackers and defenders must remain outside. Basic defense is designed to protect the goal area by placing all six players around it, forming a wall. Defense techniques are similar to those for basketball, except that more contact is allowed. Body contact with the torso is permitted, but players may not push, hold, or endanger an opponent in any way. Excessive roughness results in 2-minute suspensions.

When in attack, players are called backcourts, wings, and circle runners. Passing is the primary way to move the ball in attack. A player is allowed three steps with the ball before and after dribbling, but while stationary may hold the ball for only 3 seconds. The attacking player's task is to find a way over, around, or through the defensive "wall." This is done by using strategies similar to those for basketball, incorporating the concepts of the "give-and-go," screen, pick-and-roll, and overload. The offense may run set plays, but a freewheeling style usually dominates.

SKILLS LISTED WITH CUES

The cues listed for team handball include passing and catching (overhand pass, catching on the run), individual movement in attack (piston movement and sidestepping), shooting (general principles, set shot, jump shot), goalkeeping, defense (basic stance, individual tactics, shot blocking, small-group tactics, team defense: 6–0 zone), offense (attacking the gap, small-group tactics, team offense: fast break, 3–3 formation), and essential team handball rules.

TIPS

1. Write or call the U.S. Team Handball Federation (see the FYI section) to order the *Introduction to Team Handball* video, a televised game from the Olympics, and basic rules.
2. Set up the VCR and TV in the gym the week before you begin a team handball unit. Show the *Introduction* video and 5 minutes of the game video the first day of class.
3. Give each student a handout of the simplified rules.
4. Let students experience the game right away by giving them just a few basic team handball rules using skills they already know from other sports like basketball and softball. Add rules as the game develops.
5. After a goal is scored, the goalie puts the ball back into play right away. As a result, the defense must move back quickly. If the court is small, this practice allows more playing area than would be available if the throw-off were made at half-court.
6. Call plenty of 7-meter penalty throws on major fouls, and let the player who was fouled take the throw (a major foul is one that destroys a sure chance to score or any dangerous play, i.e., pushing, tripping, hitting, undercutting a jumping opponent, or grabbing an opponent's arm). This approach helps keep the game safe, and players will learn faster about serious fouls, clear chances to score, and dangerous play.

EQUIPMENT TIPS

1. Regulation indoor court, 20 meters × 40 meters, approximately 65 feet × 131 feet, one-third larger than a basketball court.
2. Indoors with limited space, that is, only a regulation or smaller basketball court:
   a. Try to maintain 18- to 20-meter width by using extra space outside basketball court.
   b. Small basketball court: Have no sideline boundaries, and play balls off the side walls. Reduce players to five plus a goalie.
   c. After a goal, goalie puts ball back into play with throw-off from the goal area rather than restarting from center court. Goalie cannot leave area or shoot.

3. Outdoor court: playground, grass field, sand beach. For continuous action put an extra ball and student "chaser" behind each goal. Goalie picks up extra ball when shot goes over end line, and student chases the other ball and returns it behind the goal.
4. Marking the court: The most essential lines are the arced 6-meter goal area line and the 7-meter penalty-throw line. Use gym floor tape, basketball court three-point line, cones, rope, "chalk dust," paint, or white flour on grass. The dashed free-throw line is optional (see Figure 24.1).
5. Modified goals, 2-meter × 3-meter opening: Tape on wall, portable standards made with rope or old volleyball nets, large crash mat against wall, field hockey or indoor soccer goals, goals built from PVC pipe.
6. Team handballs (about 23 inches in circumference): For safety reasons, the official men's or women's leather ball is not recommended for beginning players or coed classes. Use Sportime's "Supersafe Elite" handball, a dense foam ball, or a slightly deflated volleyball.

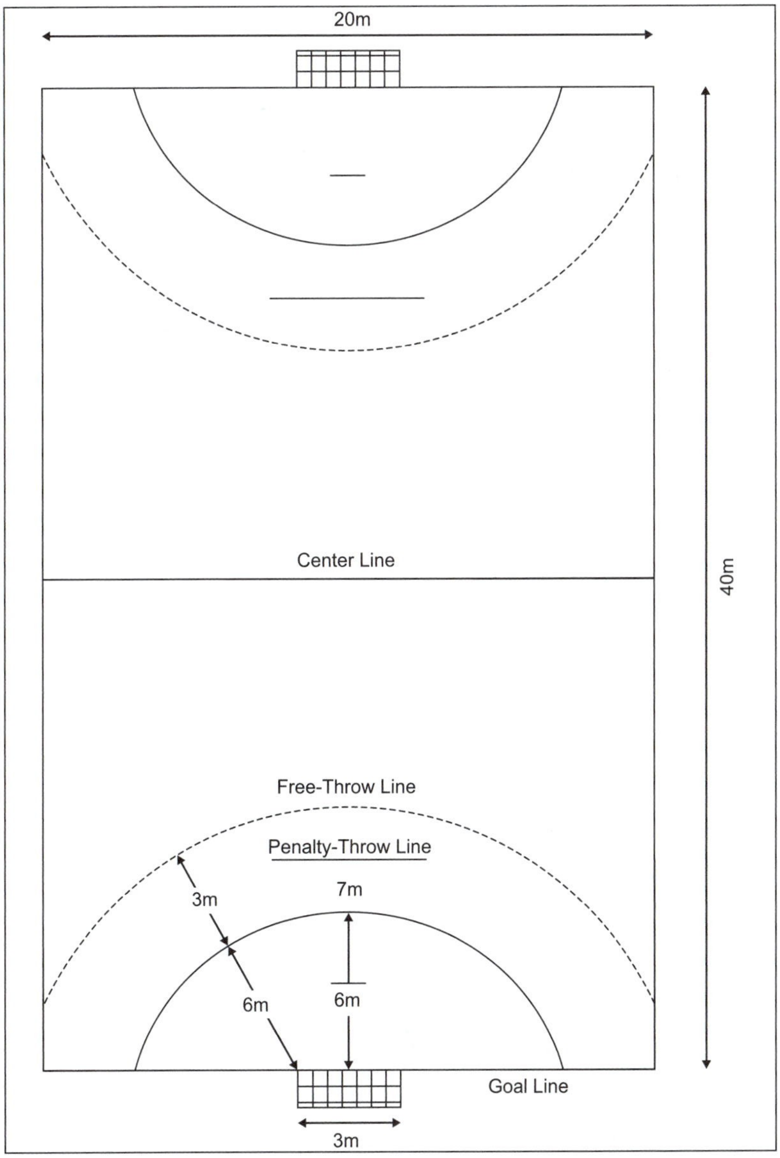

FIGURE 24.1 Team Handball Court

TEACHING IDEAS

1. Teach non-contact basketball-style defense. The official handball rules do allow some body contact, but it is not recommended for beginning players.
2. Use the "teaching rules" during scrimmage to encourage players to develop passing and shooting skills along with increasing goalie safety:
   a. Three passes before the team can shoot.
   b. No dribbling or a limited number of dribbles.
   c. Shoot only bounce shots or play without a goalie in the goal area using targets in the goal corners, that is, towels, cones, hoops, and the like. Only the designated goalie can go into goal area and put ball into play after a shot.

FYI

For further information and special help, consult the following organizations and resources.

ORGANIZATIONS

Available resources for sale: team handball basic rules sheet; team handball rule book; videos: ask for video listing; suggestions: *Introduction to Team Handball,* Olympic games, international games (designate men's or women's).

USA Team Handball
One Olympic Plaza
Colorado Springs, CO 80909
Phone: (719) 575-4036
Fax: (719) 575-4055
E-mail: info@usateamhandball.org
Website: www.usateamhandball.org

U.S. Team Handball Federation
1903 Powers Ferry Road, Suite 230
Atlanta, GA 30339
Phone: (770) 956-7660
Fax: (770) 956-7976

Team handball Special Olympics volunteer coach training school manual can be ordered here.

Special Olympics International
Sports Department
1325 G Street, Northwest, Suite 500
Washington, DC 20005-3104
Phone: (202) 628-3630

SUGGESTED EQUIPMENT COMPANIES

Sportime
Phone: (800) 283-5700
Supersafe Elite Handball (6¾ inch), practice/portable goals, and goal nets

Fold-A-Goal
Phone: (323) 734-2507
Practice, portable goals recommended for school programs

Jayfro
Phone: (860) 447-3001
Folding regulation goals and goal nets

PUBLICATION

Clanton, R., & Dwight, M. P. (1996). *Team handball: Step to success.* Champaign, IL: Human Kinetics.

The authors, physical education teachers/coaches and 1984 Olympians, present an illustrated 12-step progressive program of basic skills and strategies. An excellent teacher resource including drills for increasing and decreasing difficulty of skills, lead-up games, a student rule handout, and more. This book can be ordered from the publisher at (800) 747-4457.

PASSING AND CATCHING

SKILL	CUE	WHY	COMMON ERROR
Overhand Pass	Pass with 1 hand, catch with both		
Preparation	Fingertip grip		Holding ball in palm of hand
	Lift ball up and back with elbow flexed at 90°		Elbow too close to body—ball too close to head
	Weight on back foot		
	Shoulders perpendicular to target		
Throwing Action	Step toward target		
	Rotate and square shoulders to target		No shoulder rotation—always facing target
	Lead with elbow; whip forearm and snap wrist		The ball is pushed from shoulder and hand, and ball leads
Catching on the Run (Figure 24.2, page 322) *Preparation*	Maintain running rhythm		Stopping to catch the ball
Position	Hands up; form a triangle with thumbs and forefingers almost touching		
	Push off one leg, extend arms toward ball		
Receiving Action	Soft hands—catch while flexing elbows to give with ball		Ball rebounds off hands
	Land on other foot		

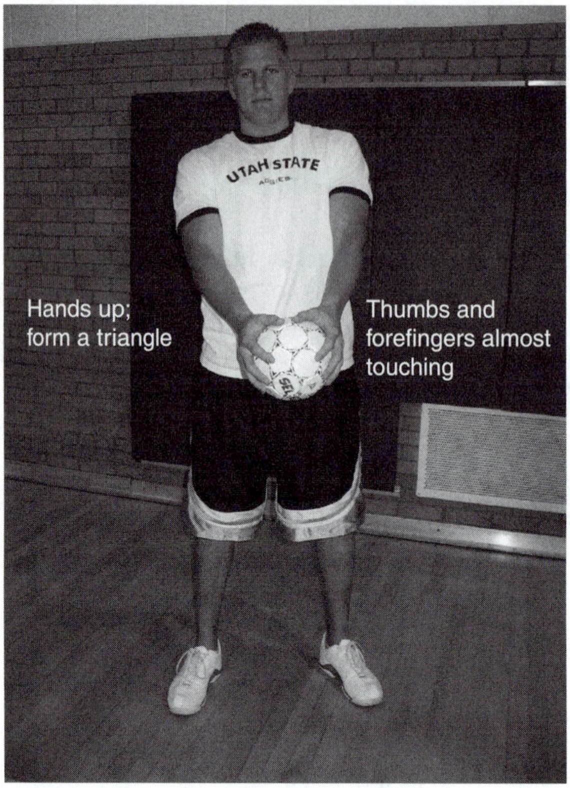

FIGURE 24.2 Catching on the Run

INDIVIDUAL MOVEMENT IN ATTACK

SKILL	CUE	WHY	COMMON ERROR
Piston Movement	Fundamental movement of backcourt players; sum of 3 actions similar to up-and-down motion of a piston in a motor cylinder		
The Three Actions	1. Run to receive; catch ball while running toward goal		Standing in 1 spot to receive pass
	2. Use 3 steps to attack goal; rules—allow 3 steps with ball (i.e., a right-hander should step left-right-left); on third step, shoot or pass, throw off foot that is opposite to throwing arm		Throwing off foot on same side as throwing arm, or passing ball while backing up
			Poor timing

continued

INDIVIDUAL MOVEMENT IN ATTACK, continued			
SKILL	**CUE**	**WHY**	**COMMON ERROR**
Piston Movement *The Three Actions, continued*	3. Back up quickly; prepare to attack again		Forgetting to back up and staying too close to defense
			Watching for action; not moving
Sidestepping	Fundamental movement for circle runners along or near 6-meter line		
Position	Balanced position; knees bent, feet shoulder width apart, hands open ready to catch		Standing upright with hands down, not ready to catch
			Not creating own space
Leg Action	Step sideways using quick, small steps without crossing feet; maintain balanced position		Bringing feet together or crossing feet
			Off balance; poor footwork

SHOOTING			
SKILL	**CUE**	**WHY**	**COMMON ERROR**
General Principles	Shoot on move—piston movement		
	Watch goalie and shoot for open corners of goal; may choose to bounce ball when shooting low		
	Take shots between 6–9 meters; avoid severe angles	Learn to dive into circle to improve angle	Shooting a set shot from a wing position
	Shoot only when there is an opening (shoot over and between defenders)		Charging into a defender or carelessly shooting a ball that hits a stationary defender

continued

SHOOTING, continued			
SKILL	**CUE**	**WHY**	**COMMON ERROR**
Set Shot			
Preparation	Run to receive and attack using 3 steps		Standing still when shooting
	Weight on back foot (same as shooting arm)		Shooting off same foot as shooting arm
	Elbow flexed at 90° or greater		
	Shoulders perpendicular to goal		Facing target, shoulders square to goal
	Head up and eyes on goalie, shoot to open corner; equals "cobwebs"		
Throwing Action	Step forward, transferring weight from rear to front foot		
	Rotate and square shoulders to goal		
	Lead with elbow, whip forearm, and snap wrist		Pushing ball forward from shoulder
Follow-Through	Momentum continues forward and arm motion continues across body		
Jump Shot	Use jump shot to shoot over a defender, or when jumping into the goal area to score		
Preparation	Run to receive and attack using 3 steps		
Jumping Action (Figure 24.3)	To jump: plant foot opposite throwing arm and drive other knee up (changing forward momentum into upward momentum)		Charging into defender; not reading spacing properly
	Raise shooting arm up and back; make an L		
	Rotate shoulders square to goal while whipping throwing arm forward (elbow, shoulder, forearm, wrist)		

continued

FIGURE 24.3 Jump Shot

SHOOTING, continued			
SKILL	**CUE**	**WHY**	**COMMON ERROR**
Throwing Action	Pike slightly at waist and land on takeoff foot		Shot lacks velocity, all power coming from strong upper-body action; poor mechanics

GOALKEEPING			
SKILL	**CUE**	**WHY**	**COMMON ERROR**
Rules	Goalie isn't permitted to 1. Leave goal area while in possession of ball (free throw) 2. Receive a pass from a court player while inside the goal area (penalty throw)		
Goal Throw	Stand inside the goal area and throw ball to a teammate		

continued

GOALKEEPING, continued			
SKILL	**CUE**	**WHY**	**COMMON ERROR**
Goal Throw, *continued*	Goal throw is awarded when 1. Ball is blocked and recovered in goal area 2. Blocked ball goes over the end line 3. Ball is thrown over end line by attacking team		
Goalie Protection	Train all beginning players in basic goalie technique; make sure each player gets a chance to play the position		
	Play with a dense foam ball at beginning level		
	Wear long sleeves and pants		
	Males wear a protective cup		
Basic Position (Figure 24.4)	Stand tall with knees slightly flexed, weight on balls of feet, hands up, eyes on ball (like a jumping jack)		Bending at waist with hands low, similar to basketball defensive position
Movement in Goal	Step out about ½ meter from goal line and follow ball by moving with quick shuffle steps, keeping body aligned with the ball		Standing in middle of goal and not moving
	Get stable prior to shot; be ready to block shot		Feeling off balance when shot is taken
	Protect near post		Poor balance
			Mechanics
Blocking High Shots			
Footwork	Take small step in direction of ball, push off leg farthest from ball, and leap in direction of shot		Leaning, reaching for ball rather than moving body
			Poor mechanics
			Fatigue

continued

FIGURE 24.4 Basic Position of the Goalie

GOALKEEPING, *continued*			
SKILL	**CUE**	**WHY**	**COMMON ERROR**
Blocking High Shots, *continued*			
Blocking Action	Extend arm(s) in path of ball and attack the ball; block ball, don't try to catch it		Ball goes through hands when trying to catch it
			Taking eye off ball
			Weak hands
			Fatigue
Blocking Low Shots			
Footwork	Take small step in direction of ball, push off leg farthest from ball		
Blocking Action	Extend opposite leg and arm(s) in path of ball to block	Strength, balance, and flexibility	Shot goes over leg—failing to block with both leg and arm(s)

continued

GOALKEEPING, continued			
SKILL	**CUE**	**WHY**	**COMMON ERROR**
Blocking Wing Shots			
Position	Stand tall close to goal; place weight on goal-side leg		
	Goal-side arm up, elbow bent about 90° with forearm in front of face, other hand out to side, bent about 90°		
Footwork	As shooter jumps into the goal area, take one step out from the goal and move with quick shuffle steps to keep body aligned with ball		
Blocking Action	Block high shots with arm(s) and low shots with leg and arm(s)		

DEFENSE			
SKILL	**CUE**	**WHY**	**COMMON ERROR**
Individual Basic Stance	Feet shoulder width apart, knees slightly bent, weight forward on balls of feet, body upright, arms out, hands up		Upper body bent forward, hands down, like basketball defensive stance
Individual Defense Tactics			
Movement	Shift along 6-meter line in direction of ball		
	See ball and direct opponent at all times		
	When your opponent attacks, step out from 6-meter line to meet attack—play basketball defense, no contact		Attacker is able to get a shot off from 7 or 8 meters

continued

DEFENSE, continued			
SKILL	**CUE**	**WHY**	**COMMON ERROR**
Individual Defense Tactics *Movement, continued*	Wing defenders should not step out, as a set shot or jump shot is not likely to be successful from such a bad angle		Attacker drives around player and jumps into goal area for a shot
	Stay between opponent and goal		
	When opponent passes the ball, recover to the 6-meter line		Leaving space for circle runner to run behind you
Shot Blocking *Action*	From basic stance, extend one or both hands into path of ball		
	Attack ball similar to volleyball blocking		Ball goes through hands toward goal
Small-Group Defense Tactics	Help triangle—when player steps out, 2 adjacent players squeeze in slightly for help on both sides		Big open space is left along 6-meter line
	Communicate—each defender should know who is stepping out, who is staying back to help	Good offensive	Two players step out to meet 1 attacker, or no one steps out to meet attacker
Team Defense *6–0 Zone*	All 6 defenders take positions along 6-meter line, forming movable wall in front of goal		
	Shift as a unit in direction of ball movement		
	Each defender is responsible for attacker in his/her area of zone—each attacker should be accounted for by 1 defender	Good offensive	One defender guarding 2 attackers, or an attacker left unguarded

OFFENSE

SKILL	CUE	WHY	COMMON ERROR
Individual Offense Tactics *Attack Gap: Space Between 2 Defenders*	Use fakes to get in a gap		
	Create a workable space from defense		Attacking too close to defenders; causing free throws, which interrupt flow of attack
	Be a threat to score; look to shoot first, then pass		Not maintaining proper passing
	Break through gap for a shot from 6-meter line		
	Create overload by drawing 2 defenders and passing to an open teammate		
Small-Group Offense Tactics	2 or 3 players work together to create scoring opportunity		
Basketball-Type Tactics	Give-and-go		
	Pick-and-roll		
	Crossing splits or scissors		
	Screens		
Three Phases of Team Offense *Fast Break*	Primary—long pass from goalie to breaking wing		
	Secondary—goalie shoots outlet pass, and team moves ball up floor quickly		
Organize into 3–3 Offense Formation; Move Ball in Support Points	3 players near the 6-meter line: left wing (LW), right wing (RW), circle runner (CR)		

continued

OFFENSE, continued			
SKILL	**CUE**	**WHY**	**COMMON ERROR**
Three Phases of Team Offense, *continued*	3 players outside 9-meter line in backcourt: left backcourt (LB), center backcourt (CB), right backcourt (RB)		
	Move ball with short, quick passes, wing to wing		
	Run to receive, play in good timing with teammates		
Execute Small-Group Tactics	Play with patience; wait for good scoring opportunity		Trying to score too often one-on-one

ESSENTIAL RULES			
SKILL	**CUE**	**WHY**	**COMMON ERROR**
Goal-Area Line or 6-Meter Line	The most important line on court		
	No one is allowed inside area except goalie; players may jump or dive into area prior to releasing ball		
Players	6 court players, 1 goalie per team		
	Throw-off starts the game and is repeated after every score		
	Offensive team lines up on center line—defense at least 3 meters away		
	Offense passes from center of court to teammate, and play begins		
Playing the Ball	Player is allowed to 1. Run 3 steps (violation = free throw)		

continued

ESSENTIAL RULES, continued			
SKILL	**CUE**	**WHY**	**COMMON ERROR**
Playing the Ball, *continued*	2. Hold ball 3 seconds (violation = free throw) 3. Dribble with no limit, with 3 steps allowed before and after dribbling (no double dribble)		
	Player is *not* allowed to 1. Throw a ball that endangers opponent 2. Pull, grab, or punch ball out of opponent's hands		
Defending an Opponent	For beginners, non-contact basketball-style defense		
Throw-In	Awarded when ball goes out of bounds on sideline or when ball is last touched by defensive player (excluding goalie)		
	Place 1 foot on sideline to throw in		
	Defense 3 meters away		
Free Throw (Minor Fouls and Violations)	Awarded to the opponents at exact spot foul or violation occurred		
	Defense must be 3 meters away; if foul or violation occurs within 3 meters of goal-area line, put ball into play at 9-meter line (free-throw line)		
	Thrower must keep 1 foot in contact with floor		
7-Meter Penalty Throw (Major Foul)	Awarded at 7-meter line when a foul destroys a clear chance to score		
	One-on-one shot with the goalie		
	All other players behind the 9-meter line (free-throw line)		

25

Tennis

INTRODUCTION

No one can describe the stress, intensity, and exhilaration one goes through when stepping up to the line to serve for the big point in tennis. No other sport can match the beating the body gets after a 3-hour match played in 105-degree weather. No other feeling can top the desire to scream a forehand past your opponent after a rally that has made your legs burn. You know it's all up to you. No other game can be as exciting, different, and rewarding for each individual point. No other situation can be as maddening, frustrating, and absolutely glorious as a match of tennis. It gets better every time you step out on the court.

Tennis is not only a sport for a lifetime, but it also helps build character. It teaches you about speed, endurance, agility, anticipation, and quick reaction time. Tennis also tests your mental skills. You learn to control your temper and stay mentally tough to earn those big points that determine who wins the match. To be successful, you must be creative in combining mental and physical skills. Once you are able to do this, you will learn to construct points. It is gratifying to put the different shots and strokes together to earn a point. The satisfaction comes when you hit a great shot. You keep coming back to the court for more.

The more you play, the more fun it gets. You can always reach for the next level. That is why tennis is one of the most enjoyable sports.

SKILLS LISTED WITH CUES

This chapter present cues for the following tennis skills: grip, set position, volley, forehand, teaching progressions for forehand stroke, backhand, teaching progressions for backhand stroke, lob, drop shot, teaching progression for the serve, serve receive, backspin, overhead smash, singles and doubles scoring tiebreaker, and strategies for singles and doubles.

EQUIPMENT TIPS

1. Tennis rackets: Go with the full-size racket unless a player is really young, because they grow out of them so fast.
2. Balls: The teacher needs lots of tennis balls, at least 10 per student.
3. Clothing: Tennis shoes and comfortable clothing are recommended.

TEACHING PROGRESSIONS

1. Teach grip and ready position. Move to forehand and backhand volley, hitting balls with forehand stroke only, then hitting balls with backhand stroke only. The next step is to alternate the forehand and the backhand. Play a game with a forehand stroke to feed the ball and get the game started using volley forehand and backhand skills. Teach the tennis serve last.
2. Try not to hit in the *doughnut hole* area—the center—of the court. Why? Because your opponent can stand there, hit the ball back and forth, and move you all over the court.
3. When working on positioning, imagine two magnets. One magnet is centered behind the baseline, while the other is at the center of the court, about one to two steps from the net. Have the magnets draw you to one of these two spots on the court. The goal for the receiver is to stay out of the doughnut hole, which is in the middle of the court. Players can pass you easily by hitting a shot deep into the court.
4. See teaching progressions after each skill.

MINI-GAMES FOR TENNIS

1. *Quarter-court games* (see Figure 25.1):
   a. Play games inside the service area using volleys, where points are quickly scored.
   b. The game is started with the ball on top of the net. Drop the ball and play it out.

FIGURE 25.1 Quarter-Court Games

c. Players begin to volley the ball back and forth.

d. Whoever has the ball can start the point.

e. You can play games to 7 points and switch sides.

2. *Half-court games:* Two players play on a half-court. The rules are the same as a ground-stroke game. Play games to 7 points.

3. *Ground-stroke points:*

   a. To put the ball in play, bounce the ball and hit it underhand anywhere in the opposite court.

   b. Singles court lines for singles games and doubles court lines for the doubles games.

   c. The ball can bounce only once in your court.

   d. Whoever has the ball can start the point.

   e. Pick a total, such as 11 points, and the first one to reach the score wins. You can play best of three or best of five and rotate with your neighbors.

   f. This drill is great for learning to put points together.

4. *Regulation tennis game, one serve:* Only hit a second serve.

5. *Regulation tennis game, two serves:* You can hit a harder first serve.

6. *Five misses:*

   a. Four players on a court at a time with "alternates" at the net post. (There can be just one player at the net post.)

   b. Players play out a ground-stroke point together, and whoever misses goes to the net post.

   c. One at a time, the alternates replace the misses.

   d. As soon as a player has five misses, the game is over and you form new teams.

   e. You can also do this game with a feeder in one of the posts. The feeder tosses the ball in the court to start play.

   f. Players rotate after each point with alternates at each net post.

FYI

For further information and special help, consult the following organization.

ORGANIZATION

U.S. Tennis Association (USTA)
70 West Red Oak Lane
White Plains, NY 10604
Phone: (914) 696-7000
Fax: (914) 696-7167
Website: www.usta.com

GRIPS

SKILL	CUE	WHY	COMMON ERROR
Forehand Grip (Right-handed) (Figure 25.2)	Lay racquet flat to get correct grip		
	Shake hands with palm behind racquet	Puts racquet in proper position	
	Hold the end of the racquet	Greater speed with a longer implement and greater reach area to contact the ball	Gripping too high on the handle
	Index knuckle on third bevel close to fourth bevel	Gives you vertical hitting surface so ball does not go into net or fly long	Gripped so racquet face is too open or too closed
Backhand Grip (Figure 25.3)	Turn racquet clockwise so palm is on top of racquet	The ball flies long if you don't rotate your grip. Remember: "Grip wrong, ball long"	
	Index knuckle on second bevel	Gives you vertical hitting surface so ball does not go into net or fly long	

continued

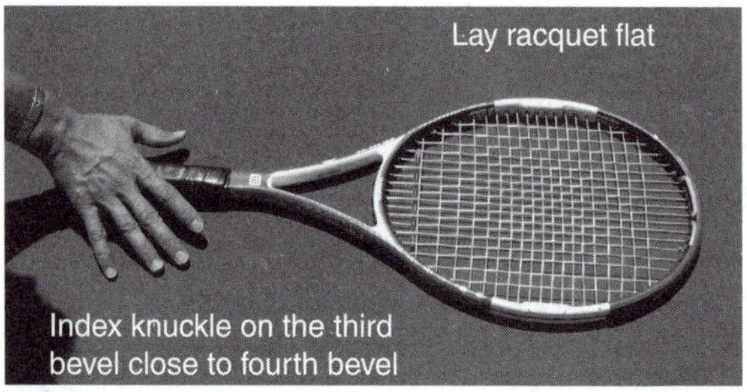

(a) Placement

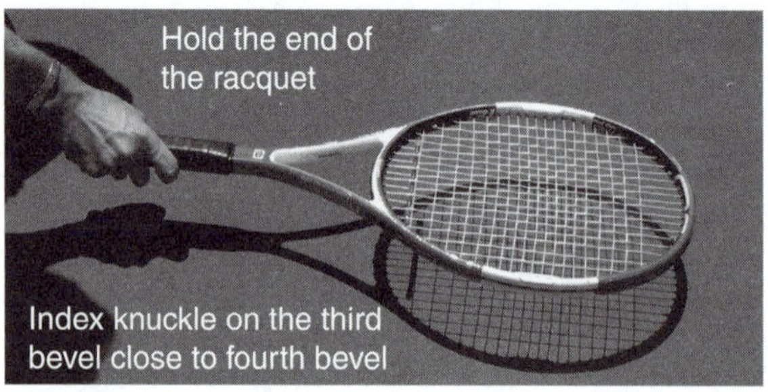

(b) Grip

FIGURE 25.2 Forehand Grip

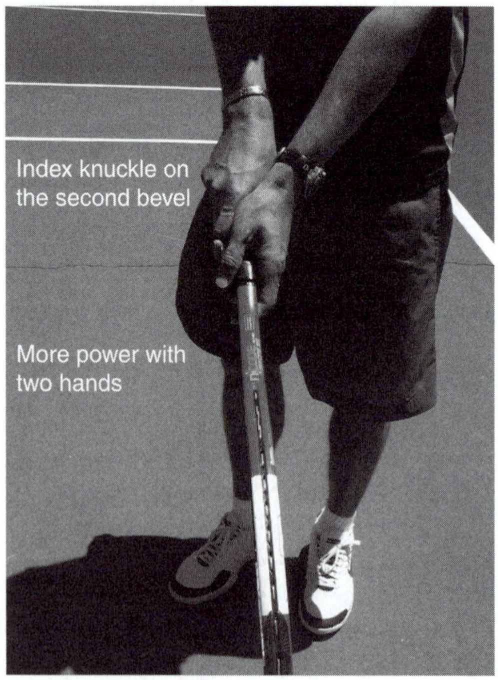

FIGURE 25.3 Two-Handed Backhand Grip

GRIPS, continued

SKILL	CUE	WHY	COMMON ERROR
Two-Handed Backhand Grip (Right-handed)	Same cues for regular backhand	Quick reaction time	Hold racquet too tight with both hands
	Keep left hand up to anticipate hitting a backhand	More power with both hands	
	Grip left hand above right hand on racquet	Proper racquet position	
	Left index knuckle on third bevel		
Bevel	Top bevel of the racquet is number 1; second bevel is number 2; third bevel is number 3; and fourth bevel, number 4		
Right-handed Players	Right-handed players rotate bevels in a clockwise direction		
Left-handed Players	Left-handed players rotate bevels in counter-clockwise direction		

VOLLEYS

SKILL	CUE	WHY	COMMON ERROR
Forehand Volley	Index knuckle on second bevel for both forehand and backhand	No time to change much for quicker reaction time to ball	Having a grand stroke grip
(Figure 25.4, page 338)	Turn shoulders to get racquet ready	Positions racquet to move straight forward	No turn
	Firm wrist, firm grip	Prevent the racquet from coming out of hand, especially if the ball is hit hard into the racquet	Dumping the head of racquet down
	Hand below ball, racquet and wrist form L; do not let racquet head drop	Firm contact when you hit the ball; better control and accuracy	
	Contact ball in font of body	Makes for better contact	Contacting ball late

continued

FIGURE 25.4 Forehand Volley

FIGURE 25.5 Backhand Volley

VOLLEYS, continued			
SKILL	**CUE**	**WHY**	**COMMON ERROR**
Forehand Volley, *continued*	Be aggressive; in this shot, go get the ball, don't wait for the ball to come to you	Places the opponent on the defensive	
	Bend at the knees and keep the back vertical		
Backhand Volley (Figure 25.5)	Same as forehand volley cues, just hitting on backhand side		Pulling racquet with right hand; lead with your left
	Bow-and-arrow position		
	Index knuckle on second bevel		

FOREHAND STROKE—RIGHT HAND

SKILL	CUE	WHY	COMMON ERROR
Grip	Index knuckle on 3rd bevel close to the 4th bevel	The ball does not go high and you can get under the ball	
Preparation (Figure 25.6)	Turns shoulders early	Early prep allows for contacting ball in front of body	Turning late
Footwork	Turning shoulders causes a pivot on the back foot and a step toward net		Allowing the ball to come to you, rather than taking a step in as you hit
Stroke Action	Turn body as racquet goes from low to high	Enhances power	Staying sideways to net
Contact Point	Contact point, racquet is in vertical plane	Accuracy	Not keeping head still
(Figure 25.7)	Hit ball even with front hip	Easier to see and hit solidly	Hitting late

continued

FIGURE 25.6 Forehand Stroke Preparation

FIGURE 25.7 Forehand Stroke Contact Point

FOREHAND STROKE—RIGHT HAND, continued			
SKILL	**CUE**	**WHY**	**COMMON ERROR**
Finish and Follow-Through (Figure 25.8)	Swing low to high and finish with belly button facing net	Using body creates power	Pulling up too quickly on follow-through
	Point elbow toward the opponent when done	To get good topspin; ball will not go out of bounds	Swinging too slow using topspin; the ball needs to be hit aggressively
	Kiss your biceps	The friction created with "over-the-ball" motion will give more powerful topspin	
	Bend knees and get low	Ball will not go into net if you get low and bend your knees	Ball goes into net

FIGURE 25.8 Forehand Stroke: Finish and Follow-Through

TEACHING PROGRESSION FOR FOREHAND

Check grip first—always, always, always

To practice the grip, have students bounce the ball with their racquet, using the appropriate grip. They can bounce the ball up or down and count how many they get.

1. Have players stand 1 to 2 feet away from the tennis fence. Start with racquet head back, and in closed position swing the racquet to contact point. Make sure the racquet is vertical. On the follow-through, racquet goes over the opposite shoulder and elbow points toward the opposite court. Swing from low to high and finish "kissing the biceps." Step 5 feet away from fence, drop the ball, and hit it into the fence.
2. When students' stroke is done with control, move to the court. Drop-hit a ball over the net. Give them a target to aim for—for example, hit down the alley.
3. Next, teach students how to toss to a partner. One student tosses a ball underhand so that it bounces 5 to 8 feet in front of his or her partner. Toss a ball back and forth until they have good accuracy. The ball should bounce at least waist high.
4. When ready, the students toss the ball to their partners. The tosser stands off to the side of the net and tosses balls to his or her partner, who is standing at the service line ready to stroke the ball (see Figure 25.9).
5. The tosser is on one side of the net and tosses balls to his or her partner, who is standing on the baseline ready to stroke the ball. Encourage students by saying it doesn't matter where the ball is landing, but stress the importance of good form on their stroke. When they have some accuracy, allow them to hit forehands back and forth with their partner.

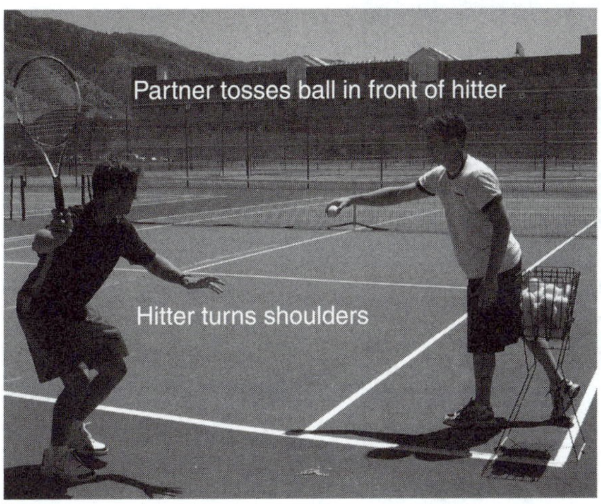

(a) Step 1

(b) Step 2

FIGURE 25.9 Partner Forehand Drill

TWO-HANDED BACKHAND—RIGHT HAND

SKILL	CUE	WHY	COMMON ERROR
Grip	Left hand up early, grab racquet	Reaction time	
	Right hand index knuckle to second bevel	Accuracy for shot	
	This hand is only there for support		
Preparation	Turn shoulders early	Early prep allows for contacting ball in front of body	Twisting late
Footwork	Shoulder turn causes a pivot on back foot and step toward net		Not taking a step into the court as you hit
Stroke Action (Figure 25.10)	Bend at knees, back vertical	Better shot accurarcy	
	Turn shoulders early	Better power, better accuracy	

continued

FIGURE 25.10 Backhand Stroke Preparation

TWO-HANDED BACKHAND—RIGHT HAND, continued			
SKILL	**CUE**	**WHY**	**COMMON ERROR**
Contact Point (Figure 25.11)	Contact point vertical and off the front hip	So ball will land in court	Not leading with the left hand
Finish (Figure 25.12)	Follow through high and finish over opposite shoulder	To achieve topspin	
	"Kiss your biceps"		

FIGURE 25.11 Backhand Contact Point

FIGURE 25.12 Backhand Stroke Finish and Follow-Through

TEACHING PROGRESSION FOR BACKHAND

1. Demonstrate the backhand grip. Line students along the fence and have them shadow-swing from low to high following the cues.
2. Partner drop-feeds the ball to partner. Hit into the fence.
3. When they feel comfortable with the stroke, line students on the baseline and partner-feed. Give them a target to hit ball in the court, down the line, or crosscourt.
4. When the students are ready, pair them up. Have one student stand off to the side of the net and toss balls to his or her partner, who is standing at the service line, ready to stroke the ball.
5. Have partner feed ball from the other side of the net.
6. Rally backhand to backhand.
7. Partner tosses the ball to alternating sides. Forehand, backhand, forehand, backhand, etc. This drill gets players to change grips, move feet to the ball, and learn how to hit backhands in a gamelike situation.
8. Teach a ground-stroke game. It incorporates all the skills students have learned and gives them gamelike practice with lots of repetitions.

GAMES FOR LEARNING FOREHANDS, BACKHANDS, AND VOLLEYS

1. See "Rally Game" in pickleball (Chapter 17).

LOB AND DROP SHOT

SKILL	CUE	WHY	COMMON ERROR
Lob	Rotate racquet opposite of backhand		
	Swing low to high	Ball goes up in air	Hitting ball too hard
	Soft touch		
	Pull racquet arm to opposite shoulder		No follow-through
Offensive	Lob must be height of fence; lob over fence		Not aiming lob
	Hit to big square	Having a place to aim gives play more control and accuracy	Lob too short; not following through
	Hit higher than the fence (good practice height)		
Drop-Shot Slice	Act like hitting a backhand or forehand, but cut shot in half	More control of ball	Full follow-through
	Soft touch at contact		

SERVE—RIGHT HAND

SKILL	CUE	WHY	COMMON ERROR
Grip	Right-hand index knuckle on second bevel	Accuracy and control	Holding racquet too tight
Foot Placement (Figure 25.13)	Point left foot toward right net post; if left-handed, right foot toward left net post	This allows for good shoulder rotation and power	
	Left foot 4 inches from baseline	Prevents foot fault	Foot too close to the baseline
	Back foot comfortable position	Stability and balance	
Toss	Hold ball in finger-tips	Control of ball	
	Hold the ball down by leg	Control and accuracy of toss	
	Gently toss the ball high	Timing for serve	Tossing too high hurts power and rhythm
(Figure 25.14)	Keep arm straight all the way up	Accuracy of toss	
	Hold arm up until ball contacts racquet	You will "feel" the ball better	

continued

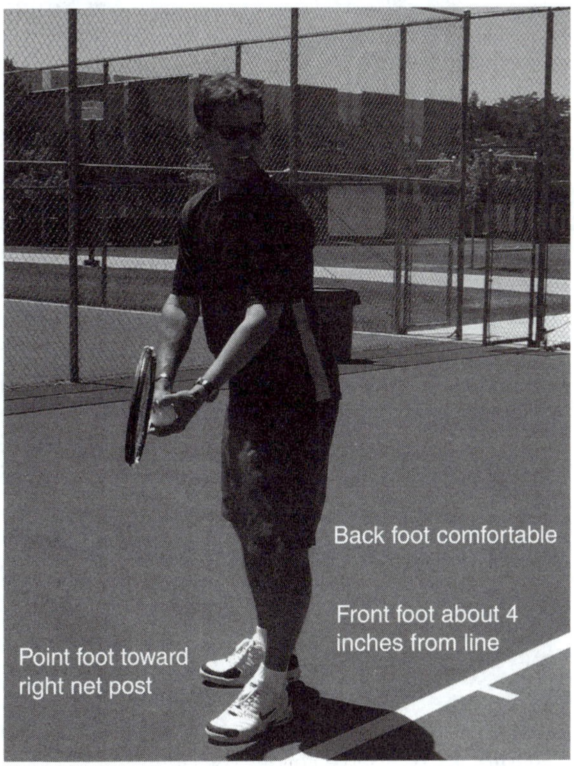

FIGURE 25.13 Serve Setup

FIGURE 25.14 Serve Toss

SERVE—RIGHT HAND, continued			
SKILL	**CUE**	**WHY**	**COMMON ERROR**
Stroking Action (Figure 25.15)	Hit high and in front of you	Power and good contact point	
	Racquet motion is like throwing a ball	Creates a powerful serve	
Follow-Through (Figure 25.16)	Arm action comes across the body	Completes the motion of your serve and power isn't lost	
	The shoulder of the arm that hits the serve rotates to where the other shoulder was	The movement naturally provides more power as body weight goes into serve	
Let	Ball hits top of net, goes over net into court; serve is taken over again		Calling it a fault or double fault (on first or second serve)
Ace	Serve is in, and receiver cannot touch it		
Double Fault	Neither of 2 serves goes into court		

FIGURE 25.15 Serve Stroking Action

FIGURE 25.16 Serve Follow-Through

TEACHING PROGRESSION

1. Teach the ball toss first. Place the racquet on the ground at a 30-degree angle and place foot at the end of the handle. Toss the ball up and try to hit the strings of the racquet.
2. Have students throw a ball into the service box. If they can throw it into the box, they can serve it into the box.
3. Teach the entire serve.
4. If the student has difficulty with the serve, have her or him start the serve with racquet up behind head.
5. Allow beginners to serve up close and then move back to the baseline when they are ready.

RECEIVING SERVE

SKILL	CUE	WHY	COMMON ERROR
Powerful Serve	Short backswing	Better control of ball	Bringing racquet too far back
	Watch ball go into racquet		Looking to the target early
	Block ball		Overhitting
			Big follow-through
	Like a volley		
Less Powerful	Hit ball into court		

SPIN AND SMASH SHOTS

SKILL	CUE	WHY	COMMON ERROR
Topspin	Racquet swings low to high		Swinging level
	Candy cane swing		
	Racquet starts knee-high and finishes nose-high		
Backspin (Slice) (Figure 25.17, page 348)	Racquet swings high to low		Swinging level
	Cut through ball		
	Watch ball hit strings		
Overhead Smash	Hit like the serve		
	Left foot in front; power with left foot		Power comes from both feet or back foot
	Point elbow to ball with left hand		Misjudging ball by losing focus of ball

FIGURE 25.17 Backspin

RULES

To start a game, the server starts behind the baseline and to the right of the center line. The server is given two serves to get the ball into the right service court of the opponent (see Figure 25.18). Whoever wins the rally earns the point.

"Love–15" would be the score if the receiver won the first rally.
"15–Love" would be the score if the server won the first rally.

The server then moves to the left of the center mark behind the baseline and serves to the opponent's left service court (see Figure 25.18). The server continues to alternate service courts each time a point is scored by either the server or the opponent. After 40, the next point wins the game. (If score is 40–40, it's deuce; players continue playing until someone wins 2 points in a row.)

After a game is completed, the opponent gets to serve. Alternate serving games until one player has won six games. See scoring cue boxes in the following tables for more information.

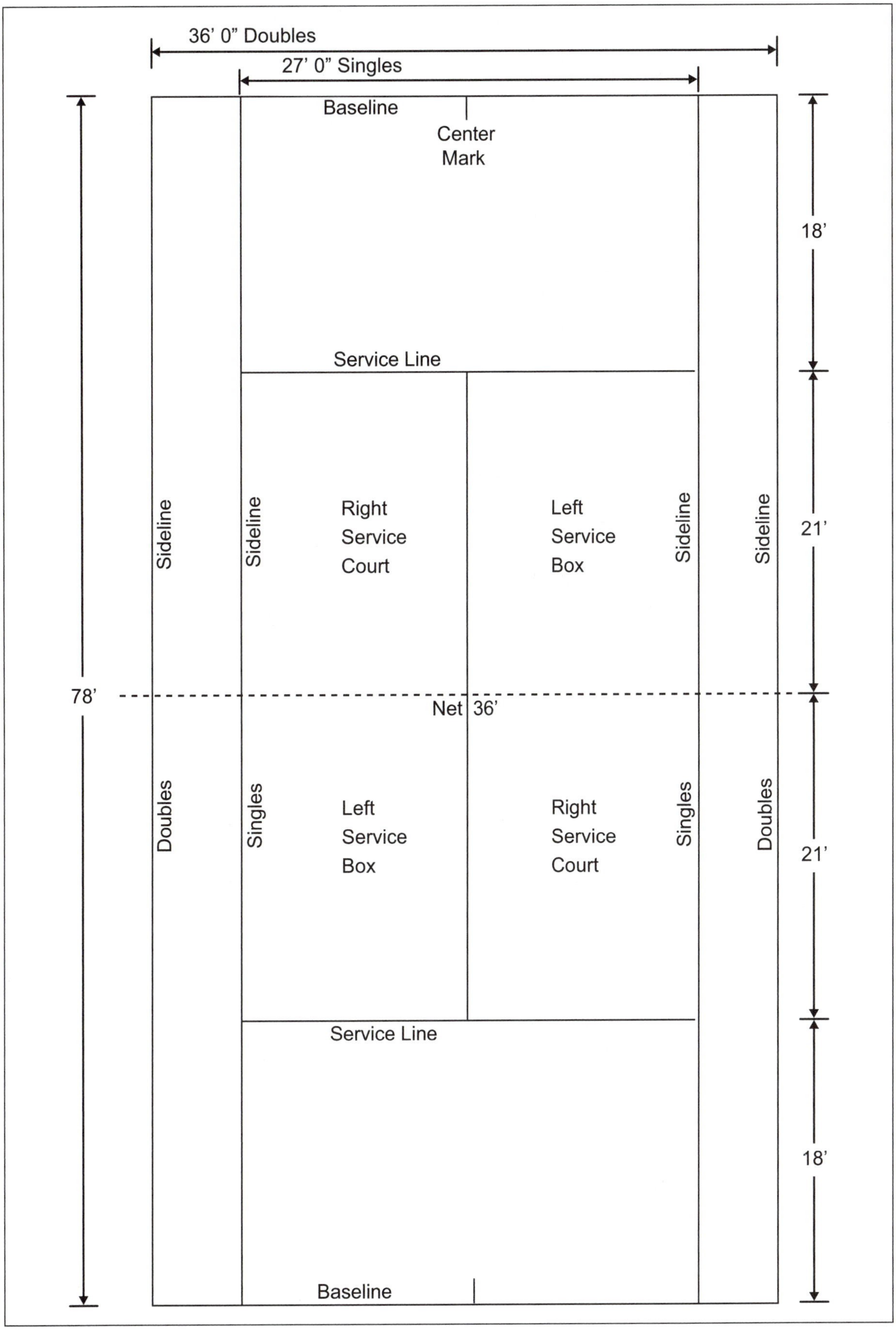

FIGURE 25.18 Tennis Court

SINGLES SCORING

SKILL	CUE	WHY	COMMON ERROR
Rules	First score is the server's score		Saying receiver's score first
	In this game, *love* means zero		
	Love (0), 15, 30, 40, game 15–0 = 15–love 0–15 = love–15 30–30 = 30 all 40–40 = deuce		
	Win by 2, deuce and ad		
	Scoring is used for game, set, and match		
	Ad in: server's advantage		
	Ad out: opponent's advantage		
	Or in "no ad": 1–2–3–game		
	No ad after 3–3		
	Next point is game point		
	Receiver chooses side on which to receive serve		
Playing a Set	Change sides on the odd-numbered games: 1, 3, 5, 7		
	Win 6 games; win by 2 games		
	If each player wins 6 games, a tiebreaker is played		
Match Play	*Women:* Win 2 out of 3 sets		
	Men: Win 3 out of 5 sets		

DOUBLES SCORING

SKILL	CUE	WHY	COMMON ERROR
Rules	Partner A1 serves 1 complete game		
	After the set you can serve 2 in a row (at the end of first set and beginning of second set, the server can serve 2)		
	Partners always serve from opposite sides of court		
	Opponent B1 serves 1 complete game		
	Partner A2 serves 1 complete game		
	Opponent B2 serves 1 complete game		
Doubles Receiver	*Deuce court* is the right side		Switching during set
	Ad court is the left side		
	At beginning of set, each player chooses which side to receive—deuce or ad court		
	Must stay in that court to receive serve		Receiver's teammate stepping into server's box
	Change sides of court every odd-numbered game		

TIEBREAKER

SKILL	CUE	WHY	COMMON ERROR
7-Point Tiebreaker	Service begins with the player who received in the 12th game		1–love
	Don't call zero–love in a tiebreaker (1–zero)		
	Player A serves first point from deuce (right) court: 1 point		
	Player B serves from ad (left) court first and then from deuce (right) court: 2 and 3 points		
	Player A (C in doubles) serves from ad (left) court first and then from deuce (right) court: 4 and 5 points		
	Player B (D in doubles) serves from ad (left) court first and then from deuce (right) court: 6 and 7 points		
	Change courts after every 6 points		Stop match by having a rest
	Cannot take more than 90 seconds		
	Grab towel and move to court		
	First player to score 7 points wins		
	Win by 2 points		

26

Touch Rugby

INTRODUCTION

Touch rugby is a highly enjoyable running game with the objective of scoring tries. Developed in Sydney, Australia, in 1960, it is a noncontact version of the rugby league game that can be played anywhere by men and women of all ages and abilities. It is a great way to raise your level of fitness and improve your ball-handling skills, and besides all that, it's just a lot of fun. It's always coed, and unlike touch football, there is no specialization in positions. It's continuous; there's no stopping to make plays, so think while you're running. The faster you are able to get in position and move the ball, the greater the advantage you will have.

SKILLS LISTED WITH CUES

The cues in this chapter cover the fundamentals of the sport such as passing and catching. It also covers offense and defense, some basic strategies, and basic rules.

TIPS

Start by teaching players how to catch and pass. Then, run wings unopposed (this is called "all-blacks"). A wing is when players line up on a 45-degree angle approximately 3 to 5 meters apart. Players advance together, holding this formation until the ball is passed to them. Once they receive the ball, they pass it to the next player in the line and retreat behind the player who now has the ball to stay onsides. When players can do this efficiently, it is time to split into teams and play a game.

EQUIPMENT TIPS

1. A rugby ball looks like a big football with rounded tips; they can be purchased on rugby Internet sites.
2. A touch rugby pitch (field) is 70 meters long × 50 meters wide. There is a halfway line with two 10-meter lines on each side of the halfway line (see Figure 26.1).
3. Pullover vests.

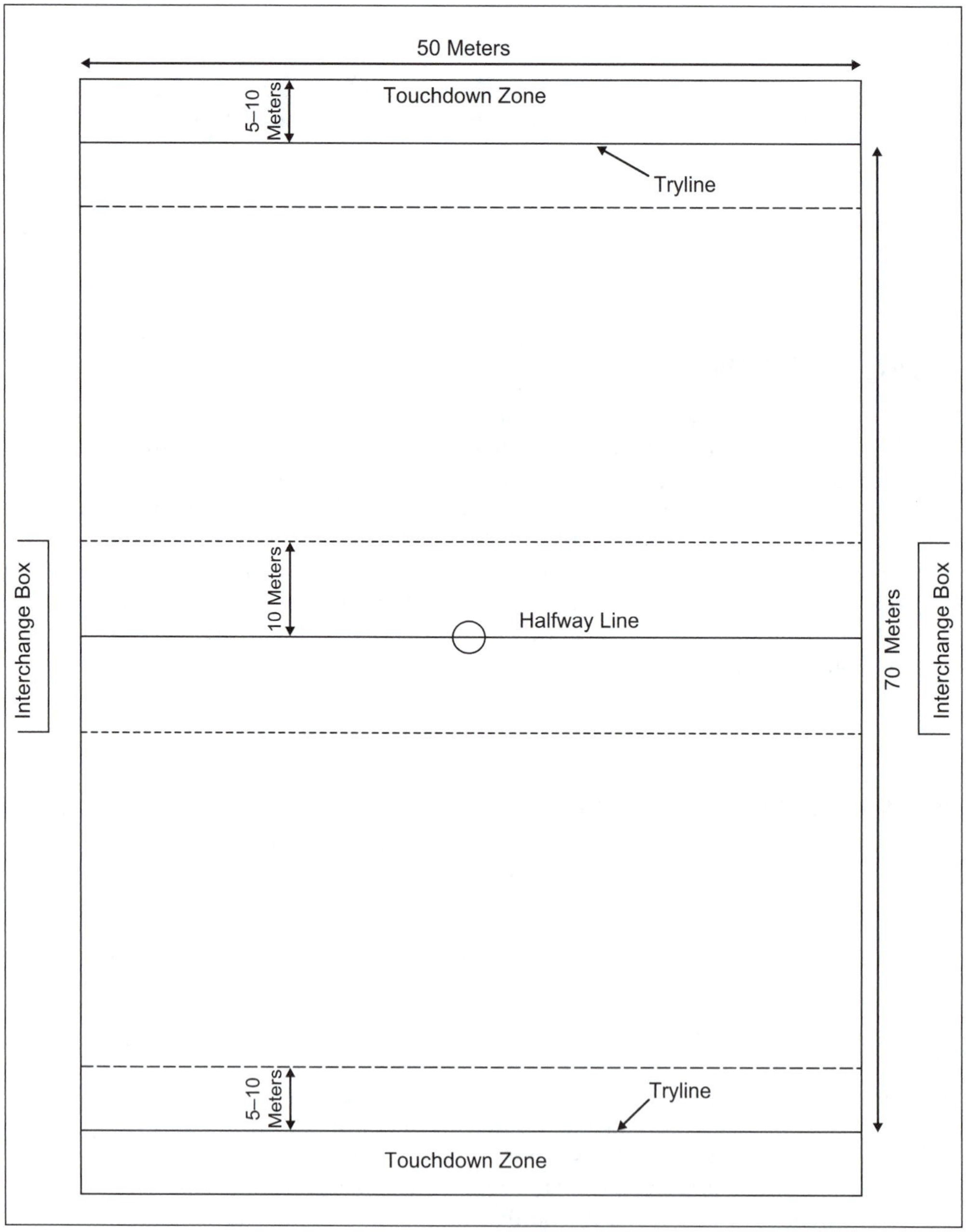

FIGURE 26.1 Touch Rugby Field

TEACHING IDEAS

1. Referee can limit the number of touches before the ball is turned over.
2. Generally played with 7 players on each team, but the game can be played with as few as 5 or as many as 10. Modify the field to account for more or less players.
3. If teams are uneven, the scrum-half (player who picks up the ball after the rollball) on the short team can run with the ball.
4. A rule can be made that any dropped ball (even if it is knocked on by the defensive team) is a turnover.
5. Rules for kicking can be adapted for more advanced teams.
6. Defense cannot advance during a rollball or tap, allowing the offense to gain momentum.

BASIC RULES AND GAME PLAY

1. Officially, the game is divided into two halves of 25 minutes each. There is a 5-minute break at halftime, and teams change direction in the second half.
2. To start the game, the ball is tapped at the halfway mark. This consists of a player releasing the ball. The ball touches his or her foot and returns to the player's hands. The ball is then live. Defensive players must be 10 meters behind the halfway mark but can advance as soon as the ball is tapped. A tap is also used to recommence play after a try is scored and on penalties (Figure 26.2 on page 356).
3. Offensive team forms wings and uses strategies to gain field advantage while attempting to score touchdowns.
4. Each team is allowed six touches before change of possession. A legal touch includes touching the ball, shoes, hair, shirt, etc. When the defense makes contact with the ball carrier they should stop, raise their hand, and call out "touch." The offense must initiate the rollball from that spot.
5. The defensive team marks players and attempts to cause the offensive team to make errors to receive possession of the ball.
6. Penalties are awarded in cases of shepherding (blocking), offside infringements, forward passes, and player misconduct. The defensive team must be back at least 10 meters on a penalty tap.
7. A rollball is used to restart play after a player is touched (Figure 26.3 on page 356).
8. During a rollball, the defense is required to be 5 meters back.

VOCABULARY

1. *Pitch:* In rugby, the field of play is called a pitch.
2. *Touch line:* This is the out-of-bounds line.
3. *Forward pass:* The ball is not passed backward or laterally, but it is passed to a teammate who is in front of the passer. This results in a penalty.
4. *Dropped ball:* Any time the ball is not caught, it is considered a dropped ball. The result is a turnover.
5. *Try zone touchdown:* This is similar to an end zone in football. To score, the player with the ball must cross into this zone and touch the ball under his or her control to the ground.

FIGURE 26.2 Tapping the Ball

FIGURE 26.3 Rollball

6. *Shepherding:* A player who is on offense and prevents a defensive player from tagging his or her teammate who has the ball is shepherding, and it is a turnover. No, this isn't football, and you can't block. It results in a penalty and the defense must start back 10 meters.
7. *Rollball:* Used to restart play after a player is touched or the ball is turned over.
8. *Offside:* An imaginary horizontal line runs across the field where the ball is situated. Players must stay on their own side of the line; if the line is crossed, the player is offside. Interference with play from an offside position is a penalty.
9. *Scrum-half/acting-half:* The player who picks up the ball after a rollball is in the scrum-half/acting-half. This player role changes with each play, depending on who is closest to the ball (the idea is to get the ball out quickly to catch the defense off guard). The scrum-half has the choice to run with the ball or pass the ball, but if this player gets touched, it is a turnover. Additionally, this player cannot score since at least one pass must be made to score.

FYI

For further information and special help, consult the following organization and resource.

ORGANIZATION

Australian Touch Association
P.O. Box 9078
Deakin, ACT 2600
Australia

WEBSITE

www.touchrugby.com

CATCHING

SKILL	CUE	WHY	COMMON ERROR
Call for Ball Support	"With you" or "On your left/right," etc.	More likely to gain field advantage if your teammates know they can pass to you	Not letting your teammates know where you are
Hands Out (Figure 26.4)	Chest level	Give a target	Hands too big; ball slides through and bounces off chest
	Form triangle—like setting in volleyball (but in front of you instead of over your head)		Hands too small, jammed fingers, dropped balls
	Hands should be just a little wider than the ball and collapse easily around the ball as contact is made		

FIGURE 26.4 Catch, Call, and Release for the Ball

PASSING

SKILL	CUE	WHY	COMMON ERROR
Eye Contact	Make eye contact with the person the ball is going to	Make sure of recipient of pass	Passing without looking
Stance	Stand sideways	Use core muscles in rotation for greater power	Facing the target
Grip	Hold with both hands		
	Hold on bottom third of ball	Harder for opponents to knock ball from hands	Grabbing middle of ball
	Thumbs point toward sky, fingers wide and spread around ball	Ball is wobbly in the air and hard to catch	Ball not vertical at time of release
	Ball is vertical		
Leg Action	Short to medium step with leg closest to target	Inaccurate	Overstriding
	Rotate at hips	Less power	No rotation
Arm Action	Arms firm	More power and accuracy in pass	Using only 1 hand
	Swing like a pendulum or an elephant's trunk across body	Uses shoulder muscles instead of arm muscles	Arms too loose or too rigid
			Trying to spin the ball (long passes will have a natural spin)
Release (Figure 26.4)	Underhand, sideways toss	Most accurate and controlled way to pass	Trying to pass like a basketball (forcing from chest rather than letting arms swing)
	Release right at the top of the pendulum swing		
	Ball must go backward or lateral	If ball goes forward, it is a turnover	Trying to pass like a lateral pass in football
			Releasing too high or too low
			Passing forward

OFFENSE

SKILL	CUE	WHY	COMMON ERROR
Rollball (Figure 26.4)	The ball is placed on the ground and rolled between the legs with either the hands or foot	To restart play after a touch or a turnover	Too slow, allowing defense to get set
	All defensive players must be back 5 meters		
Scrum-Half Pass (Figure 26.3)	An offensive player picks up the ball after the rollball and passes to another teammate (the person closest to the ball picks it up; this player is the scrum-half for that play)	Puts the ball in play; once the scum-half has both hands on the ball or passes it, the ball is live and the defensive team can attack	The scrum-half cannot score off a rollball; at least 1 pass must be made to score
	This player can run with the ball, but if touched, possession is lost	So one player cannot dominate play	
Wings	Players line up on a 45° angle approximately 3–5 meters apart	To receive the ball, you must be behind the passer; lining up like this gives you the chance to catch the ball at full speed, allowing you to advance farther	Players line up straight
	Players advance together, holding this formation until the ball is passed to them		
	They pass it on before they are tagged and retreat behind the player, who now has the ball to stay onside		Passing the ball forward
			Catching the ball flatfooted
	Run straight up the field	Running across the field takes away field space from teammates	Running sideways, trying to cut corners

continued

OFFENSE, continued			
SKILL	**CUE**	**WHY**	**COMMON ERROR**
Basic Strategies			
Loops/Wraps	First player in wing passes the ball and then loops behind teammates to take a pass on the far side; this causes an overload	If you can get a player open on the end, you can gain field advantage with an overload	Shepherding
			Not communicating
			Getting ahead of the person with the ball; can't make a pass forward
Skips	Passing past the next player in the line to an open player; can skip 1 or more players	Get the ball to a player who can break through a hole	Receiver not ready to catch
Cutting/Switching	Making a sharp cut off the hip of the player with the ball	To hit a gap and break through the defensive line	Too far away from ball carrier
Scoring (Figure 26.5)	1 point is awarded when the ball carrier crosses into the try zone and touches the ball to the ground without losing control	Losing control of ball	Results in a turnover; not touching the ball to the ground; no point awarded; roll ball 5 meters from try zone.
			Dropped ball, turnover 5 meters from try zone

FIGURE 26.5 Try Zone/Touchdown

FIGURE 26.6 Legal Touch

DEFENSE			
SKILL	**CUE**	**WHY**	**COMMON ERROR**
Tagging (Figure 26.6)	Touch the player with the ball; a legal touch includes contact with ball, shoes, hair, shirt, etc.	To stop advancement; forces the offensive team to reset; when tagged 6 times, the ball is turned over	Excessive force as called by the ref can result in a penalty
Marking	Pick a player; if that player moves, follow him or her; if he or she has the ball, tag him or her	Easier defense for beginners	Letting your man through a hole
	Watch the waist	Don't get juked—faked out	Watching the head, ball, or feet
Sliding	Zone defense rather than man	Physically easier; more fun	Not reacting fast enough
	If offensive player loops/cuts/switches, the defensive team slides to mark the new man	As in any sport, communication is important; always let your team know where you are and who you are guarding	Not communicating effectively
	If you call the end, you always mark the offensive player who is on the end; if you call 2 in, you always mark the player second from the end		Offensive team develops overload or breaks through holes, thinking your teammate will make a tag that should be yours
Interception	If you catch a pass from the offensive team, the play continues in your possession	If you make a play from an offsides positions, it is a tap penalty	You cannot hang out in the passing lane waiting for a pass; you must charge a pass from your line and catch it cleanly to gain possession
Offsides	Defensive players cannot be behind the ball; they must start 5 meters back from rollball, then must remain even with the ball during play	Results in a tap penalty	Going too far forward

27

Track and Field Events

INTRODUCTION

How can I go over the hurdle faster? How do I improve my sprint time? What's the best way to exchange the baton? Students and athletes might ask questions such as these. Are you ready to answer without giving them too much technical information?

An effective way to teach track and field skills is to provide teaching cues that are simple and to the point. Good visual teaching cues help athletes create visual images for better concentration and consequently help to perfect techniques. For example, when teaching the use of starting blocks, have students make a check mark with their hands at the starting line. The check mark cues the student to establish the correct hand position. Another example: When teaching the long jump, feedback from the coach might include saying, "Mark, I really liked how you arched your back like a C in the air; however, be sure to close the jackknife on your landing a little sooner."

Giving students or athletes visual teaching cues can make a significant difference in the outcome of a race or event. A tenth of a second faster time or one inch difference in a throw or jump could mean advancing to regionals and then state competition.

SKILLS LISTED WITH CUES

Teaching cues in this chapter include the following: pillar, sprinting form, skills and drills, relays, low hurdles, steeplechase, distance running and jumping events (long jump, triple jump, high jump), and throwing events (shot put, discus, and javelin).

Each event is broken down into its component phases, and cues are provided for each phase of the skill. The cues can be used in teaching the beginner or in helping experienced athletes perfect their technique.

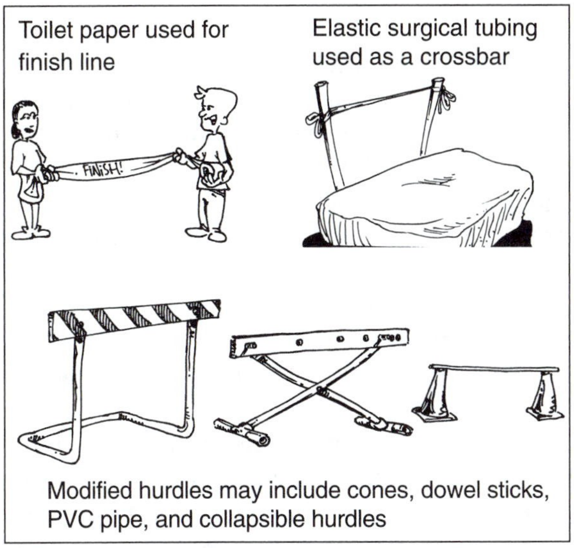

FIGURE 27.1 Equipment Ideas for a Track and Field Unit

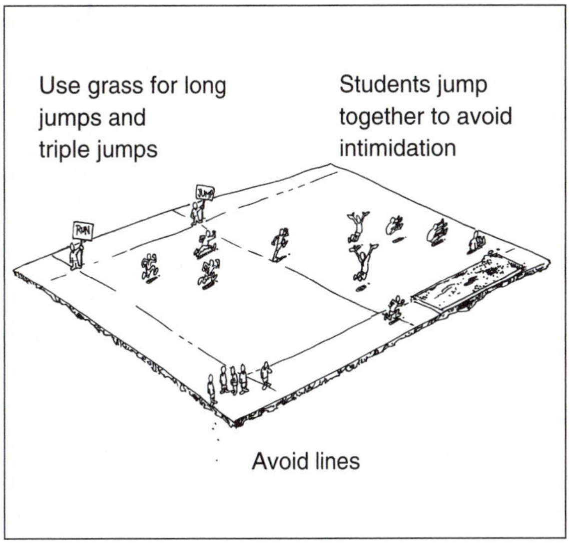

FIGURE 27.2 Teaching Long Jump to a Physical Education Class

TIP

When using a four-station rotation system for a large class, do not include more than one dangerous event. For example, do not include both shot put and high jump. The four stations might include starts, shot put (a dangerous station where the teacher should be present), distance runs, and long jump.

EQUIPMENT TIPS FOR RUNNING EVENTS

1. Starts: Blow a whistle to replace gun; use toilet paper for finish line.
2. Use large orange cones, dowel sticks, PVC pipe, or bamboo poles to make hurdles, or use foam rubber practice hurdles. Students are less likely to get hurt because foam hurdles are lightweight (see Figure 27.1).

EQUIPMENT TIPS FOR JUMPING EVENTS

1. High jump: Use elastic surgical tubing as a crossbar (see Figure 27.1).
2. Use grass for long jumps and triple jumps for large classes (see Figure 27.2).

EQUIPMENT TIPS FOR THROWING EVENTS

1. Use lightweight, safe substitutes for competitive implements. If you don't have enough equipment, introduce the event as a station activity.
2. Shot put: Use tennis balls filled with lead shot and bound in tape; or, use soft softballs.
3. Discus: Use rubber rings, small hula hoops.
4. Javelin: Use balls.

TEACHING IDEAS

1. Have all students practice long jump and triple jump together, shoulder to shoulder on the grass instead of one at a time in the pit, until they gain some proficiency in the sport. Everyone will get more practice, and students may be less self-conscious than they might be when jumping in front of their peers.
2. For the long jump, place a low hurdle or cone in sand. Have student jump over object. Place the hurdle or cone farther out or higher up to challenge the student.
3. For the triple jump, place three hula hoops equidistant on the runway. Have students run down the runway and place a foot (for each phase) in the hula hoops. Gradually lengthen the distance of the hula hoops to challenge the students.
4. Let students roll the discus on the ground, making sure the discus is coming off their index finger. See how far they can roll a discus before it falls over.
5. Teaching progression: Teach shot put first and discus second. Use modified equipment for large classes or beginners as described under "Equipment Tips."

Warm-Up

Start the warm-up with a 1- to 3-minute jog, and then move to dynamic stretches.

Dynamic Stretches

Dynamic stretching is a method of warm-up for explosive, high-speed activity. Dynamic stretches stimulate the body's ability to move faster by promoting more efficient nerve firing and more blood flow to deeper muscle tissues. Dynamic stretching is thought to be superior to static stretching because of the positive effects on the nerves. Static stretches are thought to dampen nerve firing. Dynamic stretches move the limbs through a full range of motion. Basically, the joint is moving continuously through various coordinated and sport-specific motor executions (Winkler & Schexnayder, 1998).

It is important to start gradually and then progress to greater speed and muscle recruitment. Warm up the large muscles first and then go to smaller, more specific muscles. Most of the following progressive exercises can be performed while jogging, skipping, running backward, or zigzagging (Pfaff et al., 1991, p. 50).

1. Big arm circles: Move the arms forward, backward, swimming backstroke, front crawl, and windmill type of motion—alternating one arm forward, the other arm backward. Use your imagination to create ways to move the arms while also moving the legs.
2. Bend-over sweeps: Bend over at the waist, swing the arms left and right, and move to a cross-swing.
3. Torso twist: In a standing position, straddle the legs and twist the torso from side to side.
4. Leg swings: Stretch by swinging the leg in front, back, and to the side of the body. Extend one hand to balance against a wall or partner's shoulder.
5. Speed-skater stretch: Slowly lean in squatting speed-skater position and do a stretched lunge to right and left sides.
6. Slow forward leg lunges: Take slow, long lunge steps while moving forward.

7. Ankling: Roll from the heel to toe, alternating each foot. Place heel next to instep of opposite foot, rolling forward with half steps. Swivel the hips while moving forward heel to toe.
8. Ankle rolls: Draw the alphabet with toes so ankle rotates.
9. Inverted scissors: Lie on back and roll up on your shoulders. Hands and forearms are flat on the ground or floor. Move the legs above your head in a scissors motion, forward and backward, side to side, and crossing the legs.
10. Inverted bicycles: Lie on back and roll up on shoulders. Hands and forearms are flat on the ground or floor. Move your legs like riding a bicycle.

Rule of thumb: Be creative and have fun. As long as you stay in continuous motion, you are stretching or moving dynamically.

All elite, explosive athletes, including sprinters, warm up in this dynamic manner because of its positive effect on nerve firing. These same high-level athletes avoid static stretching while warming up for high-speed performance because of its negative effects on nerve firing. This does not mean that static stretching is bad; only that it is inappropriate as a warm-up for high-speed performance (Winkler & Schexnayder, 1998).

Core Exercises

Before and during the teaching of sprinting technique, emphasize exercises that develop the core of the body from midtorso to midthigh. Core exercises develop the ability to stabilize the core into a pillarlike configuration. The core can be strengthened with exercises requiring the use of core musculature in any or all planes. A general fitness block that includes extensive core development would be appropriate to teach before beginning a skill block that includes sprint technique. See the strength training chapter (Chapter 22) for more details on the core and exercises.

FYI

For further information and special help, consult the following organization and resource.

ORGANIZATION

USA Track and Field
RCA Dome, Suite 140
Indianapolis, IN 46225
Phone: (317) 261-0500
Fax: (317) 261-0481
Website: www.usatf.org

Jamie Bennion (heptathlete)
270 N. 530 East
American Fork, UT 84003
Phone: (801) 756-4689

PUBLICATION

Carr, G. (1999). *Fundamentals of track and field* (2nd ed.). Champaign, IL: Human Kinetics Publishers.

PILLAR

SKILL	CUE	WHY	COMMON ERROR
Pillar	Critical for many sport skills	Foundation of correct body posture in most sport skills	
Head Position	Head over shoulders	Creates more efficiency in runners' sprinting technique	
Shoulder Position	Shoulders over hips		
Hip Position	Hips over feet		
	Make a pillar with your torso when performing sprinting drills and sprinting		

SPRINTING SKILLS AND DRILLS

SKILL	CUE	WHY	COMMON ERROR
Toe Action (Figure 27.3, page 368)	Toe up	To allow foot contact	
		To be as close under the hips as possible—allows for sprinting to be a pushing action, instead of a pulling action	
		Decreases time spent on the ground and places the foot in an optimal position to come up under the hip; eliminates "dangle time"	
Heel Action	Heel up	To shorten the lever as quickly as possible by bringing the heel directly under the buttocks; avoids dangle time	Leg extended behind you after it leaves the ground
Knee Action	Knee up	Increases stride length	
	Make a backwards L		
	Thigh parallel to ground		

continued

SPRINTING SKILLS AND DRILLS, continued			
SKILL	**CUE**	**WHY**	**COMMON ERROR**
Arm Action	Hold arms at 90° angle; fingers come to the eye on the front side		
	Don't pass the hip on the back side ("cheek to cheek")		
	Shoulder joint only joint to move		
	Fingers "eye to hip"		
Pillar	Run tall and make a pillar with torso: head over shoulders; shoulders over hips; hips over feet; abs like an accordion	Prevents upper body from leaning back	

FOUR PROGRESSIVE SPRINT DRILLS

Drill 1: Pawing Action

In this drill, students focus on pulling the heel directly under the buttocks and raising the thigh to a position parallel to the ground. The drill is performed by standing sideways, placing one hand on a wall, and raising the opposite leg so the thigh is parallel to the ground. The ready position is knee parallel to the ground, and standing on the balls of the feet, heel under the buttocks, toes flexed toward the knee. The student then makes a pawing action on the ground, similar to a bull threatening to charge. Throughout the whole sequence, the toe stays flexed, emphasizing contact on the ground directly under the hip.

Drill 2: Walking A's

Walking A's are similar to the pawing action. Begin by standing in the start position (knee parallel to ground, toe flexed, and heel to buttocks). Perform the pawing action one leg after the other and begin moving forward. Emphasize the cues of toe up, knee up, and heel up, arms "cheek to cheek" and keeping core tight (Figure 27.3, page 368).

Drill 3: Skipping A's

This drill emphasizes the powerful snap of the leg to the ground under the hip. A skip is performed. The student focuses on the cues, thigh parallel, toe up, and heel up, in addition to placing the foot in the optimal position under the hip upon contact with the ground (Figure 27.4, page 368). Arm action again should be cheek to cheek.

Drill 4: Running A's

Sometimes known as "High Knees." Running A's put all the drills together and emphasize frequency of contacts with the ground, not distance traveled. The student focuses on the same cues as the walking and skipping A's, emphasizing a stable core (stand tall but push abdominal wall toward spine).

FIGURE 27.3 Walking A's

FIGURE 27.4 Skipping A's

SPRINT ACCELERATIONS

A sprint acceleration is a gradual acceleration from a standing position to full speed over 100 meters. The purpose is to develop and rehearse the conceptual model of acceleration and transitioning to full speed.

SPRINT ACCELERATION AND TRANSITION SKILLS

SKILL	CUE	WHY	COMMON ERROR
Sprint Accelerations (Initial 15–30 meters)	Push back into the track on balls of feet	More time needed on the ground during the initial acceleration phase to obtain a faster top-end speed	
	Angle of body at 45°		
	Low heel recovery (heels don't come above the opposite knee)		
	Toe up		

continued

SPRINT ACCELERATION AND TRANSITION SKILLS, continued

SKILL	CUE	WHY	COMMON ERROR
Transition (through 50 meters)	Uniformly progress from an emphasis on pushing to a "pawing action"	Allows sprinter to maintain speed that has been generated from the acceleration phase	
	Foot contact gradually becomes upright under hip		
	Toe up, heel up, knee up	When the knees drop, deceleration occurs; the longer a sprinter can keep the knees up, the longer he or she will maintain full speed	
	Body must be a "pillar," stand tall		
	Transition from low heel recovery to high heel recovery (heel under buttocks)		

SPRINTING

SKILL	CUE	WHY	COMMON ERROR
Full Speed	Toe up, heel up, knee up!	When knee drops, deceleration occurs; the longer a sprinter can keep the knees up the longer he or she will maintain full speed	
	Maintain knee parallel to ground		
	Hold arms at 90° angle		
	Fingers "cheek to cheek"		
	Make a pillar with your torso (hips up, abs tight)	Prevents students from leaning back when running	
	Run tall		
	Ball of foot lands under hip		

BLOCK STARTS

SKILL	CUE	WHY	COMMON ERROR
Initial Block Setting	Front block 2 foot lengths from start line	Strongest position from which to push	Feet too far apart or too close together, or front foot is too close to or far from back foot
	Back foot 3 foot lengths from start line		

STARTING BLOCKS

SKILL	CUE	WHY	COMMON ERROR
"On Your Mark" (Figure 27.5)	Back into blocks		No routine, no order, no sequence
	Toes barely in contact with track		
	Front foot goes in first, back foot second		
	Hands make a bridge with fingers and thumb (behind starting line)	Raises center of gravity	Weight on thumb and knuckles
	Shoulders over hands	Engages forward momentum	Weight back, shoulders behind hands
	Weight forward		
	Eyes looking down	Keeps head neutral	Dropping the head
	Head is level		
	Sit in blocks		
"Set" (Figure 27.6)	Buttocks up in 1 motion	Less stress on supporting arms	Coming up too slow, buttocks lower than head
	Lean until you are just about ready to fall	Gets you ready for the 45° angle of your body	
	Shoulders over line		
	Body still like statue		Moving body
	Front leg at 90° angle		
	Back leg at 120° angle		
	Both feet pushing back hard into pedals	Gives sprinter pre-tension in legs	

continued

FIGURE 27.5 "On Your Mark"

FIGURE 27.6 "Set"

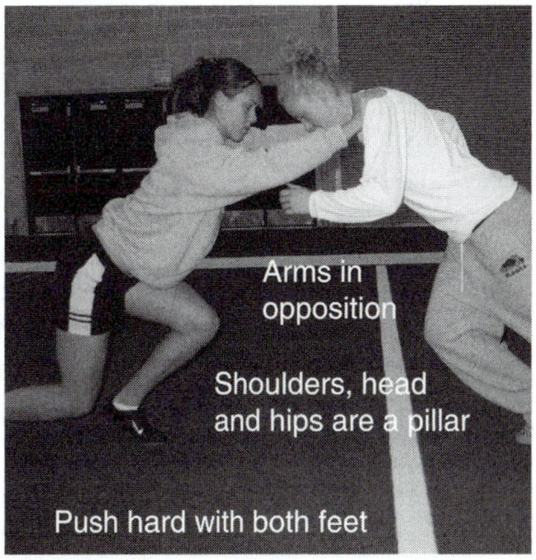

FIGURE 27.7 "Gun"

STARTING BLOCKS, continued

SKILL	CUE	WHY	COMMON ERROR
"Gun" (Figure 27.7)	Drive opposites (right arm, left leg or left arm, right leg)	Helps extend body while coming out of blocks	Right arm and right leg come out of blocks first (or left arm and left leg)
	Drive arm out and up		
	Push both legs equally hard		Stepping with forward leg first
	Explode out of the blocks at 45° angle	Helps sprinter push back into track rather than pulling	Standing straight up
			Pulling motion
	Short, quick steps		
	Feet contact track directly under hip		

ACCELERATION DRILLS/REACTION TIME DRILLS/FITNESS FUN DRILLS

Make two lines:

```
xxxxx    x  .............................................. 20 yards
       T
xxxxx    x  .............................................. 20 yards
```

1. Two students lie on their stomachs, their hands behind the line. The teacher stands behind them. On the teacher's clap, the students get up quickly and sprint 20 yards.
2. Two students lie flat on their backs, their heads on the starting line. The teacher shouts "right" or "left" and students move accordingly. The students turn over, get up as quickly as they can, and sprint 20 yards.
3. Two students lie flat on their stomachs, their hands behind the line. The teacher shouts "right" or "left." The students get up quickly and make a complete right or left turn (whatever the teacher shouts), and sprint 20 yards.

4. Two students stand up and face the teacher; they look directly into the teacher's eyes. The teacher will move the right or left thumb; the students turn in that direction and sprint 20 yards.
5. Two students sit on the ground and cross their legs. The teacher claps. The students get up without touching the ground with their hands and sprint 20 yards.
6. Two students get in a push-up position, their hands on the line. When the students hear a clap, they do one push-up—down, up—and then sprint 20 yards. Make sure students do the push-up correctly.
7. Two students perform one squat thrust and then sprint 20 yards.
8. Two students perform one squat thrust, jump, and then sprint 20 yards.
9. Students get in the on-your-mark position. The teacher says "set." The students quickly switch legs right, left, right, left and then get up and sprint 20 yards.
10. Teachers and students can design their own drills to make them fun and creative.

SPRINTING—50, 100, 200, 400 METERS

SKILL	CUE	WHY	COMMON ERROR
Racing Form			
Hip-Torso Action	Tall, as if being picked up by the hair	Allows sprinter's knees to come up to 90°	Hips turned down
	Tummy flat		
	Make a pillar with the hips and torso		
	Buttocks tucked under	Keeps hips turned up	
Arm Action	Sharp elbows		Arms crossing midline of body
	Back arm stays at 90°; "cheek to cheek"		
Hand Position	Hold a newspaper		Fists clenched
	Hold a penny		Floppy hands
Leg Action	Heel to buttocks		Not enough knee flexion
	Step over opposite knee		Knee lift too low
	Thigh parallel to ground		
	Point toe to sky		Pointing toe to ground before contact
	Claw ground with foot		
	Snap leg down		Not snapping leg down
	Ground contact with ball of foot directly under hip	Energy efficient	Stopping foot on contact with ground

RELAYS—BLIND HANDOFF UNDERHAND

SKILL	CUE	WHY	COMMON ERROR
Receiver's Arm Position (Figure 27.8)	Slam the door directly behind you, keeping arm straight	Gives the passer an accessible target	Arm extended outward
	Thumb in toward back-bone; make check mark toward ground		
Receiver's Hand Position	Steady hand and arm		Hand and arm moving
Passer's Arm Position (Figure 27.8)	Hit the palm with underhand delivery	Prevents passer from missing receiver's hand	Trying to pass before target appears
	Focus eyes on hand; hit target		
Passer's Code	Tape mark for takeoff		Leaving too early or too late
	Leave when incoming runner crosses tape with body		
Exchange (Figure 27.9)	Passer yells "hit," a signal for the receiver to lift arm back	Minimizes the time of the exchange	Passer is too fast
	Receiver and passer at full speed when exchange takes place		Receiver is not at full speed

FIGURE 27.8 Relay Hand Position

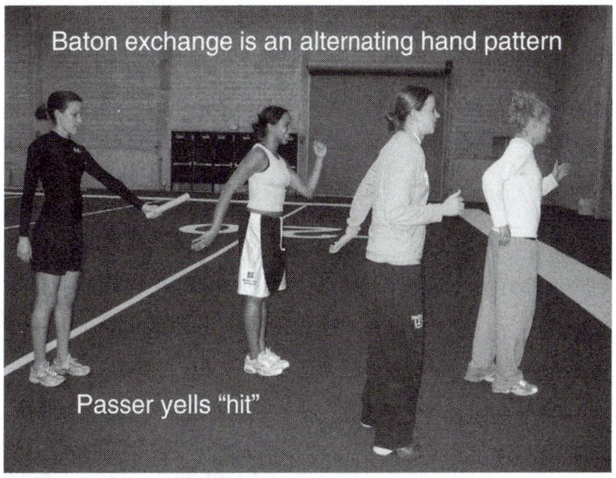

FIGURE 27.9 Relay Passer's Code Drill

RELAYS—VISUAL HANDOFF

SKILL	CUE	WHY	COMMON ERROR
Receiver	Turn head back over left shoulder toward passer; judge incoming runner's speed	To be able to match passer's speed, minimizing the time of exchange	Taking off too soon or too late
	Take 2 accelerating steps, then turn		
	Point hand at incoming runner with palm up and elbow down		
	Take the baton from the incoming runner like you're taking the money and running	Decreases the chances of dropping the baton	Dropping the money (baton)
Passer	Put baton in receiver's hand, arm fully extended at shoulder level	Decreases the chance of dropping the baton	Watching other competitors
	Full speed until receiver has baton		Slowing before pass

RELAYS—BLIND HANDOFF OVERHAND (MORE COMPLEX)

SKILL	CUE	WHY	COMMON ERROR
Receiver's Arm and Hand Position	Arm and hand parallel to ground		Hand bent up at wrist
	Elbow facing up		Arm and hand too low
	Make a check mark with palm facing up	Creates a big target	
Passer's Arm Position	Punch baton into target	Minimizes chance of passer missing the hand	Passing the baton from above shoulders coming down
	Piston-type motion		Passing baton before target appears
	Focus eyes on hand		Eyes wandering
Passer's Code	Tape mark		
	20–30 steps; leave when incoming runner hits tape	Minimizes the time of the exchange	Too soon or too late
Exchange	See target before pass		Passer is too fast, receiver not at full speed
	Passer yells "hit," the signal for the receiver to put arm back		

LOW HURDLES

SKILL	CUE	WHY	COMMON ERROR
Body Position *Before Hurdles*	Short last step		
	Pawing action (like a bull)	Prevents hurdler from going high over hurdles	Sitting, planting drive leg in front of hip
Over Hurdles	Exaggerated sprinting form over the hurdles	Maintains hurdler's speed over hurdle and in between	Jumping over hurdles
Between Hurdles	Sprinting form between hurdles		Last step before hurdle is too long
	Heel to buttocks, toe up		
	Thigh parallel to ground		
	Body erect, tall		
Trail Arm	Drive elbow back	Arms in close to body	Swings back too far
	Cut knee off with thumb		
Lead Leg	Upper leg flexed	Fast lead leg	Straight lead leg
(Figure 27.10)	Heel to buttocks		
	Extend like a switchblade		
	Snap foot downward and backward		Toe contact too far forward of hips
	Ball of foot lands under hip		
	Vigorous pawing action		
	Hips stay level		

continued

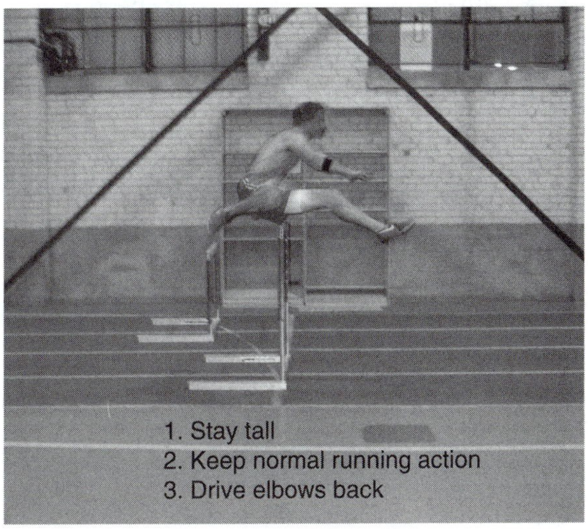

FIGURE 27.10 Going Over Low Hurdle

LOW HURDLES, continued			
SKILL	**CUE**	**WHY**	**COMMON ERROR**
Trail Leg	Hips parallel to hurdle		Hips not parallel
	Lead with knee and bring knee back to parallel	Helps maintain speed throughout race	Leading with thigh
	Toes averted		Toes pointed down
	Foot flexed		
	Snap foot down "quick"		
Equal and Opposite Reaction	Stay tall over hurdle; then tall position when foot touches ground	Similar to normal running position, which is more natural	Getting tall too soon or too late
			Leaning over hurdle

STEEPLECHASE			
SKILL	**CUE**	**WHY**	**COMMON ERROR**
Water Jump	Stay short		Standing tall
			Arms flapping around
	Lean forward	Limits amount of time over hurdle	Slowing down before the hurdle
	Keep center of gravity close to hurdle		
	Push off the back of the hurdle		Stepping on top of hurdle
Stationary Barriers	Same as 400 hurdle		
	Stay tall		
	Accelerate into the hurdle	Maintains speed going over hurdle	
	Keep up speed		
	Be conscious of trail leg		

DISTANCE RUNNING

SKILL	CUE	WHY	COMMON ERROR
Body Position	Relax the face, neck, shoulders, and arms	More energy efficient	Face, neck, shoulders, and arms are tense/tight (wasted energy)
	Body erect		
Hand Position	Thumb rests on the index finger, as if reading a newspaper (relaxed)	Limits energy lost	Clenched fist or floppy hands
Arm Position	Arms swing forward and back moving shoulder joint only	Energy efficient	Arms cross midline of the body—high arm swing
Leg Position	Use shorter steps than sprinting		Bouncing up and down
			Long stride
	Toes and knees up	Prevents runner from getting sloppy	
Foot Position	Strike heel and roll to toe	Calves won't get tired as quickly	Striking toes first
	Toes straight ahead or slightly out		Feet are pigeon-toed
Head Position	Head and eyes straight ahead	Keeps runner focused on task	Head down or up
Breathing	Breathe from stomach (avoid side-aches)	Receive more air	Breathing from the chest
	As if taking a breath to play a musical instrument		
Thought Process	Think positive thoughts: "I feel great"; "I am strong"; "Body is moving well"	Helps motivation	Thinking negative thoughts

LONG JUMP

SKILL	CUE	WHY	COMMON ERROR
Approach	Start with takeoff foot forward		Changing starting/ jumping foot
	12–18 strides; younger athletes, fewer strides; faster athletes, more strides	Get tired easily	Too many strides
	Accelerate to maximum usable speed		Changing speed of approach
	Same approach every time	Makes runway accurate	
	Knees up and tall in last strides as if being lifted by the hair		
Takeoff	Last 2 steps, like a layup in basketball—long-short	Ensures last step will be under hip	Last step too long
	Jump up and out		
	Drive up knee and opposite arm vigorously	Provides better leverage	Not driving up free knee and opposite arm
	Overemphasize knee lift and arm drive		
Action in the Air (Figure 27.11)	Body makes a curve, like a half-moon	Sets jumper up for a landing	Upper body ahead of hips
	Arch back like a C		
	Knees and feet behind hips		
	Arms above head and behind shoulders		
	Close jackknife	Brings legs up higher in air to allow for greater distance	Little or no leg action
	Extend legs and throw arms past knees		Arms are not thrown past knees
Landing	Collapse buttocks to heels upon landing	Greater distance	Feet apart
	Arms thrust forward		
	Feet together		

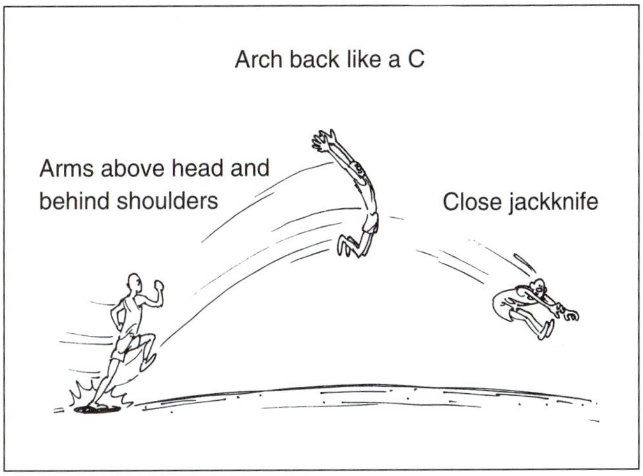

FIGURE 27.11 Long Jump

TRIPLE JUMP

SKILL	CUE	WHY	COMMON ERROR
Approach	Start with jumping foot forward		Changing starting/jumping foot (takeoff foot)
	12–18 strides; younger athletes, fewer strides; faster athletes, more strides	They tire easily	
	Knees up and tall in last 5 or 6 strides as if being lifted up by the hair		Overstriding or sitting
	Maximum speed		Last step too long
	Same approach every time	Makes runway accurate	
	Last 2 steps like a layup in basketball—long-short last 2 steps	Ensures last step will be under hip	
Hop	Take off and land on same foot	The rule	Landing on the opposite foot
	Tall upper body	Knees come up better	Leaning forward at waist
	Head and eyes level		Looking down at ground, head down
	Look ahead		
	Knee up, toe up		Straight leg

continued

TRIPLE JUMP, continued			
SKILL	**CUE**	**WHY**	**COMMON ERROR**
Hop, *continued*	Snappy, pawing action	Gets jumper ready for next phase	No pawing action
	Active landing		Leg does not snap down
Step	Long step, as if stepping over mud puddles		Hopping again
	Take off and land on opposite foot		
	Tall upper body	Knee comes up better	Leaning forward at waist
	Head and eyes level; look ahead		Looking down at the ground, head down
	Split in air		Short steps
	Wide thigh separation during step		
	Landing—snappy, pawing action	Gets jumper ready for next phase	No pawing action
	Active landing		
Jump			
Arm Action	Reach for the sky; drive arms upward	Provides better leverage	Not driving arms upward
Head and Eye Position	Head and eyes level; look ahead		Looking down
Body Action	Close jackknife		No hips
	Extend legs from hips		
	Throw arms past knees, as if driving ski poles back at the start of the race	Allows for greater distance	Reaching hands to feet
	Collapse buttocks to heels upon landing		Straight-leg landing on buttocks
Ground Contact	Even cadence throughout jump	Greater distance	Uneven cadence
	Even rhythm		
	Feet make "ta–ta–ta" sound (even–even–even step)		Feet make "taaa–ta–ta" sound (long–short–short step)

HIGH JUMP

SKILL	CUE	WHY	COMMON ERROR
Approach	Start just on the outside of the standards	Allows for better curve	
Running Stride	Make a J		Running straight at the bar
	10-step total approach		
	Get speed in run first		
	The last 4 steps start the turn for the J		
Body Position	Lean into curve		Standing tall in curve
	Inside shoulder a little lower than outside shoulder		
Running Stride	Last 3 steps medium, long, short	Ensures last step will be under hip	Last 3 steps too long or too short
Takeoff *Legs*	Take off from outside foot		Inside foot used to take off
	Foot placed parallel to bar		
	Takeoff foot down quickly, as if stepping on a bug	More power	Take off with both feet
	Plant power leg, active landing		Failing to plant power leg, no power in run or jump
	Drive the lead knee vigorously up	Provides for greater leverage	Not driving knee up
Arms	Drive both arms up	Provides for greater leverage	Using legs only
Flight *Body Position*	Arch like a banana	Makes better arch	Flat back
	Head back		
Arm Position			Hands not visible
			Dropping fists

SHOT PUT

SKILL	CUE	WHY	COMMON ERROR
Enter/Exit Position	Enter ring from rear	The rule	Entering and exiting ring from side or front
	Exit from rear	The rule	
Hold Shot	Cradle shot	Allows for better release	Dropping the elbow and having the shot roll into palm
	Hold shot on finger pads		
	Push shot firmly against neck		
	Elbow up		
Release of Shot	Push shot through head		Throwing like a baseball
	Shot leaves from neck, a "put" not a throw		
	Release is fast like a punch and at a 45° angle		Punch is horizontal
Start of Glide	Bend support knee		Hurrying start and keeping weight back
	Kick backward with nonsupport leg		Trying to throw before reaching power position
	Land both feet simultaneously still facing back		
	Hips open up quick like a baseball swing		
	Free arm swings up as if slapping a giant	Creates torque	
Explosion of Glide	Push with both legs	Makes throw more powerful	Legs collapse on thrower
	Keep shot back last		
	Release shot at 45° angle		
End of Throw	Slap and pull with free arm	Shorten lever to speed rotation	

DISCUS

SKILL	CUE	WHY	COMMON ERROR
Enter/Exit	Enter ring from back	The rule	Touching any part of the ring other than the area between entering and exiting the ring after the throw
	Exit ring from back	The rule	
Holding the Discus	Open-handed eagle-claw grip	Allows for correct release and flat disc in air	Letting discus fall from hand
	Carry a textbook		
	Relax fingertips on edge of discus		Not gripping solidly
Release	Discus leaves off index finger as if releasing a bowling ball	Better flight	Holding on to discus too long
The Wind	Twist and shout	Shout makes discus go farther	Only half winding
	Keep body wound up until throw, then shout	The more torque, the farther the disc will go	
	Keep arm back		
Explosion of Throw	Hips lead like a baseball swing	Creates torque	Throwing before reaching power position
	Hips open quick like a baseball swing		
End of Throw	Long pull (smooth like a golf swing)	Creates long lever	Hurrying the throw release (will cause discus to flutter like a dead duck)
	Head and chest up facing sector		Legs collapse

28

Ultimate Frisbee

INTRODUCTION

Ultimate Frisbee originated in Maplewood, New Jersey, in 1968. It uniquely combines high competition with the spirit of the game. "Spirit of the game" means no referees, honest playing, and positive spirits on and off the field. "Spirit" means ultimate athletes need not waste time faking out officials. Instead, efforts focus on high performance and going all out. In all other sports, players are allowed to do anything until an official informs them that an activity is illegal. (In basketball it isn't a foul unless it is called as such.) Combining skills from sports ranging from soccer and Frisbee to basketball, ultimate Frisbee is a fast-paced, highly energetic noncontact sport that isn't for the lazy or pessimistic.

SKILLS LISTED WITH CUES

The cues in this chapter include the following skills: rules, backhand throw, forehand throw (sidearm), and catching.

TIPS

1. A certain level of maturity, trust, and honesty are required for the spirit of the game.
2. Seven players per team.
   a. *Handlers* (three players) are the first players to take a "pull" (similar to the kickoff in football). Generally these players are the most accurate throwers of the seven players on the field.
   b. *Mids* (two players) are players who generally have good cutting and maneuvering skills. They provide constant "flow" of the disk downfield with back or side cuts.
   c. *Longs* (two players) are players who have the ability to run fast,

long back cuts into the end zone or at least downfield. Longs should have field sense and accurate catching skills.

3. Substitute when players get tired; keep a "fresh crew." Only when one team scores can a substitution be made.
4. You can stand only one Frisbee width from the player with the disk, and you count stalling with "1, 2, . . . 8, 9, 10." If the thrower still has the disk after the marker says 10, a turnover is called, and the other team gains possession of the disk.

EQUIPMENT TIPS

1. Use lots of Frisbees (175 grams official weight).
2. Have students wear rubber cleats, if available.
3. Use cones, lines, or flags to mark end zones and boundaries.
4. Field dimensions should be 40 yards wide × 70 yards long, with 25-yard-long end zones.
5. Have students wear colored vests.
6. Use a scoreboard.

TEACHING IDEAS

1. Play to 21, with victory margin of 2 points. Informal games can be played to other point totals or for a specified time.
2. The game starts with both teams standing on opposite end lines. The disk is thrown to the other team as a kickoff. Players move the disk down the field by throwing it to one another. If the Frisbee hits the ground or goes out of bounds, the other team gains possession. Once a player catches the disk in the end zone, a point is scored and the opposing team must walk to the far goal line and await the pull or throw-off from the scoring team.
3. The game can be played with as few as four players to a team on any flat open space available that has a fairly well marked end zone.

FYI

For further information and special help, consult the following organization.

ORGANIZATION

Items include the following teaching materials: videos, disks, publications, rules, how to start teams or leagues, college starter kit, how to teach ultimate frisbee.

Ultimate Players Association
741 Pearl Street
Side Suite
Boulder, CO 80302
Phone: (800) UPA-GetH
Website: www.upa.org

RULES

SKILL	CUE	WHY	COMMON ERROR
Basic Guidelines	The disk may never be handed—it must always be thrown		
	No player may move while in possession of the disk		
	Player may pivot on 1 foot in any direction, as in basketball		
	The disk may be thrown in any direction		
	No more than 1 player may guard a thrower		Double guarding equals a free pass on the spot
	Use both legs and hands to guard or knock down the disk		
	The defensive team gains possession of the disk whenever the offensive team's pass is incomplete, intercepted, knocked down, or goes out of bounds		
	Out-of-bounds throws are taken over by the opposing team at the point where the disk went out of bounds	If a disk goes out of bounds after crossing goal line, opposing team may throw in from either corner of end zone at goal line	
	No hand slapping to knock the disk down or out of the passer's hand		
	If disk is passed to you, must stop within 3 steps	No running with the disk	
Myths	Played only with dogs		
	You won't get a workout		

THROWING

SKILL	CUE	WHY	COMMON ERROR
Backhand (Figure 28.1, page 388)			
Grip	Stand sideways		
	Pinch disk's edge with thumb and forefinger	To control the flight of the disk	
Throw	Wipe table with back of hand, disk flat	Disk will go farther	Releasing with disk at too much of an angle
	Release, like snapping a towel	Accuracy and specific target to focus on	
	Pivot, windup, step, snap, release	Power on the disk	Using too much arm motion
	Point finger at target after follow-through		
	Step at target		
Pull (Full Throw—Same as Kickoff in Football)	Same as backhand except preparatory steps		Incorrect release angle
			Misreading wind
Forehand (Sidearm)			
Grip (Figure 28.2a, page 388)	Thumb holds inside of disk	To generate a spinning disk	
	Middle finger is pivot finger		Incorrect grip
Throw (Figure 28.2b, page 388)	Outside rim of disk lower than inside	Keeps disk flat while in the air	Too much arm motion
	Step (same side) to target, snap towel	Throw farther	Incorrect release angle will cause disk to dive into ground
	Elbow on hip—wrist snap		Throwing like a baseball
	Try not to use arm for strength on this toss		
	All wrist action		

FIGURE 28.1 Backhand Grip and Throw

(a) Forehand Grip (Sidearm)

(b) Forehand Throw (Sidearm)

FIGURE 28.2

CATCHING

SKILL	CUE	WHY	COMMON ERROR
Sandwich Catching	Watch disk come to hands	Keeps eyes focused on target	Looking away, incorrect timing
	1 big hand on top of disk, 1 big hand on bottom	Big hands gives bigger surface to hang onto the disk	Not using both hands
	Clap before you catch		
	Hands like a clam	More surface area on the disk for better control	
	Spread fingers		

OFFENSE

SKILL	CUE	WHY	COMMON ERROR
Movement	Cut, circle away, cut, circle—keep moving!	Avoids same-speed movements	Same-speed movements
	Fake and sharp cut	Keep the defensive players guessing	
	Look while pivoting; fake, pivot, fake; anticipate!	The goal is to get open	No faking movements, standing still
	Lead teammate with throw	Better option to catch the disk	
	Throw to area, not to person, on long throw		Not giving player enough lead on throw

DEFENSE			
SKILL	**CUE**	**WHY**	**COMMON ERROR**
Marking (Figure 28.3)	Stick like glue	Not letting an opposing player get open for a throw	Lack of conditioning
			Going for steal and losing opponent
	Play the annoying little brother—opponent cannot get rid of you		
	Watch midsection		Watching head and feet—getting faked out
			Overrunning opponent
	Keep hands low		
	Count to 10 slowly; thrower has only 10 seconds to throw before a violation is called		

FIGURE 28.3 Defensive Marking

29

Volleyball

INTRODUCTION

Teachers and coaches face a monumental task when preparing instructional methods for teaching motor skills. They make many decisions regarding content, method, class organization and control, evaluation, and methods of grading. When planning for content and method, the teacher should be able to answer the following questions: Why did you teach that skill the way you did? Why was the instruction sequenced as it was? Why did the group practice like that? Why did you have them use instructional aids? Why did you say what you said to them?

Most, if not all, of these answers should be based on empirical evidence rather than on opinion, tradition, or the teacher's whim. Researchers have found that modeling facilitates motor-skill learning. Magill (1985) states, "Selecting the correct cues is one of the most important elements that an instructor includes in the teaching process."

In addition to focusing a student's attention on essential elements of the model, meaningful cues reduce the amount of information that is given. Because students attend to a limited amount of new material for a limited time, such a routine will enhance learning. For example, when teaching the block, the two cues are "Hands up" and "Make Mickey Mouse ears." These cues provide "hooks" on which to hang memories of the instruction. Some teachers find that years later students can remember many of the cues they received in their volleyball classes.

SKILLS LISTED WITH CUES

This chapter presents the cues for the following skills: ready position for forearm pass, forearm pass, overhead pass, setter's position and signals, serves (underhand and overhand), spiking, blocking, preparation for dig, forearm pass dig, dig (sprawl, pancake, overhead, fist), team strategies (offensive and defensive), and individual strategies (offensive and defensive).

The cues are listed in a recommended teaching sequence. A list of alternative cues is provided to benefit students who have difficulty linking the first cue with the desired performance. The alternate cues will suggest similar mental images that students may connect to more familiar motor patterns. Teachers should experiment with the cues and match the most helpful cue to each student's need.

TIP

After each drill, have players perform a set number of push-ups and sit-ups. This allows for a more efficient use of time with the benefit of increasing strength.

EQUIPMENT TIPS

1. Use a light ball to teach the basic skills (for example, a lightweight plastic ball found at most discount department stores).
2. Leather balls are better than rubber balls in preventing arm soreness.
3. Lower the nets, or have students work back to the baseline on serving drills.
4. Use blackboard and chalk to record competitive drills and the like.

TEACHING IDEAS

1. When possible, perform drills that contain the playing sequence—that is, "pass, set"; "serve, pass, set, hit"; "dig, set, hit"; and so on.
2. Drills should always have a specific goal (i.e., targets, scores, hit a certain number in a row perfectly, create competition with score 13–13, hit until you lose, etc.).
3. Always end drills on a positive note.
4. Games take 20 to 40 minutes to play. Some drills need to be as long as game time.
5. If court space is available, play 2-on-2, 3-on-3, or 4-on-4 games.

TEACHING PROGRESSIONS

Forearm Pass

1. *Throw, hit, catch:* A player tosses the ball to a partner, and the partner passes back. The ball is caught and tossed again. Repeat 10 times.
2. *Toss, pass, pass:* Two players start with a toss and keep passing back and forth until 20 passes have been tossed (see Figure 29.1, page 392).
3. *In a line of three:* Player A passes to player B, who passes behind his head to player C, who passes long to player A. Rotate after 10 passes. Switch the person in the middle to give each player a chance to pass the ball backward over her head.
4. *Triangle:* Three players pass the ball in a triangle. This allows the passer to practice facing the ball and angling the arms. Switch after 12 passes.

Overhead Pass

1. *Throw, hit, catch:* A player tosses the ball to a partner, and the partner passes back. The ball is caught and tossed again. Repeat 10 times.
2. *Toss, pass, pass:* Two players start with a toss and keep passing back and forth until they have made 20 passes.
3. *In a line of three:* Player A passes to player B, who passes behind her head to player C, who passes long to player A. Rotate after 10 passes. Switch the

FIGURE 29.1 Forearm Pass Drill, Toss-Pass-Pass Drill

person in the middle to give each player a chance to pass the ball backward over his head.

4. *Triangle:* Three players pass the ball in a triangle. This allows the passer to practice facing the ball. Switch direction of the pass after 12 passes.

Overhead Serve

1. Serve at the wall.
2. Serve from the attack line with a partner and move back.
3. Serve and chase the ball.
4. Serve to opponents, who try to catch the ball.
5. Serve in a game situation, 3-on-3 games, played on half-courts.

Spike

1. *You go, I throw:* Players begin their approach, and you toss the ball as if they have performed the proper approach. The players need to come to you. Toss the ball as they jump, a couple of feet from the net and directly in front of you.
2. *I throw, you go:* You toss the ball to the outside. The hitters start off the court and behind the line.

Block

1. Have players practice the two-step move with an opposing partner across the net.
2. Have blocking against hitters in the spiking drill. Be careful of spikers who run under the net. Blockers tend to come down on spikers' feet and sprain their ankles. Encourage setters to set the ball off the net (not tight). This decreases the possibility of injury.

FYI

For further information and special help, consult the following organizations and publication.

ORGANIZATIONS

Provides information about volleyball coaching clinics.

Canyon Volleyball
c/o Carl McGown
3815 Riverwood Drive
Provo, UT 84604
Phone: (801) 225-9271
Fax: (801) 225-9273

USA Volleyball
715 S. Circle Drive
Colorado Springs, CO 80910
Phone: (888) 786-5539, (719) 228-6800
Fax: (719) 228-6899
Website: www.usavolleyball.org

American Volleyball Coaches Association
1227 Lake Plaza Drive, Suite B
Colorado Springs, CO 80906
Phone: (719) 576-7777
Fax: (719) 575-7778
Website: www.avca.org

PUBLICATION

McGown, C., Fronske, H., & Moser, L. (2001). *Coaching volleyball: Building a winning team.* Boston: Allyn & Bacon.

PASSES

SKILL	CUE	WHY	COMMON ERROR
Forearm			
Ready Position	Arms extended in front of body; keep low	Ready to come up and pass the ball when it comes to you	Weight on heels instead of balls of feet
	Knees bent		Knees locked straight
Execution	Wrists and hands together		
	Lifelines together	Makes a nice flat and strong surface for the ball to contact	Elbows held at sides, arms too close to body
	Forearm contact with ball		

continued

PASSES, continued			
SKILL	**CUE**	**WHY**	**COMMON ERROR**
Forearm			
Execution, continued	Hide your chest		Hitting ball on wrists
	Fat part of arms hits ball		Hitting ball on wrists
	Elbows straight and simple	This provides a smooth surface to bounce the ball off straight	
(Figure 29.2)	Make a flat surface with the forearms		Bending elbows, moving arms up and down to add power
(Figure 29.3)	Face ball, angle arms		
	Shuffle		
	Pass over lead leg		Facing target
	Beat ball to the spot		
	See the server, see the ball		
Overhead (Figure 29.4)	Big hands	Big hands allow you to cover a wide surface area of the ball, which gives you more control and accuracy	
	As if looking at the bottom of a full bowl of cereal		

continued

FIGURE 29.2 Forearm Pass (Hand Position)

FIGURE 29.3 Forearm Pass (Foot Position)

PASSES, continued			
SKILL	**CUE**	**WHY**	**COMMON ERROR**
Overhead *Execution* (Figure 29.5)	Shape early	Gives you more time to prepare to receive the ball. This is a key for correct performance. Not shaping early is the biggest cause of failure of this skill. Over-emphasize to your players to have their hands up extra early	
	Hands up at hairline		
	Extend		
	Like a basketball chest pass; elbows straighten		Ball staying in contact with hands too long—violation
			Only using arms to push ball
	Face target		
	Over lead leg		Setting over right or left shoulder, sideways

FIGURE 29.4 Overhead Pass (Ready Position)

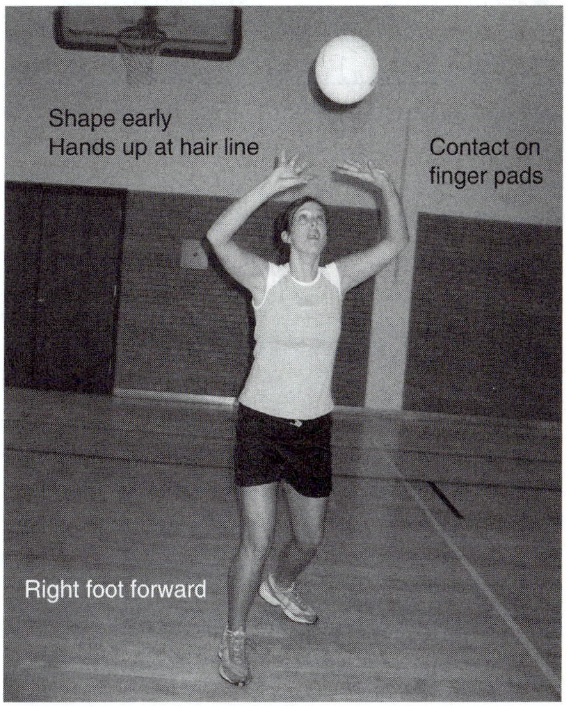

FIGURE 29.5 Overhead Pass

SETTER'S POSITION

SKILL	CUE	WHY	COMMON ERROR
Technique	Right shoulder to net	For consistent sets to spike	Not looking at pass early enough
	Stand next to or as close as possible to the net	Helps control ball	Trying to pass a serve
	Right side of court, front row		
	Shape early	Helps set the ball at hairline—not chin or chest	
	Extend	More power	
	Face target	More accuracy	Overarching the back, telegraphing the set and lowering the point of contact
Back Set	Hips forward	Helps push setting base backwards, so setter can push body weight and momentum into a reverse set	
	See setter's signals		

SERVES

SKILL	CUE	WHY	COMMON ERROR
Underhand			
Leg Action	Step toward net with foot opposite to throwing arm	More power to the ball	Stepping forward with same leg as stepping arm
Hand Position	Palm up, make a fist	Bigger surface area for ball to contact; better control of ball	
	Thumb rests on side of index finger		
	Arm close to body, brush shorts	Better efficiency	
	Elbow straight	Helps with the follow-through	Elbow bent
	Hit ball out of hand	Greater control of ball	Tossing ball into air
	Like pitching horseshoes		Arm action stops at ball contact
	Follow-through toward target		

continued

SERVES, continued			
SKILL	**CUE**	**WHY**	**COMMON ERROR**
Overhead *Ready Position* (Figure 29.6)	Bow-and-arrow action	Keeps elbow high and ready to hit ball	
	Stand sideways; left foot points at target	More power to serve the ball	
		Weight transfer from back to front foot	
	Hold ball in 1 hand	Simplifies the serve	
	Ball in left hand and up in front of hitting shoulder	Eliminates extra movement and allows accurate and consistent contact with the ball	
	Hitting elbow up	Timing to contact ball is more efficient	
Toss (Figure 29.7)	Precise toss	Simplifies timing and decreases decision making	
	Toss it (step, toss, hit)		Rotating shoulder forward, elbow stays back
	Toss in front of serving shoulder		
	Heel to target		Hitting behind or on top of ball
(Figure 29.8)	Contact ball at top of toss		
	Have a routine you do each time, like basketball free-throw routines		

continued

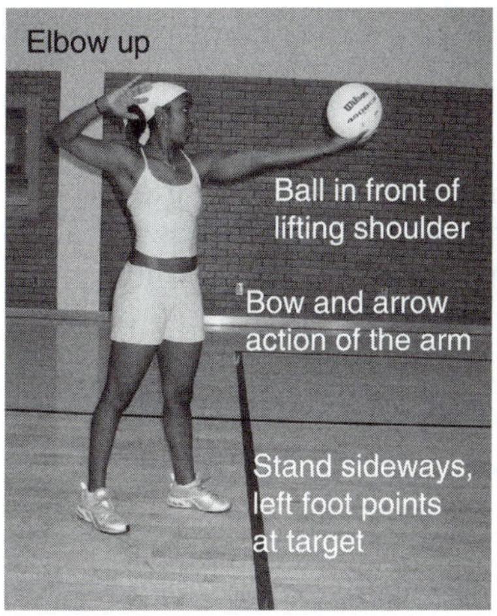

FIGURE 29.6 Overhead Serve (Ready Position)

FIGURE 29.7 Overhead Serve Toss

FIGURE 29.8 Overhead Serve (Contact)

SERVES, continued			
SKILL	**CUE**	**WHY**	**COMMON ERROR**
Floater Serve	Low, controlled toss	Easy to time the contact; server can make contact at the peak of the ball toss, where the ball has neutral energy; server can prevent the ball from spinning after contact	Throwing too high and getting poor contact (harder to time a falling ball)
	Toss the ball in front of the shoulder at 11 o'clock	Ideal position to get a flat contact with the ball without putting spin on the ball	Tossing the ball directly above shoulder, more likely to put topspin on the ball
	More front-on stance, with left foot slightly forward	Encourages a balanced and stable body position that is optimal for producing a flat contact	Side-on stance encourages body rotation through the ball, gives the ball a right-to-left spin
	Abbreviated follow-through	A short follow-through reduces the chance of putting spin on the ball	Following through usually puts backspin on the ball
	Fire abdominals	Puts power into the serve; the abs should be fired vertically rather than horizontally to avoid putting body rotation into the contact	Relying on the arm can lead to injury eventually
	Contact with a flat, solid hand	Encourages a short contact, less likely to put spin on the ball	Loose hand contact gives a longer contact
Topspin Serve	Toss with topspin	Makes it easier to generate a powerful topspin serve if you are hitting with the spin	
	Toss over shoulder, hit at 12 o'clock	At the point of contact, the hand is traveling upward and forward (ideal for hitting a powerful topspin)	Contacting the ball out in front of the shoulder, where the hand is falling from its peak; makes it harder to put topspin on the ball

continued

SERVES, continued			
SKILL	**CUE**	**WHY**	**COMMON ERROR**
Topspin Serve, *continued*	Step into the contact	Helps generate power	Lack of transfer puts pressure on the shoulder; more chance of injury in the long run
	Fire the abs	Vertically and horizontally to help generate power	
	Snap the wrist over the ball	Helps to create the maximum amount of topspin	
		Encourages a long contact, which helps to controll the direction of the ball	
Jump Serve	It is a topspin serve conducted in the air	Helps young athletes new to the serve break the skill down into two skills they can already do (learn topspin serve first)	Overcomplicating the process
	Start with a short, structured approach	Keep the skill as simple and compact as possible when learning	Taking elaborate approach patterns and using a high toss
	Toss with the right hand or both hands for right-handed servers	Keeps the toss in front of the contact shoulder, so you only have to think about the toss in two dimensions	
	Start on right foot, toss, step onto the left, then right-left-close step	Short and defined approach pattern helps the learner time the ball	
	Practice tossing the ball	The toss is the first skill in the sequence; the player must be able to produce a consistent toss to practice the serve	Producing a variety of tosses, then adjusting using inferior techniques just to make contact; forcing the athlete to focus on the outcome rather than the skill

OFFENSIVE HIT

SKILL	CUE	WHY	COMMON ERROR
Used for Balls Off of Net (Figure 29.9)	Elbow back, hand above head, rotate elbow forward, and reach up with an open hand	Rotation increases torque and translates into a faster, harder hit	
	Hit ball at highest point of reach with the heel of the hand and follow through after contact at the intended target	Increases control of the direction of the ball	
	Similar to a throwing action, with the hand above the head		
	Contact ball on bottom third	A higher contact increases the probability of the ball going over the net	
	Watch the ball hit hand	Decreases the probability of missing the ball	
		Increases the chance of a solid hit	

continued

FIGURE 29.9 Offensive Hit (Ready Position)

OFFENSIVE HIT, continued			
SKILL	**CUE**	**WHY**	**COMMON ERROR**
Used for Balls Off of Net, *continued*			
Hitting Action	Step under the ball, with the foot opposite of hitting arm	More power in the hit; lining up the hitting arm with the ball is critical for the ball hitting the hand squarely or solidly	
	The hitting arm should be lined up directly under the ball		

SPIKING			
SKILL	**CUE**	**WHY**	**COMMON ERROR**
Execution	4-step approach: R-L-R-L if right-handed; L-R-L-R if left-handed	Carry momentum and power into spike	No approach; starting approach too close to net
(Figure 29.10, page 402)	Arms forward-back-forward	Able to jump higher	Jumping off only 1 leg like a basketball lay-up
	Bow and arrow action; elbow back and high	Increases power and speed of the hitting arm	
	Fingers apart		Fist
	Hand open and firm	Increases surface area of the contact, which aids in control	
	Hand in shape of ball	To control ball and apply spin	Hand is flat, or fist, or like jelly
	Wrist somewhat stiff	Ensures firm contact	
Timing	First step when ball is set		Running too far forward; ball goes over attacker's head
	Stepping and setting		
	Trust eyes; do not guess		
(Figure 29.11, page 402)	Contact ball high and in front of you at 11 o'clock	To hit downward on ball	Contacting ball too low or behind head
	Powerful wrist snap	Controls the ball and puts spin on ball so it will go down into the court	No wrist snap
	Fast arm swing	Make a positive, decisive motion	Slow swing leads to poor timing and poor contact

FIGURE 29.10 Spike (Ready position)

FIGURE 29.11 Hitting Execution

BLOCKING

SKILL	CUE	WHY	COMMON ERROR
Setup (Figure 29.12)	Keep hands up at eye level	Shorter distance to travel to cross net	Bringing hands and arms below net, straight legs
	Knees bent, ready to jump	Preparation to react quicker to setter	
	Seal the net with body	Prevents ball from coming down on your side of net	Body too far from net
	Chin down for peripheral vision		
Arm Action	Hands up as if playing a piano		
	Fingers are firm and spread—Mickey Mouse ears		Fingers close together and not firm

continued

BLOCKING, continued			
SKILL	**CUE**	**WHY**	**COMMON ERROR**
Setup, *continued*			
Timing	Ball, setter, ball, hitter	Aware of all opponents' attacking options	Hands down at sides
			Watching only the ball
	Lead step		
	3-step move		Moving with hands down at waist
	Get over		
	Penetrate		
	Angle hands into opponent's court as if diving into a swimming pool		Being too far away from net
	Reach over		

FIGURE 29.12 The Block

DIGS

SKILL	CUE	WHY	COMMON ERROR
Dig Preparation	Anticipate spike		
	Feet apart, arms ready	Balanced position to move	Weight back on heels, standing straight up
	Ball, setter, ball, hitter; watch hitter's shoulders and head	Can adjust to ball better	Watching ball, not hitter
	Knees bent	Can move quicker	Flat-footed, rooted to spot
Forearm Pass/Dig Pass	Arms like a wall; don't swing arms	Swinging arms adds energy to the ball and makes it harder to control the direction	Swinging arms
	Absorb shock of spike; like a sponge	Absorbing energy of ball to keep in play	
	Platform underneath ball	Directs the ball up—allows teammate to get ball	Arms too close to body
Sprawling	Anticipate spike; be stopped when hitter contacts ball	Anticipate ball speed better	Still moving when hitter contacts ball
	Big step toward ball	More efficient	No tennis hop
	Close to floor, chin up	Lessens impact when you hit the floor	
	Hit ball, then sprawl	First things first	Falling over instead of moving feet
	Helping hand	Helps support your weight	
	Turn knee out	Prevents knee from getting hurt	
Pancake	Big step toward the ball	Efficient movement	Not moving feet fast enough
	Close to floor	Lowers your center of gravity, increasing the distance you can travel and lessening the impact as you hit the floor	Diving up and down means you can't reach as far—more likely to hurt yourself
	Helping hand	Use your hands to help support your weight as you hit the floor	

continued

DIGS, continued			
SKILL	**CUE**	**WHY**	**COMMON ERROR**
Pancake, *continued*	Turn knee out	Keeps knee from directly hitting floor	
	Slide hand close to the floor	Prevent friction burns	Sliding the hand across the floor can slow you down and lead to friction burns on the heel of the hand
Overhead	Tomahawk action	Solid contact to be legal and push ball upward	Contact between ball and hands is too long to be legal
	Deflection or rebound back toward net	Gives team second chance; targets middle of court	
Fist	Flat surface		

SETTER'S SIGNALS			
SKILL	**CUE**	**WHY**	**COMMON ERROR**
Setter	Quarterback of team signals with fingers to spiker and team		Other players call the signal
	Calls the set signal by using a hand signal to notify players of type of play		
Height of Set; Spiker on the Court	4 3 3 2 ——1—— net ————		
	5 4 3 2 1 A B C Setter		
Spiker's Court Position on Net	Setter signals for first number or letter Examples: 1–1 short set 5–1 long short set		Not listening or looking for signal from setter
Height of Ball Number	Setter signals for second number Examples: 5–4 high set C–4 high back set		Confusing the numbers

continued

SETTER'S SIGNALS, continued			
SKILL	**CUE**	**WHY**	**COMMON ERROR**
Short Sets	"You go, I throw"		
1–1, 3–1, *A–1, C–1*	Spiker watches ball go over shoulder		Not watching ball; moving too late or too early
	Correct timing takes practice		
	As soon as ball passes shoulder, chase the ball to net; stay with it		Becoming frustrated and quitting
Medium Sets *1–2, 3–2*	When the ball leaves setter's hands, go!		
High Sets *5–4, C–4*	"I throw, you go"		Leaving too soon
	Watch where ball is set		
	Go when the ball leaves the setter's hands		Not watching the ball leave the setter's hands

SETTER'S HAND SIGNALS			
SKILL	**CUE**	**WHY**	**COMMON ERROR**
End of Play			
Setter's Responsibility	Setter gives signal before ball is served	Setter gives signal at side of leg to prevent opponent from seeing it	
Hitters' Responsibility	Hitters look for setter's signal as soon as play is over		Forgetting to look for setter's hand signals
	Move with setter on calls net S S H H		Not looking for setter's hand signals
	Everybody watch pass, move accordingly		
During Rally			
Hitters' Responsibility	Hitters can call signals 1–5–C	Communication critical between hitter and setter	

continued

SETTER'S HAND SIGNALS, continued

SKILL	CUE	WHY	COMMON ERROR
Front Sets	Thumb, index, and middle fingers used for front sets		
Short Set	Index finger = 1–1		
	Index and middle finger = 1–2		
Middle Front Set	Thumb, index, and middle finger = 3–2		
	Four fingers = 4–4		
Long Set	Five fingers = 5–4		
Back Sets	Pinkie and ring finger used for back sets		
Short Back Set	Pinkie finger = A1		
Middle Back Set	Pinkie finger and ring finger = B2		
High Back Set	Make letter C = C4		

TEAM STRATEGIES

SKILL	CUE	WHY	COMMON ERROR
Offense	Stress passing and serving over all other skills	A good pass means players can hit and spike the ball well	
	Use all 3 contacts if possible, or other team will		
	Only attempt technically what players can do physically; do not do too much		
	Setter is the most athletic player on team, most important		
	Sets must be high in order to attack		
	Talk to each other when passing, hitting, and so forth	Communication a key to good team play	

continued

TEAM STRATEGIES, continued

SKILL	CUE	WHY	COMMON ERROR
Defense	Funnel attack to back-row players		
	First do offense, then defense		
	Front-row players stay close to net		
	Stay low, with good center of gravity		
	Front-row attackers never reach back for a dig; someone will be punched in the face		

INDIVIDUAL STRATEGIES

SKILL	CUE	WHY	COMMON ERROR
Offense	Front-row hitters, stay away from net	Gives the hitter 3- and 4-step approach, more time to get to ball and hit hard	
	When hitting, keep ball in front of you		
	Try to anticipate what will happen before it happens		
	Hit around the blockers, even if it means you cannot hit the ball as hard		
Defense	Be ready for anything, all the time	Communication key to good team play	
	Weight on balls of feet, not heels		
	Try to anticipate attacks		
	If you intend to pass or dig a ball, call for it: "I go," "Mine"		
	Talk!		

30

The Practice of Yoga and Pilates Exercises

INTRODUCTION TO YOGA

We offer people something extremely important when we teach yoga in this day and age. Although yoga today is often taught and practiced as a pursuit for health and fitness in a changing world, its spiritual roots still nourish authentic yoga teachings. We have Americanized it and turned it into a workout, so it is important that we as teachers make it restorative and rejuvenating, not miserable!

Yoga can be defined as "mindfulness," or the process of directing the attention toward whatever we are doing at the moment. Through the practice of various yoga techniques and postures, we are continually moving the attention toward the present moment using the breath. In doing so we learn to feel the action from the postures, or *asanas,* from deep within.

The practice of yoga is teaching the mind to steady or to become calm, without distraction, fixed gently on the sound and quality of our breath. Yoga grows with time. Some days are easy, and the mind is calm and the physical body is light and responsive; on other days, you may find that the mind is very busy and the body feels like heavy sand.

Why is yoga, an ancient practice, becoming so popular? Perhaps it is because the practice addresses so many modern concerns. In our fast-paced lives, we are always multitasking, rarely making decisions carefully and one at a time. The practice of yoga can benefit all types of people—from children to older adults and from athletes to couch potatoes. Yoga tones the muscles, sculpts the body, improves flexibility, builds muscular strength and endurance, and increases lung capacity while calming the nervous system and mind. It creates the range of motion needed to therapeutically work and heal all areas of the body. It heals, detoxifies, electrifies, and regenerates both body and mind at the deepest levels. One of yoga's greatest advantages is to assist in preventing injury. It is also a helpful tool for recovering from injury and for restoring loss of mobility or range of movement and loss of strength.

As teachers, we create safe environments in which students can approach the practice of yoga, including its different or awkward aspects. For example, we ask students to be barefoot, and to get into funny positions. We ask them to wear fitted clothing and to investigate what they feel. To facilitate this growth, it is crucial to attend to the environment and the attitude with which we encourage students to approach practice. The hallmark of the yoga practitioner is moderation. So as teachers, we remind ourselves and our students that the pose/posture should never take precedence over the person. We also set up appropriate boundaries (e.g., regarding touch) to support safe environments, and we encourage our students to attend to boundaries they need in order to relax. Around the world, thousands of people have benefited from yoga. Practicing with awareness, common sense, and a little basic knowledge can help ensure that yoga is a safe and healing experience for many more.

YOGA SKILLS LISTED WITH CUES

This chapter presents cues for the following: Sun Salutations A and B, standing postures/asanas, seated postures/asanas, and modified closing sequence.

EQUIPMENT TIPS

1. Consider playing quiet yoga music during instruction or using a guided relaxation (see FYI section).
2. Wear clothing that is comfortable and fitted; avoid baggy clothing.
3. Practice barefoot, without socks.
4. Use a clean yoga sticky mat, preferably one's own mat. Mat wipes or spray may be used to clean mats between users if mats are going to be shared. *Note*: These mats are thinner than the usual aerobics mat; using thick or cushy mats can create severe stress on the wrists and ankles.
5. For modification of poses, have props available—such as blankets, blocks, or straps.

PRACTICE IDEAS

1. Stomach and bowels should be empty; practice 2 to 3 hours after a meal.
2. To avoid injury, do not force the body beyond its capacity. Practice at "the edge," with enough effort to create sensation and keep you engaged, but with less effort than will create pain or an inability to breathe. Discomfort is different from pain; it should disappear once the pose is released. Even among very fit people, weaknesses will become visible during the practice—this is ok! If a pose is causing pain, try a modification or a less-strenuous pose until the body is strengthened and the original pose can be performed more comfortably.
3. If there is any persistent pain, it is a sign of incorrect practice of some physical problem. Consult with a qualified teacher.
4. Hold the postures only as long as the proper alignment can be maintained. The length of time spent in each pose will increase along with strength, flexibility, and endurance.
5. Elongate the spine before bending to maximize disk space. Normal curves keep the spine healthy. The spine bends forward and backward most easily in the lumbar region, so we tend to overwork the lower back. Forcing the spine into forward bends is one of the most dangerous things you can do in all of yoga. It is important to always return the spine to neutral.

6. Alignment principles:
   a. Scoop the tailbone under and lift the chest (telescope the ribs) to create space in the vertebrae.
   b. Draw the shoulders back, in, and down with the lower portion of the blades curling under toward the heart. (A good visual is having the arms lifted shoulder height and bent at a 90-degree angle. Draw just the elbows forward and feel how the blades curl under toward the heart).
7. Engage the internal locks, or *bandhas,* lightly throughout the practice.
   a. *Mula bandha,* or root lock, located at the perineum approximately ½ inch in from anus. Drawing the pelvic floor up will help the tailbone scoop under.
   b. *Uddiyana bandha,* or navel lock, is performed by exhaling fully and then drawing the lower belly inward and upward while simultaneously lifting the diaphragm.
   c. Children under 13 should not engage the *bandhas.*
8. Use a focal point, or *drishti,* to reduce distraction. Keep eyes softly focused on this gazing point while practicing; may be off the fingers, toes, nose, or middle of the forehead. Alternatively, one may choose to focus the gaze on a spot on the floor approximately 3 feet ahead, or lift the gaze slightly to a point on the wall.
9. Breathing techniques, or *pranayama,* aid concentration. In yoga, the breath is viewed as a sacred bridge between the tangible body and the intangible mind.
   a. Breathe in and out through the nose.
   b. Fully expand the lungs on inhalation; fully contract on exhalation. Pay attention to the exhale, and allow the inhale to simply happen.
   c. Create an audible breath, called *ujjayi pranayama,* which sounds similar to ocean waves gently crashing. While contracting the back of the throat and keeping the mouth closed, inhale making a "hsss" sound and exhale with a "hammm" sound.
   d. Use the breath as an indication of appropriate effort level. Try to keep the breath smooth . . . pause slightly and restore an even, flowing breath.

TEACHING IDEAS

1. Value students' opinions; praise and encourage them. Teach respect and compassion through example. Give them options or choices, and help them to see possibilities. Teach them to accept their limitations and where they are at this moment in time. Be playful and loving.
2. According to Sri K. Patthabi Jois, Master Yogi, the Primary Series in Astanga Yoga may be taught to ages 9 to 11. Those over 12 can begin a more serious study of this type of power yoga. Younger children generally can concentrate only for up to 40 minutes, while older ages can practice up to 60 minutes. *Do not overwork* children.
3. Teach Child's Posture and Knees into Chest first (see Closing Sequence). Encourage students to use these poses, or Downward Facing Dog, as resting poses if they become lightheaded, short of breath, or too tired during the practice.

TEACHING PROGRESSIONS

1. Breath: *Pranayama* (life current/life force)
2. Internal locks: *Mula bandha, Uddiyana bandha*
3. Alignment principles
4. Sun Salutations A and B
5. Postures
6. *Vinyasa*: a unique linking of one posture to the next in a dynamic flow
7. Closing sequence
8. Final relaxation: *Savasana*
9. Breathe 3 to 5 times while performing each posture, unless otherwise noted.

GAMES

1. Use the familiar figure of Darth Vader to introduce the breath technique of *ujjayi pranayama*. Bring hand to mouth and act as if you are steaming up a mirror to get the effect of abdominal breathing. Be playful and do not force students to participate; have fun with this.
2. Use animals and nature to portray the postures. For example: Eagle, Down-dog, Cat/Cow, Stork, Frog, Bug, Cobra, Mountain, Half-moon, Tree, etc. Be playful and creative.
3. As students become more familiar with the poses, invite them to choose a pose their body is calling for. They can practice individually during the closing sequence before going into relaxation. Offer appropriate calming poses for them to consider, such as Child's Pose or Spinal Twist.

FYI

For further information, consult the following organization and resources.

ORGANIZATION

Yoga Journal
2054 University Avenue
Berkeley, CA 94704
Phone: (510) 841-9200
Fax: (510) 644-3101
www.yogajournal.com

PUBLICATIONS

Iyengar, B. K. S. (1989). *The tree of yoga*. Boston: Shambhala Publications, 1989.

Feuerstein, G. & Payne, L. (1999). *Yoga for dummies*. IDG Books Worldwide.

MUSIC/MEDITATION—ARTISTS

Krishna Das
Prem Joshua
Shiva Rea
Sharon Salzberg

PRODUCTS

Hugger Mugger
www.huggermugger.com

Barefoot Yoga
www.barefootyoga.com

SUN SALUTATION A SEQUENCE/WARM-UP

This sequence is designed to produce heat in the body so that muscles and joints are prepared for the physical work to follow.

SKILL	CUE	WHY	COMMON ERROR
Mountain Posture *(Tadasana)*	Stand with both feet together (big toes touching), legs active, spine long; engage the *bandhas;* breathe deep	Builds awareness of feet, ankles, alignment of spine; strengthens feet, ankles, quads, hamstrings, core, and back	Pressing back into knee joint to "lock" knees *Modification:* Lift/pull up with quads to bring legs straight.
Upward Hand Pose *(Urdhva hastasana)*	**Inhale.** Raise both arms (lungs should be full just as the hands touch); gaze at the thumbs; chest upward	Lengthens spine, shoulders, and arms; strengthens hips, legs, and feet	Collapsing in low back *Modification:* Even if a slight backbend is desired, lengthen from tailbone, lifting up from waist.
Full Forward Fold *(Uttanasana)*	**Exhale.** Fold forward, taking the chest toward the knees; look toward toes. *Note:* Every Full Forward Fold *must* be done with bent knees.	Lengthens hamstrings and back; strengthens quads and abs	Not folding enough *Modification:* Pull belly button back toward spine, allowing torso to come closer to legs and protecting low back.
Look Forward	**Inhale.** Lengthen the spine, draw the chest away from belly; lengthen back of neck, look forward	Lengthens spine, neck, and hams; strengthens quads and abs	Overworking back by forgetting to use legs *Modification:* Keep legs engaged as in Mountain Posture; keep abs engaged as in Forward Fold.
4-Limb Stick *(Chaturanga dandasana)*	**Exhale.** Step back, lower from plank to 4-limb stick while gazing forward *Modification:* Drop knees, uncurl toes; elbows beside ribs if possible; hover or lie flat on the floor	Total core stability; increases strength in wrists, shoulders, triceps, quads, and hams	Collapsing in low back *Modification:* Pull in abs to help support, but also rely more on arms. To do so, make sure hands are placed right under shoulder, with fingers widespread and middle fingers pointing forward.
Upward Facing Dog, or Cobra *(Urdhva mukha svanasana)* (Figure 30.1, page 414)	**Inhale.** Straighten the arms or slightly bend at the elbows and roll onto the tops of the feet; knees lifted or dropped to floor; toes pointed; lift chest high; scoop tailbone	Increases strength in upper body; increases flexibility of chest and abs	Hyperextending elbows *Modification:* Turn arm muscles to make the inner elbows face each other.

continued

FIGURE 30.1 Upward Facing Dog

SUN SALUTATION A SEQUENCE/WARM-UP, continued			
SKILL	**CUE**	**WHY**	**COMMON ERROR**
Downward Facing Dog *(Adho mukha svanasana)*	**Exhale.** Push hips up away from floor toward the intersection of the ceiling and the wall behind; press heels toward the floor and lift the kneecaps; gaze at navel; engage the *bandhas;* remain here for 3–5 breaths	Increases arm, shoulder, quad, and ankle strength; increases flexibility in spine, hams, calves, and achilles	Resting weight on toes *Modification:* Lengthen along back of legs from hips to heels, allowing heels to descend toward floor; balance weight between hands and feet.
Walk or Jump Forward	**Inhale.** Walk or jump the feet forward in between hands; lengthen the spine, take gaze forward	Strengthens core and arms; lengthens spine	Not trying jumping! Try it! It's not as hard as it looks!
Full Forward Fold *(Uttanasana)*	See cues on page 413		
Upward Hand Pose *(Urdhva hastasana)*	See cues on page 413		
Mountain Posture *(Tadasana)*	**Exhale.** Lower arms in preparation for next Sun Salutation A or *vinyasa*	Returns the body to a neutral alignment	

SUN SALUTATION B SEQUENCE

SKILL	CUE	WHY	COMMON ERROR
Mountain Posture *(Tadasana)*	Stand with both feet together (big toes touching), legs active, spine long; engage the *bandhas;* breathe deep	Builds awareness of feet, ankles, alignment of spine; strengthens feet, ankles, quads, hamstrings, core, and back	Pressing back into knee joint to "lock" knees *Modification:* Lift/pull up with quads to bring legs straight.
Fierce Posture *(Utkatasana)*	**Inhale.** Bend knees (coming into a squat) and raise both arms to the sky; fill lungs fully; gaze toward thumbs	Stretches shoulders and arms; lengthens spine; strengthens quads, hams, abs, and chest	Staying too upright *Modification:* Move hips back behind heels as though sitting in a chair.
Full Forward Fold *(Uttanasana)*	**Exhale.** Fold forward, taking the chest toward the knees; look toward toes. *Note:* Every Full Forward Fold *must* be done with bent knees.	Lengthens hams and back; strengthens quads and abs	Not folding enough *Modification:* Pull belly button back toward spine, allowing torso to come closer to legs and protecting low back.
Look Forward	**Inhale.** Lengthen the spine, draw the chest away from belly; lengthen back of neck, look forward	Lengthens spine, neck, and hams; strengthens quads and abs	Overworking back by forgetting to use legs *Modification:* Keep legs engaged as in Mountain Posture; keep abs engaged as in Forward Fold.
4-Limb Stick *(Chaturanga dandasana)*	**Exhale.** Step back, lower from plank to 4-limb stick while gazing forward. *Modification:* Drop knees, uncurl toes; elbows beside ribs if possible; hover or lie flat on the floor.	Total core stability, increases strength in wrists, shoulders, triceps, quads, and hams	Collapsing in low back *Modification:* Pull in abs to help support, but also rely more on arms. To do so, make sure hands are placed right under shoulder, with fingers widespread, and middle fingers pointing forward.
Upward Facing Dog, or Cobra *(Urdhva mukha svanasana)*	**Inhale.** Straighten the arms or slightly bend at the elbows and roll onto the tops of the feet; knees lifted or dropped to floor; toes pointed; lift chest high; scoop tailbone	Increases strength in upper body; increases flexibility of chest and abs	Hyperextending elbows *Modification:* Turn arm muscles to make the inner elbows face each other.

continued

SUN SALUTATION B SEQUENCE, continued			
SKILL	**CUE**	**WHY**	**COMMON ERROR**
Downward Facing Dog *(Adho mukha svanasana)*	**Exhale.** Push hips up away from floor toward the intersection of the ceiling and the wall behind; press heels toward the floor and lift the kneecaps; gaze at navel; engage the *bandhas;* remain here for 3–5 breaths	Increases arm, shoulder, quad, and ankle strength; increases flexibility in spine, hams, calves, and achilles	Resting weight on toes *Modification:* Lengthen along back of legs from hips to heels, allowing heels to descend toward floor; balance weight between hands and feet.
Warrior I Pose, Right Side *(Virabhadrasana I)* (Figure 30.2)	**Inhale.** Bring right foot forward between hands and flatten back foot in 30° angle, heel away from little toe. Bend forward knee, bringing knee directly over ankle; raise hands over head with arms straight until palms touch; gaze at thumbs (this should be done in 1 inhale)	Increases strength in gluteals, legs, core, back, shoulders, arms, ankles, and feet	Forgetting to breathe! If necessary, take an extra breath.

continued

FIGURE 30.2 Warrior I Pose

SUN SALUTATION B SEQUENCE, continued			
SKILL	**CUE**	**WHY**	**COMMON ERROR**
4-Limb Stick *(Chaturanga dandasana)*	Exhale; see cues on page 415	See cues on page 415	
Upward Facing Dog or Cobra *(Urdhva mukha svanasana)*	Inhale; see cues on page 415		
Downward Facing Dog *(Adho mukha svanasana)*	Exhale; see cues on page 416		
Warrior I, Left Side *(Virabhadrasana I)*	Same as Warrior I, Right Side, but use left side	Increases strength in gluteals, legs, core, back, shoulders, arms ankles, and feet	
4-Limb Stick *(Chaturanga dandasana)*	Exhale; see cues on page 415		
Upward Facing Dog or Cobra *(Urdhva* mukha *svanasana)*	Inhale; see cues on page 415		
Downward Facing Dog *(Adho mukha svanasana)*	Exhale; see cues on page 416; remain here for 3–5 complete breaths		
Walk or Jump Forward	Inhale as you walk or jump feet toward hands; lengthen the spine while gazing forward	Core stabilization; increases strength in arms; stretches spine	
Full Forward Fold *(Uttanasana)*	Exhale; see cues on page 415		
Fierce Posture *(Utkatasana)*	Inhale; see cues on page 415		
Mountain Posture *(Tadasana)*	Exhale, lower your arms and straighten the legs in preparation for the next Sun Salutation B; gaze straight ahead	Brings spine back into neutral alignment	

STANDING POSTURES SEQUENCE

Hold all standing postures for multiple breaths, work up to 3 to 5 minutes per pose.

SKILL	CUE	WHY	COMMON ERROR
Big Toe Posture *(Padangusthasana)* *Base: Full Forward Fold*	From Mountain Posture, jump feet hip width apart. **Inhale.** Lift gaze toward sky. **Exhale.** Fold forward, clasp the big toes with middle and index fingers of each hand.	Strengthens quads and shoulders; increases flexibility in hamstrings	If cannot reach toes, clasp ankles, bend knees, bring ribs to thighs
Hand Under Foot Pose *(Padahastasana)* *Base: Full Forward Fold*	From Mountain Posture, exhale; place hand under foot with toes to wrist	Counterstretch for wrists; increases flexibility in hams; strengthens quads and shoulders	If cannot reach under feet, bring fingers to toes, or blocks, and bend knees
Extended Triangle Pose *(Utthita trikonasana)* (Figure 30.3, page 420)	From Mountain Posture, walk feet 1-leg length apart; turn right foot out and left toes in slightly. **Exhale.** Raise arms to shoulder level; shift hips to left while lengthening torso to right; rotate arms as windmill, bringing right hand to shin. **Inhale.** Come up slowly. Repeat on other side.	Strengthens quads, hams, calves, back, and abs; lengthens intercostals, waist, hip flexors, and inner thighs	If hand does not come to shin, use a block. If hand goes below shin, try to take hold of big toe.
Revolved Triangle Pose *(Parivritta trikonansana)* *Base: Extended Triangle Pose*	From Mountain Posture, step feet 1-leg length apart, front to back. **Exhale.** Turn right foot out, left toes in; square hips to the right, place right hand on sacrum; reach left arm forward, descend to shin or outside of right little toe; spiral around, open left shoulder to sky, reach up. **Inhale.** Come up slowly. Repeat on other side.	Stretches hams and hips; lengthens spine; strengthens quads, shoulders, and arms	If feet are too narrow, the pose will be wobbly. Make sure feet are at least hip width apart; may also help to shorten length of stance. Try to keep sacrum level.

continued

STANDING POSTURES SEQUENCE, continued			
SKILL	**CUE**	**WHY**	**COMMON ERROR**
Extended Side Angle Pose *(Uttihita parsvahonasana)* *Base: Extended Triangle Pose*	From Mountain Posture, step feet 3–4 feet apart, arms outstretched; turn right foot open and left foot in approximately 45°. **Exhale.** Bend right knee directly above heel, lower right hand to the floor outside the right foot (inside of foot for beginners); extend left hand up to sky. **Inhale.** Come up slowly. Repeat on other side.	Lengthens torso, outer side leg, ribs, and intercostals; strengthens hams, quads, calves, and shins	If hand does not reach floor, bring right forearm onto right thigh; place left hand on sacrum (reverse for left side)
Prayer Twist *(Parivritta parsvakonasana)* *Base: Extended Side Angle Pose*	Turn right foot out, stay up on left toes. **Exhale.** Bend right leg, knee above heel; left elbow to outside of right knee; place left and right hand into prayer position. **Inhale.** Come up slowly. Repeat on other side.	Rotation of torso; lengthens spine, groins, inner thighs; strengthens hams, quads, shins, and calves	If pose is wobbly, drop knee to floor
Expanded Leg Pose *(Prasarita padottanasana)*	From Mountain Posture, step feet 3–4 feet apart; outer edges of feet parallel, hands on hips, drawing elbows back toward each other; scoop tailbone, contract quads, telescope ribs, lift chest, and look up. **Exhale.** Fold forward, hands stay on hips, keep legs active. **Inhale.** Come up slowly.	Increases flexibility in inner thighs and outer shins; strengthens back and abs	
Hand to Big Toe Pose *(Utthita hasta padangusthasana)*	From Mountain Posture, raise right knee; grab big toe with index and middle fingers; straighten leg; hold for 3–5 breaths; open to right side; hold for 3–5 breaths	Strengthens hips, feet, and knees; stretches hams and opens groins; develops balance	If leg cannot straighten while toe is held, hold onto bent knee; may open bent knee to outside

continued

STANDING POSTURES SEQUENCE, continued			
SKILL	**CUE**	**WHY**	**COMMON ERROR**
Tree Posture *(Vrksasana)* (Figure 30.4)	From Mountain Posture, **inhale.** Lift right foot with both hands. **Exhale.** Place foot on upper-left thigh, bring hands to prayer position. Repeat on other side.	Strengthens hips, legs, and core; opens hips; increases balance	If foot cannot comfortably stay on opposite upper-left thigh, bring foot to opposite calf
Warrior I *(Virabhadrasana I)*	**Inhale.** Bring right foot forward between hands and flatten back foot in 30° angle, heel away from little toe. Bend forward knee, bringing knee directly over ankle; raise hands over head with arms straight until palms touch; gaze at thumbs (this should be done in 1 inhale).	Increases strength in gluteals, legs, core, back, shoulders, arms, ankles, and feet	Forgetting to breathe! If necessary, take an extra breath.
Warrior II *(Virabhadrasana II)* *Base: Warrior I*	From Warrior I, **exhale** and open arms parallel to floor and in line with legs. Left leg should remain at 90° angle, right foot flat at 30° angle; left knee over heel; gaze over the left middle finger. **Inhale.** Come up slowly. Repeat on other side.	Strengthens feet, ankles, knees, quads, spine, and shoulders; increases flexibility in groin, legs, and feet	

FIGURE 30.3 Extended Triangle Pose

FIGURE 30.4 Tree Posture

SEATED POSTURES SEQUENCE

Hold all seated postures for multiple breaths; work up to 3 to 5 minutes per pose.

SKILL	CUE	WHY	COMMON ERROR
Staff Posture *(Dandasana)*	Sit with legs extended in front of body, feet and knees touching. **Exhale.** Drop chin to chest; keep legs active, spine long, arms straight, hands pressing down with palms flat and back of knees pressing down.	Lengthens spine; strengthens shoulders, arms, and hands	Lifting heels off ground
Intense West Posture *(Paschimottansasana)* *Base: Staff Posture* (Figure 30.5, page 422)	From Staff Posture, raise arms up, telescope ribs, scoop tailbone. **Exhale.** Fold forward, clasp big toes with middle and index fingers, gaze at toes; keep feet and knees together; contract quads.	Increases flexibility in the hamstrings and the back; increases strength in the biceps and chest	Rounding in low back *Modification:* Straighten spine by pulling abs in and up. May keep arms at side to help lift torso.
Intense East Posture *(Purvottanasana)* *Base: Staff Posture*	From Staff Posture, place hands flat on the floor behind hips, pointing fingers toward toes. **Inhale.** Drop head back, push hips up to sky. Keep legs straight and active with feet touching and soles of feet on the floor; keep arms straight and fully engaged.	Increases flexibility in the front of the body; opens anterior shoulder	Dropping hips *Modification:* Lift from waist so body is like one plank; push into hands, and spread fingers wide.
Single Leg Forward Bend A *(Janu sirasana A)* *Base: Staff Posture*	From Staff Posture, extend left leg straight, bring right foot to inner left thigh, right knee should be at 90° angle. **Exhale.** Fold forward, clasp left foot with both hands. **Inhale.** Come up slowly. Repeat on other side.	Increases flexibility in hams; opens hips	If knee of bent leg is off floor, support it with a blanket. If cannot reach foot, may use strap around foot or clasp shin.

continued

FIGURE 30.5 Intense West Posture

FIGURE 30.6 Boat Posture

SEATED POSTURES SEQUENCE, continued

SKILL	CUE	WHY	COMMON ERROR
Seated Twist *(Marichyasana C)* *Base: Staff Posture*	From Staff Posture, bend right knee and bring right foot flat near right sitting bone. **Inhale.** Lengthen spine and take hold of right knee with left hand. **Exhale.** Begin spiraling to right and place right hand on the floor behind back. With each inhalation, lengthen spine; with exhalation, invite body to twist further. Release slowly. Repeat on other side.	Increases flexibility in back; increases range of movement in torso	"Hanging out" in pose *Modification:* Move deeper in twist with a deeper variation: place left outside elbow on outside right knee, hand up, fingers spread, and use the knee to push against.
Boat Posture *(Navasana)* *Base: Staff Posture* (Figure 30.6)	In Staff Posture, **inhale.** Lift and straighten both legs and feet together, toes spread at eye level; gaze at toes; arms straight, parallel to floor with palms facing each other.	Strengthens core, especially transverse abdominals	Collapsing in low back. *Modification:* May bend knees and hold behind them to lift out of low back; much better to start with modified version; as one develops strength to hold spine straight, work on extending legs.
Bound Angle Posture *(Baddha konasasa)* *Base: Staff Posture*	From Staff Posture, bring soles of feet together in front of groin; hold feet with fingers on top of foot (with thumbs on the soles), keeping outer edges of feet on floor; lower knees toward floor.	Increases flexibility in adductors	Ignoring knee pain. *Modification:* Try elevating hips by sitting on edge of rolled blanket or on block. Use blankets to support legs if knees are up in the air, allowing muscles to relax.

continued

SEATED POSTURES SEQUENCE, continued			
SKILL	**CUE**	**WHY**	**COMMON ERROR**
Hero Posture *(Virasana)*	Kneel on floor; bring knees and feet together, then sit on your feet	Stretches quads and outer front shin	Again, ignoring knee pain! *Modification:* Try placing rolled blanket on calves and sit back. For deeper variation, allow feet to separate just wider than hips, and sit down between feet (or on rolled blanket placed between hips).
Seated Angle Posture *Base: Staff Posture*	From Staff Posture, open feet wide, legs straight; hold feet with hands. **Inhale.** Lengthen the spine and gaze forward. **Exhale.** Release deeper into pose.	Increases flexibility in adductors	Collapsing in low back *Modification:* Imagine doing Expanded Leg Pose while seated. If hands do not reach feet, use straps around feet, or place hands on shins.
Child's Pose *(Balasana)*	On all fours, knees apart, bring glutes back and down toward heels; lengthen arms over head, forehead down on mat, abdomen between thighs; breathe deeply	Restores and rejuvenates whole body and mind; excellent rest pose. Also increases flexibility in back and hips.	
Spinal Twist	Lie flat on back; draw left knee into chest, extend right leg out; hook left toes on right quad, right hand on outside of left knee; bring left knee down toward floor on right side of body. Extend left arm with palms down on floor, allowing left shoulder to drop toward floor; look over left shoulder.	Increases flexibility in rib cage, intercostals, glutes, and lower back	

MODIFIED CLOSING SEQUENCE

End your practice with this sequence to return the spine to neutral and the body to its basal metabolic rate. Rest in Final Relaxation for a minimum of 5 minutes; 10–15 minutes is recommended. These restorative poses are actually the most important and beneficial of all.

SKILL	CUE	WHY	COMMON ERROR
Knees into Chest (Figure 30.7)	Lie flat on back; draw both knees into chest, wrap the arms around the knees and gently roll in a circular motion	Releases lower back, gently massages back; preparation for final relaxation	
Knees into Chest Twist	From Knees into Chest, open arms to side with palms facing down; draw shoulders down into sockets, drop both knees to right side, look over left shoulder. Repeat on other side.	Releases residual tension in the lower back, spine, gluteals, intercostals, and lats	
Final Relaxation/ Corpse Pose *(Savasana)*	Lie flat on back; allow feet to flop open and let arms extend along floor at 45°, palms up. Release all muscles, dissolve all tension; close your eyes and completely relax.	Allows heart rate and breath to slow to a natural, soothing rhythm; revitalizes and rejuvenates whole body and mind	

When coming out of this sequence, wiggle fingers and toes to return to awareness. Then roll onto your right side in a fetal position. When prepared, place both hands on the floor and push yourself up to a comfortable position and maintain seated lotus or any comfortable position to keep the spine tall. Take three slow breaths in and out. *Breathe in slowly.* Now the body has been cleansed and the mind is relaxed, ready to meet the rest of the day with energy and vitality!

Namaste, everyone! (My light salutes your light!)

FIGURE 30.7 Knees into Chest

INTRODUCTION TO PILATES

Pilates is a unique system of conditioning the body that uses strengthening and stretching exercises developed by Joseph H. Pilates in Germany during the early 1900s. Calling his system *Contrology*, Joseph Pilates combined the best of Eastern and Western exercises and optimal breathing to build a balanced body, focusing primarily on the *center* or *core*. Whether you are training for soccer, golf, tennis, or dance, using the core allows the body to move safely through flexibility, conditioning, and resistance activities.

Pilates principles—strength, endurance, flexibility, balance, and stability—are the same as those used for daily activities. All Pilates exercises use correct biomechanics and alignment to build optimal muscle memory. Every Pilates exercise, done with quality and precision, engages the full body; so the entire body is trained and integrated. Pilates is perfect for toning and elongating muscles, training for an athletic event, rehabilitating from an injury, and maintaining body awareness, alignment, and strength.

A conscious form of exercise, Pilates requires a blend of breath, control, and body awareness to achieve overall fitness; build strength without bulking up; and employ mental focus where quality, not quantity, brings results. Pilates work is not frenetic, mechanic, or mindless exercise; each movement requires focused concentration and flowing breath to connect mind and body and work with precision and balance. Pilates is not a quick fix or a shortcut to fitness. With total focus on detail, fewer repetitions done correctly will make the most progress; 80 reps are not better than 5.

The deep postural muscles of the abdominals, spine, and pelvic floor are the primary targets of Pilates technique to prevent other stronger muscle groups (such as the buttocks or shoulders) from "taking over" when they are not the appropriate muscles for a given movement. Pilates is a *functional* system that retrains the body to overcome its compensations, balances both sides of the body, and reduces the risk of injuries so that any motion becomes more efficient—from standing up or walking downstairs to throwing a ball or swinging a racquet.

Pilates allows conditioning of the body without punishing it; it's a gentler way to tone and strengthen, reducing stress and wear and tear on joints. By using the body correctly in proper alignment with sound muscle recruitment patterns, and doing workouts to increase their effectiveness, students can reduce the risk of injury during practice and play. Pilates benefits include streamlining the belly and waist; elongating the muscles; recovering from injury; developing a healthy, supple spine; improving balance and coordination; reducing pain and stiffness; improving posture and alignment; quieting the mind; and increasing circulation and oxygen uptake.

PILATES SKILLS LISTED WITH CUES

This chapter presents cues for the following: Pilates fundamentals and Pilates matwork exercises.

EQUIPMENT TIPS

1. Use a Pilates mat, thick towel, or a room with a thick carpet to protect the spine.
2. Wear close-fitting, nonrestrictive clothing (tights, bicycle shorts, leotard, leggings, etc.) so the instructor can see how your body is moving; use bare feet or nonslip socks.
3. Use a space with good circulation of air and enough room to avoid other students or furniture.

PRACTICE IDEAS

1. Avoid working out after a meal or when not feeling well.
2. Stay focused—avoid distracting situations (i.e., noise, loud music, TV).
3. Remind your body often to stay aligned correctly. When proper alignment is utilized, there is less stress on joints and less risk of injury.
4. Breathing properly is essential to each exercise, because each movement "rides" on the breath. The Pilates breath is full and wide, expanding the chest cavity in width, breadth, and depth (3-D breathing).
   a. Scoop the abs and inhale (a deep "sniff" through the nose) to prepare for movement, and deepen the scooping of the abs and exhale (a forceful blow or huff from an open mouth) to execute the movements.
   b. Proper exhalation allows the diaphragm to contract and activates the abdominals and pelvic floor.
   c. Most important—never hold your breath!
5. Engage pelvic floor and abs a maximum of 40 percent to keep action gentle—engaged, not gripped.
6. Avoid rushing through movements to fit in more repetitions; go for quality rather than quantity.
7. Questions to ask as you exercise:
   a. Do you overuse the muscles at the front of the thighs?
   b. Can you stabilize the pelvis as your legs move in space?
   c. Is one part of your spine more flexible than another?
   d. Do shoulders and neck feel stretched—or stressed?
   e. Is your breathing coordinated?
   f. Are your movements flowing—or jerky?
   g. Are your hip flexors working instead of your powerhouse (core)?
   h. Do you activate pelvic muscles, or are you "letting it all hang out"?
8. Never push to a discomfort level; don't strain: No pain, all gain.
9. Drink plenty of water throughout the day to avoid dehydration.
10. Be patient; progress takes time, but is well worth the wait. There are no shortcuts.

TEACHING IDEAS

1. Warm up for 3 to 5 minutes.
2. Exercise in a space warm enough to keep muscles relaxed but not hot enough to overheat the body.
3. Mastering breath may require reeducation for those who are upper-chest or belly breathers.
4. Remind students of the following concepts:
   a. Centering means that the core activates before the arms and legs move—stability *before* activation.
   b. Concentration and focus translates to quality exercising and strengthens the mind-body connection. Pilates is a mental and physical workout. Be mindful of the quality of movements rather than the quantity.
   c. Conscious exercise and awareness keeps you "present" during each Pilates exercise and allows you to sense the changes and challenges in the body.

5. Students may want to keep a journal or diary to record workouts, mental and physical reactions, and what is working or not working.

GLOSSARY OF PILATES TERMS

Alignment. The body position where the joints are in line and symmetrical.

Articulation. Movement of the spine that stacks the vertebra one at a time; segmenting or putting space between the vertebrae.

Core. The area between the bottom of the rib cage to the hips including the pubic bone, spine, buttocks, and bladder control muscles; also called "powerhouse" or "girdle of strength."

Engagement. Active contraction of a muscle or muscles during movement without gripping or bringing tension into other parts of the body.

Extension. Increasing the angle of a joint (muscle lengthens).

Flexion. Reducing the angle at a joint (muscle contracts and bones move closer to each other).

Natural or neutral spine. Correct biomechanical position. Maintaining the natural curves in the spine from shoulders to pelvis so they are not tilted forward or back, left or right.

Navel to spine. The physical and mental action of pulling the belly button toward the spine to engage the core or powerhouse (navel to spine, not spine to mat or floor).

Pilates stance. Feet in a V position (45°), heels together, knees soft, legs "zipped" or glued together to engage inner thighs.

Rotation. Twisting or turning the bone in the socket.

FYI

For further information and help, consult the following organizations and resources.

ORGANIZATIONS

Pilates Method Alliance
2631 Lincoln Avenue
Miami, FL 33133
Phone: (866) 573-4945
Website: www.pilatesmethodalliance.org

Stott Pilates
2200 Yonge Street, #1402
Toronto, ON Canada, M4S 2C6
Phone: (416) 482-4050
Website: www.stottpilates.com

The Pilates Studio
2121 Broadway, #201
New York, NY 10023
Phone: (212) 875-0189

The Pilates Center
4800 Baseline Rd. #D206
Boulder, CO 80303
Phone: (303) 494-3400
Website: www.thepilatescenter.com

The Physical Mind Institute
84 Wooster St., #405
New York, NY 10012
Phone: (800) 505-1990
Website: www.the-method.com

Peak Pilates
4865 Riverbend Rd.
Boulder, CO 80301
Phone: (800) 925-3674
Website: www.peakpilates.com

PUBLICATIONS

Alpers, A. T., & Segal, R. T. (2002). *The everything Pilates book.* Avon, MA: Adams Media Corporation.

Gallagher, S. P., & Kryzanowska, R. (1999). *The Pilates method of body conditioning.* Philadelphia, PA: BainBridgeBooks.

Pilates, J. H. (2000). *Your health and return to life through contrology* (revised and edited by S. P. Gallagher & R. Kryzanowska). Philadelphia, PA: BainBridgeBooks.

Pilates Style Magazine. www.pilatesstyle.com

Siler, B. (2000). *The Pilates body.* New York: Broadway Books.

Siler, B. (2003). *The Pilates body kit.* New York: St. Martin's Press.

Complete guide to Pilates, yoga, meditation, stress relief. (2002). Bath, UK: Paragon Publishing.

PILATES FUNDAMENTALS

Pilates fundamentals are important for every Pilates exercise; they are key to correct Pilates practice to prepare you for Pilates mat and equipment work (since they are used to execute various exercises). Use them as warm-ups and body-pattern reminders. Once you have mastered the fundamentals, they will become automatic as you do Pilates exercises.

SKILL	CUE	WHY	COMMON ERROR
Breathing and Imprinting *Repetitions: 5*	Lie in constructive rest (CR) position (knees bent, feet flat on floor). Inhale slowly and deeply into the sides and back, feeling the ribs expand and contract. Gently contract the pelvic floor muscles (bladder control muscles between pubic and tail bones), pulling abs up and in (navel to spine) on inhale and more on exhale. The lumbar spine depresses slightly toward the floor.	Helps recruit proper muscle-firing patterns during exercise Controls coordination and fluidity of movements Exhaling fully activates the core muscles Helps stabilize trunk and spine Brings focus to center	Raising shoulders Allowing stomach to pooch out Breathing without activating pelvic floor Forcing back to floor Tilting pelvis Tensing shoulders

continued

PILATES FUNDAMENTALS, continued			
SKILL	**CUE**	**WHY**	**COMMON ERROR**
Pelvic Bowl and Pelvic Tilts *Repetitions: 6–10*	Lying in CR position with knees and sitz bones in alignment, inhale and curve/tilt the pelvis forward with the tailbone moving toward the floor (arching gently). Return to neutral and then curve lumbar spine, pointing tailbone toward ceiling. Alternate between flexing and extending spine. Using a core contraction, tilt pelvis from side to side and from forward to back as though swishing water in a bowl. Circle pelvis clockwise and counterclockwise.	Teaches how to use abs and lumbar muscles to stabilize the pelvis Teaches how to find neutral pelvis	Failure to return to neutral pelvis between each tilt Heels, knees, or sitz bones out of alignment Overly arching back (hyperextending) or flattening back on the pelvic tilts
Bridging *Repetitions: 4*	Lying in CR position, exhale and peel one vertebra at a time off the mat to lift hips off floor—no pressure on neck. Return spine to floor in reverse order, one vertebra at a time, as you lower back and hips to floor.	Develops awareness of abs in relation to spine and pelvis Stretches front of hip joint and quads	Bridging before imprinting Tensing chest, neck, or shoulder muscles
Knee Stirs *Repetitions: 5 each direction with each leg*	Lying in CR position, activate core, **inhale**, fold one knee toward chest to 90° and use your hand to stir the knee in a small circle without pelvic motion. Stir in opposite direction before repeating with other knee.	Releases superficial hip flexors (TFL, rectus femoris, sartorius) while activating the primary hip flexor (iliopsoas)	Allowing pelvis to rock Using the quads/front of legs rather than "floating" the leg into the fold

continued

PILATES FUNDAMENTALS, continued			
SKILL	**CUE**	**WHY**	**COMMON ERROR**
Leg Slides *Repetitions: 6; 3 on each side, alternating*	Lying in CR position, activate core; allow one knee to lower to side and slide it to full extension; rotate to parallel and slide it back to bent-knee position; repeat on other side. Reverse by sliding leg to extension, rotating out, sliding up to side (bending knee), rotating to parallel.	Mobilizes hip joint while using only the joint Facilitates ease and economy of movement	Dropping thigh to floor Losing neutral pelvis position Moving heel off line with sitz bones
Flight *Repetitions: 4*	Lie prone, legs hip width apart, feet pressing into mat. Exhale, engage core while lifting breastbone and pulling shoulder blades down, lengthening through top of head. Return chest to mat. Repeat with arms extended forward.	Maintains stable lumbar spine and pelvis Isolates spinal extensors	Letting belly relax during exercise Overarching back Locking knees
Rib Cage and Arms *Repetitions: 3 each direction*	Lie in CR position, arms alongside body. Reach the shoulder blades down the back as the arms reach up and overhead; lower arms behind head and circle around toward legs (like angels in the snow). Reverse direction. Reach behind head only as far as you can keep lumbar spine on mat.	Stretches lats and strengthens muscles that stabilize shoulder blades	Splaying front ribs Arching back off floor Letting belly bulge Reaching behind head too far with arms so back arches
Rotating Arms *Repetitions: 10*	Lie in CR position, arms alongside body. Reach arms overhead to 70°. Rotate one arm forward (down to mat) as the other arm rotates back behind ear. Rotate in opposite direction.	Stretches lats, and muscles that attach shoulder blades to spine Increases range of motion in shoulder girdle Strengthens rotator cuff	Raising shoulder blades Not keeping abs scooped to spine

continued

PILATES FUNDAMENTALS, continued			
SKILL	**CUE**	**WHY**	**COMMON ERROR**
Cat (Figure 30.8) *Repetitions: 4 each direction*	Kneel on hands and knees (all fours). Exhaling, curve spine toward ceiling with core lifting, back rounded, shoulder blades spread wide, head curved toward chest. Reverse spinal curve allowing head, breastbone, and tailbone to lift up toward ceiling. Return to neutral.	Teaches articulation of spine Stretches trunk muscles Helps find neutral spine for upper body weight-bearing exercises	Letting go of core during arch Curving your back upward without lifting abdominals—belly to spine
Torso Twist *Repetitions: 3 each direction*	Sit cross-legged (tailor), arms crossed over chest, elbows lifted gently. Inhale and rotate torso to one side allowing head and shoulders to follow, looking over shoulder. Engage abs to initiate turn, as though wringing out a towel.	Stabilizes pelvis Rotates spine and mobilizes rib cage	Sinking into the mat Uneven weight on sitz bones Allowing navel to move

For a relaxation exercise that can be used anytime the back muscles feel tight or after doing arching exercises, kneel on mat with legs slightly apart, buttocks to heels. Bend forward to rest forehead on mat with arms alongside legs, palms up. Feel gravity draw you toward the floor. Breathe deeply to relax neck, face, shoulders, arms, and back. If legs or knees are tight, place a small pillow or rolled towel between thighs and buttocks. This is often called Child's Pose.

FIGURE 30.8 Cat

PILATES MATWORK EXERCISES			
EXERCISE	**CUE**	**WHY**	**COMMON ERROR**
Hundreds (Figure 30.9) *Repetitions: 10 sets of 10*	In constructive rest (CR) position, fold legs into tabletop position (lower legs parallel to floor)—scoop belly to spine as you curl head, shoulders, and upper spine off floor. Keep space between chin and throat as though holding a lemon under chin. Lift arms a few inches off floor, reaching fingers and arms long. Pulse arms (from the back, not the chest) up and down a few inches, breathing in for 5 pulses and out for 5 pulses. Legs may be straightened out to 45° for more core emphasis. Focus eyes on belly.	Improves circulation and warms up the body in preparation for Pilates exercises Improves breathing, expands rib cage and lungs, strengthens core, lengthens spine, focuses mind, stabilizes torso	Puny arm pumping or flopping wrists Straining or tensing neck and shoulders Letting pelvis move or rock Belly breathing instead of 3-D breathing Letting abs relax
Roll Up *Repetitions: 3–5*	Lie with legs straight, arms alongside body pressing arms and legs into mat for stability; curl head, shoulders, and spine off floor slowly, keeping navel pulled to spine. Stretch forward over legs with torso lifted over thighs. Deepen ab contraction and slowly lower body onto mat, sequencing spine one vertebra at a time, lowering head after shoulders touch mat. Keep legs squeezed together and pressed into mat.	Works the powerhouse and stretches the hamstrings Teaches how to articulate spine Mobilizes and massages spine	Moving jerky or fast Collapsing over legs Letting legs relax Flopping spine onto floor Failure to activate core or use breath to assist roll up and roll down

continued

FIGURE 30.9 Hundreds—in Table Position (L) and Legs Extended to 45° Angle (R)

PILATES MATWORK EXERCISES, continued			
EXERCISE	**CUE**	**WHY**	**COMMON ERROR**
Leg Circles *Repetitions: 6–8 in each direction with each leg*	Lie with arms alongside body; press into mat for stability. With one leg straight out and pressed into the floor, extend other leg straight to the ceiling (rotated out slightly) and begin making circles (about the size of a Frisbee), moving leg across the body outward and around; then reverse by going away from the body, out and around. Repeat sequence for the other leg.	Reveals imbalances, teaches stabilization and isolation Uses oppositional energy to reach and rotate the leg while stabilizing pelvis Facilitates internal and external rotation	Letting pelvis wobble Using the quads instead of the core to bring the leg back to center Moving hips and torso while circling leg
Rolling Like a Ball (Figure 30.10) (Don't do this on floor or a thin mat!) *Repetitions: 4*	Sit with knees bent and together, heels close to buttocks, holding lower shins; head and neck are curled forward toward the knees as you balance on tailbone. Inhale to roll back with fluid motion. Exhale to roll up, returning to original balanced position on tailbone, toes pointed just off mat. Keep body in round, compact shape throughout the exercise. A strong ab contraction and exhale on the roll up will assist getting up.	Articulates, strengthens, and massages spine Stabilizes shoulder girdle Improves balance, control, and coordination Facilitates deep, coordinated breathing	Rolling back onto head Jerky movements Flopping backward instead of rolling smoothly

continued

FIGURE 30.10 Rolling Like a Ball

PILATES MATWORK EXERCISES, continued			
EXERCISE	**CUE**	**WHY**	**COMMON ERROR**
Single Leg Stretch (Figure 30.11) *Repetitions: 10; 5 on each leg*	Lie supine; activate core. Curve into Hundreds head and neck position as you fold one knee toward chest; place same-side hand on ankle, opposite hand on knee, elbows wide, shoulders down. Extend other leg out to 45°. Double-pulse thigh to chest; then switch legs (and hands). As one leg tucks in, the other lengthens away.	Elongates spine Stabilizes and strengthens core Develops precision and coordination Builds resilient hip muscles Decompresses spine, hips, and shoulders	Moving torso during the exercise Tensing shoulders Knees losing parallel alignment Letting abs bulge
Double Leg Stretch *Repetitions: 6*	Start in Hundreds head and neck position with both knees pulled into chest, hands placed just below knees, elbows wide. Exhale to extend arms out past ears while legs extend to 45°. Inhale, circling arms wide around to shins, bringing your body back to starting position. Squeeze thighs together to support lower back.	Stretches hip muscles and the low back Strengthens upper abs	Hunching shoulders Moving torso and head Relaxing legs Arching back

continued

FIGURE 30.11 Single Leg Stretch

PILATES MATWORK EXERCISES, continued			
EXERCISE	**CUE**	**WHY**	**COMMON ERROR**
The Saw (Figure 30.12) *Repetitions: 8; 4 on each side, alternating*	Sit tall with legs extended forward, feet flexed, legs open in V position slightly wider than shoulders, arms extended at shoulder height. Rotate torso to one side, reaching opposite hand toward baby toe while exhaling as head and chest curve to thigh and back arm reaches behind you on high diagonal. Inhale to deepen core contraction as you bring torso back to starting position. Repeat movement to the other side.	Mobilizes hip joint Works the waistline Stretches the hamstrings Creates separation between lower body and shoulders for elastic energy in swinging motions Wrings out stale air from lungs	Twisting before activating core Moving hips Allowing thigh to raise off floor Scrunching neck
Spine Twist *Repetitions: 8, alternating sides*	Sit tall with legs extended forward, thighs zipped up, feet flexed, arms extended at shoulder height. Exhale to rotate torso to one side, allowing head and shoulders to follow, looking over back shoulder. Increase stretch with a 2nd exhale and greater reach. Keep belly button facing forward. Deeply inhale to return to starting position.	Stabilizes pelvis Facilitates spinal rotation Mobilizes rib cage	Sinking torso instead of maintaining tall posture Raising sitz bones off mat Shifting hips or heels Raising shoulders

continued

FIGURE 30.12 The Saw

PILATES MATWORK EXERCISES, continued			
EXERCISE	**CUE**	**WHY**	**COMMON ERROR**
Swan Prep *Repetitions: 4*	Lie prone, legs hip width apart, forearms on mat in diamond shape. Exhale, pressing arms into the mat, lifting breastbone, abdominals, and head off mat while keeping neck and spine long (look at the floor). Hold briefly before lowering.	Maintains stable lumbar spine and pelvis Isolates spinal extensors	Overarching lumbar spine Raising pubic bone off mat Dropping head back onto neck
Single Leg Kick (Figure 30.13) *Repetitions: 8; 4 on each leg, alternating*	Lie prone, propped on elbows with fists together, pubic bone on mat, abs scooped up, legs extended slightly open. Kick one heel into buttocks with double beat. Return leg to mat and kick other leg into buttocks with double beat. Alternate flexed and extended ankle.	Works hamstrings, biceps, triceps while stretching quads, knees, and abdominal muscles	Relaxing abs Moving torso Sinking into shoulders or lower back
Crisscross/Oblique Single Leg Stretch (Figure 30.14) *Repetitions: 10; 5 in each direction*	Lie on back with hands behind head, elbows wide, one leg folded toward the chest, one leg straight, head and shoulders curled into Hundreds position. Rotate torso to bring the opposite elbow toward the folded knee. Reverse the movement, extending folded leg and folding straight knee as torso twists to	Strengthens oblique abs Stretches lats Strengthens muscles that stabilize shoulder blades	Pulling on the neck or head Switching without holding the oblique position Moving too fast

continued

FIGURE 30.13 Single Leg Kick

FIGURE 30.14 Crisscross/Obliques

PILATES MATWORK EXERCISES, continued			
EXERCISE	**CUE**	**WHY**	**COMMON ERROR**
Crisscross/Oblique Single Leg Stretch, *continued*	bring opposite elbow toward folded knee. Inhale on the transition; exhale to twist toward knee. Keep pelvic muscles lifted and body anchored to mat as though stuck in cement.		
Teaser Prep (Figure 30.15) *Repetitions: 3 with each leg*	Lie on back, one knee bent, one leg extended so thighs are parallel and glued together, arms reaching past ears. Exhale and slowly lift head and torso off mat, reaching arms toward extended foot, keeping shoulders relaxed. Feel the body "float" up as though pulled by a magnet. Roll spine down to mat, returning arms overhead.	Works powerhouse and stabilizes lower body Improves balance and coordination	Gripping to rise Dropping back to mat rather than sequencing spine one vertebra at a time
Side Kicks (Figure 30.16) *Repetitions: 10; 5 in each direction, alternating*	Lie on side with elbow, shoulder, midback, and thighs aligned (stacked), legs at 45° angle in front of body. Press top palm into mat. Exhale to kick leg forward and back with double beat, keeping leg parallel to floor, foot flexed at ankle. Inhale on transition from front to back.	Works inner and outer thighs and buttocks Increases strength and mobility of hip joint	Rolling hips forward or back Sinking ribs into mat Kicking back too far, causing back to arch

continued

FIGURE 30.15 Teaser Prep

FIGURE 30.16 Side Kick

PILATES MATWORK EXERCISES, continued			
EXERCISE	**CUE**	**WHY**	**COMMON ERROR**
Mermaid (Lateral Bending) *Repetitions: 3 of each on each side*	Sit on one side with knees bent, one leg on top of the other. Hand is flat on mat directly under shoulder. Press straight arm into mat as the other arm reaches in a sweeping arc overhead in lateral bend, keeping head and neck in line with spine. Reverse the motion, stretching arm up and outward to return to starting position.	Strengthens arms, shoulders, and wrists Stretches hips and torso	Sinking into supporting shoulder Scrunching at waist Leaning instead of lifting to side
Push-Up *Repetitions: 3*	Stand in Pilates stance, scoop navel to spine. Walk hands down legs and out on the mat to plank position, body balanced on straight (not locked) arms. Lower body by bending elbows; push up to straight arms and fold at center, walking hands back toward feet, curling up to standing position.	Strengthens arms, shoulders, upper back, and chest Stretches shoulders and hamstrings	Sagging middle, or butt sticking up so body is not in straight line from head to heels (plank position)
Seal (Have fun with this!) *Repetitions: 6*	Sit with knees bent and open, heels together, hands reaching inside legs and under ankles. Roll back onto shoulders and clap heels together 3 times. Exhale to roll forward and clap heels 3 times as you balance on sits bones. Make 3 good, hearty "arfs" as you balance and clap feet.	Articulates and massages spine Stretches trunk muscles Tests balance and coordination Making sound activates core and expels stale air	Forgetting to breathe Failing to activate core to roll up Rolling onto head

References

Allsen, P. E., Harrison, J. M., & Vance, B. (1997). *Fitness for life. An individualized approach* (6th ed.) Blacklick, OH: McGraw-Hill.

Blakemore, C. (1995). *Methods of designing cues.* Provo, UT: Brigham Young University.

Christiansen, R. (1995, August 22). [Cues for teaching]. Unpublished interview.

Christina, R. W., & Corcos, D. M. (1988). *Coaches guide to teaching sport skills.* Champaign, IL: Human Kinetics.

Coker, C. (1998, January/February). Performance excellence: Making the most of natural speed. *Strategies, 11*(3), 10–12.

Darst, P. W., Zakrajsek, D. B., & Mancini, V. H. (1989). *Analyzing physical education and sport instruction.* Champaign, IL: Human Kinetics.

Docheff, D. M. (1990). The feedback sandwich. *Journal of Physical education, Recreation, and Dance, 64,* 17–18.

Fronske, H., Abendroth-Smith, J., & Blakemore, C. (1997). Critical overhand throwing cues help 3rd, 4th, and 5th grade students achieve efficient throwing patterns and increase their distance. *The Physical Educator, 54*(2), 88–95.

Fronske, H., & Birch, N. (1995). Overcoming road blocks to communication. *Strategies, 8*(8), 22–25.

Fronske, H., & Collier, C. (1993, September). Cueing your athletes on good jumping events. *Journal of Physical Education, Recreation, and Dance, 64*(7), 7–9.

Fronske, H., Collier, C., & Orr, D. (1993, February). Cueing your participants in on track events. *Journal of Physical Education, Recreation, and Dance, 64*(2), 9–10.

Fronske, H., & McGown, C. (1992, October). Visual teaching cues for volleyball skills. *Journal of Physical Education, Recreation, and Dance, 63*(8), 10–11.

Fronske, H., & Wilson, R. (2002). *Teaching cues for basic sport skills for elementary and middle school students.* San Francisco, CA: Benjamin Cummings.

Lacrosse Foundation. (1994). *The Lacrosse Foundation's parent's guide to the sport of lacrosse.* Baltimore, MD: Lacrosse Foundation, Inc.

Lawther, J. D. (1968). *The learning of physical skills.* Englewood Cliffs, NJ: Prentice-Hall.

Lockhart, A. (1966, May). Communicating with the learner. *Quest, VI,* 57–67.

Mack, G. (2001). *Mind gym.* Chicago, IL: Contemporary Books.

Magill, R. (2003). *Motor learning: Concepts and applications* (7th ed.). Blacklick, OH: McGraw-Hill.

Masser, L. (1993). Critical cues help first grade students' achievement in handstands and forward rolls. *Journal of Teaching in Physical Education, 12,* 301–312.

McGown, C. (1988). [Motor learning]. Unpublished lecture notes. Provo, UT: Brigham Young University.

Parker, D., & Bars, J. (1994). *On target for fun* [video]. Palm Beach, FL: The Athletic Institute.

Pfaff, D., Myers, B., Light, R., Freeman, W., & Winkler, G. (1991). *USA Track & Field Level II. Coaching education program: The jumps.* Indianapolis, IN: The Athletic Congress, TAC, USA.

President's Council on Physical Fitness and Sports. (2004). *The president's challenge physical activity and fitness awards.* Bloomington, IN: President's Council on Physical Fitness and Sports.

Rink, J. (2000). *Teaching physical education for learning* (5th ed.). Blacklick, OH: McGraw-Hill.

Select Marketing Groups of America. (2000). *The super study of sports participation* [print]. American Sports Data. Available: www.sgma.com/research/marketplace/superstudy_sports_participation.html.

Strand, B., Reeder, S., Scantling, E., & Johnson, M. (1997). *Fitness education: Teaching concepts-based fitness in schools.* Scottsdale, AZ: Gorsuch Scarisbrick.

U.S. Department of Health and Human Services. (1996). *Physical activity and health: A report of the Surgeon General.* Atlanta, GA: Centers for Disease Control and Prevention.

Winkler, G., & Schexnayder, I. (1998, July). *Level three coaching seminar.* Baton Rouge, LA: United States of America Track & Field.

Winkler, G., Seagrave, L., Gambetta, V., Orognen, J., Jolly, S., & Rogers, J. (1986). *Coaching Certification Level II: Sprints and hurdles.* Indianapolis, IN: The Athletic Congress, TAC, USA.

Index

Page references followed by *f* indicate figure.